Medieval & Renaissance Literary Studies

REFIGURING

the

SACRED FEMININE

The Poems of John Donne,
Aemilia Lanyer, and John Milton

THERESA M. DIPASQUALE

DUQUESNE UNIVERSITY PRESS
Pittsburgh, Pennsylvania

Published in the United States of America by
DUQUESNE UNIVERSITY PRESS
600 Forbes Avenue
Pittsburgh, Pennsylvania 15282

Section 2 of chapter 1 appeared previously as "'She sees,' 'She's seen,' and she 'hath shown': The Feminine Trinity in 'Upon the Annuntiation and Passion,'" *John Donne Journal* 23 (2004): 117–38; section 3 as "Ambivalent Mourning: Sacramentality, Idolatry, and Gender in 'Since she whome I lovd hath paid her last debt,'" *John Donne Journal* 10, no. 1–2 (1991): 45–56; and an earlier version of section 6 as "'to good ends': The Final Cause of Sacramental Womanhood in *The First Anniversarie*," *John Donne Journal* 20 (2001): 141–50. An earlier version of section 3 of chapter 3 appeared as "'Heav'n's last best gift': Eve and Wisdom in *Paradise Lost*," *Modern Philology* 95, no. 1 (1997): 44–67. All of these materials are reprinted by permission of the journals.

    Earlier versions of some of the material in chapter 2, sections 5–6, appeared in "Woman's desire for Man in Lanyer's *Salve Deus Rex Judaeorum*," *Journal of English and Germanic Philology* 99, no. 3 (2000): 356–78, copyright 2000 by the Board of Trustees of the University of Illinois. Used with the permission of the University of Illinois Press.

Library of Congress Cataloging-in-Publication Data

DiPasquale, Theresa M., 1962–
    Refiguring the sacred feminine : the poems of John Donne, Aemilia Lanyer, and John Milton / Theresa M. DiPasquale.
        p. cm. — (Medieval & Renaissance literary studies)
    Summary: "A study of the sacred feminine as it is understood in the works of John Donne, Aemilia Lanyer, and John Milton, each of whom reformed and envisioned several important Christian archetypes: Ecclesia, the Blessed Virgin Mary, Divine Wisdom, and the soul as bride of Christ"—Provided by publisher.
    Includes bibliographical references and index.
    ISBN 978-0-8207-0405-0 (cloth : alk. paper)
1. English poetry—Early modern, 1500–1700—History and criticism. 2. Christian poetry, English—Early modern, 1500–1700—History and criticism. 3. Women in literature. 4. Women—Religious aspects. 5. Femininity—Religious aspects. 6. Femininity (Philosophy) in literature. 7. Donne, John, 1572–1631—Criticism and interpretation. 8. Lanyer, Aemilia—Criticism and interpretation. 9. Milton, John, 1608–1674—Criticism and interpretation. I. Title.
    PR535.W58D57 2008
    821'.3093823—dc22

                                                              2007051592

∞ Printed on acid-free paper

For
Lee Patrick Keene
and
Dominic Jude DiPasquale Keene

Contents

Abbreviations

Note: All spellings of titles are normalized in the Donne *Variorum*'s "Short Forms of Reference for Donne's Works." I have followed suit here, but in the body of my text, I have used the titles as they appear at the heads of individual poems within the *Variorum* proper or, in the case of poems not yet covered by the *Variorum*, in Shawcross's edition.

Annun	Donne, "The Annuntiation and Passion"
BCP	*Book of Common Prayer*
BedfHon	Donne, "To the Countess of Bedford" ("Honor is so sublime")
BedfRef	Donne, "To the Countess of Bedford" ("You have refined me")
BedfWrit	Donne, "To the Countess of Bedford" ("To have written then")
Broken	Donne, "The Broken Heart"
Canon	Donne, "The Canonization"
ElBed	Donne, "Going to Bed"
ElServe	Donne, "Oh, let not me serve so"
FirAn	Donne, *The First Anniversary. An Anatomy of the World*
FQ	Spenser, *The Faerie Queene*
FunEl	Donne, "A Funeral Elegy"

Goodf	Donne, "Goodfriday, 1613. Riding Westward"
HHB	Spenser, "Hymne of Heavenly Beavtie"
HSBatter	Donne, "Batter my heart"
HSLittle	Donne, "I am a little world"
HSRound	Donne, "At the round earth's imagined corners"
HSShe	Donne, "Since she whom I loved"
HSShow	Donne, "Show me dear Christ"
HSSighs	Donne, "O might those sighs"
HSVex	Donne, "O to vex me"
HSWhat	Donne, "What if this present"
Lit	Donne, "A Litany"
MHMary	Donne, "To the Lady Magdalen Herbert, of St. Mary Magdalen"
PL	Milton, *Paradise Lost*
PR	Milton, *Paradise Regained*
Res	Donne, "Resurrection Imperfect"
Sappho	Donne, "Sappho to Philaenis"
Sat3	Donne, "Satire III" ("Kind pity chokes my spleen")
SDRJ	Lanyer, *Salve Deus Rex Judaeorum*
SecAn	Donne, *The Second Anniversary. Of the Progress of the Soul*
Sidney	Donne, "Upon the Translation of the Psalms by Sir Philip Sidney"
Teares	Spenser, *The Teares of the Muses*
Tilman	Donne, "To Mr. Tilman after He Had Taken Orders"
YP	Milton, *The Complete Prose Works*, ed. Don M. Wolfe et al.

Editorial Note

The first quotation from any particular poem or collection of poems is documented in a footnote identifying the source by editor's name, title, and page number[s]; subsequent quotations are cited parenthetically by title and line number or, where appropriate, by title, book number, and line number.

Donne's poetry is quoted from the *Variorum Edition* whenever possible: the elegies and "Sapho to Philaenis" from volume 2, the *Anniversaries* from volume 6, and the Holy Sonnets from volume 7, part 1. Poems that do not appear in the volumes of the *Variorum* published to date—the satires, the verse letters, the *Songs and Sonets,* and devotional poems other than the Holy Sonnets—are quoted from *The Complete Poetry of John Donne,* edited by John T. Shawcross. All Donne poems are cited parenthetically by short title and line number. Donne's sermons are quoted from *The Sermons of John Donne,* 10 volumes, edited by George R. Potter and Evelyn M. Simpson and cited parenthetically by volume and page number. Milton's poetry is quoted from *John Milton: Complete Poems and Major Prose,* edited by Merritt Y. Hughes and cited parenthetically by abbreviated title and line number, using the abbreviations provided in Hughes's edition. Milton's prose works are quoted from *The Complete Prose Works of John Milton,* 8 volumes, edited by Don M. Wolfe et al., which is cited parenthetically as YP by volume and page number. Lanyer's poetry is quoted from *The Poems of Aemilia Lanyer: Salve Deus Rex Judaeorum,* edited by Susanne Woods. Titles of the shorter poems and prose dedications in Lanyer's *Salve Deus Rex Judaeorum* are cited parenthetically by abbreviated title and line number; both the volume as a whole and the long title poem are referred to using the italicized title *Salve Deus Rex Judaeorum* in full or in the abbreviated form *Salve Deus*; the title poem is cited parenthetically by line number as *SDRJ*.

Except where otherwise noted, I quote throughout from the popular and profusely annotated 1560 Geneva Bible, which was the most popular Protestant Bible for many years even after the publication of the 1611 King James Version. I have discussed in my notes points at which a poet may have taken into consideration other translations, including the Bishop's Bible, the Catholic Douay-Rheims Bible, and (in works composed after 1611) the King James.

The 1559 *Book of Common Prayer* and the Elizabethan Homilies are cited parenthetically by page number as *BCP* and *Certaine Sermons*, respectively. The Articles of the Church of England are cited as *Thirty-Nine Articles* by article number.

When citing theological and exegetical works by patristic, medieval, and early modern writers, I have in most cases provided page numbers in the initial citation, but in subsequent citations have used notation that will allow interested readers to locate the passages in question in other editions or translations than the one I have used (for example, citations of Calvin's *Institution of the Christian Religion* and Hooker's *Of the Laws of Ecclesiastical Polity* by book, chapter, and paragraph). In a few cases (Calvin's *Commentaries* and Aquinas's *Summa Theologica*, for example), the translations I used are now relatively difficult to obtain in print, but are readily available in online editions; I have thus included the electronic publication information for those editions in my bibliography and have cited quotations parenthetically using notations that will allow readers to locate the quoted passages either in the online edition or elsewhere.

In quotations from original sixteenth and seventeenth century print publications and facsimile editions thereof, I have silently replaced long *s* with *s*.

Acknowledgments

This book is the fruit of many years' labor. I am grateful to family, friends, colleagues, and students who have encouraged me, put up with me, guided me, and enriched my understanding of the poetry. I am particularly indebted to my scholarly mentors Mary Free and Gordon Braden; to Susan Wadsworth-Booth, Albert Labriola, and Kathy McLaughlin of Duquesne University Press; and to the anonymous reader who commented on the manuscript for the press. All of these people read my work in progress at various stages and helped me to shape and discipline a sometimes unruly manuscript. I of course take full responsibility for the book's remaining flaws.

This study has in it—as do many scholarly books—an element of autobiography; it springs from my own experience of the sacred feminine as exemplified by the women who have inspired me, supported me in my family life and in my scholarship, and come to my assistance whenever I needed help: my grandmothers, Teresa and Lucrezia; my mother, Charlotte; my sisters, Catherine and Maria; my mother-in-law, Kathleen; and her mother, Sophie. It also reflects the love and support of my husband Lee and our son Dominic, who enable my own imperfect but ardent efforts to embody the sacred feminine.

Introduction

John Donne, Aemilia Lanyer, and John Milton each revised and renewed the Judeo-Christian tradition of the sacred feminine. Rooted in the Hebrew scriptures, further developed in the New Testament, and expanded upon in the writings of the church fathers and in a wide range of medieval and early modern liturgies, sermons, poems, and treatises, this tradition celebrates feminine archetypes of grace, virtue, and spiritual illumination. Its central figures are divine Wisdom, who appears in the book of Proverbs; the created Wisdom of the Deutero-canonical Ecclesiasticus and Wisdom of Solomon, who reflects the uncreated and creating Sapientia of Proverbs; the bride of the Song of Solomon; the Mary of Luke's gospel; and Ecclesia as she is invoked in the Pauline epistles and the book of Revelation.[1] These figures are essential to the works of Donne, Lanyer, and Milton, for all three poets are invested very deeply in the ancient and scripturally authorized belief that the relationship between God and humankind is gendered: God is father, bridegroom, king; the human soul and the church as corporate entity are daughter, bride, and consort.[2] But for Donne, Lanyer, and Milton, the essential femininity of the human vis-à-vis the divine is complicated by the fact of an individual person's biological sex: a soul's encounter with God and her place in the economy of redemption are, in these writers' poetry, indelibly stamped by the sex of the body in which that soul is housed. All three are engaged in literary projects that modify, expand upon, challenge, or rethink

I

the natures of men and women, the duties and privileges of the female sex, and the essential role played by feminine powers and influences in healing the sin-forged rift between God and men. Each resists and modifies the strict Calvinist belief that fallen Nature is radically depraved and unable to cooperate with grace; and in so doing, each counters what Rosemary Radford Ruether astutely identifies as Reformed theology's tendency to diminish the role of the Blessed Virgin and of the sacred feminine more broadly.[3] Each portrays the feminine as a reflection of the divine, and woman herself, at her best, as an agent of redemption or conduit of grace. Each understands Christian poetics as serving a function analogous to that of Mary, who gave birth to and nurtured God's Word incarnate.

Donne, Lanyer, and Milton are by no means the only three English Protestant writers invested in the sacred feminine. Edmund Spenser's corpus is largely devoted to the celebration of feminine allegorical figures who embody holiness, truth, virtue, and generative or regenerative power; George Herbert relies upon gendered images and archetypes in defining his sacramental poetics; and scholars have demonstrated that gender is also an important factor in the poems of Francis Quarles, Mary Sidney Herbert, and Henry Vaughan, to name three others.[4] But John Donne, Aemilia Lanyer, and John Milton are all, I would argue, exceptionally provocative in their approaches to sex and gender as aspects of the sacred. A tone of intellectual and spiritual self-assurance and resistance to external authority is noticeably audible in all three, albeit in different keys and in the service of very different projects. That tone is the outward sign of an inward conviction that compels each writer to undertake bold revisions of traditional materials and to do so in ways that often resist simple conformity to any officially sanctioned doctrine, including the mainstream of English Calvinism as it is enshrined in *The Thirty-Nine Articles* and the Elizabethan Homilies. While no great poet is merely or simply orthodox, Donne, Lanyer, and Milton were all particularly concerned to avoid the pitfalls of orthodoxy. None of the three would "let [his or her] Soule be tyed / To mans lawes, by which she shall not be tryed / At the last day" (Donne, *Sat3*, 93–95); "she," in each case, answered to a higher authority than any man-made institution, political or ecclesiastical. And thus each had to struggle, in one way or another, to define the precise nature of his or her relationship with the Church of England and its doctrine.[5]

John Donne, though he would be ordained a priest of the English church in 1615 at the age of 42, was born into a recusant family deeply committed to the Old Religion; his maternal great-grand-uncle was Saint Thomas More, his mother's brothers were Jesuits risking their lives for the English mission, his brother Henry died in prison after being arrested for harboring a priest, and his mother herself (who lived until 1631, dying only a few months before her son), was a lifelong recusant. The poet spent much of his youth under the influence of noble families still committed to Roman Catholicism and resistant to the Tudor monarchy's insistence on conformity, and he was deeply affected by disagreements and divisions within the English Roman Catholic community.[6] Not surprisingly, then, many of Donne's poems bear the marks of what might be characterized as his maternal heritage; as scholars such as Dennis Flynn, R. V. Young, and M. Thomas Hester demonstrate, Donne's ties to pre-Tridentine English Catholicism help to define his thought, his spirituality, and his art. Those ties have a particularly important effect, I would argue, upon his attempt to reconcile his conception of woman as a sacrament, a human conduit of grace, to the parameters of doctrine and devotion as they were defined by the English church under the self-consciously patriarchal King James.[7]

Donne's near contemporary Aemilia Lanyer was a woman deeply committed to a proto-feminist creed rooted in her radical interpretation of the New Testament. Through her narrative poem on the Passion of Christ and the dedicatory poetry she used to introduce and frame it, Lanyer rethinks the theology of priesthood and claims for women a sacerdotal privilege denied them by Protestants and Catholics alike. As scholars including

Susanne Woods, Kari Boyd McBride, Janel Mueller, and Achsah Guibbory have shown, Lanyer's poetry is genuinely radical in its implications.

No seventeenth century English poet, however, was more politically, ecclesiastically, and theologically radical than John Milton. Finding himself, as he put it, "Church-outed by the Prelats" (YP 1:823)—which is to say, kept by his antiprelatical beliefs from entering the ministry of the established church—he determined from a point very early in his career to serve God and the church as a poet and a prophetic revolutionary rather than a priest. He went on to challenge orthodox opinion on every front: in his defenses of regicide, in his divorce tracts, in *Areopagitica,* and in his poetry. Approaching Milton from a wide range of very different theoretical perspectives, scholars including Arthur E. Barker, Diane McColley, John Shawcross, Joseph Wittreich, Catherine Gimelli Martin, Michael Schoenfeldt, Stephen B. Dobranski, and John P. Rumrich have demonstrated the uncompromising independence of Milton's Christian vision, which leads him to oppose a variety of orthodoxies: he confronts the Laudian church of the Caroline period with an anti-authoritarian model of Ecclesia, parts company with many of his Presbyterian and Nonconformist political allies in espousing an essentially Arminian doctrine of good works, and embraces monism and Arianism, each of which Calvinists and Roman Catholics alike classify as heretical. Milton thus, like Donne and Lanyer before him, brings to bear upon the poetic interpretation of English Protestantism something of an outsider's perspective. All three poets have minds inclined to question and to seek out new solutions to ancient problems, and all three invite their readers to develop a deeper appreciation of the sacred feminine.

Building upon the work of the many scholars who have studied these poets with particular attention to their portrayals of woman and of the feminine, I do not seek to break new ground in defining the poetic practice of Donne, Lanyer, or Milton, but rather to enrich readers' understanding of specific works by each poet through historically grounded and intertextually sensitive formalist analysis. The intertextual element is perhaps most significant, for this study provides a sustained opportunity, more extensive than any provided in the existing scholarship, to see each poet in the varying lights cast by the other two.[8] Juxtaposing the mid- to late-seventeenth-century Milton with two writers who lived and wrote during the reign of King James, the proto-feminist Lanyer with two of the most authoritatively masculine poets of early modern England, and the deeply conflicted Donne with the fiercely resolved Lanyer and Milton allows the reader to see more clearly how each of these three very different poetic imaginations, coping with particular historical and personal circumstances, envisions the place of femininity and the role of female human beings within the economy of redemption. No overarching thesis about the three can emerge from such a process, for generalizations about the achievements of Donne, Lanyer, and Milton as a group obscure the enormous differences among them. By studying them in connection with one another, however, we may appreciate more fully each writer's unique poetic articulation of the sacred feminine: Donne's portrayal of woman as sacrament, and of divine grace made present through female flesh and feminine virtue; Lanyer's portrayal of woman as priest, and of divine grace transforming Nature herself; Milton's portrayal of woman as an earthly type of heavenly Wisdom, and of divine grace proceeding from the "consummate virtue" of a woman's son.

My subject is the poetry that presents these portrayals, not the theology or philosophy or politics underlying them, for my approach to the texts I discuss is primarily literary in intent and focus. My goal is to present illuminating new readings of poems that challenge twenty-first century orthodoxies as unflinchingly as they did early modern ones; but I wish, to paraphrase an essay by Stanley Fish, to show why all three of these poets "matter" in a literary sense by focusing upon their "aesthetic achievement[s]" and recognizing that "historical and political matters" as well as religious and philosophical ones, "matter chiefly as the material of" those achievements, not as objects of study in their own right.[9] In interpreting the varying approaches that Donne, Lanyer, and Milton take to the sacred feminine in their poems, I have thus frequently glanced backward at the long history of theological and artistic interpretation that informs scriptural, patristic, medieval, and early modern approaches to Mary the Mother of Jesus, to the idea that both the individual soul and the church are the bride of Christ, and to the image of Sapientia as she is portrayed in the book of Proverbs and in the Wisdom of Solomon.[10] I have not, however, sought to trace that history systematically or to account for all of the controversies over scriptural authorship and interpretation that began in the early Christian era and continue to the present day, for to do so would distract needlessly from my critical focus on individual works by Donne, Lanyer, and Milton and from my study of each poet's works in relation to those of the other two. And while I have read with a sense of historical context throughout this study, my objective in doing so is always primarily and finally to explore each poem discussed not as a simple product of or response to its context, but as a rich and enduring verbal artifact that rises from and redefines that context on the poet's own terms.

The following chapters are thus organized by author and work, not by themes, genres, or particular images of the sacred feminine. I begin with Donne, though Lanyer was approximately three years his senior, since Donne wrote the earliest of the poems I discuss, a 1608 meditation on "The Annuntiation and Passion." His masculine response to the Jacobean milieu in which he wrote provides an excellent point of reference for reading Lanyer's proto-feminist response to that same milieu, while his relatively conservative ecclesiology and sacramental theology act as sounding boards for the study of Milton's more radical vision.

Donne is perhaps best known to twentieth and twenty-first century readers for his fusion of sexuality and spirituality. Like King Solomon as Donne describes him in a sermon, the poet brought an amorous disposition to bear upon his encounter with the sacred.[11] A man who loves a woman, the poet laments in a sonnet on the death of his wife, can find that love to be both a means of grace and an impediment to it; and a good woman, that same poem makes painfully clear, has a weighty load of semi-otic, spiritual, and physical significance to bear before she can be "into heauen rauished" (*HSShe*, 3); she is — by her very nature as Donne understands it — a human sacrament. But the meaning of sacrament was a highly charged issue in the early seventeenth century, and questions about gender were, for Donne, inti-mately entwined with the denominational issues at play in Eng-land during King James's reign. Section 1 of my opening chapter thus surveys Donne's shift, in the first two decades of the sev-enteenth century, away from the satirical, anti-Petrarchan and often misogynous themes of the elegies and epigrams he wrote during the final years of Queen Elizabeth's reign. I seek to con-textualize the poet's frequent focus, in works composed during the early Jacobean period, upon a reverent though always witty and intellectually daring exploration of what he once called "the Idea of a Woman."[12] Section 2 of the chapter turns to one of Donne's devotional works from this period, "The Annuntiation and Passion," a poem that envisions a cooperative threesome consisting of the speaker's soul, the Virgin Mary, and the church: an earthly feminine trinity through whom the masculine Trin-ity of heaven is revealed. The meditative calm and joy of "The Annuntiation and Passion" contrast sharply with the conflicted and uneasy tone of the Holy Sonnets "Since She whome I lovd" and "Show me deare Christ." The first of these, I argue in sec-tion 3 of the chapter, is a literary receptacle into which the poet channels the ambivalent sexual and spiritual longing he feels in the absence of his much-desired spouse. Donne can confront his grief and his ongoing desire for Anne only by working through contested theological questions: whether and how sacraments convey grace, and whether and how Christians ought to venerate saints. "Show me deare Christ," like "She whome I lovd," grap-ples with the nature of nuptial love, though the spouse in ques-tion is Christ's rather than the poet's. In section 4 of chapter 1,

I argue that the sonnet's notorious concluding lines, in which the speaker imagines Christ sharing his spouse with any man who truly desires her, rely upon Donne's darkly ambivalent revision of a joyful image from the writings of his favorite exegete, Saint Augustine. The unresolved tensions of the sonnet reflect Donne's ongoing struggle with ecclesiastical and spiritual questions that are, for him, always gender questions as well.

The remaining three sections of chapter 1 deal with Donne's monumental tribute to the sacred feminine, the *Anniversaries.* Section 5 discusses the poetics of this three-part work, which invites readers to acknowledge and celebrate the sacrament of woman and to compensate for the devastating effect of her absence by participating in poetry that is also intended to function sacramentally. Section 6 focuses on *The First Anniversarie. An Anatomie of the World,* detailing the ways in which that poem confronts misogyny and celebrates the "Idea of a Woman" as Donne understands it. Section 7 reads both "A Funerall Elegie," the shorter poem that is placed between the *First* and *Second Anniversarie* in the 1612 edition of those poems, and *The Second Anniversarie. The Progres of the Soule* as works that admit to the limitations of a sacramental poetics and focus on the transcendent womanhood of female saints in heaven. Chapter 1 as a whole argues that, in the poetry Donne was writing during the reign of King James, his images of the sacred feminine—the good wife ravished by God and the nearly anonymous "shee" whose virtue is the "matter and the stuffe" of others' redeemed existence (*FirAn,* 77), the mourning Madonna beneath the cross and the apotheosized "Mother-maid" who takes "Ioy in not being that, which men haue said" (*SecAn,* 341–42), the feminine soul gazing intently upon what Christ's "imitating spouse" reveals to her, and the open-armed Ecclesia who is the object of the masculine poet's desire—all emerge from his gendered response to Jacobean theological and ecclesiastical conflict. But rather than providing clear or definitive answers to the poet's questions about sexuality, religion, or spirituality, each of these images instead animates a poem that is itself ambiguous, open-ended, and committed to engaging readers in the production of meaning.

Like Donne's *First Anniversarie*, Aemilia Lanyer's *Salve Deus Rex Judaeorum* was published in 1611, the year in which the King James Bible was first printed. Section 1 of chapter 2 thus positions Lanyer as another poet who responds assertively and creatively to the Jacobean politico-religious milieu. Lanyer's vision of womanhood and of ministry, and her vigorous commentary on marriage, social class, and sexual desire apparently found no audience in her own time. But Lanyer, whose poetry is now an established feature of the literary landscape in Renaissance studies—having become the focus of a growing number of critical and scholarly essays and books, and having been granted a place in the *Norton Anthology of English Literature*—brings real theological sophistication to bear upon her poetic treatment of matters divine and devotional, sexual and textual. Her vocabulary and her prosodic skills are limited, but her language is nevertheless wittily resourceful, sensuously textured, and fiercely insistent upon the poet's self-consciously female perspective. Section 2 of chapter 2 surveys the poetics of the *Salve Deus*, arguing that Lanyer positions herself as both prophet and priest. In this section, I extend and develop the work of previous Lanyer scholars in demonstrating the poet's reliance upon the model provided her by Mary Sidney Herbert, Countess of Pembroke. The poetry emerging from that model bears witness to Lanyer's conviction that redeemed Nature is perfectly reconciled with grace and that the Incarnation of Jesus in the womb of Mary is both source and summit of that reconciliation.

In sections 3 and 4 of chapter 2, I focus on one of the central themes springing from Lanyer's incarnational poetics, exploring how she reinterprets and vivifies the allegory of Ecclesia. Asserting that every female Christian has a vocation to live as the church incarnate, Lanyer describes that church's female ministry as more true to Christ and more spiritually efficacious than the apostolic priesthood of men. But Lanyer's ecclesiology is only one aspect of her belief in the radical implications of

Christ's incarnation. I thus turn, in sections 5, 6, and 7 of the chapter, to the portrayal of marriage and sexuality in *Salve Deus*. Lanyer, I argue in section 5, not only defines woman's relationship with the divine in erotic terms, but envisions redeemed female *eros* as authorizing women's desire for worthy men. As I go on to demonstrate in section 6, however, Lanyer presents her vision of heterosexual eros as rendering obsolete the institution of Christian marriage celebrated in Ephesians. And as section 7 of the chapter argues, reading Lanyer's longing portraits of other women in light of Donne's "Sapho to Philænis," *Salve Deus* also opens up new possibilities for sanctified homoeroticism. Chapter 2 as a whole demonstrates, then, that for Aemilia Lanyer, the virtuous woman is not a sacrament, as in Donne's poetry; she is instead a priestly minister of Christ's Eucharistic presence and an embodiment of Ecclesia doing God's work in the sinful world of Adam's sons. In the redeemed woman's experience as Lanyer portrays it, all contraries are reconciled; her relationship with God, which is no less erotic than it is spiritual, sets her free to take pleasure in the human objects of her desire, be they wise and comely men or beautiful and virtuous women.

In moving from Aemilia Lanyer in chapter 2 to John Milton in chapter 3, I make a historical leap of some 21 years, shifting from 1611, when *Salve Deus* was published, to 1632, the probable date of Milton's *Arcades*. Two turbulent decades separate Lanyer's praise of Margaret Clifford from the young Milton's tribute to the Dowager Countess of Derby, and a significant gap also separates the earlier writer's anti-intellectual stance and her sometimes unwieldy versification from the learned classicism and rich verbal craftsmanship of the young Milton. But that gap does not obscure the very real similarities that link Milton's aristocratic entertainment to Lanyer's book; each celebrates the goodness of a venerable noblewoman who has separated herself from the decadence of Stuart court culture in order to live as a virtuous embodiment of Christ's spouse, the church. But while Lanyer argues for the sacerdotal vocation of that woman and focuses on her status as the spouse of Christ, Milton—in

Arcades and in later works—is particularly interested in the luminosity of her virtue, which establishes her as an avatar of Wisdom. Every encounter with the sacred feminine in his poetry is in one way or another suffused with that sagacious light. In section 1 of chapter 3, I argue that Milton presents a Reformed alternative to the pastoral entertainments being staged at court by King Charles and his Catholic queen by portraying Alice Spencer Stanley Egerton as a type of Ecclesia endowed with the qualities of the scriptural Sapientia. Section 2 of chapter 3 continues my discussion of the young Milton's ecclesiology and further explores his interest in female personifications of Wisdom, arguing that the Lady of *A Mask Presented at Ludlow Castle* embodies his evolving notion of the church and the regenerate soul as a wise but fallible virgin-errant. *A Mask* as a whole portrays wisdom as an intellectual virtue that mirrors the moral virtue of chastity and is particularly well suited to guide any soul housed in a virginal body, as well as the church militant herself, in her journey through the wilderness.

Section 3 of chapter 3 turns from analyzing the virginal archetype of Milton's *Mask* to explore the epic portrait of a marriage in his *Paradise Lost*, which goes about justifying "the ways of God to men" (*PL* 1.26) not only by exploring the freedom that God grants all rational creatures and the obedience that can flow only from such freedom, but also by imagining—at the very center of prelapsarian life—a human relationship that is biblically tied to questions of freedom and obedience: marriage. In portraying Adam and Eve, I argue, Milton looks yet once more to the Wisdom books of the Bible, modeling their prelapsarian union upon the intimate relationship of King Solomon with Sapientia and defining Eve's prelapsarian freedom and dignity as a function of her sapiential "Virgin Majesty," which she retains even within a consummated patriarchal marriage (*PL* 9.270).

Moving from the Eden of *Paradise Lost* to the desert landscape of *Paradise Regained*, section 4 of chapter 3 focuses on Milton's Jesus and on his status as the son of Mary, exploring how the Savior portrayed in Milton's brief epic puts into practice the *sapientia creata* God affords all men and women. In doing so, Jesus reveals that he is not only his Father's valiant son, but also his wise mother's dutiful child and attentive pupil. Chapter 3 in its entirety thus demonstrates that Milton returns again and again to the scriptural figure of divine Wisdom as his inspiration for female figures whose created human wisdom both mirrors and nurtures the divine Sapientia.

The coda that follows chapter 3 returns to a theme touched upon in each of the preceding three chapters: Marian poetics. Donne, Lanyer, and Milton all look to the Virgin Mother of the Redeemer as a model of sacred creativity; Mary's maternal work provides each writer with inspiration for his or her own poetic work. All three thus have in common a deep affection for and commitment to that most exalted human embodiment of the sacred feminine: Mary, full of grace.

DONNE

John Donne's poetics, his explorations of human sexuality and love, and his portrayals of spiritual struggle are all intricately entwined with his response to post-Reformation theological issues. Whether a Donne persona is hoping to turn a bug bite into a seduction (as in "The Flea"), complimenting English ladies while traveling abroad in Catholic France (as in "A Letter to the Lady Carey and Mrs. Essex Rich"), or contemplating the image of the crucified Christ (as in "What if this present?"), his discourse will be loaded with theological freight.[1] For Donne was raised on the language of religious debate, having grown up in a fiercely committed recusant family, and he came to embrace the English church only, as he would put it in a famous passage from the preface to *Pseudo-Martyr*, after he had *"suruayed and digested the whole body of Diuinity, controuerted betweene ours and the Romane Church"* (B3r).

This process of surveying and digestion never really ended for Donne. Though he ceased at some point to call the Roman Catholic Church his own (the precise date remains uncertain), he never abandoned the ecumenical spirit with which he undertook the study of debated theological and ecclesiastical questions. He would eventually become a priest of the English church, dean of St. Paul's, a preacher, and a Protestant theologian of great subtlety and depth, but his commitment to the Church of England did not prevent him from continuing to believe what he asserted in a 1609 letter to his friend Henry Goodyer: "that in all Christian professions there is way to salvation" and that the Roman Catholic and English Protestant churches are "sister teats of [God's] graces, yet both diseased and infected, but not both alike" (Donne, *Letters,* 100, 102).

This graphic gynecological image is a good starting point for reflection upon Donne's idea of Ecclesia, which acknowledges both the painful mastitis of the established church (the breast at which he was feeding by 1609) and the more deadly cancer that he and other English Protestants believe to be afflicting the Roman breast. Both ecclesiastical paps, Donne implies, nourish souls; grace flows through each. But neither is untouched by the corruption of the fallen world. In light of this image, it is no surprise to find that the poems Donne was writing during the same period as the letter grapple constantly with gender-oriented versions of the questions central to the theological and ecclesiastical issues debated by Roman Catholics and English Protestants of various persuasions during the early seventeenth century: To which incarnation of the bride of Christ should one be loyal? And what does the true bride look like? What role does the mother of Jesus play in our salvation, and how should we honor her? Is grace made manifest in physically tangible ways? And, if so, how are we to respond to the streams of grace that flow through maternal and material channels?

Donne's poems never provide simple, definitive answers to these questions. Even in the sermons he preached after he was ordained in 1615, his theology and ecclesiology are nuanced in ways that defy easy categorization. But in much of the poetry he wrote during the Jacobean period—from "The Annunciation and Passion" in 1608, through "Since She whome I lovd" (which grapples with the 1617 death of his wife) and "Show me deare Christ" (which may have been written as late as 1620)[2]—Donne seeks answers to the theological, political, cultural, and ecclesiastical issues of his time and to his own spiritual, emotional, and physical desires through encounters with and meditations on female figures. The church, the Blessed Virgin, the "shee" of the *Anniversaries*, and his own beloved Anne all serve as sacramental intermediaries between God and man, between the spiritual and the physical, between the sacred and the profane.

These encounters vary in part because they take place within several different genres. In "The Annuntiation and Passion," a 46-line meditative poem inspired by the liturgical and political events of 1608, Donne's persona is filled with quiet awe, and his vision of a feminine Trinity is unclouded by fear or doubt. In the sonnet on Anne's death, however, and in "Show me deare Christ," the speaker is vexed and uncertain, torn by conflicting emotions Donne associates with the sonnet form itself; his vision is blurred or blocked, and the poet's deepest anxieties—about God, about woman, and about church—are laid bare. But Donne's greatest works from the early Jacobean period break free from the narrow confines of a sonnet's little world; the *Anniversaries* (written 1610–11; published 1611–12) undertake a meditation of near-epic proportions. In these poems, Donne's "Idea of a Woman" is his guiding principle as he dissects a fragmented and decaying world and envisions a celestial realm beyond the reach of denominational controversy or gender hierarchy.

1. Donne in the Late Elizabethan and Early Jacobean Milieux

In his erotic elegies, which probably date primarily from the 1590s and which are among his earliest extant poems, Donne repeatedly uses gendered imagery—much of it arguably misogynous or pornographic—to deal with then current theological questions and religio-political issues.[3] Indeed, the personae of these Ovidian poems, the speakers of Donne's satires (which were written in the late 1590s), and "the anti-Petrarchist, anti-Neoplatonic outlaw lover of [his] lyrics" are all hopelessly caught up in what M. Thomas Hester punningly calls "sectual politics" ("'this cannot be said,'" 374).[4] In the elegy "Oh let not me serve so," for example, the speaker begins by deploring the kind of courtiership that earns honor only through financial ruin and false flattery; he does not want to be known as his mistress's servant unless he really is just that: "Oh then let mee / Fauorit in ordinary or no fauorit bee."[5] He proceeds to warn his unfaithful addressee that if she continues to abuse his loyalty to her, he

> shall
> As Nations do from Rome, from thy Love fall.
> My hate shall outgrow thyne, and vtterly
> I will renounce thy dallyance: and when I
> Ame the Recusant, in that resolute state
> What hurts it me to be excommunicate?   (ElServe, 41–46)

The promiscuous beloved is described as a queen, a lady served— as Elizabeth was—by many who seek her favor and court her with amorous language. At the same time, she is a church of indeterminate denomination: both the whore of Babylon abandoned by the secular principalities of Reformation Europe, and the English church spurned by a nobly unyielding "Recusant." Here and in many other poems of the same genre, Donne elides sexual freedom and spiritual freedom, roundly mocking the Petrarchan veneration of Elizabeth by such poets as Spenser and Ralegh. In "To his Mistress going to bed," Donne targets in particular Ralegh's colonial ambitions. The poem parodies the Elizabethan fantasy of possessing a virgin "America," a "new-found land" one is licensed to explore (as Ralegh was licensed by Elizabeth to explore Virginia). Donne taps the subversive potential of Ovidian elegy in order to critique both Ralegh's New World ambitions and the Protestant queen whose court culture glorified the Petrarchan ideal of the unobtainable beloved, establishing Elizabeth as a secular, Protestant replacement for the Blessed Virgin Mary.[6]

Why, then, did Donne move during the early Jacobean period from writing Ovidian elegies that muddy, mock, or invert exalted images of female beauty and purity to writing poems that take the sacred feminine seriously? The answer, I would argue, has to do with regime change. When Elizabeth died in 1603, her passing was an opportunity for some writers to amplify and intensify the cult of the virgin queen that Donne had burlesqued in his elegies. Others, however, displayed a less than reverent attitude; the monarch's death elicited from some of her subjects a sardonic response very much in keeping with the spirit of Donne's elegies and satires: "Wee worshipt noe saintes, but wee prayd to ladyes, in the Q[ueenes] tyme," remarked an Inns of Court wit named Edward Curle; "This superstition shall be abolished, we hope, in our kinges raigne."[7] As Hackett suggests, Inns of Court students like Curle were no doubt perceiving in Elizabeth's demise "the welcome end of an unduly feminised, extravagant culture" (Hackett, *Virgin Mother, Maiden Queen,* 226). No more Petrarchan posturing; no more quasi-papistical adoration of the Virgin, no more bowing to a woman! Donne was no longer at the Inns of Court in 1603, but he had studied at Lincoln's Inn from 1592 to 1595, and elegies like "To his Mistress going to bed" had been composed in the same milieu that fostered the wit of the young Curle. The author of that daring poem would probably have laughed at Curle's joke.

Even as late as 1617, a little over two years after Donne was ordained to the priesthood, one can detect a related form of wit, muffled by solemn context but still discernable, at work in a sermon. On March 24, 1616/17, the anniversary of Elizabeth's death and James's accession, Donne preached on Proverbs 22:11: "He that loveth pureness of heart, for the grace of his lips, the king shall be his friend." In the sermon, Donne thus comments both upon various kinds of love and on the qualities of a virtuous monarch. The former subject occasions a long digression (*Sermons,* 1:199–203) on the spiritual danger of loving women too much or in inappropriate ways, one example of which, he claims—almost as if to flash his Protestant credentials before *"the Lords of the Council, and other Honorable Persons"* gathered at Paul's Cross (*Sermons,* 1:183)—is the belief that the Blessed Virgin Mary contributed to human beings' salvation as much as Eve contributed to their downfall. "She, more then any other woman, and many other blessed women since," Donne concedes, "have done many things for the advancing of the glory of God, and imitation of others" (*Sermons*, 1:200). But, given the weakness of men, members of the female sex — Mary included — are still temptations to idolatry.

Later in the sermon, Donne recalls the day of Queen Elizabeth's death as an occasion of sadness mingled with joy at the proclamation of James's kingship, and while he stresses the goodness of the late queen, he does so more in order to magnify James (as a king so virtuous that he need not resent the praise of his predecessor) than to look back nostalgically upon Elizabeth or to compare her to the Blessed Virgin. Interestingly, the portions of the sermon devoted to Elizabeth stress how *old* she was when she finally went to her reward:

> In the death of that Queen, unmatchable, inimitable in her sex; that Queen, worthy, I will not say of *Nestors* years, I will not say of *Methusalems*, but worthy of *Adams* years, if *Adam* had never faln; in her death we were all under one common flood, and depth of tears. But the *Spirit of God moved upon the face of that depth*; and God said, *Let there be light, and there was light, and God saw that that light was good.* (*Sermons*, 1:217)

The opening chapter of Genesis is applied here to portray the reign of James as a new creation, the dawning of God's light following the primeval darkness that preceded it. The old monarch, Donne says, "reigns now with Christ, the other reigns here over us *vice Christi*, for Christ. . . . [S]he was fittest in that fullness of years, to be chosen and assum'd into heaven; and he fittest . . . to choose to stay upon earth, for our protection, and for our direction" (*Sermons*, 1:218–19). It had, in short, been time for her to go: out with the old woman, in with the New Man.

A similar gender dynamic, as well as a similar use of messianic imagery in praise of James, animates *Sorrowes Ioy*, a collection of poems published immediately following Elizabeth's death and James's accession in 1603.[8] The verses in this anthology of pieces by various Cambridge University men repeatedly stress that a virtuous queen has been replaced by a divinely appointed king and that the sorrow subjects feel at the loss of the former is amply comforted by their joy in welcoming the latter: "For her I grieve, in him I take delight," Thomas Bradburie writes, "To him I give the day, to her the night" (9). According to Thomas Byng, when God "reft away / The aged mother of these orphane lands; / The children wayled for their dames decay"; in answer to their prayers, God has sent them James: "Comfort, my sheep," the Lord says, "a Shepheard I have found, /.../ Him will I giue, he shall you rule aright. / Your Mother gon, he shall your Father hight" (8). As these elegies and Donne's 1617 sermon bear witness, the gender codes informing Elizabethan Protestantism were revised when the queen died and James came to the throne. Elizabeth's "lawes / Still new like fashions" had insisted that the English reject the whore of Babylon and "thinke that shee"—Elizabeth, no less than the church she headed—was "onely perfect" (Donne, *Sat3*, 56–57, 58, 59). With James's succession, that cruel fair was replaced by a king who cultivated a patriarchal self-image, asserting himself (in such venues as the Hampton Court Conference and with such projects as his new Bible translation) as a wise and authoritative *paterfamilias,* an English Solomon able to resolve all difficult questions.

Donne praises the king as such a figure in the preface to *Pseudo-Martyr,* his 1610 contribution to the oath of allegiance controversy. Donne hopes, through the service he renders the king by writing and publishing this treatise, to share "by this meanes, their happinesse, of whome, that saying of the Queene of *Sheba,* may bee vsurp'd: Happie are thy men, and happie are those thy Seruants, which stand before thee alwayes, and heare thy wisedome" (fol. A3v). This is a bid for court preferment, an expression of Donne's desire to be one of the king's "men"; but in order to achieve his desire, Donne finds it expedient to quote a judicious woman: it is through the female voice of the Queen of Sheba that he can woo James's favor. Clearly, the time for the witty misogyny of his elegies is past; with the death of the aged virago who had inspired much of the prickly antifeminism that animates those works, Donne finds himself presented with new opportunities and new motivations to explore images of female wisdom, discretion, and blessedness.[9]

Indeed, the reign of the man-loving, patriarchal James seems — ironically enough — to have provided Donne with a context in which such images became particularly essential to his poetics. For, despite the clear preference for masculine rule conveyed by his 1617 sermon on the anniversary of James's accession, Donne's poetic practice in the early years of James's reign would have been a deep disappointment to Curle, who had hoped for the abolition of lady worship under the new king. All of Donne's flattering Petrarchan verse letters to the Countess of Bedford, as well as the reverent poems he addressed to the Countesses of Huntingdon and Salisbury, date from the reign of James. So, too, do the divine and meditative poems that are the focus of this chapter; in "The Annuntiation and Passion," the *Anniversaries*, "Since She whome I lovd," and "Show me deare Christ," a self-consciously masculine speaker celebrates various incarnations of the sacred feminine — the Blessed Virgin, the church, the saintly wife, the soul that embraces holiness — in an attempt to find the God that this multiform "she" both veils and unveils.

2. THE FEMININE TRINITY IN "THE ANNUNTIATION AND PASSION"

Queen Elizabeth's death and King James's accession fell on the eve of the Annunciation, March 24, 1603; poets made much of the emotional and political contrasts afforded by the occasion and of the liturgical resonance of the date.[10] But they had nowhere near as rich a paradox to work with as Donne did five years later, when Good Friday fell on March 25. A virgin queen's expiring on the eve of Lady Day is one thing; but it is far more compelling to find oneself mourning the death of the King of Kings on the day set aside to celebrate his conception. John Donne celebrated this rare liturgical event with "The Annuntiation and Passion," which explores the Virgin Mary's preeminent place in salvation history, Ecclesia's role as Christ's "imitating Spouse" (39), and both of these feminine figures as objects of the Christian soul's contemplation. The results of the exploration are dramatic, for the poet defines these three—Mary, church, and the soul—as a female trinity, envisioning a triple manifestation of sacred femininity in an attempt to find the masculine Trinity toward whom only "she"—that divine Trinity's creaturely, feminine reflection—can guide him.

As a former Catholic with ongoing sympathy for English recusants, Donne was badly in need of guidance to help him pick his way through the religio-political minefield of spring 1608. One persona James Stuart had cultivated as he ascended the throne of England in 1603 was that of Rex Pacificus. The king had been highly pleased by works like John Harington's congratulatory poem celebrating the monarch's alleged power to unite, not only the realms of England and Scotland, but also the various religious factions dividing Britain:

> Joy, Protestant; Papist, now be reclaymd;
> Leave, Puritan, your supercillious frowne,
> Joyn voice, hart, hand, all discord be disclaymd.
> Be all one flock, by one great sheppard guided.[11]

The image of James as such a shepherd no doubt appealed to the ecumenically minded Donne, who must have watched with great interest as James fielded petitions from Roman Catholic recusants and strict Calvinists eager for more stringent reform within the established church, as well as various overtures from Protestant and Catholic powers on the Continent. But any plans the king may initially have entertained to relax government policies toward recusants were abruptly curtailed on November 5, 1605, by the discovery of the Gunpowder Plot, which made the threat of terrorism the focal point of James's domestic policy, justified his demand that all his subjects take an oath of allegiance denying the authority of the pope, and precipitated a new wave of intense anti-Catholicism in England.

In his 1608 treatise *Triplici nodo, triplex cuneus,* James claimed that he had initially been willing to bestow "Benefits and Gracious fauours...vpon Papists," but that the Gunpowder

Plot had shown him just how misplaced those benefits and favors were.[12] His response, he went on to explain, was to require of his Roman Catholic subjects an oath of allegiance that would do no more than distinguish "betweene the Ciuilly obedient Papists, and the peruerse Disciples of the Powder-Treason" (*Triplici nodo*, 46–47). As M. C. Questier has demonstrated, this claim was very likely insincere, for the oath was in fact precisely what the papal see took it to be: a "diabolically effective polemical cocktail" designed to force English recusants into an impossible bind, "an extraordinarily forceful act of government which, for a time, seemed to threaten the existence of English Romanism in a way that no conventional 'persecution' ever could" (Questier, "Loyalty, Religion," 311, 328).

In response to the English law establishing the oath (3 James I c.4; June 22, 1606), Pope Paul V had issued a *breve* (September 22, 1606) forbidding English Catholics to swear it. When the imprisoned archpriest George Blackwell nevertheless did subscribe, the pope issued another *breve* (August 23, 1607) stressing that he meant what he said the first time; in addition, Cardinal Robert Bellarmine wrote a letter to Blackwell (September 28, 1607) urging him to recant his subscription to the oath even if doing so meant martyrdom. It was to these three documents— the two papal *breves* and Bellarmine's letter—that James was responding in *Triplici nodo, triplex cuneus:* a triple wedge to cut through a triple knot, first published anonymously (though all of Europe knew the author's identity) in February 1608.[13]

In this work, James insists (referring to himself in the third person to retain anonymity) that if only the pope had deigned to indicate "what special words he quarrelled in that Oath," then, "it might haue bene that his Maiestie for the fatherly care he hath, not to put any of his Subiects to a needlesse extremitie, might haue bene contented in some sort to haue reformed or interpreted those wordes" (*Triplici nodo*, 7). Though contrasting the English monarch's alleged willingness to discuss specifics with the pope's "flat and generall condemnation of the whole Oath," James's claim that he feels "fatherly care" for his people makes clear to English recusant readers that they must choose which father they will obey. For the king here echoes the language used by Paul V in his first *breve* forbidding Catholics to take the oath, a document reprinted within *Triplici nodo* itself. The pope had addressed the English Catholics as his "WElbeloued sonnes," saying that he was *"compelled"* to forbid the taking of the Oath *"by our Fatherly care which we doe continually take for the saluation of your soules"* (*Triplici nodo*, 9, 10).

Not surprisingly, Donne viewed both sides of the oath of allegiance debate with a certain degree of skepticism, and his response to it was complex. As Dennis Flynn ("Irony") demonstrates, *Biathanatos* (written ca. 1608) and *Pseudo-Martyr* (published 1610) may both be read—especially in relation to each other—as ironic reflections on the controversy surrounding the oath, rather than as a serious defense of the martyrdom *Pseudo-Martyr* called suicide and a straightforward argument in favor of avoiding such suicide by taking the oath. When the patriarchal heads of Mother Church's earthly incarnations insist that men choose between them, a sincere son of that mother must, it would seem, take refuge in irony. Or, perhaps, in a witty appeal to *her* authority.

Though it is not framed as a direct response to the oath of allegiance controversy, "The Annuntiation and Passion," written just one month after James's *Triplici nodo* was first published, reflects the poet's unwillingness to let two warring would-be fathers define his faith or his religious practice. While the Jacobean church and its Roman rival barrage one another with paternalistic rhetoric, Donne gazes upon an image of the sacred feminine that arises from his own, idiosyncratic fusion of Roman Catholic and Reformed theology and from a liturgical event that unites apparent opposites. From the vantage point of a Lady Day that is also Good Friday, he envisions an earthly feminine trinity capable of revealing the divine Father, Son, and Holy Spirit.

As Jeffrey Johnson demonstrates, a conception of the Holy Trinity as "divine community" is central to Donne's theology and "illuminates every corner of his religious imagination" (*Theology of John Donne*, 5). In the sermon he preached at Lincoln's Inn on Trinity Sunday 1620, Donne observes, "it is a lovely and a religious thing, to finde out *Vestigia Trinitatis*, Impressions of the Trinity, in as many things as we can" (*Sermons*, 3:144). According to Saint Augustine, one of the most important of these "Impressions" is the human soul, made in the image of the triune God and engaged in acts of memory, understanding, and will. Augustine detects a trinitarian structure in other aspects of human experience as well, finding—for example—that in an act of loving, "there are three, the lover, and what is being loved, and love."[14] Augustine also detects a trinity in the sense of sight, which involves the interaction of three distinct but related things: "the thing we see," "the actual sight or vision," and that which "holds the sense of the eyes on the thing being seen..., namely the conscious intention" (*The Trinity*, 11.2). Similarly, in an act of cogitation, the will joins a remembered thing with the internal vision or impression of that thing in the mind's eye (*The Trinity*, 11.6).

In "The Annuntiation and Passion" (entitled, in some manuscripts, "Upon the Annunciacion and Passion fallinge upon one day 1608"), Donne finds a created reflection of the triune deity in three feminine figures: the cogitating Christian soul, the woman upon whom her mind's eye gazes (the Blessed Virgin), and her guide (the church). Each member of this triad has a distinct identity, but all are—in another sense—united as one "Shee": she who "sees," she who is "seen," and she who "hath shown" how a Christian ought to respond to the triune God. The poet's construction of this threefold figure is grounded in his use of the word "she(e)" as the prevailing nominative pronoun throughout the poem: it refers first to his soul (the *anima* being grammatically and theologically feminine), then to the Virgin (hailed by Gabriel as "blessed...among women" [Luke 1:28]), and finally to the church, Christ's "imitating Spouse" (*Annun*, 39). The poem has a tripartite form established by the speaker's movement through these three figures, each of whom is defined in visual language as seeing, being seen, or showing.

The poem begins with a section in which the speaker focuses upon the visual banquet afforded his soul on a day when his body is deprived of its usual nourishment.[15] Commanding his flesh to "abstaine to day," he establishes himself as self-consciously devout and masculine, for the stance he takes in relation to his flesh is that of a husband addressing a wife, a "weaker vessel" (1 Pet. 3:7) in need of discipline: "Tamely fraile body'abstaine to day; to day / My soule eates twice, Christ hither and away." But while the first-person speaker—the intellect addressing the body—clearly feels authorized to govern and command his flesh, he can provide the body with adequate reason for fasting only by pointing to his soul, which is itself—as one would expect, given the demands of both Latin grammar and Christian tradition—gendered feminine. And as the speaker tells his "fraile body" (1) what his soul perceives, he repeatedly underscores the latter entity's feminine identity. The two-word clause "She(e) sees" appears four times in the first 12 lines.

On this day when two different but profoundly interconnected liturgical events coincide, the soul observes a series of paradoxes that arise not only from the falling together of the Annunciation and Passion, but more fundamentally from the miracle of the Incarnation itself, which begins at the moment of Christ's conception and comes to fruition on the day his human flesh suffers and dies for the sins of humanity. First, "She sees" Christ as "man" (3) completing the "circle" that is "embleme" (4) of both man and God; just as in a circle "first and last concurre" (5), so on "this doubtfull day / Of feast or fast, Christ came, and went away" (5–6). The geometric figure of the circle forms a zero, and though it seems a contradiction to say that one sees when there is nothing to be seen, nothingness is the next object of the soul's perception: "Shee sees him nothing twice at once, who'is all" (7); embracing simultaneously the near nonentity of the embryo and the corpse, the quintessence of Being comprehends nothingness.[16] The related paradox of divinity made flesh, of alpha in omega, informs the speaker's third rendering of his soul's vision: "Shee sees a Cedar plant it selfe, and fall, / Her Maker put to making, and the head / Of life, at once, not yet alive, and dead" (8–10). The cedar, Gardner notes, symbolizes God, the everlasting One; but here it is also a mortal thing, an evergreen that is planted and dies. In this context, such an image evokes the tree of the cross on which Christ "did rise and fall," as Donne puts it in the poem he would write five years later for Good Friday 1613 (*Goodf*, 13).

The gender of the soul that "sees" these images of divine paradox is reinforced by the reference to Christ as "*Her* Maker" (9; emphasis mine); and in the fourth "She sees" clause, the object of her perception is the paragon of feminine gender and female sex, the Virgin Mary: "She sees at once the virgin mother stay / Reclus'd at home, Publique at Golgotha" (11–12). Whether meditating privately in her chamber on the day of the Annunciation or mourning openly at the foot of the cross on Good Friday, the Virgin is a model for the speaker's soul. Both must prove humbly receptive to the miracle of the Incarnation; both must stand as one of many witnesses to the Crucifixion. The "shee" of the poem is, then, not only the see-er; she is also—in the person of the Virgin—an essential part of what is "seen" by the devout soul.

Lines 11 and 12, the last two lines of the poem's opening section on what the soul sees, are also the first two lines of the poem's second section, which tells of the Blessed Mother. As the verb "sees" occurs several times in the first 12 lines, so the passive form of that verb looms large in the lines on Mary: "Sad and rejoyc'd shee's seen at once, and seen / At almost fiftie, and at scarce fifteene" (13–14). The repetition of "seen" in line 13, with the second instance of the verb serving as a rhyme word, clearly sets up a connection between the perceiving soul and the perceived Madonna. In addition, the quick segue from line 11's "She sees at once" to line 13's "Sad and rejoyc'd shee's seen at once" blurs the line between the two figures, making it seem for a moment that the speaker's soul is the figure who appears "Sad and rejoyc'd at once"; nor is that impression entirely false, for the reader does perceive a mixture of sorrow and jubilation in the soul's visual banquet of paradoxes. The soul who sees and the Virgin who is seen are not entirely separate. They are mother and daughter; Mary becomes the mother of the Savior when "Gabriell gives Christ to her," and the mother of all Christian souls when, on Good Friday, Christ gives "her to John" (16) with the words "Beholde thy mother" (John 19:27). But like the divine Father and Son, this human mother and daughter are also one; Mary and the individual soul of each Christian share both the gift of the Annunciation and the bereavement of Good Friday. Line 15 — "At once a Sonne is promis'd her, and gone" — applies to the soul even as it does to Mary, "For vnto *vs* a Childe is borne, & vnto *vs* a sonne is giuen" (Isa. 9:6; emphasis mine), as it was to all of his apostles that Jesus said, "a litle while, and ye shal not se me" (John 16:16). Like the soul that has not yet given birth to the good works that are the fruit of grace, the Virgin of the Annunciation is "Not fully'a mother" (18). And as "Shee's in Orbitie" (18), mourning the death of her only child, so the human soul mourns the death of the Son of Man.

If one counts the lines overlapping with the poem's first section and the quotation in line 22 of the *Ave* Gabriel addressed to Mary, the poem's portrait of the Blessed Mother, like the section on the soul's seeing, occupies 12 lines. But before those 12 lines are completed, the poem's third and longest section is anticipated by the introduction, in line 19, of yet another visually oriented verb. The speaker sums up what the soul "sees" and what is "seen" of Mary's experience, commenting, "All this, and all betweene, this day hath *showne,* / Th'Abridgement of Christs story, which makes one / (As in plaine Maps, the farthest West is East) / Of the'Angels *Ave,*'and *Consummatum est*" (19–22; first italics mine). These lines on what is "showne" by the liturgical "Abridgement" of the Gospel lead into the work's third section. Beginning with line 23, the speaker focuses on the church, the feminine figure who has arranged for the meditative possibilities "this day" affords by "some times, and seldome joyning" Good Friday and the feast of the Annunciation. This third and final part of Donne's poem moves from what the soul "sees" and how Mary is "seen," to what the church "showes" (27) and "hath shown" (33) to her members, and in particular to the speaker's own "Soule," who observes and responds to all that Ecclesia demonstrates.

The final section is the longest. Indeed, since the first two 12-line sections overlap, and thus occupy only lines 1–22, the 24-line section extending from line 23 through line 46 represents just over half the poem. The church, after all, includes both the Blessed Mother who is a type of Ecclesia, and the individual soul who—like the church as a corporate entity—is called to be the spouse of Christ. The portion of the poem dealing with the church is long enough to subsume the lines on the two more individuated feminine figures because the church is the most important of the three in mapping out the Christian way of life; though not infallible, she is a reliable guide. Like the polestar, which is not itself the pole but nevertheless proves a clear indicator of which direction is north, the church is the best indicator we have of God's will:

> As by the selfe-fix'd Pole wee never doe
> Direct our course, but the next starre thereto,
> Which showes where the'other is, and which we say
> (Because it strayes not farre) doth never stray;
> So God by his Church, neerest to him, wee know.   (25–29)

These lines avoid dealing with the question, so important in "Satyre III" and in Donne's sonnet "Show me deare Christ," of which earthly incarnation of the church is the best or truest. Rather than seeking to determine which ecclesiastical denomination strays least from God, they acknowledge the universal church, the bride of Christ who is "neerest to him" even when the human institutions that represent her *do* stray "farre" from his wounded side.

"[T]he virgin mother" (11) and the soul who is both her daughter and her reflection or likeness are, so to speak, the first and second persons of an earthly feminine triad, corresponding to the Father and the Son of the heavenly Trinity. Not surprisingly, then, Donne's speaker emphasizes the connection between the church and the Holy Spirit. Alluding to Exodus 13:21, he follows up the image of the polestar that "strayes not farre" with an image of the church as the guide of an errant people: "wee"—the faithful—"stand firme, if wee by her motion goe; / His Spirit, as his fiery Pillar doth / Leade, and his Church, as cloud; to one end both" (29, 30–32). Helen Gardner recounts in her gloss on line 32 the traditional Christian interpretation of Exodus 13:21, in which "the Lord went before" the Israelites "by day in a piller of a cloude to leade them the way, & by night in a piller of fyre to giue them light": the pillar of cloud represents the Old Testament, in which God manifests himself only through what Milton calls "shadowy Types," while the pillar of fire is a type of the New Testament, which moves "From shadowy Types to Truth, from Flesh to Spirit" (*PL* 12.303). "Donne's interpretation," however, which makes the pillar of cloud a type of the church and the pillar of fire a type the Holy Ghost, Gardner believes to be "original"; she notes further that, "In many places 'cloud' is glossed generally as 'flesh' and particularly as 'the humanity of Christ'. Donne may be extending this to the Church, which is Christ's body" (Gardner, *The Divine Poems*, 97). But the church is the mystical body of Christ, not his fleshly humanity, and Donne is here defining her relationship with the third person of the Trinity rather than the second. Perhaps, then, Donne represents the church as the pillar of cloud because she is not herself the Holy Spirit who descended on the apostles in tongues of fire (Acts 2:3), brought the church to life, and illuminated Christ's disciples in their time of darkness; but she is "neerest to him," as the pillar of cloud in Exodus is the daytime partner to the pillar of flame. Fire is a masculine element, water a feminine one, so the Spirit to whom Jesus refers using the masculine pronoun manifests himself in flame, while the church is figured forth in the colder, damper medium of cloud.

Her ministry, the speaker believes, is well summed up by her joining of feast and fast; the fact that the church is the force binding those opposites together is underscored again and again, with the word "joyning" in line 24, and "joyne" in lines 33 and 39. This copulative function reinforces the parallel between the church as the third person of Donne's feminine trinity and the Holy Spirit as the third person of the divine Trinity. For in Augustine's *De Trinitate*, the Spirit is the love that unites the Father and the Son (*The Trinity*, 6.7). Similarly, the church's orchestration of the liturgical overlap of Good Friday and Lady Day brings together the Virgin and the soul, the mother and the daughter, the object seen and what Augustine calls its "quasi-offspring," the image in the beholding eye (*The Trinity*, 11.9, 11).[17]

The speaker of Donne's poem completes the description of what his soul perceives through a catalog of different expressions summing up the lesson that the liturgical occasion teaches; the "Church, by letting these daies joyne, hath shown" that

> Death and conception in mankinde is one.
> Or 'twas in him the same humility,
> That he would be a man, and leave to be:
> Or as creation he had made, as God,
> With the last judgement, but one period,
> His imitating Spouse would joyne in one
> Manhoods extremes: He shall come, he is gone.
>
> (*Annun*, 33–40)

The church as "imitating Spouse" is here a feminine mirror to the masculine God; but her imitation is more than mimicry. She shows that humanity reflects the divine, since the paradoxes of the Incarnation are reflected in the paradoxes of human existence itself. "Death and conception...is one" (34) in mankind because the embryo is subject to death from the start; the mortal sin of Adam and Eve infects the soul of each newly begotten baby from the moment it is conceived. And yet, for the Christian, death is the gate of life. The church also reproduces divine truths on a human scale, thus—like Mary—giving birth to Emmanuel, God-with-us. As God made "creation.../ With the last judgement, but one period" (37–38), so the church plays out in liturgical time the eternal simultaneity of the alpha and omega, making intimate and immanent what would otherwise remain distant and transcendent.[18]

Like the Christ she imitates, moreover, the church is extravagant, providing an embarrassment of spiritual riches. By overlapping Good Friday and Lady Day, she provides an overabundance of spiritual resources to "busie" the industrious soul and to bankroll her business:

> Or as though one blood drop, which thence did fall,
> Accepted, would have serv'd, he yet shed all;
> So though the least of his paines, deeds, or words,
> Would busie'a life, she all this day affords;
> This treasure then, in grosse, my soule uplay,
> And in my life retaile it every day.   (41–46)

The financial metaphor that is quite explicit in the final couplet is introduced subtly in the first half of the larger analogy, Christ's act of atonement being considered in quantitative terms as a literal redemption or buying back that could have been accomplished with but one drop of his infinitely precious blood. The offer, if "Accepted" by the one to whom the debt was owed, would have "serv'd"—the word reminds us that the Redeemer is the suffering servant of Isaiah. But as the suffering servant is not content to do only as much as is required to complete his task, so the church is not content to supply souls with only one of his "paines, deeds, or words" as a subject for contemplation or an inspiration to action. Any of them alone would "busie'a life": keep a contemplative in constant meditation, keep an ordinary soul laboring in the vineyards, and overdetermine every line of every work a witty devotional poet writes. But the church "all this day affords," with "affords" carrying overtones of both its generic meaning—"To manage to give, to spare" (*OED*, v. def. 4)—and its more specifically financial meaning—"To have the means, be able or rich enough; to bear the expense" (*OED*, v. def. 3). With that observation, the poem comes full circle, returning to the first feminine figure, the speaker's soul. If the church is generous enough to provide such "treasure," the speaker's soul must in turn "uplay" it, invest it soundly, so as to have available an inexhaustible source of sacred currency, coin applicable to the spiritual demands of daily life.

With this conclusion in mind, one can more fully appreciate the first two lines of the poem: "Tamely fraile body'abstaine to day; to day / My soule eates twice, Christ hither and away." The sense of superabundance in the poem's concluding lines is first evoked here, the image of the soul's double banquet providing a rich counterpoint to the body's fasting and abstention on Good Friday. Even more importantly, the eating metaphor ushers in the four "She sees" clauses that follow and thus defines the soul's visual perception as a kind of feeding, its eating as a way of seeing. Indeed, the sequence "eates...Christ" / "sees...Christ" demonstrates that the speaker has answered the invitation of Psalm 34:8: "Taste ye & se, how gracious the Lord is." As Johnson demonstrates, this imperative would come to define Donne's pastoral objective as a clergyman. "While the center of Donne's theology is the essential community of God revealed in the doctrine of the Trinity," Johnson explains, "the theological goal divulged in his preaching, as well as in his administration of the sacraments, is to bring the individual, through the visible Church, into loving conformity with God. To that end, the tasting and seeing by which one receives the grace offered to all in Christ's passion serves as the antitype to the eating of the forbidden fruit."[19] Thus, though Donne was still seven years away from ordination in 1608, and though he was faced that year with new challenges to finding in any "visible Church" the feminine ideal his poem envisions, "The Annuntiation and Passion" reflects the theological goal he would go on to pursue as a priest in the Church of England. The speaker's reflections allow his soul to "taste and see" the abundant divine goodness poured out in the Incarnation and the atonement. Thus fed, she becomes one person of the triune "shee" who shows men how to mirror the triune God.

Nor is that God hard to digest. As Donne explains in "A Litanie," another poem that he wrote circa 1608, the "Blessed glorious Trinity" is "Bones to Philosophy, but milke to faith" (28, 29).[20] "A Litanie" begins with three stanzas addressed to the three persons of the Trinity and continues with a fourth that calls upon the Trinity in its entirety. In this fourth stanza, the speaker muses that, while the Trinity as an intellectual concept is as indigestible as "Bones," it is nevertheless the spiritual "milke" that nourishes the faithful soul. This evocative image of godhead as the mildest of foods, the milk a mother produces for her infant, feminizes divinity itself. But if God is milk, it is a human female who expresses that milk. The speaker proceeds immediately, in stanza 5, to a prayer thanking God for the Virgin Mary, "that faire blessed Mother-maid, / Whose flesh redeem'd us; That she-Cherubin, / Which unlock'd Paradise" (37–39). The woman in "Whose wombe... / God cloath'd himselfe, and grew" (41–42) is thus portrayed—like the church in line 29 of "The Annuntiation and Passion"—as "neerest to" God. In "A Litanie," the nearness is physical and prosodic as well as spiritual, for it is the flesh of a woman (worn by her son) that redeems humanity, and the stanza giving thanks for the redemptive power of Mary's flesh follows directly after the one on the Holy Trinity.[21]

No earthly father is afforded such dignity; even when, in stanza 7, the speaker of "A Litanie" turns to praise "The Patriarches," he calls them "Those great *Grand*fathers of thy Church, which saw / More in the cloud, then wee in fire" (56–57; emphasis mine). Here the pillar of cloud represents Nature, which preceded both Mosaic law and the new covenant of grace as God's means of manifesting himself in the world; the patriarchs are the distant male ancestors "Whom Nature clear'd more, then us grace and law" (58). In these lines, fully legitimate spiritual

patriarchy is a thing of the past; the Christians of 1608, whichever ecclesiastical father they acknowledge, see less clearly
than the ancient grandfathers.[22] But as "The Annuntiation and
Passion" confirms, one may escape such blindness by turning
to a feminine model of grace. Joining herself with Mother Mary
and with a feminine rather than patriarchal version of Christ's
"imitating Spouse," a soul can—within a poem's space, at any
rate—evade the triple knots and triple wedges of earthly masculine authority and open herself to the infinite goodness of the
Father, the Son, and the Holy Ghost.

Outside the frame of Donne's poem, however, there was no
single universal church by whose "motion" Donne could "goe"
(30); and "The Annuntiation and Passion" bears implicit witness to that fact, alluding in subtle but definitive ways to the
poet's denominational preference. In midpoem, the speaker
refers to the church as "Gods Court of faculties" (23), the court
of faculties being a specifically English ecclesiastical institution, a tribunal of the Archbishop of Canterbury able to grant
dispensations and allow appointments that would otherwise be
illegal due to a conflict of interest (such as the overlap of two
seemingly incompatible liturgical occasions). The church that
decides "some times, and seldome" to allow the coincidence
of Good Friday and Lady Day is *God's* court of faculties, not
Archbishop Bancroft's, for that coincidence has occurred from
time to time in every Christian calendar, Orthodox and Western,
Julian and Gregorian: Protestants and Roman Catholics the
world over experienced it most recently in 2005. But in 1608,
English Protestants did not share the same calendar with Roman
Catholics on the Continent, and Donne's poem thus focuses on
a liturgical event that was occurring only in England and a few
other Protestant countries that year. All of Western Christendom
was observing Good Friday on the same day that England was;
but for Catholic Europe, which had abandoned the Julian calendar for the Gregorian, the date of Good Friday in 1608 was April
4, not March 25. Thus, when the speaker of "The Annuntiation
and Passion" speaks of what "This Church" has demonstrated

by "letting these daies joyne," he is in fact responding to the outward and visible actions of a specific ecclesiastical communion. Though the soul may gaze upon the idealized motions of Christ's mystical spouse, the "fraile body" must "tamely" submit to the liturgy, the calendar, and the governance of one earthly institution.[23]

3. Donne's Ambivalent Mourning:
Woman as Mortal Sacrament

"The Annuntiation and Passion" avoids confronting the gap between an archetypal image of Christ's "imitating Spouse" and the less-than-perfect reality in which that spouse's body is weakened by denominational fractures. In his own marriage, Donne could not escape the harsh truth that the soul of even the most godly and virtuous wife dwells in a mortal body. Of course, he did exercise his wit in an effort to lighten the burdens of corporeality. In a 1613 letter to his friend Henry Goodyer, Donne commented on his freedom during a period when his wife, Anne, was recovering from childbirth: "I have now two of the best happinesses which could befall me...which are to be a widower and my wife alive" (Gosse, *Life and Letters*, 2:18). This quibble on present absence, life, and death seems to allude to the sexual abstinence imposed upon him by Anne's condition and to celebrate it as a blessedly impermanent taste of chaste widowhood. But as the sonnet on Anne's death bears witness, his little joke turned out to be no laughing matter. In the wake of a later, fatal pregnancy, Donne endured two of the worst sadnesses which could have befallen him: he was still a husband, not yet truly widowed, and his wife was dead.

"Since She whome I lovd" is an attempt to cope with those sadnesses, to define who and what the poet has lost and, in so doing, to redefine himself; for Anne remains, even beyond this life, bone of his bone and flesh of his flesh. He remains her husband, though he knows that he must become a bride of Christ. As, in life, Anne bore many children fathered by John Donne, so in death—and in the sonnet—she bears a wealth of symbolic meanings that the poet's ever-masculine mind seems unable to cease begetting. Death has deprived him not only of the woman he loves, but also of a human sacrament, a tangible sign that both revealed and concealed divinity.

Toward this sign, this woman—and part of Donne's problem is that neither word will do on its own—the poem directs a mixture of passionate devotion and ingenious anxiety. Such a divided mood is typical of Donne's work; but the sonnet's imagery and theme evoke in particular the unresolved conflicts in Donne's sense of the sacramental. His response to the absent presence of Anne parallels his response to the Eucharist, the most hotly debated absent presence of the period. And his fears about marriage reflect his fears about the efficacy of both baptism and the Eucharist, for he defines these two sacraments in conjugal terms, as the earthly means by which the soul is wedded to God.[24] The sonnet suggests that Donne's profound ambivalence toward sacramental signs, including Anne herself as such, springs from the difference between sacramental experience and anagogical orientation. As Donne explains in a 1626 Easter sermon, "there are mysteries of two kindes":

> [S]ome things are [mysteries]…Because, though the thing be near enough unto me, yet somthing is interposed between me, and it, and so I cannot see it: And some things are so…because they are at so remote a distance, as that…my sight cannot extend to them.…[S]acraments are mysteries, because though the grace therein bee neare mee, yet there is *Velamen interpositum*, there is a visible figure, a sensible signe, and seale, between me, and that grace, which is exhibited to me in the Sacrament.…[whereas] the resurrection is a mystery, because it is so farre removed, as that it concernes our state and condition in the next world. (*Sermons*, 7:98)

In the sonnet, Donne contemplates both kinds of mystery and finds that they are in tension with each other. He looks to the "state and condition" his soul is to assume "in the next world" when he will be wedded to the celestial bridegroom who now woos him; but even as he resolves to ponder such "heauenly things" (4), his thoughts remain preoccupied with more earthly mysteries, and particularly with Anne herself as a "visible figure" that came between him and the "grace ... exhibited to" him in her.

Anne's spiritually salutary role in Donne's life is defined in lines 5–6 of the sonnet: "Here the admyring her my Mind did whett / To seeke thee God; so streames do shew the head."[25] Gazing upon Anne's goodness was a powerful aid to his salvation; for, as the English church's marriage ceremony reminds brides, husbands may be won for Christ "while they behold [their wives'] chaste conversation" (BCP, 298).[26] But for Donne, Anne was more than a model of virtue; she was a sacramental sign, a stream that showed the Head. The image recalls a commonplace based on John's Gospel: Christ's body was, as Donne puts it in a sermon, "the spring-head of both Sacraments" (Sermons, 9:333); after his death, water and blood flowed from the wound in his side. Like the fluid elements of baptism and Eucharist, Anne was a stream flowing out from the Lord; she was able to "shew" the godhead, to direct human perception toward her divine source.[27]

Though Anne could not provide a Eucharistic banquet, she was the sacramental appetizer that stimulated Donne's piety and prepared him for a full spiritual meal. With a pun that tastes of gastronomic, religious, and erotic arousal, Donne declares that Anne *whetted* his mind to seek the one who could truly drench his parched soul. And in line 7, he tells the Lord that his search has been successful: "I haue found thee,'and thou my thirst hast fed." It is through participation in the Lord's Supper, the soul's banquet, that Donne can make such a proclamation; the virtuous wife has shown her husband the way to the Communion table. But now she is gone.

The sonnet begins with the widower's reflection on what has happened and how it has altered his perspective:

> Since She whome I lovd, hath payd her last debt
>   To Nature, and to hers, and my good is dead
>   And her Soule early into heauen rauished,
> Wholy in heauenly things my Mind is sett.   (1–4)

Donne's thoughts are fixed upon things celestial because Anne's death was the end of his earthly "good," the good of marriage itself. The passing of the wife returns her husband to the aloneness of Adam before Eve's creation, to the solitude that God pronounced "not good."[28] It also deprives him of the good promised in Psalm 128, a wife like a "fruteful vine."[29] For Anne was nothing if not fertile.

The fruitfulness of her womb was, of course, a mixed blessing, for she died of complications attendant upon the birth of her twelfth child. Donne may thus be punning on "whome" in the opening line; the "She whome [he] lovd" was the she-womb he made almost constantly pregnant, and he is reflecting on the implications of how she died. In observing that Anne has "payd her last debt / To Nature, and to hers," Donne genders even that most generic of human experiences, death. As Faulkner and Daniels explain, Anne has discharged not only "her debt to Nature as a human being (all must die)" but also her debt "to her own nature as a woman (the danger peculiar to all women of dying in childbirth)" ("Donne's *Holy Sonnets* XVII"). And because 1 Timothy identifies childbearing as a woman's best assurance of salvation, Donne can hope that the labor that killed her body is the seal of her soul's new life, a life in which all earthly "debts" are canceled.

But behind the death that canceled all of Anne's obligations, behind the fatal pregnancy itself, lay her frequent fulfillment of one obligation in particular: the "marriage debt" she owed as a wife. Saint Paul asserts the doctrine that a husband's body is not his own, nor a wife's her own, and that they must fulfill their conjugal duties to one another (1 Cor. 7:3–4). The payment of this debt may involve a different way of being "into heaven rauished": that is, the "death" of sexual climax. And whether or not Anne experienced such expiration on a regular basis, we may assume that her husband believed she did. Given the Renaissance theory that female satisfaction is necessary for conception, there was certainly plenty of evidence. At any rate, Anne had clearly paid the marriage debt "to hers" time and again; but as Donne goes on to admit in lines 8–9 of the sonnet, he still thirsts for "more Love." Thus, in saying that Anne "hath payd her last debt," he is acknowledging her release from all earthly obligations even as he ponders the melancholy fact that she will never again make love to him.

Not surprisingly, Donne's ongoing desire for Anne is riddled with guilt; there is too direct a relation between his conjugal activities and their lethally fruitful consequences. As the cause of his wife's pregnancy, the collector of her marriage debt, he is implicated as the agent of her undoing. He has been the death of his own "good." And the sonnet's conclusion implies that, if God had not intervened, she might — on a more spiritual level — have been the death of him.[30] Donne's carnal thirsts might eventually have destroyed his soul even as they did destroy her body. If God had allowed him to continue embracing Anne as his "good," he implies, she would have become his god: no longer a "thing diuine" (12) — a sacramental intermediary connecting man and God — but rather a thing *divinized,* an idol standing between and dividing them. As Donne puts it in a sermon (citing Augustine as his source), the things God gives us as helps may destroy us if we misuse them. Men must be certain to use marriage "to pay a debt, not to satisfie appetite; lest otherwise she prove *in Ruinam,* who was given *in Adjutorium,* and he be put to the first mans plea, ... *The woman whom thou gavest me, gave me my death*" (*Sermons,* 2:345). In other sermons, Donne speaks of sacraments in the same biblical language he uses here to refer to wives: they are gifts given *in adjutorium,* "helps, which God in his Church hath afforded us" (*Sermons,* 6:175).[31] Yet, as is clear in his homiletic discussion of the two kinds of mystery, he also stresses that a sacrament is "somthing...interposed between" human perception and the divine (*Sermons,*

7:98). As sacramental wife, then, Anne was the first kind of mystery; she both "shew[ed] the head" and veiled it. Deprived of her, the poet looks to the other kind of mystery, to that which is at such a distance that his "sight cannot extend" to it (*Sermons*, 7:98). This mystery is "the resurrection, [in which] they nether marie wiues, nor wiues are bestowed in mariage, but are as the Angels of God in heauen" (Matt. 22:30).[32]

In one of his wedding sermons, Donne would attempt to explain this disconcerting text by urging that "mariage is ordained for *mutuall helpe* of one another," but in heaven, "God himself shall be intirely in every soul; And what can that soul lack, that hath all God?" (*Sermons*, 8:99). His question is, of course, rhetorical; a soul that *has* "all God" can lack nothing. But what of the soul that is *offered* God's all? The sonnet makes clear that, until a soul possesses that offering fully, it will persist in longing and questioning: "A holy thirsty dropsy melts mee yett. / But why should I begg more Love, when as thou / Dost woe my Soule, for hers offring all thine[?]" (8–10). In these lines, Donne's continuing thirst is partly for the celestial wedding feast yet to come, but it is also for conjugal joys now past. Unable to separate devout apocalyptic yearnings from potentially idolatrous desire, he remains suspended between a sacramental mystery—Anne the earthly bride—and an anagogical mystery: God the celestial bridegroom. He longs to have "more Love" from God than can be conveyed in any earthly sacrament, but he also thirsts for "more Love" from a woman called More.

Her name is expansive and abundant; it suggests copiousness, plenty, even excess. And there's the rub. For according to Pauline and Augustinian theology, the husband is a type of the reason, while the wife is a type of the flesh over which the reason should rule. The flesh is the *caro conjux*, the complaining wife who forever leads her better half astray.[33] Thus, though Anne the woman was a saint, More the wife symbolizes a part of Jack that has always caused him trouble: like Jack Falstaff, he has "*more* flesh than another man, and therefore *more* frailty" (*1 Henry IV*, 3.3.167–68; emphasis mine). In a sermon, Donne argues that practically every sin "comes within the name of *workes of the flesh*" and that all manner of "abundance and superfluity begets these workes of the flesh" (6:197). In the sonnet, God has taken away his abundance—his More—but he still thirsts for that fleshly abundance, and thus finds himself still wedded to carnal desire.

He admits this hard fact even as he tries to deny it in line 4: "Wholy in heauenly things my Mind is sett," he says, imagining thought as a mode of penetration. The poet's mind is not *on* but *in* the objects of contemplation. Though his body can no longer enter Anne's, and his soul cannot yet enter heaven, his thoughts find their way into a delightful enclosure. Donne's assertion that his mind is set "Wholy" in such a matrix resonates four lines later in the description of a "holy thirsty dropsy"; but clearly, neither the way his mind is "sett" nor his craving for "more Love" is wholly holy. In fact, wholeness of any kind eludes him, for he is inwardly torn between his continuing husbandly emotions and his need to become a bride of Christ. As Anne's husband, he has not come to terms with what he sees as a rape, a violation of his spousal rights. But the God who has "into heauen rauished" Anne's soul (3) is also pursuing Donne's. If he is to respond to the divine suitor, he must abandon his masculine role and prepare to live in a mansion where Christ, not he, is the head of the household.[34]

In some ways, Anne's sacramental function in his life has helped him to prepare for this unmanning. For, though John was Anne's "head" according to Ephesians 5 ("the housband is the wiues head, euen as Christ is the head of the Church" [5:23]), she was his leader in the search for God. In the phrase "so streames do shew the head," Donne conflates direct and indirect objects, himself and Christ; Anne shows the One Head of the whole mystical body *to* her "head," her husband. The conflation underscores the ironic implications of Anne's directive role; as God's sacramental instrument, she is a spiritual support to Donne, a "helpe mete" (Gen. 2:18) for one who has authority over her. But she helps him by directing his attention toward a higher marriage in which he is to take the subordinate, feminine position.

The gender crisis evoked by the language of the sonnet ironically recasts the allegory of regeneration outlined in Romans 7. Comparing the Old Law to a first marriage, Paul explains that a Christian is like a woman whose first husband has died and who is therefore free to remarry. Under the Law, he explains, "we were in the flesh" and "the motions of sinnes...had force in our membres, to bring forthe frute vnto death. But now we are deliuered from the Law...wherein we were holden" (7:5–6). Paul stresses that the New Testament's abrogation of the Law does not imply that the old covenant was evil; but though "holie, and iust, & good" (7:12), the Law could not bring salvation. Similarly, Anne's marriage to Donne was not evil, but within it Donne's soul remained fleshly, and procreation meant death; Anne's flesh was impregnated with children who were literally "frute vnto death." Only the second marriage—that of the soul and God—can bring life. Donne's problem is that he can take personal comfort from Paul's allegory only if he learns to identify with the wife who survives her husband and joyfully remarries. In the 1560 Geneva Bible, the gloss on the passage from Romans explains: "Bothe in this first mariage & in the seconde, the housband & the wife must be considered within our selues: the first housband was Sinne, and our flesh was the wife: their children were the frutes of the flesh.... In the seconde mariage ye Spirit is the housband, the new creature is the wife, & their children are the frutes of the Spirit." But the language of the sonnet shows that Donne has not properly internalized the allegory; the circumstances surrounding Anne's death still lead him to think of Anne as flesh and of himself as "the first housband...Sinne" whose conjugal embraces of that wife "bring forthe frute vnto death." From one perspective, then, the sonnet is Donne's attempt to read Romans 7 aright, to realize that despite his status as sorrowful widower, he must conceive of himself as a newly liberated widow and bride-to-be if he is to enter into the joy of spiritual union with God.

To read Romans 7 correctly would be to understand and embrace the full implications of baptism, for Paul introduces the allegory of the newly liberated widow precisely in order to explain the difference between carnal existence and the new life of those "dead to sinne" through the sacrament (Rom. 6:2). In lines 13–14 of Donne's sonnet, however, an allusion to the liturgy of baptism makes clear that the poet remains uncertain about the validity of his own baptismal vows. In these lines, Anne's death is associated with, if not directly attributed to the Lord's "tender iealosy" in the face of three deadly rivals: "the World," the "fleshe," and the "Deuill" (14). These are the three forces formally rejected during baptism, the marriage ceremony that weds the soul to God. Just as the bride and groom promise that they will "keep" themselves "only to" one another, "forsaking all other" (BCP, 291, 292), so in the rite of public baptism, the new Christian vows to "forsake the devil and all his works, the vain pomp, and glory of the world, ... [and] the carnal desires of the flesh, so that [he will] not follow, nor be led by them" (BCP, 273). In the sonnet, then, Donne seems to feel that despite Anne's personal virtue, she was symbolically that uncooperative "wife," the flesh; she was his own fleshly part, and it was necessary for him to cease following or being led by her. Indeed, she had to die if he was to hold himself truly baptized, truly wedded to Christ; for baptism is a dying with Christ in which the sinful flesh—"the bodie of sinne"—is "destroyed" (Rom. 6:6).

The death of the flesh in baptism should, according to Colossians, lead to a new, more spiritual existence: "If ye then be risen with Christ, seke those things which are aboue, where Christ sitteth at the right hand of God. Set your affections on things which are aboue, and not on things, which are on the earth" (3:1–2).[35] But this is where Donne discovers the catch-22. The counsel provided by the epistle does not solve his problem, for his dead wife is now one of "the things which are aboue," one of those heavenly things in which his mind is set. As one of the "Saints and Angels, things diuine" (12), Anne looks all the more like the deity who is her rival for Donne's love.

Indeed, Anne's new, heavenly status by no means puts an end to idolatrous possibilities. In some ways, it makes things even more difficult; for although a wife is a "helpe mete" while she is on earth (Gen. 2:18), the Protestant husband must no longer call upon her after her death.[36] Although saints' prayers may assist us, the dean of Saint Paul's explains, we should address only God in our prayers: "all that can be had, is to be asked of him, and him onely[;]...a man...cannot take the water so sincerely, so purely, so intemerately from the channell as from the fountaine head" (*Sermons*, 5:360). Streams that show the head may be abused even when they have become heavenly; as long as Donne is still tempted to refresh himself with downstream waters, Anne remains dangerous, and God must fear "least [Donne] allow / [His] Love to Saints and Angels" (11–12).

As a divinely inspired poet whose thoughts are turned toward heaven yet still marred by idolatrous tendencies, Donne has an illustrious precedent in the book of Revelation. The author — who happens to have the same name as the poet — twice falls down to worship an angel and is twice told that he must not do so (Rev. 19:10 and 22:8–9). John first tries to worship his "fellowe seruant" immediately after the angel has proclaimed blessing upon those invited to the wedding feast of the Lamb (19:9).[37] Similarly, the peril of idolatry becomes an issue in Donne's sonnet as soon as the poet begins to reflect upon the divine bridegroom who wishes to wed his soul. In Revelation, John hears and records the very promise that might comfort a man melted by "holy thirsty dropsy" — "I wil giue to him that is a thirst, of the well of the water of life frely" (21:6) — yet he remains prone to idolatry; in the last chapter of the Bible, Revelation 22, having been shown "a pure riuer of water of life, cleare as crystal, proceding out of the throne of God, and of the Lambe" (22:1), John once again abases himself before the angel (22:8–9).[38] Donne, too, is continually tempted to worship the guide who shows him the way to divine refreshment.

Has Donne's spiritual peril been increased by God's transformation of a fleshly wife into a heavenly saint? The concluding section of the poem suggests that the tactics of the divine suitor are problematic:

> [Thou] dost not only feare least I allow
>> My Love to Saints and Angels, things diuine,
> But in thy tender iealosy dost doubt
> Least the World, fleshe, yea Deuill putt thee out.   (11–14)

Something is wrong here.[39] The idea of a jealous God is, of course, a commonplace of the Hebrew scriptures, but Donne's emphasis seems inverted. If he is trying to explain why God went so far as to take away his saintly wife; it *should* say something like, "Thou dost not only fear lest I love the World, the Flesh, and the Devil; but in thy tender jealousy dost doubt lest holy saints and angels put thee out." Donne would thus confirm Anne's goodness even as he took comfort in God's remarkable solicitude. But the poem puts it the other way; God is so careful that he worries *not only* about the dangers involved in loving saints and angels *but even* about the threat posed by the world, the flesh, and the devil. The forces of evil are cast as the lesser threats; it is as though a woman were to say to her husband, "You're jealous not only of your tried-and-true friends, but even of Don Juan, Casanova, and the Vicomte de Valmont." The emotional logic is twisted: it is the logic of Leontes in *The Winter's Tale*, sure that his best friend *is* most likely to have cuckolded him; it is the logic of Donne's own resentment, filtering through and warping his portrait of God's jealousy; it is the logic of a fallen world where sacraments are sinful, where marriage is adulterous, where "woo" is spelled "woe" (10), and where husbands — both human and divine — are destructively possessive of their spouses.

   Donne's concern with the idea that God's love may not be enduring, that the soul may lose it through too great an attachment to a creature, is by no means confined to the sonnet on his wife's death. As Potter and Simpson point out, the sermon Donne preached to Queen Anne at Denmark House some four months after Anne Donne's death deals with "ideas...that reflect the

mood of" the sonnet (introduction to *Sermons*, 1:135). The text
of the sermon is Proverbs 8:17: "I love them that love me, and
they that seek me early shall find me." Donne quotes throughout
from Augustine's *Confessions*, highlighting passages in which
the penitent saint laments his profane loves and the belatedness
of his conversion to love of God. In the sermon, as in "Since
She whome I lovd," God seeks to wed man's soul: "The love of
God," Donne tells Queen Anne and the others in his auditory,
"is the consummation, that is, the marriage, and union of thy
soul, and thy Saviour" (*Sermons*, 1:243). But the fear, in the sermon as in the sonnet, is that the deficiency of a human being's
response to that love will put an end to it: "except we love too,
God doth not love with an everlasting love: God will not suffer
his love to be idle, and since it profits him nothing, if it profits
us nothing neither, he will withdraw it" (*Sermons*, 1:244). The
speaker of the sonnet is comparatively optimistic, for he insists
that God will go to any length to avoid being "putt...out" of the
heart he loves.

Indeed, A. J. Smith argues that the God of the sonnet is even
willing to share his beloved. In his edition of Donne's poems,
Smith preserves the manuscript punctuation emended in the
Variorum and in other editions, putting the pause in line 10 after
"hers": "thou / Dost woo my soul for hers; offering all thine"
(*John Donne*, 316). On the basis of this punctuation, Smith
argues that God is wooing John on Anne's behalf, intending to
reunite the couple in heaven ("Two Notes," 405–07).[40] Though
Gardner is certainly right to see such a reading as "inconsistent
with the...theme of God's 'tender jealousy'" (*Divine Poems*,
154), Donne is nothing if not inconsistent. And here he does
want to have his bride and be one too. God is a suitor in his
own right, but the line stresses that God courts Donne by offering him all that is God's, and Anne is thus a part of the bride-
price. A human bridegroom "endow[s]" his new wife "with all
[his] worldly goods" (*BCP*, 293); and God—marrying himself to
Donne's soul—endows it with all heavenly goods, including all
heavenly souls. Donne cannot hope to renew his marriage with

Anne, but he can anticipate their reunion as members of the one body, which is the bride of the Lamb.[41]

His soul can also look forward to a reunion with its "wife": the risen body. In a Lincoln's Inn sermon preached circa 1620, Donne envisions the Resurrection and contrasts earthly experience with the existence to come:

> gladnesse shall my soul have, that this flesh, (which she will no longer call her prison, nor her tempter, but her friend, her companion, her wife) that this flesh, that is, I, in the reunion...of both parts, shall see God.... It was the flesh of every wanton object here, that would allure it in the petulancy of mine eye.... And in the grave, it is the flesh of the worm; the possession is transfer'd to him. But, in heaven, it is *Caro mea, My flesh*, my souls flesh, my Saviours flesh. (*Sermons*, 3:112–13)

In heaven, Donne will at last be the only one. The tired, old feeling of suspicion and jealousy, so familiar to readers of the *Songs and Sonets*, is at last to be fully relieved in an ecstatic confirmation that he is the sole possessor of the body he loves.[42] Though taken away through death, the flesh Anne represents—and in another way Anne herself—will finally be restored. At the resurrection, they will be all the more Donne's because they have become God's.

The sonnet, however, is not as joyful as the sermon on the reunion of body and soul; Martz observes that "the ending is a most precarious resolution" ("The Action," 108). We are left with the image of the poet's divine spouse as full of doubt, uncertain that the poet will remain faithful to his baptismal wedding vows. Insofar as God's fears reflect the poet's own jealousy over Anne's ravishment, they testify to a persistent masculinity of perspective, which is—in the spiritual order of things—Donne's most serious problem (compare Rollin, "'Fantastique Ague,'" 145). He has professed his thoughts' entry into a heavenly matrix, declaring that now "in heauenly things [his] Mind is sett"; but the ingressive masculine stance of that image is in tension with the sonnet's final image. In the closing lines, the question is not what place John Donne's thoughts will occupy, but who or what will occupy John Donne.

He cannot accept the feminine role of responsive spouse as long as he continues to focus on the "Here" (5), the physical realm in which he occupies his male body. And that is precisely what he is doing in composing a sonnet; for when he tells God that "Here the admyring her my Mind did whett / To seeke thee" (5–6), he is at the same time redirecting his focus from the "heauenly things" of line 4 back to the "Here" of the physical world and of the sonnet's microcosm. "Here," he is no bride of Christ; "Here," he is a sonneteer sighing—as male sonneteers do in the Petrarchan tradition—for love of an inaccessible mortal woman. "Here" even puns on "her." And as long as he continues "*Here* the admyring *her*," as long as he confines himself to the lovelorn sonnet form, he will find it difficult to escape imprisonment in the narrow confines of his earthly masculine role. He will remain—to paraphrase the proverbial lament— "Always a bridegroom, never a bride."[43]

The anguish he feels in this situation is no doubt due, at least in part, to the fact that his vocation as a priest of the English church commits him to a very different form of discourse, to preaching the Word of God in spoken prose rather than to confronting God in written verse. When he was ordained in 1615, two years before Anne's death, Donne no doubt would have made his first attempt to "sett" his mind "Wholy in heauenly things." We get a glimpse of how he thought about the effects of ordination in a poem he addressed to Edward Tilman on the occasion of Tilman's ordination. The piece begins by addressing Tilman as "Thou, whose diviner soule hath caus'd thee now / To put thy hand unto the holy Plough" (*Tilman*, 1–2).[44] As Shawcross explains, these lines allude to Luke 9:62, in which Jesus responds to a would-be disciple who wishes to delay following Christ in order to bid farewell to family: "No man, [that] putteth his hand to the plough, and loketh backe, is apte to the kingdome of God." Following Anne's death in 1617, Donne would no doubt have read with even greater emotion verse 60, in which Jesus responds to a man who puts off discipleship in order to bury his father: "Let the dead burye their dead: but go thou and preache the kingdome of God."

In the sonnet on Anne's death, Donne is barely clinging to belief in his own salvation, much less preaching the kingdom to others as his vocation requires. But even in the poem to Tilman, he seems uncertain that becoming God's minister will assure the reorientation of mind and heart: "how is thy mind / Affected...?" he asks Tilman, "Dost thou finde / New thoughts and stirrings in thee? and as Steele / Toucht with a Loadstone, dost new motions feele?" (*Tilman*, 5–8). Has he, in other words, achieved the focus upon "heavenly things" that the Donne of the sonnet so longs to maintain? Are you, he goes on to ask Tilman, now more like a heavenly angel than a man? More specifically, he wants to know if the newly ordained preacher feels a new kind of love: "as we paint Angels with wings, because / They beare Gods message, and proclaime his lawes, / Since thou must doe the like, and so must move, / Art thou new feather'd with cœlestiall love?" (*Tilman*, 19–22). If so, Donne remarks later in the poem, the preacher resembles not only an angel, but also the Blessed Virgin: "*Maries* prerogative was to beare Christ, so / 'Tis preachers to convey him, for they doe / As Angels out of clouds, from Pulpits speake" (*Tilman*, 41–43). Being a preacher and a priest is, Donne concludes, a matter of bringing together "the heavens which beget all things here, / And the'earth our mother, which these things doth beare, / Both these in thee, are in thy Calling knit, / And make thee now a blest Hermaphrodite" (*Tilman*, 51–54). The priest wholly absorbed by his vocation is no longer limited by his male sex; he bridges gender roles and unites in himself heavenly masculinity and earthly femininity.[45]

It is perhaps not surprising, then, that in the Lincoln's Inn sermon on the reunion of resurrected body and soul (ca. 1620), Donne's joy seems dependent on the fact that he is *not* preoccupied with gender distinctions. The flesh "allured" by "every wanton object...in the petulancy of mine eye" is both the scented and beckoning vixen of Proverbs and the foolish young man she entices. And the soul in heaven is an *anima* reunited with "*her* wife." In Donne's sermon preached to Queen Anne, the confusion of gender is even more dramatic, for the divine Wisdom who speaks in Proverbs 8:17 encompasses both sexes:

> To shew the constancy and durableness of this love, the lover is a he, that is Christ; to show the vehemency and earnestness of it, the lover is a shee, that is wisdom…[;] all that is good then, either in the love of man or woman is in this love; for he is expressed in both sexes, man and woman; and all that can be ill in the love of either sex, is purged away, for the man is no other man then Christ Jesus, and the woman is no other woman, then wisdom her self, even the uncreated wisdom of God himself. (*Sermons,* 1:239)

A man might speak of this divine lover as "She whome I lovd" without anxiety or reservation. But such liberating options are not available to Donne in the sonnet on Anne's death, where he and the God who seeks his love are both stubbornly masculine. Donne's diction throughout the poem shows how much he still clings to a husband's role, which he must abandon in order to become a bride in the heavenly wedding feast. His wife is dead, but he is—alas—no widower. Thus, when he speaks of Anne, she is at once the celestial model he emulates and the beloved woman on whom, *in* whom, his amorous thoughts are wholly set. The dilemma of his all-too-husbandly soul is that it cannot gaze upon the example of her femininity without responding to it as a man. He looks to the absent bride of Christ that he may become, like her, a responsive and utterly wifely creature; but in doing so, he makes present to himself the earthly bride he still desires. In showing her husband how to welcome the bridegroom, Anne cannot help but remind him of how good it felt to be one.

4. DONNE'S "SHOW ME DEARE CHRIST" AND AUGUSTINE'S
EXPOSITION OF PSALM 33

"Since She whome I lovd" was apparently a very private poem; it and two other Holy Sonnets—"Show me deare Christ" and "Oh, to vex me"—survive in only one seventeenth century artifact: the Westmoreland manuscript inscribed by Donne's friend Roland Woodward. In the manuscript, these three are the seventeenth, eighteenth, and nineteenth Holy Sonnets, following the 16 others that are preserved in multiple manuscripts and in the seventeenth century print editions of Donne's poetry. No evidence suggests that Donne intended the sonnets unique to the Westmoreland manuscript to be read in conjunction with one another; but they are related thematically, for they all deal with the thorny issues arising from the intersection of spirituality and gender. Specifically, the masculine sexual identity that proves so spiritually precarious in the sonnet on Anne is also a problem for the speaker of "Show me deare Christ," who prays that his "amorous Soule" be allowed to "court" Christ's spouse, and for the persona of "Oh, to vex me," who presumes to "court God" (*HSVex*, 10; see Low, *Reinvention*, 79–85). Reading "Show me deare Christ" in the wake of the sonnet on Anne's death, one cannot help but feel that the poet has turned from unresolved resentment over God's ravishment of *his* spouse to ask for a glimpse of *Christ's* bride: if I can't have mine, at least let me "court" yours.

Donne's request, Anthony Low points out,

> crosses the wires between the two traditional versions of the biblical marriage trope: the marriage between Christ and his Church, and the marriage between God and the soul. On its surface,...the sonnet seems to be based only on the marriage of Christ and his Church.... But the sestet unexpectedly introduces a version of the individual marriage trope.... Donne substitutes the Church for God...in the usual trope...and incorporates additional imagery from the courtly, romance love tradition. (*Reinvention*, 76–77)

The resulting mixed metaphor reflects both the speaker's uncertainty about the identity of the true church and his own identity as a male Christian whose spiritual longings take the form of heterosexual fantasy. His desire to play a masculine rather than feminine role in the heavenly marriage is most shockingly delineated in the concluding lines of the sonnet:

> Betray kind husband thy Spouse to our Sights,
>   And let myne amorous Soule court thy mild Dove,
> Who is most trew, and pleasing to thee, then
> When She'is embrac'd and open to most Men.
>
> (HSShow, 11–14)

The request in lines 11–12 is scandalous, and the declaration that follows is both theologically controversial and emotionally disconcerting.

In an attempt to resolve the considerable problems these lines raise, Helen Gardner drains them of their sexual implications; the speaker, she says, "prays that we may see the Spouse of Christ appear to men, as a wife who delights to welcome all her husband's friends, and whose husband, unlike earthly husbands, delights in her approachability" (*Divine Poems of John Donne*, 122). By bleaching out of her paraphrase the scandalous implications of "Betray," "amorous," "court," "embrac'd," and "open," Gardner is able to reduce Donne's shocking image to a portrait of a gracious hostess, whom she identifies as "the Church Universal, at present hidden from our sight by the divisions which obscure her unity in her Lord." For Gardner, this reading supports Evelyn Simpson's contention that the sonnet is "perfectly compatible with loyalty to the Church of England" (Simpson, *Study of the Prose Works*, 101). Indeed, Gardner contends, "it could hardly have been written by anyone but an Anglican," since "The Anglican, at this period, differed from the Roman Catholic and the Calvinist in not holding a doctrine of the Church which compelled him to 'unchurch' other Christians" (Gardner, *Divine Poems of John Donne*, 122).[46]

But the final lines of the poem do not present the comforting image of a husband who delights in his wife's sociability, as Othello initially delights in Desdemona's virtuous urbanity. On the contrary, the lines say that Christ finds his spouse most "pleasing" when she throws herself "open" to all her wooers, including (or perhaps even especially) a quasi-blasphemous sonneteer. The wife who would comply with such a husband would be the strumpet Iago leads Othello to imagine, not the innocent Desdemona he kills; and it was the Roman church, not the English church or "the Church Universal," that was represented as a strumpet in the controversies of Donne's time. The sonnet gives a nod to the usual anti-Catholic imagery when the speaker initially asks, in ironic tones, whether Christ's spouse could possibly be "She, which on the other Shore / Goes richly painted" (2–3). The church the speaker envisions in the final lines—the wife pandered by her husband—thus has more in common with the "richly painted" hussy of the first quatrain than with the Protestant church that "Laments and mournes in Germany and here." As Lukas Erne points out,

> The painted Roman woman of the beginning of the sonnet—initially denied to have any resemblance with the true Church—ends up in association with the spouse who is "embraced and open to most men" at the sonnet's close. Moreover, the whore's openness "to most men" appears to make her an advocate of the catholicity which Donne knew would be associated with the Roman Church. Perhaps it is not by accident that Helen Gardner refrains from commenting on how the image of the whore, once referring to the Roman Catholic Church, once to Christ's spouse, goes full circle. (222–23)

That "Donne knew" the image of a church "open to most men" would be associated with Roman Catholicism is suggested by a Lincoln's Inn sermon Erne quotes, in which Donne laments that any man "zealous of the house of God" and willing to "say any thing by way of moderation, for the *repairing* of *the ruines* of that house, and *making up the differences* of the Church of God," is bound to be labeled "a *Papist*" (*Sermons*, 2:58). Erne concludes his essay with no more than a modest observation that the sonnet demonstrates "several years after [the poet's] ordination, how complex and divided a person Donne remained" ("Donne and Christ's Spouse," 225). But the point he makes about the concluding image is quite provocative; it supports the idea that the sonnet evokes its author's preference (expressed often in his private correspondence, as well as in the *Essays on Divinity*) for a church more catholic—that is, more universal and inclusive—than the Church of England as he knew it. And it reminds the reader that medieval Catholicism, regardless of its corruptions, was a more universal incarnation of the church militant than any post-Reformation institution.

As Claude Summers points out, however, the sonnet's figure of the Protestant church (she "which rob'd and tore / Laments and mournes in Germany and here" [*HSShow*, 3–4]) recalls a quite venerable and positive figure, the black-robed Una as she appears in the opening cantos of *The Faerie Queene*; for Redcrosse's lady has the look of "one that inly mournd" (1.1.4:6) and comes to the court of the Faerie Queene as a damsel in distress. The connection to Spenser seems likely, Summers argues, when one considers the uncharacteristic chivalric imagery in lines 9–10 of the sonnet, which ask, "Dwells She with vs, or like adventuring knights / First trauaile we to seeke and then make Love?" For Summers, however, the allusion to Spenser is ironic; for,

> If Spenser could confidently associate the Church Triumphant with Protestantism, Donne emphatically could not.... The daring and moving conclusion to the sonnet beautifully expresses Donne's sincere desire for communion with Christ's spouse the Church, but the extended sexual conceit simultaneously exposes the poet's recognition of the preposterous irony involved in any quest for true religion that identifies Christ's spouse with a temporal institution. The courtship of

the "amorous soule" and the "mild Dove" can take place only in some future time and place. ("The Bride," 76, 81)

Summers's argument is a powerful one; the sonnet is no doubt designed to shock the certainty out of any reader who equates the English church or the Roman church (or any other visible institution) with the church triumphant.

But it seems unlikely that the sonneteer—writing, most scholars agree, in a year postdating his ordination to the English priesthood—would reject the words of the satirist who, some 20 years earlier, had run through a catalog of all the lousy options, only to conclude that "unmoved thou / Of force must one, and forced but one allow; / And the right" (*Sat3*, 69–71). Given this imperative, the speaker of Satire III advises his readers that they *should* resemble what the sonnet calls "adventuring knights" who "First trauaile…to seeke" their beloved and only then "make Love" to her: "Be busie to seeke her, beleeve mee this, / Hee's not of none, nor worst, that seekes the best" (*Sat3*, 74–75). Donne did recognize all established Christian denominations as parts or "branches" of the one true church.[47] But the poet himself "Of force" did choose one embodiment of the church militant in which to "stand / Sentinell" as God's soldier (*Sat3*, 30–31). Not surprisingly, then, though none of the versions of the church mentioned by the sonnet's speaker resembles the glorified bride of Revelation, the figure most evocative of the church militant is the weeping and battle-scarred avatar of German and English Protestantism. Though she is, to use Gardner's phrase, as "unbridelike" as her "richly painted" rival, her penitential mien makes her a better candidate for the process of cleansing through which Christ transforms the church militant into the church triumphant. In Ephesians 5:25–32, Saint Paul exhorts husbands to love their wives "euen as Christ loued the Church, & gaue him self for it, That he might sanctifie it, & clense it by the washing of water through ye worde, That he might make it vnto him self a glorious Church, not hauing spot or wrincle, or anie suche thing: but that it shulde be holie and without blame." Erne quotes this passage and argues that Paul's imagery underlies Donne's sonnet at least as clearly as that of Revelation. As I have already noted, however, Erne sees the sexual imagery of the sonnet's conclusion as pointing *away* from the dark Protestant figure, who seems to me the best candidate for cleansing "through ye worde." As Erne sees it, the final lines instead bring the reader "full circle," pointing back toward the "richly painted" Roman whore whose implied willingness to be "embrac'd" by "most Men" is, in light of the closing image, no longer so clearly a bad thing.

On one level, the sonnet offers an image of Protestantism as a feasible and defensible, though less than spirited, image of the church militant, while on another level it implies that the church triumphant is a sanctified version of Roman Catholicism, stripped of her paint, scrubbed "bright," and offered freely to all by her divine spouse. How, if at all, can the sonnet's rather staid Spenserian implications be reconciled with its shocking fantasy of an all-embracing church considerably more catholic (and decidedly less protesting) than the one in which the poet himself travails? The answer, given Donne's notorious penchant for self-contradiction, is that it probably cannot be reconciled. But it is still important to recognize precisely *how* the two contradictory levels of meaning work side by side. And in order to do so, one must acknowledge a previously unacknowledged source of Donne's concluding image. The female figure open to "most Men" is not simply Donne's warped reworking of the traditional bride of Christ image; rather, she is his version of a comparably shocking image painted by his favorite exegete, Saint Augustine. In an effort to clarify the mixed message conveyed by Donne's sonnet, I would offer an intertextual reading, considering the ways in which the poem recalls and transforms two powerful passages from the works of Augustine: one from the *Confessions* and the other from his *Expositions of the Psalms*.[48]

In his *Confessions*, Augustine speaks of falling in love with the "created wisdom" of Ecclesiasticus 1:4, which he calls "the intellectual order of being which by contemplating the Light

becomes light itself" and identifies with the church triumphant:
"the rational, intelligent mind of [God's] chaste city. That city
on high is our mother." He then addresses himself to this bright,
clear church: "O lightsome house, so fair of form, I have fallen in
love with your beauty, loved you as the place where dwells the
glory of my Lord, who fashioned you and claims you as his own.
My pilgrim-soul sighs for you, and I pray him who made you to
claim me also as his own within you" (Confessions, 12.20–21).
In "Show me deare Christ," Donne, like Augustine, has his heart
set on seeing and embracing the fair form that God "claims...as
his own."

The shocking quality of Donne's conclusion, however, is
even more clearly reminiscent of a passage from another of
Augustine's works, in which he is discussing not the "created
wisdom" of Ecclesiasticus, but the divine Sapientia of Proverbs
8–9. Augustine, as was traditional, interprets this figure as a representation of the second person of the Trinity. But what makes
Augustine's portrait of Wisdom exceptional, and provides a
precedent for Donne, is that he envisions the church's ultimate
union with God as a paradoxically chaste orgy, in which Wisdom
is passionately embraced by all her lovers at once:

> The love of a carnally-minded person is inevitably accompa-
> nied by baneful jealousy; if he manages to see naked a woman
> whom he has desired lustfully, does he want someone else to
> see her too? Chastity is preserved only if the sole person who
> sees her is he who has a right to....
>
> With the Wisdom of God it is not so. We shall see her face
> to face; we shall all see her, and none of us will be jealous. She
> shows herself to all, and for all she is inviolate and chaste. Her
> lovers are changed into her likeness; she is not changed into
> theirs. She is Truth, she is God.... I don't want to be the only
> one magnifying the Lord, I don't want to be his only lover, I
> don't want to embrace him all by myself. It is not as though
> there will be no room for any others to put their hands, if I am
> embracing him. God's Wisdom is so wide that all souls can
> embrace and enjoy her.[49]

Like Donne's language in the sonnet, Augustine's language in this passage startles the mind and tests the limits of propriety.

Of course, there are important differences between Augustine's Wisdom and Donne's bride of Christ. One *is* God; the other is God's spouse. And while Donne takes liberties with the idea of wifely fidelity and husbandly kindness, Augustine violates the gender hierarchy underlying the doctrine of Christ's marriage to the church, imagining God *her*self, in the person of Wisdom, as the female figure who will be embraced by "all souls" rather than as the bridegroom who invites them in. Thus, Augustine does not quite anticipate Donne's image of Christ as *mari complaisant* (though his reference to the "sole person who...has a right to" see a woman naked points in that direction). Like Donne, however, Augustine challenges his listeners to imagine divine love in terms that transcend the bounds of human sexual propriety; and, like Donne, he does so by turning inside out the sacred "mystery" of Christ's marriage to the church as Paul describes it in Ephesians. Responding to Frank Kermode's opinion that "the main point" of Donne's concluding image "is the glorious difference of this from a merely human marriage," Erne observes, "Yet the glorious implication of the marriage between Christ and his spouse the Church is not normally a promiscuous wife but a polygamous husband" ("Donne and Christ's Spouse," 222). Instead of a divine bridegroom wedded to a whole church full of feminine souls, both Donne in the sonnet and Augustine in his commentary imagine a heavenly female ogled and groped (very chastely, of course) by a whole church full of masculine souls.

And what, one may ask, could possibly be the pastoral point of such an image for the illustrious bishop of Hippo? The answer strengthens the connection between Augustine's imagery and Donne's, for Augustine's startling description of a wide-open Sapientia glosses verse 4 of Psalm 33: "Magnify the Lord along with me." His point is to argue that God's lovers should be unified rather than divided by jealousy and the pride that leads to schism:

> Stir up this love in yourselves, my brothers and sisters, and shout to every one of your friends and relatives, *Magnify the Lord along with me!* Let this love burn in you.... If the body of Christ is dear to you, if you love the unity of the Church, seize them all and bring them along to enjoy it; say to them, *Magnify the Lord with me!*
>
> *And let us exalt his name together.* Why does it say, *Let us exalt his name together?* Because it means "in unity"; many codices indeed have *Magnify the Lord along with me, and let us exalt his name in unity....* Seize all those you can, then; seize them—by exhortation, by bringing them along bodily, by questioning and disputing and putting sound arguments before them (though gently and with kindness); seize them and drag them to love, so that if they magnify the Lord they may do so to promote unity. (Augustine, Exposition 2 of Psalm 33:6–7)

Donne's speaker, though his "questioning" seems addressed to Christ or to himself rather than to friends or neighbors, might well be said to "drag" readers toward unity through an ironic commentary on disunity. And though the shock tactic of his final image may alienate some, his goal is not only to suggest the difference between Christ's joyfully unified bride and any one of her flawed reflections but also to "promote unity" by imagining a bridegroom who values *caritas* and its unifying effect even more than he values perfect fidelity to doctrine.

Donne's post-Reformation Christendom is in some ways very different from the church of Augustine's time, for Augustine can speak confidently in the first person plural of a church that still coheres, still knows herself, and has only to reach out to those heretical members who have broken away from her. Specifically, Augustine hopes to call the followers of Donatus back into the Catholic fold:

> If the Donatist sect thinks it is magnifying the Lord, has it any reason to be offended if the whole world does so? Brothers and sisters, it is our job to say to the Donatists, *Magnify the Lord with me; and let us exalt his name in unity.* Why do you want to magnify him by amputation? He is one, so why do you try

to create two peoples for God? Why seek to dismember the body of Christ?...

Let us shout and wail with all our might, *Magnify the Lord along with me, and let us exalt his name in unity*. It is the Church that is shouting to them; the voice is the Church's voice, crying out to those who have cut themselves off. How did this severance come about? Through their pride. But Christ teaches humility when he entrusts his body and blood to us. (Augustine, Exposition 2 of Psalm 33:7)

No one denomination of Donne's time could be equated with the Donatists, who broke with the church rather than accept the validity of sacraments administered by *traditors,* priests and bishops guilty of apostasy, who had betrayed the church in one way or another during times of persecution. Both Donne in his sermons and Hooker in his *Laws* associate Donatism with the Anabaptists, who rebaptized those whose baptisms they deemed invalid.[50] And surely the author of *Pseudo-Martyr* must also have seen some correlation between the Donatists, who glorified martyrdom, and the English recusants, who denied the validity of the English church's clergy and of the Eucharist they administered. But the most relevant detail in Augustine's commentary on the psalm is his insistence that love and humility reunite the church that pride dismembers. The Donatists would not deign to accept the body of Christ from the hands of a sinner; they would sooner deny the integrity of that body by breaking off from communion with the church. In lines 5–6 of Donne's sonnet, the speaker alludes incredulously to comparable arrogance, evident in the hubristic claims of both Protestants and Roman Catholics. One side insists that the true church has been asleep for "a thousand" years and "peepes vp" only now that the Reformation has restored her primitive purity (*HSShow*, 5); the other proclaims itself infallible "selfe truth," yet often "errs" (*HSShow*, 6). Both are guilty of the pride Augustine attributes to the Donatists, of being "offended" that anyone but they presumes to magnify the Lord, and to call themselves "church." But Donne's speaker imagines Christ as a Donatist's worst nightmare; he is the ultimate *traditor,* willing to "Betray...[his] Spouse to [the] Sights" of imperfect men, to open up his church to anyone who will "court" her as an "amorous Soule" (*HSShow,* 11, 12).

But Donne's sonnet does not do what Augustine exhorts his congregation to do; it does not invite readers to invite others to join in undivided glorification of God. It is a sonnet, not a sermon or pastoral lecture; and the speaker is a typical sonnet persona, isolated and frustrated. Augustine presumes that his listeners are sure of their place in the church, and thus he can urge them to cry out with one voice, the church's voice. It rings with joy as it shouts to friends and foes alike; it invites all to converge in the collective embrace of a gender-indeterminate divinity who is at one moment called "her" and at the next, "him." But Donne's speaker is an alienated and very masculine lover who sees around him only wounded and splintered images of a feminine beloved. Stanley Stewart argues that the speaker's "intensely devout posture asserts what the implied statement" of the sonnet "denies, namely, that the speaker is himself the Bride of Christ" (*Enclosed Garden,* 20). And insofar as every Christian soul is a bride of Christ, Stewart's point is valid. But the mind of this particular bride, as Stewart acknowledges, "is jaded by the factions of competing religious claims" (21); and whatever the bridelike status of the speaker's soul, his mind expresses its bitter weariness in terms that are clearly gendered masculine. It is only wishful thinking that allows Robert S. Jackson to assert that the speaker undergoes a gender transformation during the course of the sonnet, with his "shift in tone gradually reveal[ing] his feminine character" (*Donne's Christian Vocation,* 166). No doubt the speaker does seek Ecclesia not only by wooing her ideal image but also by trying to speak with the voice of her corporate identity; he uses the first-person plural three times in the third quatrain, and the sonnet's conclusion emphasizes plurality in terms nothing short of shocking. But the "vs" and "we" of the poem are "adventuring knights" on a masculine quest; "our Sights" are the penetrating glances of the male gaze;

and the phrase "most Men," while it may mean "most human beings," takes its force in the scandalous metaphor of the final lines from the more limited definition, "most male lovers." The voice of the speaker is thus not the voice of the bride, nor even the voice of one of the bride's flawed reflections; it is the voice of one particular "amorous Soule," a soul that inhabits a body of the male sex.

Indeed, the sonnet's speaker resembles the persona of Donne's Petrarchan love lyric "The Broken Heart," in which frustrated love of an ideal figure has "shiver[ed]" the speaker's heart "as glasse." His "breast hath all / Those peeces still, though they be not unite"; thus, what remains for him is a refraction of love into "lesser" emotions: "as broken glasses show / A hundred lesser faces, so / My ragges of heart can like, wish, and adore, / But after one such love, can love no more" (Broken, 24, 27–28, 29–32). In "Show me deare Christ," the speaker's soul remains "amorous," but a similar sense of disillusionment keeps him from being able to enshrine a single, perfect image in his heart. No wonder, then, that he speaks only as a potentially adulterous groomsman rather than as a bride of any sort. And no wonder that his musings reflect only the "lesser faces" of a divided Christendom. Their deformities, it would seem, come between him and the embrace of a divine Wisdom "wide" enough for "all souls" to "embrace and enjoy." He has read Augustine; he knows Wisdom is out there and that the earthly bride of Christ must be remade in her image. But hemmed in by the genre he has chosen, imprisoned in his own masculinity, and worn down by the ceaseless conflicts that surround him, he can conclude only with an indecent proposal, and not with Augustine's rapturously erotic rendering of the beatific vision.

One can, to be sure, interpret the ending of Donne's sonnet more positively; one may argue that it, no less than Augustine's sermon, provides an alternative to the limited, dichotomous human perspective in which wives are either faithful or unfaithful, women either madonnas or whores, and churches either true or false. The sonnet may be said to challenge readers to step outside the box within which their own presuppositions have enclosed them, to rethink sexuality, gender, and the sacred in terms that transcend socially determined gender hierarchy, postlapsarian sexual shame, and limited notions of God's love.[51] But, while this alternative reading is deeply appealing, I do not believe that it is valid. The very limited context within which Donne circulated "Show me deare Christ," the fact that he released the poem only to a very small and trusted audience, must have been due at least in part to its controversial theme. As Grierson argues, a man who was either a priest of the English church, or soon to be so ordained, could not openly broadcast his unresolved doubts about the relative merits of the Roman Catholic and Reformed churches (see Grierson, *Criticism and Creation*, 2:235). It is the potential scandal of Dr. Donne as irresolute Protestant that underlies the scandal of Christ as wittol.

Of course, a radically liberal revision of traditional ideas about sexuality and ecclesiology might also warrant limited circulation; not many readers of any age could be relied upon to appreciate such a sonnet, joyful though its implications might be for an enlightened few. But when read in conjunction with the tortured images and anguished tone of the sonnets that precede and follow it in the Westmoreland manuscript, "Show me deare Christ" definitely leaves an acrid aftertaste—rather than a hint of ambrosial sweetness—on the reader's tongue. "Since She whome I lovd" ends with God himself in "doubt" about the state of the speaker's soul; and the concluding claim of "Show me"—that the Lord's spouse is "most trew, and pleasing to" him when she embraces "most Men"—seems particularly problematic when one moves from that paradoxical image of faithful infidelity to the opening of "Oh, to vex me," in which a related oxymoron, constant inconstancy, is the source of the speaker's spiritual dismay, "pleasing" neither to him nor to the God he woos.

Whether or not Donne meant "Show me deare Christ" to be read in conjunction with the other two sonnets he kept in such restricted circulation, those three—as well as "What yf this

present were the worlds last night," with its blazon of Christ and
its recollection of "all my profane Mistressis" (*HSWhat*, 10)—all
demonstrate the poet's self-conscious use of the sonnet to evoke
spiritual turmoil as deep, as painful, and as frustratingly oxymoronic as any Petrarchan lover's "ridlingly distemperd" suffering
(*HSVex*, 7). Within the space afforded him by the 14-line wooing
apparatus known as a sonnet, Donne cannot escape vexation. Its
Petrarchan heritage makes it, for Donne, a self-defeating engine;
and its "imagind corners" (*HSRound*, 1) are too sharply defined
to be softened by any pliant image of feminine receptivity. Even
the speaker of "Batter my hart," with his famous request that
God "rauishe mee" (*HSBatter*, 14), conceives of that "mee" only
in order to advance the agenda of a stubbornly erect and masculine "I": the speaker prays "orethrow *me*" only "That *I* may rise,
and stand" (*HSBatter*, 3; emphasis mine). In "Show me deare
Christ," too, Donne's sonneteer persona is a man with a man's
desires; and though he longs to know the church, to be enfolded
in the arms of Christ's spouse, he remains unsure of his place in
her all-embracing bosom.

5. Sacramental Poetics and Right Reading
in the *Anniversaries*

Donne finds a sacred application for his persistently masculine point of view in another genre—the extended verse meditation that he undertakes in his *Anniversaries*. Addressing his
readers as an authoritative anatomist, prophet, and priest, the
poet-speaker of *An Anatomie of the World* and *The Progres
of the Soule* examines gender questions and theological issues
through the lens of a sacramental poetics that takes as its subject a "blessed maid,.../ Whose name refines course lines, and
makes prose song" (*FirAn*, 443, 446). The poems that celebrate
her transcend the limits of a sonnet's "litle World" (*HSLittle*, 1)
and confront "the frailty and the decay / of this whole world."[52]
The speaker of these works does not reflect upon his own sinfulness in self-contained isolation, but emerges—in print—as

a priestly and prophetic poet seeking a community of engaged and participatory readers. For them and with them, Donne dissects a corrupt macrocosm and anticipates the better realm toward which that "Immortall Mayd" (*SecAn*, 33), the redeemed soul, progresses.

As I have argued elsewhere, Donne seeks to invest his own poems—sacred and secular—with an efficacy akin to that of the sacraments. He defines this efficacy according to a broadly eclectic Reformed theology that draws upon and synthesizes a variety of very different authorities, from Ambrose and Augustine to Aquinas, Scotus, Luther, and Calvin.[53] In his *Devotions*, Donne praises the God he calls "figurative" and "metaphorical" as a maker whose words and works always produce their desired effect. "None of thy indications are frivolous," he says, expressing not only gratitude but also professional admiration: "thou makest thy signs seals, and thy seals effects, and thy effects consolation and restitution" (*Devotions*, 129). No human poet can make such perfectly effective signs, but Donne nevertheless attempts to do so again and again in a variety of genres, from the seduction poem to the formal verse epistle. One can also see sacramental poetics at work in a liturgically inspired poem like "The Annuntiation and Passion," where Donne's goal is to bring his own soul and that of the reader into communion with Mary and the church and, through them, to "taste" the goodness of God.

In the *Anniversaries*, however, the stakes are particularly high because of the works' status as printed poems; for as Donne told his friends Henry Goodyer and George Garrard in letters sent soon after the appearance of the 1612 volume that included both *Anniversaries*, he considered the act of "Printing any thing in verse" a "descent," a form of ignoble literary materialism, "which though it have excuse even in our times, by men who professe, and practise much gravitie; yet I confesse I wonder how I declined to it, and do not pardon my self" (*Letters*, 75, 238). Donne here penitently endorses a commonly accepted early modern belief in what has been dubbed the "stigma of print"; he defends his identity as a refined amateur by expressing shame at having produced an artifact meant to be sold in bookshops. But within the poems themselves, he clearly seizes the opportunity that print affords him, an opportunity to reach a wider audience and to offer them a poem not merely inscribed on paper, but stamped upon it as a permanent impression. If print publication is a social "descent" for Donne, it is also a means of emulating the God who condescends to incarnate his word in mortal flesh, to make his "signs" into effectual "seals."

As Donne sees it, all poetic signs have the potential to function in this way. He declares in *The First Anniversarie* that "Verse hath"—like a sacrament—"a middle nature" (*FirAn*, 473); it moves in the ambiguous space between the physical and the spiritual, serving as a dynamic act of anamnesis that not only "enroules" the "fame" of the departed (*FirAn*, 474), but also brings readers into an active relationship with the one remembered.[54] The poet summons these readers to become members of a community of "new creatures" (*FirAn*, 76) whose understanding of Elizabeth Drury's "worth" (*FirAn*, 73) will lead them to a regenerate life; he declares them to be the inhabitants of "a new world" grown "from the carcasse of the old" (*FirAn*, 76, 75).[55] The "matter and the stuffe" of this world, the poet explains, is one young girl's "vertue, and the forme our practise is" (*FirAn*, 77, 78).

As the *Variorum* commentary on lines 77–78 explains (Parrish, *Variorum*, 6:383), many scholars have noted that "matter" and "forme" are Aristotelian terms used in Scholastic philosophy, *form* being—according to the *OED* definition—"the essential determinant principle of a thing; that which makes anything (matter) a determinate species or kind of being; the essential creative quality" (n. def. 4a).[56] It is just this sense of "forme" as essence that operates in line 37 of *The First Anniversarie*, when Donne says that the dead girl's name "defin'd" the world and gave it "forme." But in lines 77–78, Donne uses the terms "forme" and "matter" in a way that reflects a related but distinct theological usage: "a sacrament is said to consist of *matter* (as the water in baptism, the bread and wine in the Eucharist) and *form*, which is furnished by certain essential formulary words" (*OED*, "form," n. def. 4b). As an example of this usage, the *OED* cites the 1597 edition of Hooker's *Laws:* "To make complete the outward substance of a sacrament, there is required an outward form, which form sacramental elements receive from sacramental words" (*Laws*, 5.58.2). Hooker here concurs with Aquinas, who says, "in the sacraments, words and things, like form and matter, combine in the formation of one thing, in so far as the signification of things is completed by means of words" (*Summa Theologica*, 3.60.6).[57]

When the Anatomist says that "The matter and the stuffe of" the new world is Elizabeth Drury's "vertue," while "the forme our practise is" (*FirAn*, 77, 78), he is thus tapping the language of sacramental theology in order to explain the relationship between the goodness of one exemplary virgin and the lives of those who acknowledge her excellence. Elizabeth Drury's "vertue" is the "matter" (*FirAn*, 77) or "sacramental [element]" (Hooker, 5.58.2) of which the new world and its creatures are "Elemented" (*FirAn*, 79). "Vertue" here means not only "Conformity of life and conduct with the principles of morality" (*OED*, n. def. 2a), but also "Efficacy of a moral nature; influence working for good upon human life or conduct" (n. def. 9c), and even "An embodiment of" the "power or operative influence inherent in a supernatural or divine being" (n. def. 1b).[58] Clearly, female virtue here extends far beyond passive chastity, silence, and obedience; it is a powerful force, potentially capable of transforming those with whom it comes in contact. But this efficacy is not operative, this "matter" or "substance" is not "complete," to use Hooker's terms, until it is made into a sacrament by the addition of "sacramental words." In the case of the "new world" to arise from the virtue of Elizabeth Drury, the operative sacramental words are those of Donne's poem as it is received by readers open to the dead maiden's virtuous influence. It is the cooperative effort of the poet and his readers, their devout engagement with the "essential formulary words" (*OED*, "form," n. def. 4b) of the *Anniversaries*, that applies Elizabeth's "vertue" and makes it live.

As Donne later notes in a sermon, various kinds of Christians disagree about what constitutes the "word" that gives a sacrament its form. Roman Catholics, he says, think of the word added to the sacrament as the formula of Eucharistic consecration, pronounced by the priest, while many nonconformist Calvinists insist that the only essential word is God's Word preached. Donne inclines in the Protestant direction, but tempers the emphasis on preaching by paraphrasing Augustine: "There is a necessity of the *word*" in a sacrament "not because the word is *preached*, but because it is beleeved" (Donne, *Sermons*, 5:128).[59]

In *The First Anniversarie*, too, the receiver's believing participation is all-important. As Stanwood puts it, Donne "As priest...transforms...the vulgar world." He does so, Stanwood asserts, "by means of the grace available through Christ and embodied in Elizabeth Drury" ("'Essential Joye,'" 395). But the poet's words can bring about this renewal only in and through readers' responses to them, in and through their participation in the spiritual community implied by the liturgical first-person plural of the phrase "our practise" (*FirAn*, 78).

Donne's sacramental poetry, like the Eucharist as English Protestants conceived of it, will benefit only the "worthy receiuer," the reader possessed of "a right understanding," to use the phrasing of the Elizabethan homily on the Lord's Supper (*Certaine Sermons*, 2:198). In order to ensure that his readers may possess such understanding, the poet must first help them to recover their lost "sense and memory" (*FirAn*, 28). He must make them realize "who it is that's gone" (*FirAn*, 42), give them the opportunity to "[understand] / Her worth" (*FirAn*, 72–73), and thus make it possible for them to reflect her lingering light (*FirAn*, 70–72). But that task, as it turns out, is a formidable one. Despite (or perhaps partly because of) Donne's efforts to make reader-response a key element in the *Anniversaries*, their meaning is notoriously obscure. Scholars have long debated many aspects of the poems, and in particular the identity of the mysterious "shee" they mourn and celebrate. Though the title pages of both the 1611 and 1612 editions announce that the poems within are written "BY OCCASION OF / the...death of Mistris ELIZABETH DRVRY," many readers have concluded that these monumental works cannot really be about a deceased 14-year-old, but must in fact be mourning someone or something more important, more significant, more exalted.

Considering the historical resonance of Elizabeth Drury's first name, not a few readers have interpreted the *Anniversaries* as commemorating Queen Elizabeth, who had died a little less than eight years before the distinctly undistinguished Mistress Drury and to whom the poems' hyperbolic praises might, so the theory goes, be applied more decorously than to the obscure daughter of Donne's patron. *The First Anniversarie* begins, after all, by calling the deceased virgin a "Queene" who "ended here her progresse time / And, as t'her standing house, to heauen did clymbe" (*FirAn*, 7–8). These lines have led readers to recall the virtues of King James's much-beloved predecessor and to read the poem as a veiled tribute to her.[60] But such readings oversimplify Donne's work. Those who think the *Anniversaries* are "really" about Queen Elizabeth mistake likeness for identity; they assume that, when Donne describes a young gentlewoman in terms that seem applicable to a famous monarch, he can no longer be talking about the humbler figure. It was not Elizabeth Tudor, however, who was "loth to make the Saints attend her long" (*FirAn*, 9); Elizabeth Drury died before her fifteenth birthday, while the Virgin Queen lived to what was, in her day, a ripe old age, making the "Saints" wait 69 years before she would join them to become "a part both of the Quire, and Song" (*FirAn*, 10).

More importantly, in calling Elizabeth Drury a "Queene," Donne proceeds from the assumption that that title is, in a spiritual sense, due to every soul that becomes a bride of Christ the King. Aemelia Lanyer, as chapter 2 will demonstrate in more detail, makes the same assumption in her *Salve Deus*

Rex Judaeorum. Though Lanyer's principal addressee, Margaret Clifford, was in actuality no more than a dowager countess, Lanyer nonetheless praises her in language that might have been addressed to the late Queen Elizabeth: "So you (deere Ladie) still remaine as Queene, / Subduing all affections that are base, / Unalterable by the change of times" (*SDRJ*, 1557–59). These lines not only assign Clifford a royal title, but also recall the motto of Elizabeth I, "Semper eadem," always the same. Given Lanyer's admission that she has decided to "applie / [Her] pen" to Margaret Clifford only "Sith *Cynthia*" has left this world (*SDRJ*, 9–10, 1), her lines praising the countess as "Queene" may well have been originally intended for Elizabeth. But for Lanyer, there is no need to reword these lines when she presents them to a woman of lower social rank; the virtues of chastity and constancy crown any woman who practices them, making her a sovereign in her own right. Indeed, after addressing the first two prefatory poems of her volume to Queen Anne and her daughter the Princess Elizabeth, Lanyer turns "To all vertuous Ladies in generall," urging them to attend "this faire Queene" (Anne), but implying that they are royal personages in their own right. They are called, she says, to ride in the sun's chariot, "Attended on by Age, Houres, Nights, and Daies, / Which alters not your beauty, but gives you / Much more, and crownes you with eternall praise" ("To all," 6, 45–47). Clearly, one need not be Anne of Denmark or Elizabeth I to wear the diadem of poetic hyperbole.

Donne himself says as much (though rather sardonically) in an April 1612 letter to his friend George Garrard; the poet mentions the reports he has heard of individuals criticizing "my Anniversaries" and notes in particular that some women feel he has "said too much" in praise of Elizabeth Drury. Donne responds:

> My defence is, that my purpose was to say as well as I could: for since I never saw the Gentlewoman, I cannot be understood to have bound my self to have spoken just truths, but I would not be thought to have gone about to praise her, or any

other in rime; except I took such a person, as might be capable of all that I could say. If any of those Ladies think that Mistris *Drewry* was not so, let that Lady make her self fit for all those praises in the book, and they shall be hers. (*Letters*, 239)[61]

The first point of this *apologia* is to establish Donne's conviction that "just truths" are *mere* facts, paltry details irrelevant to the task of representing "such a person, as might be capable of all that I could say," one who provides the template or model for virtue.[62] The second and even more important point is to make clear that "Mistris *Drewry*" is the subject of the poems and that her status as anonymous nobody is part of what makes her right for the job. Not everyone can be Queen Elizabeth I, but any woman who truly wishes to do so can be "She, of whom th'Auncients seem'd to prophesie, / When they call'd vertues by the name of shee" (*FirAn*, 175–76).

One hears a similar conviction in the poet's response to his formidable friend Ben Jonson, a response recorded in William Drummond's account of his conversations with Ben. Jonson told Drummond "that Dones Anniversarie was profane and full of Blasphemies," and added "that he told Mr Donne, if it had been written of ye Virgin Marie it had been something." According to Jonson's recollection (and Drummond's account of it), Donne answered this objection by saying "that he described the Idea of a Woman and not as she was" (Jonson, "Conversations," 133; qtd. in Parrish, *Variorum*, 6:240). In light of Donne's letter to Garrard, it is clear that the difference between "the Idea of a Woman" and what "she was" is not, in Donne's mind, a simple contrast between the ideal and the real, or between fiction and truth. Instead, the "Idea" figures forth the best, not merely of what "was," but of what can be in anyone who will "make her self fit for all those praises in the book."

But if the "shee" of the *Anniversaries* is, in fact, the unremarkable Elizabeth Drury, some critics have argued, then Elizabeth Drury must be a symbol. Marius Bewley, for example, argues in a 1952 article that "*The Anniversaries* are...*secretly* celebrating...Donne's apostasy from the Roman Catholic Church"

("Religious Cynicism," 622).[63] The "true religious Alchimy" by which Elizabeth was able to "purifie / All" (*FirAn*, 181–82) seems to Bewley "a clear reference to the Catholic Sacramental system," and, as he goes on to explain, "although the Anglican Church had copied that system to some extent, Donne is referring to the original and not the copy, for he insists on the fact that she is dead.... [Only] in her ghost—or the image of Elizabeth Drury dead—[do] we have the image of Anglicanism" ("Religious Cynicism," 626–27). Bewley's reading of the *Anniversaries* as a skeptic's paean to a dead religion is slightly more accurate than the theory that the poems are really about Queen Elizabeth, for he correctly perceives the loss of sacramental grace as a central issue in Donne's *Anniversaries*. But his conclusions are nonetheless problematic because he, like those who embrace the Queen Elizabeth reading, mistakes analogy for symbolism, arguing that Elizabeth *stands for* Catholicism because she performs some functions resembling those of the Roman church.

Both Bewley's theory and the argument that "shee" is actually Queen Elizabeth underestimate what Donne believes Elizabeth Drury to be in her own right. The implications of the girl's death are huge, as Donne sees them, not because she is a symbol of something larger than herself or a conveniently named stand-in for another, more important virgin. Rather, her death is significant because, in losing her, humankind has lost a female human being who was—while she lived—the sacramental means of grace God intended her to be. As Lindsay Mann explains, "Donne evokes various specific symbolic associations for Elizabeth Drury but stresses their inadequacy or incompleteness. Thus Donne draws on all the mythological and biblical associations of an idealized woman for Elizabeth Drury; yet the 'shee' of the poems *is* Elizabeth Drury as one embodiment of the creative and sustaining quality of all virtuous women, throughout the whole of time, and bearing the seed of the righteousness divinely intended" ("Typology of Woman," 338).[64]

Edward Tayler, too, rejects the theory that Elizabeth Drury is a symbol. Citing Donne's explanation to Ben Jonson that his poem described "the Idea of a Woman and not as she was," Tayler explains that the word "Idea" here has its scholastic meaning of "intelligible species" — "that which makes the thing what it really is" (*Donne's Idea of a Woman*, 30).[65] In light of this definition, Tayler argues that when Donne "answered [the objections of Ben Jonson by saying] that he described the Idea of a Woman and not as she was," he "had in mind the basic distinction between essence and accidents": Thus, "When in the context of this distinction we 'see' the Idea we do not see a Symbol.... Rather, we come to know Elizabeth for what makes her what she is, no longer occluded from our view by the individuating properties of matter" (ibid., 30).[66] In *The First Anniversarie*, Donne makes it his business to restore "our view." But his task is monumental; for the diseased perception of man is no longer capable of discerning any pure "Idea," much less the gracious essence of the sacramental gifts "sent / For mans reliefe" (*FirAn*, 101–02), divine largesse that includes not only baptism and the Lord's Supper, but also woman, whom the *Anniversaries* define as the model for all other sacraments, ecclesiastical and poetic.

In an effort to restore the reader's appreciation for such gifts, the poet explores Elizabeth Drury's "worth" in language charged with sacramental significance. Donne begins the poem by insisting on how important it is to "celebrate" (*FirAn*, 2) "that rich soule which to her Heauen is gone" (1). Such celebration is necessary, the poet explains, since one can "know" one has a soul only if that soul "see, and Iudge, and follow worthinesse, / And by Deedes praise it" (2, 4–5). Donne's verbs "know," "see," and "Iudge" in this passage suggest that the poem's praise of Elizabeth is a sacramental action, for they recall Hooker's description of how Holy Communion affects devout receivers: "in the Eucharist we so receive the gift of God, that we *know* by grace what the grace is which God giveth us, the degrees of our own increase in holiness and virtue wee *see* and can *judge* of them" (*Laws*, 5.67.1; emphasis mine). The problem with the world Donne addresses in his poem, however, is that it is incapable of such sacramental knowledge, vision, and judgment; it cannot know it has a soul because it, in fact, no longer does. The world is a "carcasse" (*FirAn*, 75) because "shee which did inanimate and fill / The world, [is] gone" (68–69). And because the world is dead, it cannot celebrate, receive, or partake of Elizabeth. Again, Hooker's discussion of the Eucharist provides a gloss: "The grace which we have by the holy Eucharist doth not begin but continue life. No man therefore receiveth this Sacrament before Baptism, because no dead thing is capable of nourishment" (*Laws*, 5.67.1). Just as man cannot receive the Eucharist if he is spiritually dead, so the world cannot "celebrate" Elizabeth (*FirAn*, 2)—can neither "speak [her] praises..., extol" her (*OED*, "celebrate," v. def. 5), nor "perform publicly and in due form" (v. def. 1) the ritual of poetic praise that acknowledges and embraces her—as long as the world is "dead, yea putrified" (*FirAn*, 56). In its "speechlesse" state, it has returned to infancy; and having "lost" its "sense and memory" (*FirAn*, 30, 28), it is as helpless as an unbaptized infant. As Hooker explains, "in our *infancy* we...receive the grace of [Christ's] Spirit *without any sense* or feeling of the gift which God bestoweth" (*Laws*, 5.67.1; emphasis mine).

But as Donne's next, explicitly sacramental image makes clear, the world's state is more desperate than that of an unbaptized child, for it has forgotten and thus betrayed or annulled its baptism. In failing to discern the intelligible species of "that rich soule which to her Heauen is gone" (*FirAn*, 1), the world has returned to the senseless and nameless infancy that preceded "her" sacramentally efficacious "comming" into its life:

> Thou hast forgot thy name, thou hadst; thou wast
> Nothing but she, and her thou hast o'repast.
> For as a child kept from the Font, vntill
> A Prince, expected long, come to fulfill
> The Ceremonies, thou vnnam'd hadst laid,
> Had not her comming, thee her Palace made:
> Her name defin'd thee, gaue thee forme and frame,
> And thou forgetst to celebrate thy name.   (*FirAn*, 31–38)

These lines associate Donne's "Idea of a Woman" with sacramental grace while at the same time evoking a whole range of ways in which such grace is subverted, thwarted, or corrupted in Donne's world; the overdetermined language of the passage works on at least three levels.

First, the poet indicts the world for failing to "celebrate" the name that is both Elizabeth Drury's and its own (*FirAn*, 38), the name "Christian." This communal name—even more than an individual's given name (Elizabeth, John) which is bestowed in baptism and that gives "forme and frame" (37) to the one who receives it—determines who and what that person truly *is*. Amid the religious wars and persecutions of the sixteenth and seventeenth centuries, hurtful labels like "papist" or "Puritan" have become more important than the true baptismal name of "Christian," the name by which all Christendom once knew itself.[67] The world's failure to remember its baptismal name is its failure to "practise" (78) Christianity. Its amnesia cuts it off from Christian identity, from the Christian life of sacramental "celebrat[ion]" (38) and thus from sacramental grace.

Beneath the charge of impious forgetfulness, however, is a second stratum of negative meaning; for, as the poet reminds the world of the christening it has forgotten, he describes the forgotten baptismal rite itself as having been tainted by profane considerations. The christening took place, he says, only when a royal personage arrived to serve as godparent to the child and give it "Her name" (*FirAn*, 37).[68] The baptism was delayed for as "long" as it took this "Prince" (34) to arrive. It is a disturbing image. The infant was "kept from the Font" for reasons of secular patronage; the sacrament was made to depend upon the will and pleasure of a sovereign. This scenario does not directly disparage the English Protestant commingling of church and state, but it weaves a subtle antiestablishment thread into the fabric of Donne's text. What is wrong with the world, the Anatomist says out loud, is that it has become irreligious; it has forgotten its baptism. But the analogy quietly hints that this is what comes of a state religion in which the role of godparent is entrusted to the temporal ruler.

The complexity of Donne's analogy is not limited, however, to the explicit critique of forgetfulness and the implicit indictment of politicized religion. On a third, less obvious level, the lines tempt the reader to equate Elizabeth Drury with Christ. Like the Messiah for whom the people of Israel waited many centuries, the departed virgin was "a Prince, expected long" (*FirAn*, 34). The world was her "Palace" (36) just as "the whole world is"—to cite a phrase from Donne's *Sermons*—"[Christ's] Court" (*Sermons*, 5:137). "The name of Christ hath been shed upon us all in our baptisme," Donne says in another sermon (7:109); and in the poem, it was Elizabeth who bestowed "Her name" (*FirAn*, 37) at the font. Following the scent of these tantalizing analogies, William Empson declares that Donne's poem does not make sense unless one accepts "Elizabeth as the Logos" (*English Pastoral Poetry*, 84).

At the very deepest level of meaning, however—which is less a fourth layer of meaning than another way of understanding the third—the reader is invited to participate actively in the analogy between a godly young woman and Christ, and to maintain a clear sense of the distinction between them. A reader who does so will discern that "she" (*FirAn*, 32) was not Jesus *himself*, but the sacramental "comming" of his grace that "fulfill[ed]" the outward "Ceremonies" at "the Font" and without which the world was "Nothing" (36, 34, 35, 33, 32). Her "comming" (36) was—to quote a distinction Donne makes in a sermon for Pentecost—one of the "commings of Christ," but her arrival was not the first Advent "when [Jesus] came in the flesh"; it was, rather, a sacramental coming, what the sermon defines as "an Advent of grace, in his gracious working in us, in this life" (*Sermons*, 6:328).[69]

On this most equivocal level of meaning, Donne foregrounds both Elizabeth Drury's resemblance to Christ and the fact that she is *not* him; the reader is challenged to maintain the perilously fine distinction between *sacramentum* (the sacramental

element or outward sign) and *res sacramenti* ("Christ," who—as
John Calvin puts it—"is the mater, or...substance of all sacra-
mentes" (*Institution of Christian Religion*, 4.14.16). The poetry
thus poses the challenge central to every Protestant text on the
sacraments. Elizabeth resembles Christ, since—the Elizabethan
Homilies put it—"If Sacraments had not a certaine similitude
of those things whereof they bee Sacraments, they should bee no
Sacraments at all" (*Certaine Sermons*, 2:133). Nevertheless, the
reader must not mistake Elizabeth for her divine referent; for,
though "a Sacrament is a thyng nothyng worth, if it be severed
from the truth thereof," yet, as Calvin says, citing Augustine,
"euen in the very conjoynyng nedeth a distinction" (*Institution
of Christian Religion*, 4.14.16). Man must receive the sacramental woman who conveys God's grace as a vibrantly transparent
sign of that grace. He must read her aright, lest he—as Donne
comes perilously close to doing in his sonnet on Anne's death
and as Adam does in book 9 of Milton's *Paradise Lost*—replace
his God with his "good," the giver with the gift.

In the same way, readers of the *Anniversaries* seeking to
understand Donne's "Idea of a Woman" must, like the communicants exhorted in the Elizabethan homily on the Lord's
Supper, "celebrate that mystery" (*Certaine Sermons*, 2:198).
They must "celebrate" (*FirAn*, 2, 38) the "best, and first origi-
nall / Of all faire copies" (227–28). But they must do so only in
the spirit that the poet endorses; as the homily puts it, "Neither
can he be deuout, that otherwise doth presume then it was giuen
by the author. We must then take heed,...lest of two partes, we
haue but one, lest applying it for the dead, we lose the fruit that
be aliue" (*Certaine Sermons*, 2:198).[70] The homily on the sacrament mentions "applying" the Lord's Supper "for the dead"
in order to repudiate the Roman Catholic practice of offering
masses for human souls in purgatory; but the homilist's remark
is an important warning for readers of *The First Anniversarie* as
well. The poet says that Elizabeth Drury's luminescence—her
"vertue" as sacramental woman—has not gone out of the world
entirely; he detects—or, to use the language of English Protestant

Eucharistic theology, *discerns*—the "glimmering light" that "Her Ghost" casts and that "Reflects from her, on them which vnderstood / Her worth" (*FirAn*, 70, 72–73). In portraying the deceased Elizabeth Drury as a sacrament lost to mankind, then, Donne does not set her up as a unique exception to the rule of female depravity and weakness. Rather, he takes her death as the occasion to anatomize man's alienation from and abuse of the sacramental means of grace God has afforded him, including not only the ecclesiastical sacraments of Baptism and Eucharist, but also the sacrament of woman as Donne defines her.

6. The Final Cause of Sacramental Womanhood in *The First Anniversarie*

According to Donne's understanding of Genesis, woman's status as a "helpe mete" to man implies that she was created to be a conduit of grace, that her final cause is the good of man; and Elizabeth Drury, as *The First Anniversarie* portrays her, was the perfect embodiment of woman thus defined. She was the link between matter and spirit, heaven and earth. Man, "this worlds Vice-Emperor, in whom / All faculties, all graces are at home" (*FirAn*, 161–62) is so only by virtue of his relation to the sacramental woman who makes God immanent in his world. Before the Fall, he was graced by the physical beauty of the sinless Eve, that *hortus conclusus* "in whom"—as in Elizabeth Drury—"all white, and redde, and blue / (Beauties ingredients) voluntary grew, / As in an vnuext Paradise" and "from whom / Did all things verdure, and their lustre come" (*FirAn*, 361–64). After the Fall, when God, "loth t'attend / Till man came vp, did downe to man descend" (167–68), he did so by becoming incarnate in the womb of Mary, where the Word made flesh—like "Vertue" in Elizabeth Drury—grew "to such maturity,...that it must die" for the good of man (413–14).[71] But without the woman whose beauty and virtue figures forth the grace that dignifies him, "This man, so great, that all that is, is his, / Oh what a trifle, and poore thing he is!" (169–70). The event that

The First Anniversarie mourns, Elizabeth Drury's death, is but an outward and physical sign of the divorce that divides man from the grace the sacramental woman embodies: "when he did depart / With her, whom we lament," the poet explains, "he lost his hart"; and "The heart being perish'd, no part can be free" (173–74, 186). Donne thus attempts—through poetry that is meant to serve a sacramental function—to generate a new communal body made up of those who remember Elizabeth Drury and whose memory of her "from the carcasse of the old world, free, / Creates a new world" (75–76). The poet makes clear that there is no cure for the old world's infections; it is a corpse to be anatomized. But he does hold out hope that the dissection itself will prove a means of protecting the creatures of the "new world." They will more likely retain their unstained feminine virtue, their own status as "weedlesse Paradises" or enclosed gardens "Which of themselues produce no venemous sinne" (82, 83) if he can protect them against that phallic embodiment of masculine evil, the "forraine Serpent" who does "bring...in" such poison (84). He thus proceeds to tell the creatures of the "new world" about "The dangers and diseases of the old" (88); and, in doing so, he makes clear that unhealthy gender relations are among the worst of humanity's ailments.

The first section of the poem's main body (lines 91–190) describes the bodily and spiritual disorders of human beings, in whom—to quote the first line of this section—"There is no health" (*FirAn*, 91). In this section, Donne echoes the voices of women in order to comment upon humanity's "ruinous" state: "poore mothers crie, / That children come not right, nor orderly, / Except they headlong come, and fall vpon / An ominous precipitation" (95–98). Mothers cannot change the postlapsarian irony that, in obstetrics, right-side-up is wrong, that the healthiest babies tumble into the world upside-down. They can only see and mourn that truth, their cries in childbirth acknowledging humanity's fallenness even as the pain they feel is itself a punishment for that fall. Though they are in one sense only sinful daughters of Eve, the mothers in these lines are in another sense

grief-stricken prophets whose cries make manifest man's per-
versity; and it is to the latter role that the poet himself aspires.
In the conclusion of *The First Anniversarie*, he will invite a
comparison between his own work and Moses' prophetic song in
Deuteronomy. But the cries of anonymous women, rather than
the composition of the male patriarch, are the first models of
prophesy in Donne's poem.

In the lines that follow the "poore mothers" image, as many
critics note, Donne evokes the photo-negative of his exalted
"Idea of a Woman," seemingly rehashing the misogynous doctrine of woman as man's confusion. But this passage is introduced by an ultra-Donnean question that should influence one's
interpretation of what follows. "How witty's ruine?" the poet
asks (*FirAn*, 99), prompting readers to watch for comparable wit
in the poetry that pits itself against ruin:

> How witty's ruine? how importunate
> Vpon mankinde? It labour'd to frustrate
> Euen Gods purpose; and made woman, sent
> For man's reliefe, cause of his languishment.
> They were to good ends, and they are so still,
> But accessory, and principall in ill.
> For that first mariage was our funerall:
> One woman at one blow, then kill'd vs all,
> And singly, one by one, they kill vs now.
> We doe delightfully our selues allow
> To that consumption; and profusely blinde,
> We kill our selues, to propagate our kinde.   (*FirAn*, 99–110)

These lines do *play upon* conventional misogyny. But to say
that they *express* it is to ignore both the witty interrogative that
introduces the apparent misogyny and the rueful joke about male
orgasm that follows it.[72] Read within this frame, the claim that
women are "accessory, and principall in ill" and that woman
is to blame for the Fall does not—to say the least—resonate
as entirely earnest. On the contrary, these lines are reflections
on the wittiness of ruin, on the deep ironies of fallen existence
already touched on in the lines about childbirth. The point, I

would argue, is not to impugn women's status as individuals capable of good as well as evil, but to reflect wryly on woman's relationship to man's goodness and sinfulness.

Woman is a gift sent by God "For mans reliefe" — to correct the aloneness that God said was "not good" (Gen. 2:18) and, as Manley points out in his observation that the line has "slight sexual overtones," to relieve his sexual longing (Manley, *John Donne*, 135). Milton's Adam, who calls Eve "Heav'n's last best gift" (*PL* 5.19), would agree. As a helpmeet for man, one who changes the "not good" of solitude to the grace of married love, woman was and still is "to good ends" (*FirAn*, 103). As Elizabeth L. Wiggins explains, Donne is here using Aristotelian terms for different aspects of causality. The passage refers both to "*final cause* or *end*," the purpose for which something is made, and to "*principal* and *assisting efficient causes*" ("Logic in the Poetry," 56). The principal efficient cause is the primary force actualizing or bringing about a thing's final cause or end, while an assisting efficient cause is something that affects but does not primarily determine the motion of a thing toward its end. Donne is exclaiming at the irony that a woman's ability to be both the principal efficient cause of her own sin and an assisting efficient cause of a man's sin thwarts her good final end or purpose, her final cause as defined in Genesis, which is to be a help to man, an accessory to his goodness. Even in the postlapsarian world, she can realize her final cause as a "helpe mete" (Gen. 2:18) by becoming the [assisting efficient cause] of a man's movement toward a good end; but no woman can be the principal efficient cause of good in a man. He must be that for himself.

So far, so *good*. But how can Donne argue that "in ill," woman is not only "accessory" but "principall" as well? The answer lies in Donne's elision of the philosophical definition of the word "principal" with other meanings applicable in this context. In lines 385–86 of *The Second Anniversarie*, Donne says, "Still before Accessories doe abide / A triall, must the principall be tride." He thus uses the noun "principall" very clearly in its legal sense: "A person directly responsible for a crime, either as the actual perpetrator (principal in the first degree), or as present, aiding and abetting, at the commission of it (principal in the second degree)" (*OED*, n. def. 2b). It is this legal meaning that is most clearly paired with and opposed to "accessory." The noun "principal" was also used as late as 1660 to refer to an "original document, drawing, painting, etc., from which a copy is made" (*OED*, n. def. 5a). And as an adjective, too, "principal" could mean "original" (*OED*, adj. def. 6, 8). When one considers these definitions in relation to the scholastic ones we have just been exploring, the full force of Donne's wit in *The First Anniversarie* passage becomes apparent. A woman can be the secondary efficient cause of a man's sin, the instrument he uses in moving toward an evil end, a means by which his sin is carried out, or an accessory to the crime. She may also be a principal efficient cause of her own wrongdoing; and in the case of Eve, the action that made her the principal cause of her own sinfulness also made her the principal sinner, the original one merely imitated or copied by Adam. A clever Lincoln's Inn lawyer might argue, moreover, that Eve was the "principal in the first degree," the "actual perpetrator" of the original sin; whereas Adam, who was merely "present, aiding and abetting, at the commission of" her crime, was no more than a "principal in the second degree." Donne knows quite well that Eve's sin was not the principal efficient cause of Adam's; he has not forgotten Romans 5:12, which specifically says that "by one *man* sinne entred into the worlde, and death by sinne" (emphasis mine). But he wittily explores the tension between that verse and Genesis 3:6, in which Eve "did eat" *first*, and then "gaue also unto her housband with her, and he did eat." Whether or not Donne would have described Adam's transgression as Milton did, as a "completing of the mortal Sin / Original" (*PL* 9.1003–04), he is obviously fascinated with the tangled web of causation and legal responsibility, as well as with the seductive pseudo logic of the *post hoc ergo propter hoc* fallacy. Within the space of five lines, he says that "One woman...kill'd vs all" by her acting as principal in the principal or original crime (*FirAn*, 106), that all women "singly, one by one,...kill vs now," acting as assisting efficient causes of man's depletion in intercourse (107), and that "We kill our selues," that men are principal efficient causes and principal perpetrators of their own demise (110). In short, there is less misogyny here than scholastic and legal wit, which is the poet's response to the wittiness of ruin itself, to its ingenious perversion of woman's final cause or "good ends" (103) as defined in Genesis, chapter 2.

"The Idea of a Woman" as figured forth in Elizabeth Drury is the counterpoint and antidote to the dark ironies of fallen gender relations. But does Donne's "Idea of a Woman" have anything to do with woman, or does Donne celebrate Elizabeth Drury only by separating her from her sex and thus canceling or erasing her gender? Poststructuralist readers insist on the latter notion. For Ronald Corthell, Donne's "project...depends upon an emptying of Elizabeth's corporeal womanhood" ("Obscure Object of Desire," 131); and according to Elizabeth Hodgson, Donne "construct[s] Elizabeth Drury not only as a figure of idealized femininity, but also by her very perfection a desexed, desexualized, *almost* masculinized figure" (*Gender and the Sacred Self,* 175). In support of this argument, Hodgson quotes lines 177–82 of the *Anatomie,* in which Donne praises Elizabeth as

> She in whom vertue was so much refin'd,
> That for Allay vnto so pure a minde
> Shee tooke the weaker Sex, shee that could driue
> The poysonous tincture, and the staine of *Eue,*
> Out of her thoughts, and deeds; and purifie
> All, by a true religious Alchymy.

For Hodgson, these lines both define Elizabeth "as a 'super' woman capable of circumventing the curse on her sex, and [identify her] with something entirely other than woman which chooses in a Christlike kenosis the female form for a habitation" (175).

The Christology underlying this interpretation seems to me to be confusingly heretical. An analogy between Elizabeth and

Christ founded upon Donne's own, more orthodox conception of the hypostatic union would imply that, whatever is other-than-womanly in Elizabeth's nature, she is no less truly a woman than Christ is truly a man. But the language of the passage in question is alchemical, and when Donne uses such language in his sermons, he is usually not addressing ancient Christological dogmas and heresies, but rather attacking Roman Catholic doctrines contested by Protestants during his own time. For example, Donne says that defenders of the doctrine of purgatory are like "our Alchymists," who claim to find their art in the writings of Virgil, Ovid, Moses, and Solomon: "so these men can finde such a transmutation into gold, such a foundation of profit, in extorting a sense for Purgatory . . . out of any Scripture" (*Sermons*, 7:191). Even more relevantly, he uses the image of alchemists in another sermon to denigrate Catholic sacramental theology, impugning both transubstantiation and the doctrine that attrition is sufficient for a good confession: "Our new *Romane Chymists* . . . , they that can *transubstantiate bread into God*, they can change any foulness into cleanness easily. . . . A sigh of the *penitent*, a word of the *Priest*, makes all clean, and induces an absolute pureness" (*Sermons*, 1:203, 204).

Donne's language in *The First Anniversarie* associates Elizabeth Drury with a legitimate version of such sacramental transformation and purification. At first, he presents her as a prudent metalworker rather than an alchemist, as "She in whom vertue was so much refin'd, / That for Allay vnto so pure a minde / Shee tooke the weaker Sex" (*FirAn*, 177–79). Here, Donne presents Elizabeth's earthly existence as consubstantial; her female body and her sexless, divine intellect formed an alloy in which both "metals" coexisted like bread and the Body of Christ in the Lutheran conception of the Eucharist. Yet the following lines describe a positive, autoreflexive version of the alchemistic sacrament Donne's sermon impugns: Elizabeth "could driue / The poysonous tincture, and the stayne of *Eue*, / Out of her thoughts, and deeds; and purifie / All, by a true religious Alchimy" (*FirAn*, 179–82). These lines propose seriously a sacramental purgation that the sermon mocks as spurious. Elizabeth eliminated all that was imperfect in the female principle; because she was able to "driue /...the stain of *Eue*, / Out of her thoughts and deeds," she was no longer an alloy; instead, the "pure" (that is, unmixed) essence of her "minde" transmuted "All" of her, imparting its own essential "purity" to the whole that was Elizabeth, including her female body. Her sex was thus no longer "weaker" in any sense, though she was still biologically a woman. In the transubstantiation of the Eucharistic elements, the physical properties of bread and wine, the tangible accidents, remain, but their essence changes. Elizabeth, too, was transformed by a kind of transubstantiation. She made her postlapsarian female self—body, mind, and soul—into pure, unalloyed virtue.

The poet's language assures the Protestant reader that the transubstantiation of Elizabeth's female sex was no deceptive magic like that of "our new *Romane Chymists*...that can *transubstantiate bread into God*," but a "true religious Alchymy" (*FirAn*, 182). However, even as the qualitative adjectives "true" and "religious" insist on a distinction between Elizabeth's transformed nature and any other alchemy—metallurgical or theological—the noun they modify preserves the analogy. In losing Elizabeth, the world has lost the true sacramental alchemy that transmutes base material elements into spiritual gold.[73] Now that she is gone, man's ability to perceive the virtue she embodied is impaired. As Edward Tayler argues in his study of the *Anniversaries*, man can no longer grasp the "Idea of a Woman," her unalloyed essence.[74]

In the next four meditative sections of *The First Anniversarie*—reflections on the world's loss of "cohærence" (213), "proportion" (252), "Colour" (340), and "correspondence" (396) between heaven and earth—Donne continues to anatomize the corpse of a world devoid of "true religious Alchymy" (182). Without its binding force, the fabric of human society is not what it once was; the loss of "cohærence," the "crumbled" state of "all Relation" (213, 212, 214) suggests the breakdown of community that must result when men are no longer united in Holy Communion, which the Council of Trent calls "a symbol of that unity and charity with which [Christ] wished all Christians to be mutually bound and united."[75] It is the sacrament, as the Elizabethan Homilies declare, "wherein they that eate...should bee knitte together" and "ioyned by the bond of loue, in one mysticall bodie" (*Certaine Sermons*, 2:203). In saying that Elizabeth Drury was "She that had all Magnetique force alone, / To draw, and fasten sundred parts in one" (*FirAn*, 221–22), Donne thus elides the function of sacramental Woman with that of the Eucharist. To lose one is to suffer the same consequences as those that ensue from the loss of the other, for without woman, who is the guarantor of paternity and the source of physical and spiritual nourishment, man is stripped of all that the Homilies' "bond of loue" affords, "All iust supply, and all Relation" (214). In the world in which communion is sundered and womanly grace is spurned, "Prince, Subiect, Father, Sonne, are things forgot, / For euery man alone thinkes he hath got / To be a Phœnix, and that there can bee / None of that kinde, of which he is, but hee" (215–18).

Born only of themselves, alone in their uniqueness, the would-be phoenixes of this passage contrast violently with the famous hermaphroditic phoenix of Donne's "The Canonization," whose "ridle hath more wit," which is to say both more complexity and more depth, in being identified with man and woman *joined:* those "two being one, are it. / So, to one neutrall thing both sexes fit" (*Canon* 23, 24–25). The phoenix of "The Canonization" is an emblem of resurrection rather than of disintegration and chaos; its sexual energy is a sacrament of heterosexual love, or to use the Greek-derived synonyms the words of the poem evoke, a mystery of eros: "Wee dye and rise the same, and prove / Mysterious by this love" (*Canon,* 26–27). All such erotic sacramentality is lost to the world of *The First Anniversarie,* and the world is therefore "crumbled out againe to his Atomis" (*FirAn,* 212).

The sacramentality of the feminine, which is lost to the self-generating male phoenixes of *The First Anniversarie,* is beautifully evoked in the section of the poem devoted to color:

When nature was most busie, the first weeke,
Swadling the new-borne earth, God seemd to like,
That she should sport herselfe sometimes, and play,
To mingle, and vary colours euery day.
And then, as though she could not make inow,
Himselfe his various Rainbow did allow.   (*FirAn*, 347–52)

This passage poignantly revises the image of "poore mothers"
crying out at the topsy-turvy births of children into a world
turned awry by sin (*FirAn*, 95–98); for in lines 347–352, a joyful
mother, Nature herself, rejoices at the birth of the infant earth, a
perfect baby whom she swaddles in a glorious range of hues. The
God of this passage seems inspired by the deity of Proverbs 8,
who works in concert with a female Wisdom. "The Lord hathe
possessed me in the beginning of his waie," Wisdom declares in
that chapter, "I was before his workes of olde.... When he prepared the heauens, I was there,... when he appointed the funda-
cions of the earth, Then was I with him as a nourisher, and I was
daily his delite reioycing alwaie before him, And toke my solace
in the compasse of his earth: & my delite is with the children of
men" (verses 22, 27, 29–31). Rejoicing—"*ludens*" in the Vulgate's
Latin—the Wisdom of Proverbs and Nature as she appears in
these lines of *The First Anniversarie* both play, as will Milton's
Wisdom and her sister Urania, "In presence of th'Almighty
Father" (*PL* 7.11). Even the rainbow, God's own fatherly addition to the colors of Nature, is provided only "*as though
she could not make inow*" (*FirAn*, 351), not *because* she could
not. As the Wisdom of Proverbs is a "nourisher," so the *Natura*
of *The First Anniversarie* provides sustenance to "the children
of men": it is she who provides "colours" (*FirAn*, 350), and color
is that which "Sight," man's "noblest sense.../..."feed[s] on"
(353–54). The idea of the eye feeding on color is a world away
from the pale, abstract exhortation of lines 187–88, in which
the Anatomist urges the reader to "feed...on /...Religion."[76] No
such colorless mandate had been necessary "If she whom we
lament had not beene dead" (*FirAn*, 360); for in her—in this sacramental woman—"all white, and redde, and blue / (Beauties

ingredients) voluntary grew, / As in an vnuext Paradise" (*FirAn*, 361–63) that provided all the nourishment man needed.

No paradise can exist on earth, however, without a regenerate Eve. The "medicinall" effect of Elizabeth Drury's virtue (*FirAn*, 404) cannot work in her absence; for, "as some Serpents poison hurteth not, / Except it be from the liue Serpent shot, / So doth her vertue need her here, to fit / That vnto vs; she working more then it" (*FirAn*, 409–12). These lines suggest an analogy between Elizabeth and Christ, who was lifted up on the cross as the serpent was lifted up in the desert (John 3:14) and whose power to save those who look to him for healing proceeds from what Hooker calls "his personal and true presence" in the sacrament of his Body and Blood (*Laws*, 5.67.11). Just as the virtue or efficacy of the Eucharist and its influence on human lives depends upon Christ's living presence, so Elizabeth's sacramental "vertue" depends upon her presence.[77] But because "Shee, shee is dead," that presence would be lost to the world save for Donne's poem and the readers he addresses as "her creatures, whom she workes vpon" (*FirAn*, 458–60). Through their response to the "blessed maid" "Whose name refines course lines" (443, 446), Elizabeth's "true religious Alchimy" (182) still purifies both the language of poetry and the metal of the human soul. Though even in life "she could not transubstantiate / All" into gold (417–18), her virtue now "workes vpon" (455) those who "celebrate" Elizabeth (2, 38, 450) by devoutly receiving Donne's "tribute" to her (447); it effects in them a purifying "concoction" (456) and whets their appetites for "the rich ioyes.../ Of which shee's now partaker, and a part" (433–34).

7. MOVING BEYOND EARTHLY WOMANHOOD IN "A FUNERALL ELEGIE" AND *THE SECOND ANNIVERSARIE*

In the final lines of *The First Anniversarie*, the Anatomist speculates that some readers may object to his work and "In reuerence to" Elizabeth Drury, "thinke it due, / That no one should her prayses thus reherse, / As matter fit for Chronicle, not verse" (*FirAn*, 458–60). In response, he cites as a divine precedent the song Moses sings in Deuteronomy 32. God knew, he argues, that his people would

> let fall,
> The Law, the Prophets, and the History,
> But keepe the song still in their memory.
> Such an opinion (in due measure) made
> Me this great Office boldly to inuade.   (*FirAn*, 464–68)

But the wording of this self-defense, is, to some extent, an admission of guilt; invasion is a violent act. He is seeking to constrain in poetry some part of a person who now inhabits a far better realm:

> Nor could incomprehensibleness deterre
> Me, from thus trying to emprison her.
> Which when I saw that a strict graue could do,
> I saw not why verse might not doe so too.
> Verse hath a middle nature: heauen keepes soules,
> The graue keeps bodies, verse the fame enroules.
>   (*FirAn*, 469–74)

These lines admit that he has chosen to ignore the disembodied Elizabeth's status as someone or something incomprehensible: not only "beyond the reach of intellect" (*OED*, adj. def. 2), but uncontainable (def. 1) and incapable of being "grasped...taken hold of (physically) [or] caught" (def. 3). Struggling to distinguish poetic inscription or (circumscription) from interment, he insists that "verse" is an intermediate locus between the soul's heaven and the body's place of burial; but the "strict grave" is nevertheless his morbid inspiration, the enclosure that leads him to presume that his poetry, too, may "emprison" Elizabeth. He can maintain poetry's place between heaven and the grave only by making heaven itself a container, a locus capable of holding within itself the otherwise incomprehensible soul, and by projecting "fame" as a third component of the human entity, an aspect of the individual that is neither her living soul nor her dead body, but that is closer to the latter, if the line break after "soules" and the pairing of "graue" and "verse" in the final line is any indication.

The possibility that a poem may be more tomb than sacrament, more prison than means of grace, is the subject of a poem that follows *An Anatomie of the World* in both the 1611 and 1612 editions. This shorter work, "A Funerall Elegie," was probably written earlier than the *Anatomie,* immediately following Elizabeth's Drury's death, though the order of composition is not certain.[78] Whichever poem Donne wrote first, however, he chose to position the shorter piece after the longer one. As a follow-up to *An Anatomie of the World,* "A Funerall Elegie" reads like a reining in of the Anatomist's lofty ambitions. "Can we keepe her... / In workes of hands, or of the wits of men?" the Elegist asks (*FunEl,* 9–10), implying that the answer is a resounding "No." "Can shee," he continues, "who no longer would be shee, / Being such a Tabernacle, stoope to bee / In paper wrap't; Or, when she would not lie / In such a house, dwell in an Elegie?" (15–18). A maiden who has vacated her own perfect "materials," the "Pearles, and Rubies" that were her divinely fashioned body (7, 5), will never consent to be the "soule" of "Carkas verses" that are mere "workes" of a man's "hands" (14, 10). To insist that such a virgin be "in paper wrap't" would be to commit *raptus,* to force her to "lie" where she "would not."

In disassociating himself from such violent compulsion, the poet-speaker is, as usual in Donne's poetry, eliding gender concerns with theological ones; for his use of the term "Tabernacle" suggests that he is not only a man refusing to confine a woman against her will, but also a priest who will not presume to conjure the real presence of the one whose memory he invokes. His poem, like the sacrament of the Eucharist as Donne understands it, cannot "liue" without the cooperation of the one who is remembered; if his lines' "soule is not shee," they will be but "Carkas verses" (*FunEl,* 14). And yet the poet, like the priest, must avoid claiming to imprison that crucial someone in the "workes of hands" (10). Protestant polemicists such as John Bale asserted that papist presumption and error were summed up in the way Roman Catholic priests "boxed / pyxed / and tabernacled" (*A mysterye of inyquyte*, fol. 34r) the consecrated host. And for Calvin, transubstantiation was an attempt to "shut [Christ] up in the bread" and to "compasse him in" (*Institution of Christian Religion*, 4.17.19). Forbidden by Article 28 of the *Thirty-Nine Articles* to reserve the sacramental species, the priest of the English church could make no attempt to house Christ's Eucharistic presence in containers such as the "Marble chest" or "Tabernacle" referred to in "A Funerall Elegie" (2, 16). Rather, stressing the language of "remembrance" (*BCP*, 263, 264), he presented the sacrament of the Lord's Supper as a commemorative act.

In "A Funerall Elegie," the poet-speaker likewise stresses that "these memorialls" (11) can be no more than a gesture of anamnesis, a past-tense celebration of Elizabeth's now-absent flesh as having fulfilled, in life, a sacramental function. Elizabeth's "cleare body" was almost ethereal: "so pure, and thin, / Because it neede disguise no thought within. / T'was but a through-light scarfe, her minde t'enroule, / Or exhalation breath'd out from her soule" (*FunEl*, 59–62). The phrase "through-light scarfe" anticipates Donne's homiletic definition of a sacrament as a mysterious "*Velamen*" that comes between man and grace, but also is the means by which grace is "exhibited" (*Sermons*, 7:98).[79] But the translucent "scarfe" or veil of Elizabeth's body has been "demolish'd" (*FunEl*, 9). Its sacramental capacity to "enroule" her otherwise intangible "minde" is lost to those "Who liue, and lacke her" (48). It can no longer "wrap up or enfold" that mind ("enroll," *OED*, v. def. 7a), or "inscribe" upon itself as though it were a "roll or parchment" (v. def. 1, 4), the perfect "thought within." For Elizabeth is no longer willing to be enrolled even upon so "pure, and thin" a vellum.

In both the spiritual quality of her body and her short stay on earth, the dead girl resembles the resurrected Jesus. Donne's poem "Resurrection, imperfect" describes Christ's risen body in terms very similar to those used to describe Elizabeth's body in "A Funerall Elegie"; it, too, has so little of the carnal in it that it seems like a soul:

> Had one of those, whose credulous pietie
> Thought, that a Soule one might discerne and see
> Goe from a body,'at this sepulcher been,
> And, issuing from the sheet, this body seen,
> He would have justly thought this body'a soule.
>
> (*Res*, 17–21)[80]

It is Christ's risen body that communicants receive through their participation in the Eucharist, but no such sacramental contact with Elizabeth's body is possible, for only when earthly existence comes to an end will Elizabeth's "graue...restore / Her, greater, purer, firmer, then before" (*FunEl*, 45–46). And, as I have observed in connection with the sonnet on Anne Donne's death, sacramental mysteries that convey grace to man in this life are in tension with the mystery of the eschaton, when sacraments will no longer be needed. "Heauen may say" that Elizabeth's body will be restored and made better at the resurrection, "and ioy in't"; but "We lose by't" (*FunEl*, 47, 51).

Without any hope of restoring Elizabeth's sacramental presence, the poet-speaker of the "Elegie" turns away both from meditations on Elizabeth's body and from attempts to make verse that can house her as worthily as that body did. From line 83 forward, the dominant metaphor of the poem is that of Elizabeth's life as prose text, a "sad History" (*FunEl*, 83) that appears as an abruptly curtailed episode in the "booke of destiny" (84). Those who "come to reade" this volume (84) will be perplexed and confused by the apparent incompleteness of the narrative; but each of those who, like her, "dare true good prefer," shall be "her delegate":

> They shall make vp that booke, and shall haue thankes
> Of fate and her, for filling vp their blanks.
> For future vertuous deeds are Legacies,
> Which from the gift of her example rise.

> And 'tis in heau'n part of spirituall mirth,
> To see how well, the good play her, on earth.
>
> (*FunEl*, 98, 99, 101–06)

In these concluding lines, the implicit analogy between Jesus and Elizabeth continues: like Christ, Elizabeth writes nothing but the text of her death; like Christ, she leaves her example as the inspiration of the virtuous. And like Saint Paul, who by suffering for the church is able to "fulfil the rest of the afflictions of Christ in [his] flesh" (Col. 1:24), the "delegate[s]" of Elizabeth complete the story of her life by "filling vp [the] blanks" that she and "fate" have left in it (*FunEl*, 99, 102).[81] But this scenario specifically denies the value of texts written in ink; a poem cannot house Elizabeth's ghost, nor can the book of destiny fully record the "History" of her life. The only writing that can fill up the blanks left in Elizabeth's story — create presence where there is now absence — is neither poetry nor prose, but the extemporaneous drama of a life well lived. The "spirituall mirth" generated by the virtuous actors' performance belongs, moreover, to the audience "in heau'n," not to the performers "on earth" (*FunEl*, 105, 106). It does not attain the status of a liturgical celebration bridging space and time, uniting heaven and earth in an eternal moment; the celestial observers smile down from their lofty vantage point, but the play they watch is a fiction staged for their delectation. And "A Funerall Elegie" itself is less than that; its "ragges of paper" (*FunEl*, 11) describe the theater of virtue but do not perform in it.

In *The First Anniversarie*, the poet's belief in his work's sacramental efficacy allows him to lead a congregation of readers in celebrating Elizabeth Drury and effecting her continued presence in the "new world" they comprise by impressing upon the "matter and the stuffe" of her undying "vertue" the "forme" their "practise" provides (*FirAn*, 76, 77, 78). But in "A Funerall Elegie," Donne seems determined to work in the spirit of John 20:11–18, which was often invoked by Calvin and his successors as a proof-text in their argument against the Roman Catholic definition of Real Presence. When Christ told Mary

Magdalene, "Touche me not: for I am not yet ascended to my Father" (verse 17), he was, Donne explains in a sermon, issuing a warning to the communicant: "Dwell not upon this passion-ate consideration of my bodily, and personall presence, but send thy thoughts, and thy reverence, and thy devotion, and thy holy amorousnesse up, wither I am going" (*Sermons*, 7:267).[82] Donne turns precisely in this direction in *The Progres of the Soule: The Second Anniversarie*.

Having dissected the world's corpse in the *Anatomie* and admitted the limitations of his own "Carkas verses" in "A Funerall Elegie," the poet abandons dead bodies to focus on life in heaven, where the soul is free from the confines of the mortal flesh, and visible signs of invisible grace are no longer needed because the saints "[enjoy] / The sight of God, in fulnesse" (*SecAn*, 440–41). Those who experience the "essentiall ioye" of the Beatific Vision (443) see God directly, not masked by the accidents of water, bread, wine, or the beauty of a young girl whose body was such that "eies might read vpon the outward skin, / As strong Records for God, as mindes within" (505–06). Seeking to prepare readers to join Elizabeth, the speaker of *The Second Anniversarie* stresses what the poem's title page calls "the incommodities of the Soule / *in this life*"; he vilifies the body and urges readers to turn away from the flesh. Yet the poem ministers to the soul through the eyes and ears it denigrates, and it looks forward to the soul's reunion with a glorified body. *The Progres of the Soule* is thus a poetic *viaticum*; like the Eucharist offered to a dying man, it is perceived by the senses, but meant to prepare the soul for departure from the body and entry into a state where no sacrament is needed.

Sacraments and sacramental poems, thus conceived, are not unlike mothers: they nourish you and sustain you and clean you up when you are dirty, all so that, eventually, you won't need them anymore; or, at any rate, not in the same way. As Edward Tayler explains (*Donne's Idea*, 64), Donne urges his own soul and the reader's to "shake of" the "Pedantery, / Of being taught by sense, and Fantasy" (*SecAn*, 291–92) by getting "vp vnto the watch-towre" of pure intellection from which one can "see all things despoyled of fallacies" (294, 295). And yet, Tayler says, Donne relies upon Aristotelian and Thomistic notions of cognition whereby imagination mediates between the senses and the intellect. According to this model of the mind's operations, the imagery of Donne's poems—including the image of the "watch-towre" itself—mediates between sensory perception and intellect, earth and heaven, bringing the reader *through* "sense, and Fantasy"—not in spite of them—to a vision of "essentiall ioye" that transcends those lower faculties and perfectly unites the known and the knower, "the obiect, and the wit" (*SecAn,* 443, 442).

It is perhaps no surprise, however, that Donne's speaker—who so zealously urges the understanding's transcendent apprehension of a truth beyond sensory perception and imagination, as well as the soul's joyful emergence from its fleshly matrix—is also intent upon weaning his readers from all things motherly; or, at any rate, from an attachment to motherhood as we know it in this life. *The First Anniversarie* concludes with an image of the body as a "wombe" from which the soul emerges at death (*FirAn,* 453). *The Progres* recasts motherhood in terms that urge the soul to scorn that blighted fruit of the womb, the body.

As Maureen Sabine argues, *The First Anniversarie* "spell[s] out the consequences of casting female nature aside from the order of grace," suggesting "that a world systematically deprived of higher feminine value is no fit place to live" (*Feminine Engendered Faith,* 96). Sabine goes on to argue, however, that the two *Anniversaries,* taken together, surrender the cause of woman, turning away from the Blessed Virgin and embracing an exclusively patriarchal Protestantism. The speaker of *The Second Anniversarie,* Sabine concludes, "promulgate[s] a male eschatology which denies the sexual and maternal importance of women" (92). I cannot entirely disagree; Donne proclaims near the conclusion of *The Second Anniversarie* his Protestant refusal to invoke any saint, and he doubtless wishes to impress upon the reader the primacy of his devotion to the divine Father.

Raymond-Jean Frontain argues persuasively that the work is a "Protestant *Paradiso*," "designed specifically to undercut Marian 'mis-deuotion'" by replacing "Dante's [Virgin] Mary...with a Protestant Everywoman" ("Donne's Protestant *Paradiso*," 113, 114, 123). But precisely insofar as it focuses on a female exemplar rather than a male one, stressing the entry of a peerless young *woman* into a heaven where her nearly perfect body will be further perfected at the resurrection, the poem's descriptions of paradise do not evoke a wholly "male eschatology"; Donne's heaven, like Augustine's, is the ultimate destination for glorified bodies of both sexes. As *The Second Anniversarie* presents it, moreover, the closest thing to heaven on earth is the Eucharist, represented in the poem by an archetypal female symbol, the "bowle" or chalice. Nor are the work's passages on motherhood incompatible with Catholic thought; in commenting on maternity and on the female sex as it will exist beyond maternity, in glorified female bodies at the resurrection, Donne draws on Aquinas as well as Augustine.

He first broaches the subject early in the poem when the speaker—articulating Donne's own concerns as poet—implies that neither motherhood nor the female sex are good enough for the girl he celebrates:

> my life shalbe,
> To bee hereafter prais'd, for praysing thee,
> Immortal Mayd, who though thou wouldst refuse
> The name of Mother, be vnto my Muse,
> A Father since her chast Ambition is,
> Yearely to bring forth such a child as this.
> These Hymes may worke on future wits, and so
> May great Grand-children of thy praises grow.
> . . . .
> For thus, Man may extend thy progeny,
> Vntill man doe but vanish, and not die.
> These Hymns thy issue, may encrease so long,
> As till Gods great Venite change the song.
>
> (*SecAn*, 31–38, 41–44)

An eschatological orientation drives these lines; earthly music serves only as prelude to the "great Venite." But why the gender warp? Why does the poet beg a girl to be a father, and cast his own creative ambition as a mother? Sabine suggests a plausible answer that supports her reading of the *Anniversaries* as a hail and farewell to the Blessed Virgin Mary: "Elizabeth could be described as [a] 'Father' in so far as she was the formal cause of the *Anniversarie* poems in the first place; but she was not to be mistaken for his Muse. In declaring that his Muse's 'chast Ambition is, / Yearely to bring forth such a child as this,' Donne...suggest[s] tacitly that a Virgin Mother [is] still" his inspiration (*Feminine Engendered Faith*, 100). As in *La Corona*, the woman who was her "Makers maker" (*La Corona*, 26) is the model for a sacramental poetics.[83]

But even more to the point, because Elizabeth Drury was *not* the Blessed Virgin Mary, she was obliged to "refuse / The name of Mother" in order to retain her virginity. Had she lived, the sole heir of Robert Drury would almost certainly have become a wife and mother; in a Protestant world devoid of convents, dying young was her only way to join what the speaker later refers to as the "squadron" (*SecAn*, 356) of consecrated virgins. In saying that she would "refuse / The name of Mother," Donne thus interprets Elizabeth's death as her choice to be one of those "who thought that almost / They made ioyntenants with the Holy Ghost, / If they to any should his Temple giue" (*SecAn*, 353–55). These lines recall "A Funerall Elegie," where a temple metaphor describes Elizabeth as a highly sought-after match, a lady "whom, who ere had worth enough, desir'd; / As when a Temple's built, Saints emulate / To which of them, it shall be consecrate" (*FunEl*, 64–66). Elizabeth eludes all the suitors with financial and moral "worth enough" to woo her and dies, as the "Elegie" puts it, "Cloath'd in her Virgin white integrity; / For mariage, though it doe not staine, doth dye. / To scape th'infirmities which waite vpone / Woman, shee went away, before sh'was one" (*FunEl*, 75–78). The "infirmities which waite vpone / Woman" are not only the sinful tendencies of the

putatively weaker sex, but also the physical sufferings of maternity (pangs imposed in Genesis 3:16 as punishment for original
sin) and the imperfections of the husband, whose weight upon
his wife "doth dye" them both with the death of orgasm, bur-
dening her with its weighty consequence, pregnancy. Aquinas
argues that original sin is handed down through descent "from
Adam by man's seed" (*Summa Theologica*, 3.31.1); hence, the
"infirmities which waite vpone / Woman" are also the flawed
little creatures planted in her womb. All this heavy bag-
gage Elizabeth Drury avoids when she "refuse[s] / The name
of Mother."[84]

But why does Donne describe his muse as aspiring to be what
Elizabeth would not? Given the Thomistic account of human
conception, doing so is a humble way to describe his relationship with the human being who inspires him. For Aquinas,
"the mother supplies the formless matter of the body," which
"receives its form through the formative power that is in the
semen of the father"; he, the active partner, is the "principle" of
generation "in a more excellent way than the mother" who is "a
passive and material principle" (*Summa Theologica*, 2.26.10). In
The Second Anniversarie, Donne's muse, the feminine personification of his wit, talent, and ambition, provides the matter of
the poetry: the ink on the page, the audible sounds of the words.
But its essence, its form, is supplied by the girl whose name
appears on the title page. Acknowledging the imparadised soul's
liberation from matter and from the passive role of *mater*, the
poet calls her *pater*, acknowledging that she imprints form on
the formless matter of his verse.

Has Elizabeth, then, become a man in heaven? Is Donne, as
H. L. Meakin asserts, "re-member[ing] Elizabeth here by giving
her a male member, the Phallus" (*John Donne's Articulations*,
221)? By the end of the work, the answer is clearly "no." Donne's
poem ultimately confirms the view of Augustine, who took
issue with the belief that all glorified bodies would be male. At
the resurrection, Augustine insists,

all defects will be taken away from [our] bodies, but their natural state will be preserved. The female sex is not a defect, but a natural state, which will then know no intercourse or childbirth. There will be female parts, not suited to their old use, but to a new beauty, and this will not arouse the lust of the beholder...but it will inspire the praise of the wisdom and goodness of God, who both created what was not, and freed from corruption what he made. (*City of God*, Book 22.17)

Donne's lines dissociating Elizabeth Drury from physical motherhood subtly evoke Augustine's vision of transfigured female sexuality when one reads them in conjunction with the portrayal of heaven near the end of *The Second Anniversarie*. In paradise, Donne's speaker declares, the souls of the saints "Ioy that their last great Consummation / Approaches in the resurrection; / When earthly bodies more celestiall / Shalbe, then Angels were" (*SecAn*, 491–94). Among those souls, the girl who "refuse[d] / The name of Mother" awaits reunion with her glorified flesh, the feminine beauty of which is evoked when the speaker says that, in dying, she "left such a body, as euen shee / Onely in Heauen could learne, how it can bee / Made better" (501–03). The speaker also recalls Augustine's contention that, at the resurrection, woman's body will provoke men not to desire her but rather to augment their praises of the God who made her body. For he says that lust is recast as holy desire through the death of a girl who, "Long'd for and longing for'it, to heauen is gone" (509). Those in heaven and those on earth both still yearn for her; but their desire is like the saintly soul's own hunger for heaven, not like a man's lust for a woman. The longing for heaven and the longing for Elizabeth are all but indistinguishable, "since now no other way there is / But goodnes, to see her, whom all would see" (*FirAn*, 16–17). In paradise, Elizabeth both "receiues, and giues addition" (*SecAn*, 510); the line evokes the heraldic definition of the term "addition": "Something added to a coat of arms, as a mark of honour; opposed to abatement or diminution" (*OED*, n. def. 5). The presence of female beauty in heaven adds to the honor of woman and to the glory of the God who made her.

What is left for men on earth when the ideal young woman "refuse[s] / The name of Mother" and ascends to a place where glorified bodies "know no intercourse or childbirth"? For Donne, there can be only one answer: an even holier vessel. The vision of the progeny Elizabeth will beget upon his muse thus concludes with a Eucharistic image; her "issue" may, he says, stretch from the *Anniversaries* to the Last Judgment: "Thirst for that time, O my insatiate soule," he urges himself, "And serue thy thirst, with Gods safe-sealing Bowle. / Bee thirsty still, and drinke still till thou goe; / T'is th'onely Health, to be Hydropique so" (*SecAn*, 44–47).

However, even the "safe-sealing Bowle" that is the vessel of divine grace has earthly limits. The verb "serue" is ambiguous; the chalice of the Eucharist may be said to assuage thirst, and in that sense to serve—that is, help alleviate–a longing for the divine. But in another sense, the wine of the Eucharist can "serue" the speaker's spiritual thirst only by sustaining and fueling it, making him more "insatiate" than ever for the moment when God will bid him come to the wedding feast of the Lamb. As is clear in the sonnet on the "holy thirsty dropsy" that still "melts" him after the death of his wife (*HSShe*, 8), Donne is exquisitely aware of this duality—a combined satisfaction and whetting of spiritual need—in all sacraments, including the sacrament of woman. In the sonnet, Donne's thirst is both the holy longing for more of God than he can have on earth, even in the sacraments by which the Lord his "thirst [has] fed" (*HSShe*, 7) and an ongoing carnal desire for the wifely More that God has taken from him. In *The Second Anniversarie*, the Eucharist is a "Bowle" or chalice, an archetypal feminine symbol familiar from grail legend, a vessel that will slake the thirsts of the human soul for precisely as long—so Donne hopes—as "shee" whom he celebrates will be honored in poetry. Thus, though Elizabeth Drury has eschewed the fleshly role of mother, she is still associated with the feminine principle at work in the streams or bowls or vessels of divine grace that feed the thirsts of men.

For Donne, whose poetry overflows with spiritual thirst, access to the Eucharistic cup has deep significance. In rejecting the "mis-deuotion" of Catholic France (*SecAn*, 511), the poet loses the opportunity to "inuoque [the] name" of any female saint; he may not call on the "Immortall Maid" Elizabeth (*SecAn*, 516) to intercede for him, nor may he pray to the Blessed Virgin, whom the Litany of Loreto calls "Vas spirituale, Vas honorabile, Vas insigne devotionis."[85] But he does gain access to another singular vessel of devotion: the chalice from which he had been excluded as a Catholic layman. The speaker of *The Second Anniversarie* clearly takes great comfort in his resolution to drink from the Eucharistic vessel that the Church of England proffers; the intense need expressed in the lines on "Gods safe-sealing Bowle" bespeaks his affinity for an aspect of Eucharistic participation that, as a son of the Roman *mater ecclesia*, Donne would have been able to experience only spiritually and not through the physical act of raising a chalice to his lips. The price he paid for that sacred libation was great, for even after becoming a Protestant, as R. V. Young demonstrates, Donne clung to the idea of the Real Presence and grappled continually with the difficulty of affirming it in a Protestant doctrinal framework (*Doctrine and Devotion*, 95–99). And the *Anniversaries* make clear that it was no small matter for him to forego Marian devotion. Yet the longing for the cup—dismissible though it might be on an intellectual level by the Catholic doctrine that Christ's undivided body and blood are wholly present in both species—prevailed in him.

And what of that most glorious vessel of divinity, the Blessed Virgin herself? Donne's speaker seemingly repeats his slight to motherhood in his lines on Mary. In heaven, the speaker says, the soul will "see the blessed Mother-maid / Ioy in not being that, which men haue said. / Where shee'is exalted more for being

good, / Then for her interest, of mother-hood" (*SecAn*, 341–44).
Most editors glossing the line read "not being that, which men
haue said" as a denial that Mary is the Immaculate Conception,
the one human being other than Christ to be conceived without
the stain of original sin.[86] The line is vague, but it does seem to
hint at Donne's agreement with Aquinas, who argues, "If the
soul of the Blessed Virgin had never incurred the stain of original
sin, this would be derogatory to the dignity of Christ, by reason
of His being the universal Saviour of all" (*Summa Theologica*,
3.27.2). In a 1624 sermon, Donne asks, "may I not say, that I
had rather be redeemed by Christ Jesus then bee innocent?"
(*Sermons*, 6:183). The line in *The Second Anniversarie* evokes
the same preference in Mary.[87]

The speaker's assertion that the Blessed Virgin is "exalted...for being good" also implies an opinion similar to Aquinas's.
St. Thomas Aquinas says that Mary was sanctified by God while
still in her mother's womb, and that "the rebellion of the lower
powers against the reason" was "fettered" in her "by reason
of the abundant grace bestowed on her in her sanctification"
(*Summa Theologica*, 3.27.3). He concludes that Mary "committed no actual sin" (3.27.4) and that she possessed "a threefold
perfection of grace": "in her sanctification she received grace
inclining her to good: in the conception of the Son of God she
received consummate grace confirming her in good; and in her
glorification her grace was further consummated so as to perfect her in the enjoyment of all good" (3.27.5). The Virgin in
Donne's poem, "exalted...for being good," rejoices in precisely
the "enjoyment" Aquinas attributes to her.

Perhaps less innocuous, however, is Donne's follow-up to
that line, his speaker's claim that the Virgin is "exalted more
for being good, / Then for her interest, of mother-hood" (*SecAn*,
343–44). But is there any real devaluation of Mary's motherhood
here? Donne seems to be playing on Luke 11:27–28, where a
woman cries out, "Blessed is the wombe that bare thee, and the
pappes which thou haste sucked." Jesus replies: "Yea, rather

blessed are they that heare the worde of God, and kepe it." While both the scriptural passage and the lines of Donne's poem might be read as downplaying Mary's greatness and motherhood's spiritual importance, the point in Luke seems to be that Jesus recognizes mothers as more than female bodies. Christ's mother is the model of sanctity because she internalizes the Word and makes him a part of her, not only physically, but spiritually as well. Not denying the synecdoche that claims sanctity for Mary by declaring blessed her uterus and her lactating breasts, Jesus supplements it with a literal description of the woman who raised him to do the will of God and, in doing so, kept faith with the Father of her child. Motherhood here is not divorced from physical realities, but it extends beyond them. What *The Second Anniversarie* calls Mary's "interest, of mother-hood" is her unique claim to greatness *as a mother*, humbly acknowledged by the greeting of her cousin Elizabeth: "Blessed art thou among women, because the frute of thy wombe is blessed. And whence cometh this to me, that the mother of my Lord shulde come to me?" (Luke 1:42–43). Donne's speaker acknowledges that such "interest" belongs to Mary, and he does not rule out the idea that her exaltation is due partly to that "interest"; he merely stresses that the Virgin's unsurpassed virtue is even more relevant in determining her preeminence. The Madonna's cousin might be said to agree, for after greeting Mary, Elizabeth goes on to praise her for the virtue of faith: "And blessed is she that beleued: for those things shalbe performed, which were tolde her from the Lord" (Luke 1:45).

It was perhaps some consolation to Elizabeth Drury's own mother, Anne, to read that virtue is ultimately more important than "interest, of mother-hood." For in the epitaph she commissioned for her husband and herself—a Latin inscription almost certainly authored by Donne—is included a description of Anne Drury as "NEC INFÆCVNDA NEC MATER TAMEN / DORO-THEÆ. ET ELIZABETHÆ, FILIARVM, ORBA" (24–25): "neither barren nor a mother, having been bereaved of her daughters Dorothy and

Elizabeth."[88] In this vale of tears, those who do not "refuse / The name of Mother" are too often stripped of it and its consolations by death; but the greatest comfort to a woman thus deprived is to look to the resurrection. In that "last great Consummation" (*SecAn*, 491), Donne's poem assures her, the souls of her daughters will be reunited with the female bodies she bore in her womb, "earthly bodies" made "celestiall" (*SecAn*, 493).

LANYER

Aemilia Lanyer's *Salve Deus Rex Judaeorum* is concerned with ecclesiastical, theological, social, aesthetic, and political issues. But for Lanyer, gender is the *terminus a quo* for every question she considers and the *terminus ad quem* for every argument she presents. Lanyer's anticourtly stance, her vision of the church, her expressions of desire, and her impassioned response to the class distinctions that separate her from her addressees all arise from her fundamental concern with the experience of women as such throughout history, her attention to the attitudes and actions of prominent women of her time, and her belief in her own vocation as a female poet. Lanyer writes in self-conscious reaction to Stuart court culture as she sees it—that is, in condemnation of a society that centers itself upon praise of a male monarch and relegates women to ancillary and subservient roles. In doing so, she makes a specifically anti-Jacobean contribution to the ongoing debate over the nature of womankind that originated in the antifeminist polemics of the patristic and medieval periods and included defenses of woman by Christine de Pisan in the fifteenth century, Cornelius Agrippa in the early sixteenth century, and a range of early modern English writers from the mid-sixteenth century on. But Lanyer is not really concerned with defending the idea that woman is as good as or better than man, an idea she takes as an established premise; rather, she asserts as female privileges a sacerdotal vocation and a uniquely unfallen and untainted sexuality, both of which arise from what Lanyer believes to be woman's unique place in the economy of redemption.[1]

For Lanyer, Christian women—including the Blessed Virgin, the Marys at the tomb of Jesus, the Countess of Cumberland, the other virtuous women addressed in *Salve Deus,* and she herself—are not only feminine conduits of grace, but female agents of salvation, priests and living incarnations of the church through whom God redeems fallen man and ameliorates the fallen world. They do not—as in the traditional Roman Catholic and English Protestant notion of priesthood—represent Christ, the head of the church, but rather figure forth the church herself, the feminine body of which Christ alone is head. Thus, like Saint Paul, John Donne, and the Christian tradition more broadly, Lanyer defines the church as feminine; but at the same time, more radically, she insists that woman is church. Critiquing the apostles Jesus ordained as priests and, by implication, their male successors, Lanyer articulates a new, gynocentric ecclesiology. She does not seek to reform the institutional church, nor does she feel the need to declare allegiance to any one Christian denomination; rather, Lanyer believes that each virtuous woman is Ecclesia incarnate and that the community of virtuous women across history *is* the church, the body of Christ at work in the world.

Lanyer's belief that women are the most loyal disciples of Jesus and that flesh and spirit are reconciled in their experience leads her not only to claim the priesthood for womankind, but also to define the erotic desire of virtuous women as a grace-filled impulse, whether it be directed heavenward, toward honorable men, or toward other women. Rejecting the notion that the female is naturally more fleshly and libidinous than the male and thus necessarily subordinate to him, Lanyer recasts woman's experience of eros—both sacred and profane—as holy, liberating, and redemptive. Not surprisingly, the poet defines love of God as the highest and most perfect expression of womanly desire; and for Lanyer, a woman may become more perfectly one with Christ than a man ever can. But in the lives of female human beings, Lanyer believes, nature and grace, eros and *caritas*, spirit and flesh are in no way opposed; she thus envisions untainted female eros as the exhilarating, proactive, and even redemptive alternative to a range of ills. The love of Christ is the alternative to sinful worldliness and to the victim status afforded those who choose unfaithful human males as lovers; unsubmissive love for a worthy man is the alternative to the unendurable subjugation of marriage as it is defined by Ephesians 5 and 1 Peter 3; and a woman's love for another woman challenges the ironclad rules that alienate the commoner from the noblewoman. Lanyer cannot fully realize her vision of human-directed eros purged of all sin and sorrow; both woman's desire for man and woman's desire for woman are ultimately subverted or thwarted in the world as she portrays it, and Christ remains the only paramour who never disappoints. But the alternative reality Lanyer imagines nevertheless resonates, audible beneath her *fortissima* strains in praise of the divine Lover.

1. Lanyer as Anti-Jacobean and Neo-Elizabethan Translator of Scripture

One of the most important contexts for Aemilia Lanyer's *Salve Deus Rex Judaeorum* is its Jacobean, or—more accurately—anti-Jacobean frame of reference. Like Donne as he represents himself in his verse letters to Lucy, Countess of Bedford, Lanyer was an outsider to the Stuart court, observing it from a distance with a mixture of disdain and frustrated desire. As Barbara Lewalski points out, Donne's poems for Lucy, written circa 1608 through 1612, portray the countess as "the embodiment or incarnation of virtue" and explore how such "complete virtue" can possibly "exist in, act in, or manifest itself to an essentially wicked court" (*Writing Women*, 113). These poems assert that King James's "Court...is not vertues clime" (*BedfRef*, 7); but Donne's *Satyres* and *Elegies* reveal that he had thought the court of Elizabeth at least as seamy and morally bankrupt in the 1590s. Donne's quarrel is with courtly culture as such; "vertue'in Courtiers hearts," he says, "Suffers an Ostracisme, and departs" (*BedfWrit,* 21–22). Lanyer, however, targets what she sees as the faults peculiar to the court of James. While her poetry never explicitly criticizes the monarch—she was audacious, not suicidal—Lanyer conveys her disapproval of James, of his regime, and of the court culture that surrounded him through a variety of techniques, making clear that it is not just courtly debauchery or idolatry or misogyny that she condemns, but the specifically Jacobean versions of these evils.

Lanyer was not alone in thinking the court of James more corrupt than that of his relatively austere predecessor. As Maurice Lee Jr. explains,

> Murderous greed and backbiting, conspicuous consumption, and sexual misbehavior were nothing new in Whitehall in 1603. Tudor courts [had been] vicious places, too, in all senses of the word. Moral decay [had been] a theme of Elizabethan as well as Jacobean verse. The public face that Henry VIII or Elizabeth [had] presented to the world [had] succeeded in concealing a great deal of the nastiness, however. By contrast, James's public image accentuated the nastiness and made him appear to be personally responsible for it. (*Great Britain's Solomon,* 158)

The king's language was often crude, he drank profusely and spent money extravagantly, he blatantly flaunted his contempt for the common people, and his attraction to young men did not go unnoticed.[2] Yet this decadent man took it upon himself to commission a new, authoritative translation of the Scriptures and arrogated to himself a quasi-divine authority more exalted than any Queen Elizabeth had claimed. In a speech to Parliament in March 1610, James asserted that "Kings are not onely GODS Lieutenants vpon earth, and sit vpon GODS throne, but euen by GOD himselfe they are called Gods... they make and vnmake their subiects... [and are] accomptable to none but God onely" (James I, *Political Writings,* 181). Finally, and perhaps most damningly from Lanyer's perspective, James was a misogynist. As Michael Young explains, "It was not just that James loved men; he actively disliked women" and made a point of drawing attention to his attitude. "The French ambassador," Young notes, "thought that James's attitude was so hostile as to merit comment"; the English king, the ambassador wrote, "piques himself on great contempt for women...he exhorts them openly to virtue, and scoffs with great levity at all men who pay them honour'" (*King James*, 16, quoting von Raumer, *History*, 2:196). Even in the most solemn circumstances, James would seize any opportunity to make a sexist comment. William Barlow's record of the Hampton Court Conference records a scene in which a divine raised the issue of the "churching of women," a ceremony to which Puritans objected; Barlow reports that "his Maiestie very wel allowed it, and pleasantly said, that Women were loath enough of themselues, to come to Church, and therefore, he would haue this, or any other occasion, to draw them thether" (*Svmme and Svbstance*, 76). This remark may reflect James's exasperation with Queen Anne's religious proclivities; many suspected her of being a crypto-Catholic, and she had refused to take Communion in Westminster Abbey at her coronation.[3] But the joke is clearly meant to mock women in general; they are, James invites his learned interlocutors to agree with a rueful shake of their heads, creatures constitutionally inclined to neglect things spiritual. Such a remark, so prominently published in print, would not have endeared the king to Lanyer.

One can only shudder to imagine how she would have reacted to his unpublished poem "A Satire against Woemen."[4] This piece begins with 40 lines containing 40 separate "As..." clauses, each of which names a bird, an animal, or a fish and its most prominent instinct. The speaker claims that, as these various creatures "are by nature" (1) prone to their various tendencies and must "followe nature ruling them allwaye / Whose will obeye they must butt lett or staye. / Even so all wemen are of nature vaine" (41–43), unable to keep a "secrett" (44), implacable in their "disdaine" (45), vapidly loquacious, shamelessly "Ambitious" (49), greedy, and apt to use "craft" despite being generally "foolish" (53). All of the vices these lines attribute to women are commonplaces of the antifeminist tradition, but the accusations are rendered particularly offensive by the comparative context in which they are made: women, like the beasts cataloged in the first 40 lines of the poem, are classified as subhuman creatures bound to obey their unsavory natural tendencies. The poem's concluding stanza is particularly insidious, for it establishes as the work's implied readers and beneficiaries those virtuous women who have, through the exercise of reason, managed to quell their instinctual vices:

> Expose me right ye Dames of worthie fame
> Since for your honours I employed my caire
> For wemen bad hereby are lesse to blame
> For that they followe nature everiewhaire
> And ye most worthie prayse, whose reason dants
> That nature, which unto your sexe, so hants.   (55–60)

It is unlikely that Aemilia Lanyer would have had the opportunity to read James's poem, a manuscript piece that no doubt circulated only within a small courtly coterie. But it uses the sort of rhetoric she most detested, for it seeks to divide women, encouraging those who consider themselves morally excellent to adopt an attitude diametrically opposed to that which Lanyer promotes in her prose preface "To the Vertuous Reader." Any "Dames"—as the king calls them—willing to "Expose" the king's satire as "right" would, in Lanyer's terms, be "fall[ing] into so great an errour, as to speake unadvisedly against the rest of their sexe"; and women who slander other women, she says, "can shew their owne imperfection in nothing more." She wishes that

> they would referre such points of folly, to be practised by evill disposed men, who forgetting they were borne of women, nourished of women, and that if it were not by the means of women, they would be quite extinguished out of the world, and a finall ende of them all, doe like Vipers deface

the wombes wherein they were bred, onely to give way and utterance to their want of discretion and goodnesse. ("To the Vertuous Reader," 14–17, 18–24)

The viper image here is particularly telling, for it reads like an answer to the king's catalog of creatures and their natural tendencies, attributing to misogynous men an "evill," snakelike instinct that leads them to attack their own mothers. And while James's poem treats woman as an inferior species, Lanyer's preface reminds them that they are not only of the same taxonomic group as men, but that the human species depends upon them for survival.

How, then, does Lanyer's *Salve Deus Rex Judaeorum* register the poet's negative reaction to James and his court? First, Lanyer positions herself to undermine Jacobean patriarchal assumptions by addressing readers she has reason to think may be receptive to such a message. Many of the women to whom Lanyer addresses prefatory poems were themselves, as Barbara Lewalski demonstrates, actively resistant "to the patriarchal construct of women as chaste, silent, and obedient" (*Writing Women*, 2). The three who were members of the Stuart royal family (Queen Anne, Princess Elizabeth, and Arabella Stuart) all "placed themselves" by various personal, political, and social means "directly and publicly in opposition to King James, providing at the highest level examples of female resistance to the greatest patriarch" (4). And three of the noblewomen to whom Lanyer addressed herself—Lucy Harrington Russell, Countess of Bedford; Anne Clifford, Countess of Dorset; and Anne's mother, Margaret Clifford, Countess Dowager of Cumberland, who was Lanyer's principal addressee—worked to "rewrite patriarchy by using contemporary institutions and interpreting contemporary discourses so as to claim with them rights and status normally denied women" (5).

Second, Lanyer describes her principal addressee as a woman who has deliberately detached herself from the court of Queen Elizabeth's successor in order to live a celibate life that recalls that of the unmarried queen. Margaret Clifford as Lanyer portrays her maintains an Elizabethan form of virtue, "Unalterable by the change of times" (*SDRJ*, 1559), unmoved by the relative decadence and worldliness of James's reign. Having noted in the first line of the volume's title poem that she will address her poem to the Dowager Countess "Sith *Cynthia* is ascended" to heaven, Lanyer begs pardon in the third stanza for presenting a narrative poem on the Passion of Christ in place of the poem she claims that Margaret Clifford actually commissioned:

> And pardon (Madame) though I do not write
> Those praisefull lines of that delightful place,
> As you commaunded me in that faire night,
> When shining *Phoebe* gave so great a grace,
> Presenting *Paradice* to your sweet sight,
> Unfolding all the beauty of her face
>> With pleasant groves, hills, walks, and stately trees,
>> Which pleasures with retired minds agrees.
>>> (*SDRJ*, 17–24)

The point of this stanza is not really to excuse the poet for failing to write a country house poem (in fact, "The Description of Cooke-ham" does appear at the end of the volume, following *Salve Deus*). Rather, it is to introduce Margaret Clifford as the lady who loves Cookham: that is, as one devoted to an unspoiled rural "*Paradice*" bathed in the light of "*Phoebe*," whose shining in the night sky recalls the ascended "*Cynthia*"/Queen Elizabeth toward whom Lanyer has gestured in the poem's opening line.[5] The countess's mind is "retired," and the only temporal "pleasures" she desires are those afforded by the beauties of a feminine landscape bathed in the moon's feminine light. She does behold a "glorious Sunne" as well, but it is neither the material sun in the sky nor the royal "sun" King James whose "beams," in Jonson's 1605 *Masque of Blacknesse*, "shine day and night" and possess quasi-divine powers (Jonson, *Complete Masques*, 56). Rather, Margaret Clifford gazes on "the glorious Sunne / Of th'all-creating Providence" (*SDRJ*, 25–26). And while the "face" of the moon illuminates the physical beauty of Cookham's "groves, hills, walks, and stately trees," so those things reveal to her God immanent: "thou (deere Ladie)," Lanyer says, "by his speciall grace, / In these his creatures dost behold his face" (31–32). Able to gaze upon the divine Sun in a moon-lit country landscape, Margaret Clifford rejects "worldly plea-sures...as toyes" (35) and cares nothing for the "vaine delights" (42) court life affords.

The countess's king is the conquering warlord of the biblical Psalms, not the self-proclaimed *Rex Pacificus* of England, James, whose irenic foreign policy so frustrated the crown prince Henry and other English Protestants eager to advance the cause of the Reformation in Europe. The God who is the countess's advocate and protector is described in a long digression extending from line 73 to line 144: he is "That great *Jehova* King of heav'n and earth" who "spreads the heav'ns with his all powrefull hand," mounts a "Chariot" of cloud, and is preceded by "Consuming fire" that will "burne up all his en'mies round about" (*SDRJ*, 137, 82, 89, 99, 100).[6] And it is "The Meditation of this Monarchs love" (153), that keeps Margaret Clifford fighting injustice; the countess, who had been struggling since her estranged husband's death in 1605 to assert their daughter's inheritance rights, is a Christian stoic, unmoved by worldly "joyes and griefes" (155). "They have no force, to force [her] from the field" where she "Continues combat, and will never yield / To base affliction; or prowd pomps desire, / That sets the weakest mindes so much on fire" (156, 158–60).

Lest the reader have any doubt where those "weakest mindes" reside, Lanyer's next stanza makes explicit her anti-court sentiments: "Thou from the Court to the Countrie art retir'd," she tells the countess, "Leaving the world, before the world leaves thee: / That great Enchantresse of weake mindes admir'd, / Whose all-bewitching charmes so pleasing be / To worldly wantons" who "yeeld themselves as preys to Lust and Sinne" (*SDRJ* 161–65, 167). The evil "Enchantresse" here is not one of the poor women King James interrogated during the Scot-tish witch hunts and attacked in the smugly misogynous prose of his *Daemonology*; nor is she one of the rat-wearing, timbrel-shaking hags whom Ben Jonson and Inigo Jones designed in response to Queen Anne's request for some sort of "foil or false masque" to open the 1609 *Masque of Queenes* (Jonson, *Complete Masques*, 122). The stereotyped witches of that antimasque are designed to precede and be dispersed by the glorious entry of Anne and her ladies; but the "Enchantresse" of Lanyer's poem is the embodiment of those ladies' lived reality; she is the wicked "world" itself as encapsulated in the microcosm of King James's debauched court.

Lanyer does not think secular royal courts are evil by definition; her prefatory poem "To the Queenes most Excellent Majestie" freely admits that she feels great nostalgia for the time when "great *Elizaes* favour blest my youth" ("To the Queenes," 110). And this poem to Anne—the first in the volume—is clearly a bid to become a part of the Stuart queen's own court, a social and economic entity distinct from the king's court and often at odds with it, given the strained relationship between Anne and her royal spouse. As Lewalski points out, the masques Anne commissioned and performed in during the early years of James's reign tended, despite their requisite flattery of the king, to "subvert the representation of James as exclusive locus of power and virtue by means of texts and symbolic actions which exalt[ed] the power and virtue of the Queen and her ladies—and, by extension, of women generally" (*Writing Women*, 29). In Samuel Daniel's *The Vision of the Twelve Goddesses* (1604), for example, the queen appeared as Pallas, the "virgin warrior and goddess of wisdom" who "would evoke Queen Elizabeth to a contemporary audience, carrying associations of female power and militant internationalism that were anathema to James" (Lewalski, *Writing Women*, 30).

Lanyer's prefatory poem to Anne, Lewalski points out, thus portrays the queen as "another Juno, Venus, Pallas, and Cynthia, attracting Muses and artists to her throne." By depicting her in this way, the poet demonstrates her awareness "of the Queen's oppositional politics and subversive masques" (*Writing Women* 221).

And with that sense of Anne in mind, Lanyer further reinforces her work's anti-Jacobean stance, inviting James's queen to behold in the *Salve Deus* Rex *Judaeorum* (emphasis mine) an alternative model of monarchy, one established by God in the person of Christ the King,

> That mightie Monarch both of heav'n and earth,
> He that all Nations of the world controld,
> Yet tooke our flesh in base and meanest berth:
>> Whose daies were spent in poverty and sorrow,
>> And yet all Kings their wealth of him do borrow.
>
> For he is Crowne and Crowner of all Kings,
> The hopefull haven of the meaner sort,
> Its he that all our joyfull tidings brings
> Of happie raigne within his royall Court.
>> ("To the Queenes," 44–52)

The poet herself is, of course, one "of the meaner sort"; her "wealth within [Christ's] Region stands, /...Yea in his kingdome onely rests my lands, / Of honour there I hope I shall not misse: / Though I on earth doe live unfortunate" (55, 57–59). These lines essentially make Lanyer's own position preferable to Anne's, for the "happie raigne" of Christ empowers her more than James's "royall Court" does the queen consort.

Lanyer clearly hopes to be recognized not only by Christ but by Anne, for she makes a clear bid for royal patronage, expressing unabashedly her hope that the queen "will accept even of the meanest line / Farie Virtue yeelds" ("To the Queenes," 70–71). And yet, while making this bid for female royal favor, the poet still defers to her icon of anticourtly values, the Countess of Cumberland. After describing herself as one who "live[s] clos'd up in Sorrowes Cell, / Since great *Elizaes* favour blest my youth," she proceeds to spend several stanzas of the poem to Queen Anne singing the praises of Margaret Clifford as a noblewoman who shares voluntarily in the sufferings of the lowly. The countess has—according to Lanyer—gone so far as to adopt the late Elizabeth's motto, *semper eadem,* as her own: "this great

Ladie whom I love and honour," she says, has become a kind of Protestant nun, "This holy habite still to take upon her, / Still to remaine *the same,* and still her owne: / And what our fortunes doe enforce us to, / She of Devotion and meere Zeale doth do" (109–10, 115, 117–20). As Judith Scherer Herz observes, the stanzas on the Countess of Cumberland have the effect of "slightly displacing the Queen from her own dedication" ("Aemilia Lanyer," 127 n. 11). Indeed, so odd is the effect in this section of the poem that at least one critic misreads it as describing Anne herself, and takes the Roman Catholic imagery as a tribute to her rather than (as I would argue it is) a way of presenting a Protestant exemplar in language designed to appeal to a queen of allegedly Roman Catholic leanings (see Holmes, "Love of Other Women," 177).

Lanyer's poem to Queen Anne is a politically charged gesture. In addressing her volume's first prefatory poem to the queen, she presents the work as a whole to King James's most prominent and well-known female adversary. The poet mentions James directly only once in the course of her work, on the title page, which says that *Salve Deus* was

> Written by Mistris *Æmilia Lanyer,* Wife to Captaine
> *Alfonso Lanyer* Servant to the
> Kings Majestie.

This imprint is certainly, on one level, a way of claiming a court connection rather than of distancing herself from the royal milieu: the author is a loyal helpmate to the king's man; her lord's lord is her lord, too, at one remove. But in another sense, the title page text distances Aemilia from service to her husband's master. She is identified, on the uppermost and longest line of the imprint, as writer of the work and wife to a "Captaine." The officer's name appears below hers, separated from his military rank, and identified only as a "Servant." Finally, on the bottom line, separated from "Mistris Aemilia," by that "Servant," we find the "Kings Majestie" himself, looking conspicuously unmodified and uncomplimented when compared with "the Queenes most Excellent Majestie" as she appears in the title of the volume's first prefatory poem. That piece begins by addressing Anne of Denmark as "Renowned Empresse, and great Britaines Queene, / Most gratious Mother of succeeding Kings" ("To the Queenes," 1–2). She is, in short, more to be praised as the mother of Prince Henry (the martial young Protestant champion and heir to the throne to whom a specially bound copy of *Salve Deus* was at some point presented) than as the wife of King James.[7]

Perhaps even more important to Lanyer was Anne's status as the mother of a royal virgin named Elizabeth. In the poem addressed to the queen, Lanyer calls the daughter of James and Anne "The very modell of your Majestie" and begs, "O let my Booke by her faire eies be blest" ("To the Queenes," 92, 95). Not surprisingly, then, the next prefatory poem in the volume is addressed directly "To the Lady *Elizabeths* Grace":

> Most gratious Ladie, faire ELIZABETH,
> Whose Name and Virtues puts us still in mind,
> Of her, of whom we are depriv'd by death;
> The *Phœnix* of her age, whose worth did bind
> All worthy minds so long as they have breath,
>   In linkes of Admiration, love and zeale
>   To that deare Mother of our Common-weale.
>
> Even you faire Princesse next our famous Queene,
> I do invite unto this wholesome feast,
> Whose goodly wisedome, though your yeares be greene,
> By such good workes may daily be increast,
> Though your faire eyes farre better Bookes have seene;
>   Yet being the first fruits of a womans wit,
>   Vouchsafe you favour in accepting it.

Though addressed to Elizabeth Stuart rather than to Elizabeth Tudor, and though asserting that the late monarch's virtues are alive in her namesake, this 14-line poem still functions as a sonnetlike tribute to a lady now in heaven. Like Donne, who recalls how "admyring" his wife led him to God (*HSShe*, 5), Lanyer celebrates a woman to whom she still feels bound by "linkes of Admiration" and "love." The male poet, lamenting a wife who died due to complications of childbirth, ponders the mixed blessing of physical motherhood as both fruitful and fatal. Lanyer, writing to a virgin of a virgin, meditates not on the goodness of a wife and child-bearer, but rather on the spiritual fruit produced by a mateless and matchless female "*Phœnix.*" The idea of maternity in Lanyer's piece thus contrasts sharply with the vision of fatal motherhood in Donne's "Since She whome I lovd." While the physical bearing of children leads to bodily death and spiritual redemption for Anne More Donne, different versions of fecundity prevail in Lanyer's poem.[8]

First, the political motherhood of Elizabeth Tudor brings forth the common good of England; Lanyer holds her up as an inspiration for the Stuart princess whose name she bears. The poem's rhyme scheme, which is one rhyme shy of rhyme royal (*ababacc* instead of *ababbcc*), implies that the young addressee must rise to the challenge of emulating her namesake.[9] Of course, the Princess Elizabeth is also to follow in the footsteps of her own mother; having told Queen Anne that she "is the welcom'st guest" at the banquet the poem affords ("To the Queenes," 84), Lanyer proceeds to tell Princess Elizabeth that, "Even you faire Princesse next our famous Queene, / I doe invite unto this wholesome feast" ("To the Lady *Elizabeths* Grace," 8–9). The "famous Queene" in question is most obviously Anne, but the context established by the first stanza of the poem to the princess, in which the young addressee is identified as successor to the name and virtues of England's *most* famous queen, gives lines 8–9 another level of meaning: they invite Elizabeth Stuart to join the late Elizabeth I as a guest at Lanyer's feast. Eliding the Stuart queen mother and the Tudor mother queen, Lanyer provides herself with a heavenly reader to enhance the audience of earthly royals she woos.

The most important mother in the poem, however, is the woman who gives birth to it and to the sacred opus it heralds. Lanyer speaks with matriarchal authority as she addresses an immature shoot of the royal family tree, telling the princess that

Salve Deus Rex Judaeorum may increase her virtue, for the prin-cess's "goodly wisedome, though [her] yeares be greene, / By such good workes may daily be increast" (10–11). Again, Lanyer's lan-guage is ambiguous; the good work in question is both her poem on the Passion and the virtuous action the princess will perform "in accepting it" (14). Both the phrase "good workes" and the words "worth" (4) and "worthy" (5) are, of course, loaded terms in a post-Reformation context; Lanyer is careful, as she pro-motes the goodness of her literary work and compliments the virtue of a Protestant princess and her crypto-Catholic mother, not to violate the spirit of Article 11 of the *Thirty-Nine Articles:* "We are accompted ryghteous before God, only for the merite of our Lord & saviour Jesus Christ, by faith, and not for our owne workes or deseruinges." The poet accommodates this doctrine, first of all by addressing herself not simply to "To the Lady Eliz-abeth," but rather to "The Lady *Elizabeths* Grace." On the one hand, "Grace" is "A courtesy-title...used in addressing a king or queen" (*OED*, n. def. 16b), and thus merely acknowledges the princess's royal status; but on the other, it identifies any action the princess will perform in response to Lanyer's request for "favour" (14; a synonym for "grace") as either the fruit of God's grace working in her or a metaphor for the divine grace that made possible the poet's own good (literary) work. Thus understood, Lanyer's poem is a witness to her faith, for as Arti-cle 12 of the *Thirty-Nine Articles* specifies, all the good works of those justified by faith "are the fruites of fayth" and in fact "do spring out necessaryly of a true and liuely faith, in so muche that by them, a lyvely fayth may be as euidently knowen, as a tree discerned by the fruit."

A poem, of course, is a fruit not only of faith but also of poetic talent; and because the *Salve Deus* is her first publication, Lan-yer calls it "the first fruits of a womans wit" ("To the Lady *Eliz-abeths* Grace," 13). This phrasing further underscores her piety, for the construction "first fruits" has biblical connotations. In the book of Proverbs, the sage advises, "Honour the Lord with thy riches, and with the first frutes of all thine increase" (Prov. 3:9).

Lanyer's presenting her poem as the "first fruits" of her wit is thus a gesture of sacrifice and an announcement that she offers up her work for the greater glory of God. An offering of this sort is, moreover, mandated by the Law of the Hebrew scriptures; in Leviticus, God commands the Israelites to make a sacrifice of thanksgiving at harvest time: "When ye...reape the haruest..., then yee shall bring a sheafe of the first frutes of your haruest vnto the Priest, And hee shal shake the sheafe before the Lord, that it may be acceptable for you" (Lev. 23:10–11).[10] Lanyer's image of firstfruits thus places Princess Elizabeth in the role of the priest, hinting at the idea of priesthood as a female vocation. Lanyer will develop this notion more fully in her other prefatory poems and in the title work of the volume, but she clearly has it in mind already here. Even more powerfully, the image of poetry as "first fruits" parallels the Savior who dies for humankind and the narrative poem that celebrates his sacrifice. As the Lamb offered to God to expiate man's sin, Christ was an unblemished firstfruit of the flock.[11] His death has restored life, and thus his Resurrection is a foretaste of the final day when all the dead will rise: "Now is Christ risen from the dead, and was made the first frutes of them that slept" (1 Cor. 15:20).[12] It is this "Paschal Lambe," Lanyer claims in her poem to Queen Anne, that she presents to her readers through the *Salve Deus* ("To the Queenes," 85). And as Christ was the firstfruits of his virgin mother's womb, so Lanyer's poem is the firstfruits of a female poet's imagination. The audacity of this parallel is undercut somewhat by the poet's admission that Princess Elizabeth has no doubt seen "farre better Bookes" (12). But the best of all books, the Bible, is Lanyer's primary source for the Gospel story her title poem retells; and she is confident, as she puts it in her poem to Queen Anne, that her work "agree[s]...with the Text" of Scripture ("To the Queenes," 76).

Lanyer's fruitful ambiguities do not end with the bold suggestion that her poetic firstfruits resemble the Christ they offer up. The strained grammar of the sonnet's conclusion might also be interpreted to assert that Princess Elizabeth herself is "the first fruits of a womans wit." In composing "To the Lady *Elizabeths* Grace," Lanyer conceives a version of the Princess Elizabeth as the reincarnation of her great namesake, offering her addressee the literary/spiritual nourishment that will help her to mature in virtue and thus working to bring forth a new embodiment of Queen Elizabeth's "worth," her rich example as a paragon of virtue, which "did bind / All worthy minds" (4–5) to admire, love, and zealously imitate her. Again, Lanyer avoids any theological impropriety through language that carefully accommodates Protestant scruples. She neither addresses herself to the virtuous "Mother" now in heaven, nor claims that Queen Elizabeth's "worth" earned her a place there. Instead, she acknowledges the late queen's achievement in nurturing the English "Common-weale" or general good (*OED*, n.1 def. 1), a political good work that—to paraphrase Article 12 of the *Thirty-Nine Articles*—springs out necessarily of a godly monarch's true and lively faith, manifesting it to all "worthy minds," including the poet's. Nor is the term "worthy" problematic, for the *Book of Common Prayer* uses it to describe those who have properly prepared themselves to perform a sacred duty.

Lanyer and her worthy contemporaries are "[put] in mind" of the late queen by the "Name and Virtues" of the living princess ("To the Lady *Elizabeths* Grace," 2), or, to be more precise, by the name and virtues of that princess as they are conceived in Lanyer's poem. There is no need for the poet to mourn Elizabeth I, for she can write into being a lady in whom the worth of that queen lives on; and if the new Elizabeth lives up to her name, she will guarantee the well-being of a realm Lanyer calls a "Common-weale" rather than a kingdom. Princess Elizabeth's mother, Anne, is queen of the united *kingdom* of England, Scotland, and Wales, which King James has recently dubbed "Great Britain." In her poem to the Stuart queen, Lanyer acknowledges Anne's place in that patriarchal monarchy, calling her "great Britaines Queene, / Most gratious Mother of succeeding Kings" ("To the Queenes," 1–2). But Queen Elizabeth I was the "deare Mother of our Common-weale" ("To the Lady *Elizabeths* Grace," 7), our mutual good, where "our" is not gender-neutral, but fraught with a sense of feminine community. Speaking *to* a woman, *of* women, in a book that will champion the cause of woman, Lanyer elevates the late Tudor monarch as an icon of female solidarity and empowerment. Though the historical Queen Elizabeth in fact did nothing to change the political or social status of women, Lanyer holds up for the daughter of her male successor an idea of queenship as the matrix that gives birth to "our Common-weale" as women, as human beings, as Christians. With such a mother as her model, the living girl is as inspiring and potentially as valuable to Lanyer as the dead woman; Princess Elizabeth's "favour in accepting" the poet's *Salve Deus Rex Judaeorum* would lend a stamp of royal legitimacy to the work's radical rewriting of the Scriptures and confirm it as a Christian feminist *Cyropedia* for a promising Protestant princess.[13]

The poem Lanyer presents to Elizabeth Stuart and to her other addressees includes a woman-centered retelling of the Gospel as well as a defense of Eve that the poet claims "agree[s]...with the Text" of Genesis more accurately than do the misogynous interpretations of "more faultie men" by whom women are "so much defam'd" ("To the Queenes," 76, 78). As Achsah Guibbory points out, one may thus read Lanyer's book as a feminist response to the King James Bible, the new translation that was begun after the Hampton Court Conference in 1604 and published in 1611, the year in which *Salve Deus* also appeared:

> In the very year that the "Authorized Version" of the Bible was published...and dedicated to King James as "the principall moover and Author of the Worke" (sig. A2v), Aemilia Lanyer published her version of the Passion, proclaimed her authority as a woman to read and interpret the Bible, and asked for the queen's patronage of her work. Might we not, then, see the *Salve* as in some sense constituting an oppositional alternative to the monumental biblical project of James? ("Gospel According to Aemilia," 193)

We may indeed, for Lanyer would certainly have known about the translation project while it was underway. The king's plans

for a Bible free of the Geneva translation's potentially seditious marginal commentary had been reported to the public in
Barlow's 1604 *Summe and Substance of the Conference,* the
same work that recorded James's joking remark about wom-
en's laxness in coming to church. James, Barlow notes, found
particularly objectionable the Geneva gloss on Exodus 1:19,
in which the Israelite midwives defy the pharaoh's command
to kill all the male babies born to Hebrew women and cover
their disobedience with a clever lie about how the strong and
"liuely" Hebrew women always managed to deliver before they
could arrive. "Their disobedience herein was lawful, but their
dissembling euil," says the Geneva comment, thus—James
fumed—"allow[ing] *disobedience to Kings*" (Barlow, *Svmme
and Svbstance,* 47). For a woman like Lanyer, who would have
approved both of the ancient midwives and of the modern gloss,
the king's call for a translation eliminating "notes very partiall,
vntrue, seditious, and sauoring, too much, of dangerous, and
trayterous conceipts" (47) would have given her ample motivation to provide an alternative to the work of the king's all-male
translation team.

In seeking to do so, Lanyer opens herself to accusations of
overreaching, of seeking to climb to inappropriate heights.
Knowing this, she invokes classical myths traditionally associated with rash ambition but tweaks their imagery in an interestingly maternal way. Her muse, she says, will be thought an
"*Icarus*" or "*Phaeton*" (*SDRJ,* 275, 285) trying to fly before it can
crawl; in response to such objections, she deliberately associates
her work as a woman poet with the lowly duties of a mother trying to keep her baby on a proper nap schedule:

> thy poore Infant Verse must soare aloft,
> Not fearing threat'ning dangers, happening oft.

Thinke when the eye of Wisdom shall discover
Thy weakling Muse to flie, that scarce could creepe,
And in the Ayre above the Clowdes to hover,
When better 'twere mued up, and fast asleepe;
They'l thinke with *Phaeton,* thou canst neare recover,

But helplesse with that poore yong Lad to weepe:
    The little World of thy weake Wit on fire,
    Where thou wilt perish in thine own desire.

(SDRJ, 279–88)

The strained juxtaposition in these lines of classical allusion, fal-
conry terms, and childcare imagery captures perfectly Lanyer's
sense of her own situation; as a female poet and a commoner
attempting the loftiest of subjects, she is out of her element,
trespassing in the realm of the noble and the learned. A woman
of her class is expected to be minding babies, making sure that
little folk who "scarce [can] creepe" are "fast asleepe" when they
should be. But her "Infant verse" has wings; it is a baby falcon
that she refuses to keep "mued up."

The wise will, if she fails, judge her a fool; but she will not
quash her "desire," for she is motivated by love and devotion,
and Christ's preference for the weak and despised assures her
that he will empower her apparently inferior muse:

    the Weaker thou doest seeme to be
    In Sexe, or Sence, the more his Glory shines,
    That doth infuze such powerfull Grace in thee,
    To shew thy Love in these few humble Lines;
    The Widowes Myte, with this may well agree,
    Her little All more worth than golden mynes,
        Beeing more deerer to our loving Lord,
        Than all the wealth that Kindgoms could affoard.

(SDRJ, 289–96)

As Woods notes in her edition, this stanza alludes to the incident in the Gospel when Jesus goes to the temple and observes
"how the people cast money into the treasurie" (Mark 12:41); he
sees the large amounts that "riche men" (Luke 21:1) contribute,
but tells his disciples that the greatest gift is that of "a certaine
poore widow" who "threw in two mites" (Mark 12:42). For,
Christ explains, "they all did cast in of their superfluitie: but she
of her pouertie did cast in all that she had, euen all her liuing"
(Mark 12:44). The widow's penury does not hold her back from

giving all that she has; and so her "Myte" becomes her "might." Lanyer vows to follow in the poor widow's footsteps, and she is confident that her Lord will consider "Her little All" (*SDRJ*, 294) more precious than the *copia* casually cast into the treasury of sacred verse by learned men.

By invoking the widow of the Gospels, moreover, Lanyer once again aligns herself with and appeals to her principal patroness, the widowed Countess of Cumberland who—according the "The Description of Cooke-ham"—does not translate the Bible, but enters its pages and, through oneness with the beauties of Nature, interacts freely with the principal male figures of Scripture:

> In these sweet woods how often did you walke,
> With Christ and his Apostles there to talke;
> Placing his holy Writ in some faire tree,
> To meditate what you therein did see:
> With *Moyses* you did mount his holy Hill,
> To know his pleasure, and performe his Will.
> With lovely *David* you did often sing,
> His holy Hymnes to Heavens Eternall King.
> And in sweet musicke did your soule delight,
> To sound his prayses, morning, noone, and night.
> With blessed *Joseph* you did often feed
> Your pined brethren, when they stood in need.
>
> ("Cooke-ham," 81–92)

The countess is clearly made one with God both through the book of creatures and through the book of Scripture; her using a "faire tree" as a bible-stand sums up beautifully Lanyer's sense of Nature and Grace united.[14] We cannot know what translation the countess used on the occasions Lanyer recalls, or even if Lanyer really witnessed such moments, as opposed to imagining them.[15] Perhaps it was a copy of the Bishop's Bible, or perhaps the popular Geneva translation that King James so detested. But Lanyer's goal in her poetry is to provide Margaret Clifford with a new rendition of "holy Writ," one through which the virtuous reader may converse not only with Moses, David, Joseph, and the apostles, but also with such biblical heroines as Deborah, Judith, the Queen of Sheba, the wife of Pilate, the Blessed Virgin, and the Marys at Jesus' tomb.

2. LANYER'S INCARNATIONAL POETICS

In order to write the Scriptures anew and open their meaning for readers, the poet must be both prophet and priest; Lanyer believes she is called to just such a dual vocation. As prophet, she rewrites the Bible from a female perspective, proclaiming the radical implications of Christ's incarnation in a body born of woman; as priest, she offers that body—in all its beauty and sweetness—for the delectation and nourishment of her readers. Her inspiration for re-inscribing Holy Writ comes in part from her reading of Mary Sidney Herbert's psalm translations, works that Lanyer sees as performing functions both prophetic and priestly. Donne would later hail as divinely inspired these poems in which the Countess of Pembroke and her brother Philip were—as "*Davids* Successors"—able to "re-reveale" what the Holy Spirit first "Whisper'd to *David*" (Donne, *Sidney*, 33, 34, 32). Lanyer, too, sees Mary Sidney as no less a prophet and seer than King David, who composed the Hebrew psalms she translates; and thus, as Debra Rienstra argues, "Pembroke makes possible the woman poet devising on Scripture. She opens the door, with the approval of God himself, to...female exegesis" ("Dreaming Authorship," 92). In Lanyer's dream-vision poem, "The Authors Dreame to the Ladie *Marie*, the Countesse Dowager of *Pembrooke*," the poet witnesses a scene in which pagan goddesses join Mary Sidney in singing "Those rare sweet songs which *Israels* King did frame" ("The Authors Dreame," 117), and a marginal note explains that the line refers to *The Psalms written newly by the Countesse Dowager of Penbrooke*" (see Loughlin, "'Fast ti'd unto them,'" 146). As Rienstra observes, the adverb "newly" here "effectively erases the 'old versions' in a remarkable gesture, similar to Donne's, toward Pembroke's interpretive authority" ("Dreaming Authorship," 87).

The countess is no less priestly than prophetic, for her works mediate between things otherwise divided. Her psalm translations, as sung by classical muses and graces, unite Judeo-Christian poetics with pagan antiquity; and in her presence, Art and Nature end their rivalry and agree to live in "perfit unity" ("The Authors Dreame," 81, 90). Her priestly power is most vividly revealed, however, in her works' status as sacramental seals that make her virtues accessible to future readers and, in doing so, unite their author with God:

> With contemplation of Gods powrefull might,
> She fils the eies, the hearts, the tongues, the eares
>
> Of after-comming ages, which shall reade
> Her love, her zeale, her faith, and pietie;
> The faire impression of whose worthy deed,
> Seales her pure soule unto the Deitie.
>
> ("The Authors Dreame," 159–64)

The imagery of this passage is reminiscent of Donne's sermons, in which he often uses the Calvinist definition of sacraments as wax impressions or seals (see, for example, *Sermons*, 5:149, 6:160). The Countess of Pembroke's "worthy deed," her literary achievement, is here—as in Article 12 of the *Thirty-Nine Articles*—a fruit of her "faith" ("The Authors Dreame," 163, 162), a good work springing from it. But the lines may also be read to say that "faith" is but one of several virtues that *are* the countess's work, a text to be read for years to come. She thus reconciles not only paganism and Christianity, Art and Nature, but also the false dichotomy between faith and works.

Lanyer, however, aspires to a vocation even more explicitly priestly than Pembroke's.[16] In translating the psalms, Mary Sidney has "*written newly*" an Old Testament text, the book of Psalms inscribed by David who, though the anointed monarch of Israel, was but a type of Christ, the true *Rex Judaeorum*. Lanyer's stanza describing the psalms stresses the fact that they predate the Incarnation: they are "Those rare sweet songs which *Israels* King did frame / Unto the Father of Eternitie; / Before his holy wisedom tooke the name / Of great *Messias*, Lord of unitie" ("The Authors Dreame," 117–20). Portraying David as a mouthpiece for the not-yet-incarnate Wisdom of the Father, who addresses himself to that Father through David's songs, Lanyer implies that Pembroke's ability to unite seemingly disparate forces springs from the Incarnation itself, which effects—through the "Lord of unitie"—a perfect union joining creature and creator. Lanyer, in writing anew not only the Hebrew scriptures, but the New Testament that proclaims Christ as God incarnate and supreme mediator, presumes to offer that "Lord of unitie" himself through her poem: "Receive him here by my unworthy hand," she says to the countess ("The Authors Dreame," 221). This is one of several points in *Salve Deus* when, as many scholars have observed, Lanyer represents her poem on the Passion as a Eucharistic feast and, in doing so, takes upon herself a sacerdotal function. Perhaps the most explicit such reference comes in the prefatory poem to Queen Anne, in which Lanyer announces, "here I have prepar'd my Paschal Lambe," and issues a formal invitation to the banquet: "This pretious Passeover feed upon" ("To the Queenes," 85, 89). Lanyer thus defines her poem as a sacrament through which her readers may encounter "even our Lord Jesus himselfe" ("To the Ladie *Margaret*," 7).[17]

She thinks herself, moreover, as capable as Mary Sidney when it comes to avoiding the supposed conflict between Art and Nature. In the poem to Queen Anne, she begs "pardon" for any apparent presumption. It is "Not," she insists, "that I Learning to my selfe assume,"

> Or that I would compare with any man:
> But as they are Scholers, and by Art do write,
> So Nature yeelds my Soule a sad delight.
>
> And since all Arts at first from Nature came,
> That goodly Creature, Mother of Perfection,
> Whom *Joves* almighty hand at first did frame,
> Taking both her and hers in his protection:
>   Why should not She now grace my barren Muse,
>   And in a Woman all defects excuse.
>
> ("To the Queenes," 145, 147–56)

In these lines, feminine Nature is the matrix of Art; the woman who writes unaided by "Learning" is one of *Natura*'s children, under the "protection" of the God who made "both her and hers." Lanyer thus declares the alleged division between Art and Nature a problem only for "any man" who "Learning to [himself] assume[s]."[18] As a woman, she is an artist, a poet, *by* nature.

More astonishingly, this passage implies a resolution of all conflict between the order of nature and the order of grace. Unfallen *Natura* was "at first" a "goodly Creature, Mother of Perfection." And now, according to Lanyer's prefatory epistle, "To the Vertuous Reader," the world has been redeemed by one "borne of a woman, nourished of a woman, obedient to a woman;...[who] healed woman, pardoned women, comforted women" ("To the Vertuous Reader," 44–46). In the Creation restored by such a Savior, Mother Nature is the equivalent of sanctifying grace for the female poet: "Why should not She now grace my barren Muse[?]" the poet asks the queen, "And in a Woman all defects excuse" ("To the Queenes," 155–56). Nature can change a sterile imagination into a womb pregnant with sacred poetry; she can compensate for "all defects," spiritual and artistic.[19] Lanyer's poem to the possibly crypto-Catholic Anne thus gestures subtly toward a maternal intercessor who pleads for sinful humanity before the throne of her Son. By invoking the "Mother of Perfection" who will "in a Woman all defects excuse," Lanyer endorses devotion to the "goodly Creature" whom the Litany of Loreto calls "Mother of Divine Grace," though Nature herself, rather than the Virgin Mary, here fills that role.

Many of Lanyer's ideas about poetry, nature, grace, female priesthood, and the body of Christ come together in an ambiguous but evocative passage from the dedicatory essay she addresses to her principal addressee, Margaret Clifford:

> As Saint *Peter* gave health to the body, so I deliver you the health of the soule; which is this most pretious pearle of all perfection, this rich diamond of devotion, this perfect gold growing in the veines of that excellent earth of the most blessed Paradice, wherein our second *Adam* had his restlesse

> habitation. The sweet incense, balsums, odours, and gummes
> that flowes from that beautifull tree of Life, sprung from the
> roote of *Jessie,* which is so super-excellent, that it giveth grace
> to the meanest & most unworthy hand that will undertake to
> write thereof. ("To the Ladie *Margaret,*" 9–18)

Saint Peter, who heals a lame man, is the impecunious poet's
model; he declares, "Siluer and golde haue I none, but suche as
I haue, that giue I thee: In the Name of Iesus Christ of Nazaret,
rise vp and walke" (Acts 3:6). But whereas the apostle's miracle
is confined to the realm of physical healing, Lanyer claims to be
able to give her readers a more spiritually significant good, "the
health of the soule," a poetic Eucharist that presents in verbal
form the treasures most essential to Christian well-being. First,
she promises her noble reader "this most pretious pearle of all
perfection": both the "perle of great price" which is the kingdom
of God in Jesus' parable (Matt. 13:45–46), and the priceless body
of the King himself. Next, she calls the gift she offers "this rich
diamond of devotion": both the many-faceted poetic work that
celebrates Christ, and Christ himself, the diamond more precious than any other gem. But most intriguingly, Lanyer claims
to offer to her patroness "this perfect gold growing in the veines
of that excellent earth of the most blessed Paradice, wherein
our second *Adam* had his restlesse habitation." The welter of
prepositional phrases makes the passage hard to dissect, but it
is worth close scrutiny.[20] The "perfect gold" here offered is the
precious blood of Christ. Punning on "veines" as conduits of
blood and layers of ore, Lanyer evokes the idea of Christ's body
as a sacred garden, the soil of which is laced with lodes of precious metal. While the first Adam's body was fashioned from
the "dust of the grounde" (Gen. 2:7) and only afterwards "put"
into the garden God had "planted...Eastwarde in Eden" (Gen.
2:8), the flesh of the second Adam is the "excellent earth, of
the most blessed Paradice" itself, Eden restored. That the body
in which the Lord dwelt was a "restlesse" habitation Lanyer
knew from Matthew 8:20, where Jesus sighs, "The foxes haue
holes, and the birdes of the heauen haue nestes, but the Sonne

of man hathe not whereon to rest his head." On another level, the "excellent earth of the most blessed Paradice, wherein our second *Adam* had his restlesse habitation" is the body of his mother, whose womb is the alembic in which grows the "perfect gold" of his body and blood. Mary's pregnant body was a "restlesse habitation" in that she traveled "into the hill countrey" to visit Elizabeth and journeyed from Nazareth to Bethlehem in the final days of pregnancy (Luke 1:39, 2:4–5). As is ever the case in Lanyer's work, woman's experience and Christ's experience, woman's holiness and Christ's holiness, the female body and Christ's body are closely elided.

To receive the Lord's body through the language of Lanyer's sacred poetry is, then, to regain paradise, to see *Natura* restored to her original perfection. For as the church is the body of Christ, so the body of Christ is, in Lanyer's vision, a perfect manifestation of unfallen Nature: "that beautifull tree of Life, sprung from the roote of *Jessie*" ("To the Ladie *Margaret*," 15–16). This line in praise of Christ elides Isaiah's image of the Messiah as a shoot of Israel's royal stock (Isa. 11:1; echoed in Rom. 15:12) with scriptural passages that refer to the tree of life in the garden of Eden, suggest its antitype in the life-giving cross of Christ, and attribute feminine gender to both. Of Wisdom—whom Christian exegetes often interpret as the second person of the Trinity—the sage of Proverbs declares: "She is a tre of life to them that laie holde on her" (Prov. 3:18). In heaven, the book of Revelation promises, the redeemed will eat of this tree's fruit: "To him that ouercometh, wil I giue to eate of the tree of life which is in the middes of the Paradise of God" and "which bare twelue maner of frutes, & gaue frute euerie moneth" (Rev. 2:7, 22:2).[21] In calling the body of Christ the "tree of Life," then, Lanyer's dedicatory essay again feminizes Christ's *corpus*. Lanyer herself is the beneficiary of this messianic tree, for the "sweet incense, balsums, odours, and gummes" flowing from it give "grace to the meanest & most unworthy hand that will undertake to write thereof" ("To the Ladie *Margaret*," 14–15, 17–18). Thus graced, Lanyer's hand is capable of offering to the countess (who, in "The Description of Cooke-ham," memorably bestows a kiss upon her favorite tree) an intimate poetic encounter with the tree of life.

For Donne, the poet's priestly function is to imitate Christ by bridging the gap between earth and heaven, nature and grace; to make an impression upon fallen eyes, ears, and hearts; to bring readers to an awareness of their own "Letargee" (*FirAn*, 24); and then, through the celebration of Elizabeth Drury, to arouse them from their stupor and let them glimpse the heavenly transfiguration of body and soul. For Lanyer, too, poetic priesthood involves celebrating female virtue, evoking Eucharistic presence, and directing her readers heavenward; but it also means bearing witness to what she believes to be the complete reconciliation, through Christ, of female Nature and Grace on earth. The contrast between Donne's vision and Lanyer's appears most vividly when one reads Lanyer's stanzas on the Blessed Virgin Mary in relation to Donne's lines on the Virgin in *The Second Anniversarie*. Both poets' images of Mary are polyvalent and subtle; neither unambiguously advances one particular Marian doctrine. But Donne's brief portrait of "the blessed Mother-maid" who takes "Ioy in not being that, which men haue said," and is "exalted more for being good, / Then for her interest, of mother-hood" (*SecAn*, 341–44) plays a key role in advancing the *Second Anniversarie*'s turn away from earthly motherhood and sacramentality toward a vision of the transfigured, spiritualized matter of the resurrected body as it will exist at the end of time. Lanyer, by contrast, stresses what Donne calls Mary's "interest, of mother-hood"; and her woman-centered spirituality leads her, despite her avoidance of any direct request for Mary's intercession, to pronounced expressions of Marian devotion that affirm the goodness and redemptive power of the flesh as we know it in this life.

Perhaps most dramatically, Lanyer harbors no Reformed scruples about declaring Mary "full of grace." The Vulgate account of the Annunciation renders the angel's greeting as "have gratia plena" (Luke 1:28); in the Catholic Douay-Rheims translation,

these words are translated "Hail, full of grace," and it is this language (modified to include Mary's name) that begins the popular rosary prayer known as the "Ave Maria" or "Hail Mary."
Wycliffe and Tyndale use the same language in their early Protestant translations of the New Testament, but in the Bishop's
Bible, the word "grace" disappears, and the angel says, "Hayle
freelie beloued." In the even more studiously Reformed 1560
Geneva Bible, Luke's Greek is again translated, "Haile thou that
art freely beloued." As Calvin makes clear in his commentary
on the passage, the Catholic rendering, which declares Mary
"full of grace" before the enactment of Christ's redemptive
sacrifice on the cross, and thus supports Catholic belief in the
Immaculate Conception, is highly problematic from a Protestant perspective. As Calvin reads the Greek, the angel's words
are "a commendation of the grace of God," not praise for Mary,
"For the participle κεχαριτωμένη which Luke employs, denotes
the undeserved favor of God."[22] In keeping with this argument,
the 1599 Geneva Bible gloss on verse 28 asserts that the point is
God's choice of Mary rather than the state of her soul: "It might
be rendered worde for word, full of favour and grace, and hee
sheweth straight after, laying out plainely vnto vs, what that
fauour is, in that he saith, the Lord is with thee."[23] The 1560
Geneva Bible glosses the angel's next statement — "for thou hast
founde fauour with God" (Luke 1:30) — with the stern reminder:
"Not for her merites: but onely through Gods fre mercie, who
loued vs when we were sinners." Lanyer, however, retains the
Catholic language, not qualifying the idea of "grace" by rendering it as "favor." Indeed, she goes further: by including both the
Douay-Rheims' "full of grace" and the Reformed translations'
"freely beloued," she underscores both Mary's worthiness and
the force of divine eros: "He thus beganne, Haile *Mary* full of
grace, / Thou freely art beloved of the Lord, / He is with thee"
(*SDRJ*, 1041–43). The phrase "freely…beloved" perfectly suits
Lanyer's purposes, for it implies both that God freely offers his
love to Mary and that her accepting his offer will in no way sub-
jugate her. Next, reflecting on the Virgin's affirmative response

("Beholde, the seruant of the Lord: be it vnto me according to thy worde" [Luke 1:38]), Lanyer steps entirely outside the Protestant pale: "Thus beeing crown'd with glory from above, / Grace and Perfection resting in thy breast, / Thy humble answer doth approove thy Love" (1089–91). Here, only the crown of "glory" need descend from above; "Grace and Perfection" are already at home in the bosom of Mary. She is indeed, as the Roman Catholic Litany of Loreto acknowledges, the "Mater Divinae gratiae" (Mother of divine grace).[24]

Lanyer's sense of the mother of Jesus as perfect does not necessarily imply that she believed in the Roman Catholic doctrine of the Immaculate Conception, which declares that Mary not only avoided any actual sins during her lifetime, but was from the moment of her conception preserved by God from the taint of original sin. This, of course, is the doctrine Donne seems to be rejecting in *The Second Anniversarie* when he says that the Virgin rejoices "in not being that, which men haue said" (*SecAn*, 342). But it is not impossible that Lanyer would have been sympathetic to the belief in Mary's freedom from original sin, for the arguments most often used to defend that doctrine from the Middle Ages through the seventeenth century arose from a Franciscan theology that was, like Lanyer's own theology and poetics, heavily incarnational in character. As Sarah Jane Boss demonstrates, the medieval proponents of the doctrine tended to base their arguments upon "an optimistic understanding of humanity's, and the physical world's, capacity for goodness and redemption" (*Empress and Handmaid*, 132); they insisted upon the continuity between Mary's Immaculate Conception and the Incarnation, pointing to the sinless body of Mary as the substance out of which the body of Christ was to be formed.[25] It is precisely this idea of Mary that informs Donne's stanza on Mary in "A Litanie" (ca. 1608), in which he calls her

> that faire blessed Mother-maid,
> Whose flesh redeem'd us; That she-Cherubin,
> Which unlock'd Paradise, and made
> One claime for innocence, and disseiz'd sinne.   (*Lit*, 37–40)

Lanyer, too, asserts that it is Mary's "faultlesse fruit" in which "All Nations of the earth must needes rejoyce" (*SDRJ*, 1025, 1026). This "fruit"—what Donne calls her redeeming "flesh"—is, of course, her son, Jesus, who takes his flesh from her. But Lanyer's image of "faultlesse fruit" is even more provocative, for it not only evokes Christ himself, but also hints that the atonement he accomplishes is the outcome or "fruit" of Mary's perfect response to God. It is her "faultlesse" openness to God's will in making her his "Faire chosen vessell" (1030) that bears the "fruit" able to reverse what Milton will call "Man's First Disobedience, and the Fruit" of death that sprang from it (*PL* 1.1).

Of course, Lanyer might well have objected to the idea of the Immaculate Conception on the basis of the same logic Donne would use in a 1618 sermon preached at Whitehall, when he mused that for Jesus "to dye for all the world, and not for his mother, or to dye for her, when she needed not that hell, is a strange imagination" (*Sermons*, 1:307). But just such a "strange imagination" seems to be at work in Donne's "Goodfriday, 1613. Riding Westward," where he portrays the "miserable mother" of Jesus as "Gods partner here," who "furnish'd thus / Halfe of that Sacrifice, which ransom'd us" (*Goodf*, 30, 31–32), thus making her deferral to the will of the Father essential to the atonement and portraying her, if not as co-redeemer, then as someone to whom the rest of "us" are indebted.[26] Lanyer's portrayal of the Passion, too, stresses the Virgin's sacrifice while deemphasizing the idea that she herself benefited from her Son's death. Jesus "prize[s] all mortals" and dies "To save their soules" as well as "partly to fulfil his Fathers pleasure" (*SDRJ*, 1102, 1104, 1105); but his doing so causes his mother pain; she cannot "choose...but mourne, / When this sweet of-spring of [her] body dies" (1129–30).

Indeed, Mary as Lanyer portrays her is exposed and vulnerable on the road to Calvary in precisely the way that a secular queen mother would be on the occasion of her son's deposition and execution: "How could shee choose but thinke her selfe undone,

/ He dying, with whose glory shee was crowned?" (*SDRJ*, 1013–14). Mary's loss is greater than that of an earthly queen, for Jesus is not only her son, but also the divine image of his Father: "None ever lost so great a losse as shee, / Beeing Sonne, and Father of Eternitie" (1015–16). And as the type of Ecclesia, she is painfully aware that she is losing her spouse and her redeemer as well as her child; Christ is "Her Sonne, her Husband, Father, Saviour, King" (1023). Lanyer's Blessed Mother is, however, no passive victim; like Jesus himself, she willingly endures sorrow and humiliation, realizing that they are necessary for the redemption of humanity:

> Her teares did wash away his pretious blood,
> That sinners might not tread it under feet
> To worship him, and that it did her good
> Upon her knees, although in open street,
> Knowing he was the Jessie floure and bud,
> That must be gath'red when it smell'd most sweet.
>
> (*SDRJ*, 1017–22)

Despite what appears to be some textual corruption, these lines convey the Virgin's exceptional understanding of her son's mission, her ability to see clearly the truth that, in Lanyer's earlier account of Jesus' arrest and trial, sinful men fail to "discerne" or "understand" (505, 506).

Even more interestingly, the passage hints at Mary's status as her Son's sinless partner in the work of redemption. Lanyer pointedly distinguishes between the Virgin and the "sinners" who would "tread" upon Christ's "pretious blood," stressing that Mary's tears keep the sinners from deeper transgression. In washing Christ's blood with her tears, Mary not only preserves it from desecration, but also ensures that it may do the work of atonement, for the new "Covenant" must be written "with his pretious blood" ("To the Ladie *Katherine*," 47). Sinners would merely "tread it under feet," as in Hebrews 10:29, where the apostate Christian is defined as one who "treadeth vnder fote the Sonne of God, and counteth the blood of the Testament as

an vnholie thing"; but the "faire soule" of a redeemed Christian can, thanks to the Virgin's tearful intervention between the
blood of Christ and the feet of sinners, "bathe her in that flood"
(To the Ladie *Katherine*," 48).

Mary's knowing collaboration in her Son's redemptive sacrifice would perhaps be even clearer in the stanza describing her
tears were it not for an obvious error in the printed text. The
enjambment "That sinners might not tread it under feet / To
worship him" (*SDRJ*, 1018–19) makes no sense, so it seems likely
that the infinitive phrase "To worship him" (1019) was meant to
be linked to the prepositional phrase "Upon her knees" (1020).
Mary sheds her tears not only so that she may wash Jesus' bleed-
ing body and protect his blood from desecration, but also so that
she may share in his humiliation, which is the source of all spiritual benefit: "That sinners might not tread it under feet / [And
that it did her good to worship him] / Upon her knees, although
in open street," bearing witness to him as the flower of the Jesse
tree (Isa. 11:1), the "faultlesse fruit" of her womb in whom "All
Nations of the earth must needes rejoyce" (*SDRJ*, 1025, 1026).[27]
Whatever humiliation she may endure as the Mother of Sorrows,
Lanyer's Mary is glorified because she is, as Donne would call
her in "Goodfriday, 1613," "Gods partner" (31) in the redemption of man, offering the fruit of her womb to reverse the effects
of the forbidden fruit, bearing supreme witness to the idea that,
even in this life, the flesh may be in harmony with the spirit,
and Nature an agent of Grace.

3. The Womanhood of the Church and the
Priesthood of Woman

Susanne Woods asserts that Lanyer's "portrait [of the Vir-
gin] contains no hint of Mary as mediator or co-redeemer, but
instead presents her as the chief exemplar of all the womanly
virtues Lanyer praises throughout the *Salve Deus*" (*Lanyer*,
138). This claim, I would argue, underestimates Lanyer's sense
of womanly virtue as a force that unites human nature with the

divine. Lanyer's Mary is indeed a "chief exemplar," but what she models is the mediating and co-redemptive function that Lanyer believes *all* virtuous women ought to fulfill. Only the Blessed Virgin actually gives birth to the body that dies on the cross; yet every devout Christian woman is, Lanyer believes, a living, priestly incarnation of that body.

Thus, while Lanyer represents herself as exercising a priestly function through the practice of poetry, it is not poesis that she believes makes her a priest; rather, her biological sex and the gender characteristics that accompany it do so. For Lanyer, virtuous women are at once the truest icons of the church—the best representations of who and what she is—and the sacerdotal agents by means of which she ministers to human beings. That is to say, women are the rightful heirs to the apostolic succession, despite Christ's original commissioning of Peter and the other apostles. For, though the men Jesus originally chose had bodies of the same sex as his physical body, the female sex is better suited to figure forth his mystical body, Ecclesia. And unlike the male apostles Jesus ordained to assist him in his ministry, women are unwaveringly true to Christ; they do not abandon him in his hour of need. Jesus himself recognized this fidelity, Lanyer believes, for after Jesus had been crucified by men, he rose from the dead in a glorified body "so faire, / So sweet, so lovely" that it—like the body of the bridegroom in the Song of Songs—resembled a woman's as much as a man's (*SDRJ*, 1305). And in that body, he "appeared first to a woman, [and] sent a woman to declare his most glorious resurrection to the rest of his Disciples" ("To the Vertuous Reader," 49–50).[28]

At other points in *Salve Deus*, Lanyer evokes the typological interpretation of the church as Christ's bride, the same New Testament, patristic, and medieval tradition that Donne draws upon for his own purposes in poems like "The Annuntiation and Passion" and "Show me deare Christ." As Eve was made from Adam's rib, so the church is born of the blood and water that flow from the side of the new Adam, Christ. The church is thus closely identified with the Blessed Virgin Mary, the second Eve;

Mater Ecclesia, like the mother of Jesus, mediates between God and humankind, offering the body of Christ to all who hunger for redemption.[29] All these correspondences operate in Lanyer's poetry, yet she recasts and transforms this traditional conception of the church, for *Salve Deus Rex Judaeorum* vivifies the allegory of the church as woman, depicting ecclesiastical ministry as women's work.

The exclusion of women from the Christian priesthood is traditionally supported by a variety of arguments that take as their point of departure several key Pauline and Deutero-Pauline texts: 1 Corinthians 11:7 ("For a man oght not to couer his head: for asmuche as he is the image and glorie of God: but the woman is the glorie of the man"), 1 Corinthians 14:34 ("Let your women kepe silence in the Churches: for it is not permitted vnto them to speake; but they oght to be subiect, as also the Law saith"), and 1 Timothy 2:12–14 ("I permit not a woman to teache, nether to vsurpe autoritie ouer the man, but to be in silence. For Adam was first formed, then Eue. And Adam was not deceiued, but the woman was deceiued, & was in the transgression"). As Ida Raming explains in her historical investigation of the Roman Catholic canon law that excludes women from ecclesiastical office, these passages are in turn based on "the Jewish-rabbinical tradition of Genesis interpretation," which interprets the creation of Eve from Adam's rib in Genesis 2 as an indication that males are made in the image of God, while woman is made in man's image and is therefore at one remove from the divine image (*Exclusion of Women*, 111). As Raming also notes, "the traditional Catholic concept of church office"—which remained essentially intact in the official doctrine of the seventeenth century English church, despite Calvinist influence—understands "one who possesses the presbyterial and episcopal office" as "the representative of Christ, as one who in his functions of office and especially in the liturgical celebration portrays and represents Christ" (117). This understanding of the priesthood, combined with Pauline/Deutero-Pauline notions of female subordination, leads to the argument that "Christ, the bridegroom and head of the church...could not be represented by a woman, who is subject to man and as a passively receiving being could not be called (like him) the 'head'" (119).[30]

Remarkably, Lanyer's seventeenth century poem anticipates Raming's scholarly twentieth century objections to this argument:

> New Testament statements about church as "body" and "bride of Christ," which in themselves reveal the relationship of the exalted Lord to the church *in its totality*, are erroneously referred in traditional ecclesiology to the relationship between church officials and the lay congregation.... Thus office and representation are understood to mean taking the position of Christ as head and life-giving bridegroom of the church.... Outward, biological likeness to the historical Jesus—from which a spiritual likeness and similarity of nature is too quickly concluded—...becomes the main requirement for official representation, always of course with the presupposition of sacramental ordination. (*Exclusion of Women*, 120, 121, 122)

Of course, it was the Reformation's emphasis on the priesthood of all believers that began the assault on the "presupposition of sacramental ordination." Lanyer takes up a revolutionary extension of that doctrine advanced by some of the more radical Protestant sects and claims the priesthood for women.[31] In doing so, she takes a very different tack than do twentieth and twenty-first century Roman Catholic scholars like Raming, who are seeking to redefine the sacerdotal function in terms that make women's ordination possible, but not to eliminate the idea of an ordained priesthood; for Lanyer implicitly dispenses with the institutional church as such, not so much arguing for a community of faith that operates without ecclesiastical discipline, prescribed liturgy, or an ordained ministry, as proclaiming that this community already exists and is the true church. Thus, rather than begging Christ, as Donne does, to show her his "Spouse, so bright and cleare" (*HSShow*, 1), Lanyer essentially sings his praises for having revealed that spouse in the words and deeds of women from his own day to the present.

In the spontaneously charitable and unstructured church that Lanyer's poetry portrays, women are the self-appointed, unpaid pastors whose priesthood empowers them to do all that is necessary for the redemption of humankind. Indeed, Micheline White explains, Lanyer "suggests that [her female dedicatees] wield certain priestly powers,...depicts [the] women [of the Gospels] as the true disciples and founders of Christ's healing Church, and...positions Jacobean women as the spiritual heirs of these female disciples" ("Woman with Saint Peter's," 324). As Lanyer sees it, women preach the Gospel—she does so herself in her poetic alternative to the authorized translation also published in 1611; they baptize—the Countess of Cumberland renders the "waves of woe" in which she is "plunged" by the injustices of men (*SDRJ*, 34), a baptismal inundation that frees her from the world; and, in place of the Communion service of the *Book of Common Prayer*, women offer Christ present in the "holy feast" of a Eucharistic poem ("To the Ladie *Susan*," 6) and "feed [Christ's] flocke" by spending what God has bestowed on them in sustaining "the poore" ("To the Ladie *Anne*," 134, 136).

The poet claims Christian priesthood for women partly on the basis of her radical reinterpretation of the atonement. As Saint Paul teaches in Romans, Christ's Incarnation and death free human beings from the bondage of sin; as Lanyer sees it, it also frees women from the tyranny of men. As Richard Duerden puts it,

> Not only did Christ end the period of the patriarchs by fulfilling and superceding the old law, as was conventionally believed, but his life exemplified and his Passion occasioned a recognition that women are not to be subordinate. Lanyer notes that Christ personally obeyed, blessed, chose, and sent women ["To the Vertuous Reader," 49–50], but she also suggests that when Christ is sent to the cross, patriarchy is toppled. ("Crossings," 143)

Lanyer expresses this idea through the voice of Pilate's wife in what has become one of the best-known passages of *Salve Deus:*

the crime of the men who crucify Jesus is far greater than the transgression of Eve, and the subjugation of woman to man in punishment for Eve's sin is thus rescinded in the wake of the Crucifixion. Indeed, as McBride points out ("Gender and Judaism," 35), Pilate's failure to "listen to his wife" when she tells him not to harm Jesus mirrors and reverses the moment in Genesis when Adam sins in response to Eve's offering of the forbidden fruit: "Eve's sin, imputed to all women, had allowed men 'to over-rule us all,' says Pilate's wife, but Pilate's 'indiscretion,' imputed to all men, 'sets us free'" (SDRJ, 760–61). Man, as deicide, is no longer worthy of political or spiritual authority.[32]

This argument against masculine precedence and rule is, however, only Lanyer's point of departure for a more comprehensive reinterpretation of priesthood as essentially feminine in character. As many critics have observed, the Christ of Salve Deus is portrayed as meek, beautiful, obedient to his father, silent, long-suffering.[33] Lanyer thus reveals the Jesus of the Gospels, the one and only high priest of the New Covenant (as he is described in the Epistle to the Hebrews), to be possessed of virtues that her culture defines as feminine rather than masculine. Women, as members of the sex that is expected to embody those virtues, are thus particularly well placed to serve as living, dynamic images of that high priest's body, the church.

Lanyer's image of woman as church and church as woman first takes shape in her portrayal of the Passion, when she turns from a description of Christ's Crucifixion to address her patroness, the Countess of Cumberland:

> This with the eie of Faith thou maist behold,
> Deere Spouse of Christ, and more than I can write;
> And here both Griefe and Joy thou maist unfold,
> To view thy Love in this most heavy plight,
> Bowing his head, his bloodlesse body cold;
> Those eies waxe dimme that gave us all our light,
>   His count'nance pale, yet still continues sweet,
>   His blessed blood watring his pierced feet.
>
> (SDRJ, 1169–76)

Susanne Woods's footnote to line 1170 correctly observes that this address to the countess plays upon "the convention that the Christian soul is the bride of Christ"; but at the same time, and even more powerfully for Lanyer's purposes in the poem at this point, the countess is here the embodiment of the church as Christ's spouse. The poet's emphasis on her status as a witness to Christ's suffering parallels Margaret Clifford with the Blessed Virgin, whose grief during the carrying of the cross Lanyer addresses five stanzas earlier: "How canst thou choose (faire Virgin) then but mourne, / When this sweet of-spring of thy body dies, / When thy faire eies beholds his bodie torne[?]" (1129–31). The eyes of Mary and the eyes of the countess are one, for both behold the tortured body of the Savior with grief and love.[34] Indeed, were the addressee of lines 1169 and forward not identified by a marginal gloss that reads *To my Ladie of Cumberland*," the reader might well mistake those lines as a continuation of the poet's address to Mary, for the mother of Jesus is herself the spouse of Christ; in witnessing the Crucifixion, Mary gazes on the death of "Her Sonne, her Husband, Father, Saviour, King" (1023). And though the Blessed Virgin sees the scene on Calvary with her bodily eyes, she, as a type of Ecclesia, looks also "with the eie of Faith" (1169), feeling not only a mother's "Griefe" at the death of her son, but the church's "Joy" (1171) at the redemption of humankind.

Lanyer's portrayal of the church's womanhood is further developed when the poet-narrator of *Salve Deus* tells the story of the female disciples who go to Christ's sepulcher on Easter morning, planning to anoint his body, only to discover that he is risen.[35] The passage begins as an account of the scene narrated in the synoptic gospels but becomes a meditation on the church's sacramental ministry:

> The *Maries* doe with pretious balmes attend,
> But beeing come, they find it to no end.
>
> For he is rize from Death t'Eternall Life,
> And now those pretious oyntments he desires

Are brought unto him, by his faithfull Wife
The holy Church; who in those rich attires,
Of Patience, Love, Long suffring, Voide of strife,
Humbly presents those oyntments he requires:
   The oyles of Mercie, Charitie, and Faith,
   Shee onely gives that which no other hath.

These pretious balmes doe heale his grievous wounds,
And water of Compunction washeth cleane
The soares of sinnes, which in our Soules abounds;
So faire it heales, no skarre is ever seene;
Yet all the glory unto Christ redounds,
His pretious blood is that which must redeeme;
   Those well may make us lovely in his sight,
   But cannot save without his powrefull might.

(SDRJ, 1287–1304)

In these stanzas, the church is defined in highly traditional terms both as the spouse of Christ and as his body.[36] As White observes, Lanyer here "revitalizes and radicalizes ... [an] exegetical tradition that linked the Maries with the Bride/Church from the Song of Songs" ("Woman with Saint Peter's," 335).[37] Christ's "faithfull Wife / The holy Church" administers the balms of sacramental ministry, ointments that heal the Lord's body of all its wounds: the marks of the nails and spear, but also the sins of each member of that body, since sin is what made the sacrifice of the Crucifixion necessary. The "*Maries*" who come to Jesus' tomb are thus both literal representations of the allegorical Ecclesia and models of ideal priesthood, garbed in vestments to which no Puritan could object: "those rich attires, / Of Patience, Love, Long suffring, Voide of strife" (*SDRJ*, 1292–93).[38] The ordained clergymen of Lanyer's own time, she implies, are legitimate heirs to the ministry the women performed only insofar as they robe themselves in the same feminine virtues that led the Marys to come to the tomb bearing "pretious balmes" (1287). The action those female disciples performed was "to no end" (1288)—unnecessary—in that Jesus' physical body was in fact no longer dead and awaiting embalming. But as the model for the sacramental ablution and anointing to be administered to Christ's mystical body throughout the ages, it is "to no end" in another way; it is a ritual action that does not and should not cease.

In stressing that Ecclesia is the keeper of a chrism able to bless and restore sinful humankind, the dispenser of "oyles" which "Shee onely" can give, Lanyer interestingly uses imagery that projects a conservative rather than a radically reformed ecclesiology; the liturgical use of consecrated oils was an ancient practice to which English Nonconformists of the sixteenth and seventeenth centuries objected strenuously.[39] The poet thus stresses that the "oyles" she refers to are virtues rather than literal ointments, and she concludes the passage with a caveat that denies belief in the redemptive power of ritual substances and actions: "Those well may make us lovely in his sight, / But cannot save without his powrefull might" (1303–04). Nevertheless, Lanyer clearly believes in the power and importance of the outward signs of grace administered by Ecclesia as she conceives her; to be "lovely in [the bridegroom's] sight" is no small matter for a bride.

The image of the church washing "cleane / The soares of sinnes" (SDRJ, 1298–99) reminds the reader that Jesus has entrusted to his church the power of the keys, the authority to forgive sins; she has the skill to heal souls so effectively that "no skarre is ever seene" (1300). In the Gospel, as Lanyer knows very well, Jesus grants this power to a group of men, telling Peter and the other apostles that "I wil giue vnto thee the keyes of the kingdome of heauen, and whatsoeuer thou shalt binde vpon earth, shalbe bound in heauen: and whatsoeuer thou shalt lo[o]se on earth, shalbe lo[o]sed in heauen" (Matt. 16:19).[40] But Lanyer seeks out and underscores a lesser-known scriptural passage that bestows a version of such jurisdiction on a woman, and a pagan woman at that. The Queen of Sheba, whom tradition recognizes as a type of the church and of the Christian soul, traveled from afar to ask King Solomon questions and to hear him speak. Doubting the veracity of the Hebrew ruler's reputation for sagacity, the queen sought him out, "communed with him of all that was in her heart" (1 Kings 10:2), came to believe in his wisdom, and glorified God for setting him on the throne of Israel (verses 6–9). In the same way, Lanyer stresses, the church and each individual Christian must seek out divine Wisdom incarnate and celebrate his reign: "No travels ought th'affected soule to shunne, / That this faire heavenly Light desires to see: / This King of kings to whom we all should runne, / To view his Glory and his Majestie" (*SDRJ*, 1625–28). Jesus sets up this typological parallel when the scribes and Pharisees have the impudence to ask him for "a signe": "The Quene of the South shal rise in iudgement, with the men of this generacion, and shal condemne them: for she came from the vtmost partes of the earth to heare the wisdome of Solomon, and beholde, a greater then Solomon is here" (Luke 11:31; see also Matt. 12:42). For Lanyer, these words commission the queen as an adjudicator whose words will carry weight with God on the Day of Judgment:

> that Heathen Queene obtain'd such grace,
> By honouring but the shadow of his Love,
> That great Judiciall day to have a place,
> Condemning those that doe unfaithfull prove;
> Among the haplesse, happie is her case.[41]   (*SDRJ*, 1681–85)

The Queen of Sheba cannot, of course, equal Lanyer's patroness: "This great majesticke Queene comes short of thee," the poet tells the Countess of Cumberland; for "a greater thou hast sought and found / Than *Salomon* in all his royaltie" (*SDRJ*, 1690, 1697–98). While the Queen of Sheba honored "an earthly Prince" (1691) known for his splendid wealth as well as for his wisdom, Margaret Clifford devotes herself to a King clad "in lowly shepheards weed[,] / A seeming Trades-mans sonne, of none attended, / Save of a few in povertie and need" (1714–16). In the spirit of Matthew 25:40 ("in as muche as ye haue done it vnto one of the least of these my brethren, ye haue done it to me"), the countess cares for the wretched of the earth:

Sometimes imprison'd, naked, poore, and bare,
Full of diseases, impotent, and lame,
Blind, deafe, and dumbe, he comes unto his faire,
To see if yet shee will remaine the same;
Nay sicke and wounded, now thou do'st prepare
To cherish him in thy dear Lovers name:
    Yea thou bestow'st all paines, all cost, all care,
    That may relieve him, and his health repaire.
                    (*SDRJ*, 1353–60)

The countess's engagement in the corporal works of mercy is not merely an expression and proof of her faith; it is the exercise of her function as the embodiment of the church's sacerdotal ministry, obeying Jesus' mandate to Saint Peter: "Fede my lambes" (John 21:15).

She is thus granted the priestly prerogative Christ bestowed upon that same apostle:

Thy faith, thy prayers, and his speciall grace
Doth open Heav'n, where thou behold'st his face.

These are those Keyes Saint *Peter* did possesse,
Which with a Spirituall powre are giv'n to thee,
To heale the soules of those that doe transgresse,
By thy faire virtues.   (*SDRJ*, 1367–72)

As White observes, the shift from the corporal works of mercy to the keys of Saint Peter here involves a remarkable, "nonchalant fusion of feminine and clerical vocabulary. The Countess performs pious activities expected of women, yet in inspiring imitation she also provides spiritual healing" as only a priest can ("Woman with Saint Peter's," 326). While the Queen of Sheba, type and foreshadowing of the church, is granted only the power to condemn sinful men at the end of time, Margaret Clifford, Ecclesia incarnate, has full access to the power of the keys. She can "heale" transgressors (*SDRJ*, 1371), restoring them to the ranks of the redeemed. In her, man-made conflicts between faith and works, grace and virtue, are reconciled. The countess's "faith," her "prayers," and the "speciall grace" God vouchsafes her (1367) work together to "open Heav'n" (1368).

And the countess is not alone in her ministry. Lanyer does not limit priestly vocation to herself as the maker of a Eucharistic poem or to the Countess of Cumberland as emblem of the church's pastoral ministry. As White points out, Lanyer's prefatory poem "To the Ladie *Anne*, Countesse of Dorcet" makes "subtle use of clerical language" to praise the addressee, daughter of Margaret Clifford and heir to her virtues, as a "Faire Shepheardesse" whose duties are those of the Christian pastor ("Woman with Saint Peter's," 328).[42] And in the poem addressed "To all vertuous Ladies in generall," every praiseworthy Christian woman is also called to sacerdotal ministry. "Annoynt your haire with *Aarons* pretious oyle," Lanyer urges, associating them with the Old Testament priesthood established in Exodus 28–30 ("To all," 36).[43] But the poet also extends an invitation that establishes all virtuous ladies' share in the womanly priesthood of the New Covenant as she envisions it; for she invites them to be clothed in the vestments worn by Christ's feminine body, the church. The "wedding garments" Lanyer's readers are to don ("To all," 8) recall the garments that are required attire for the royal nuptials in one of Jesus' parables (Matt. 22:2–14), while the "Lamps" they must "fill...with oyle of burning zeale" ("To all," 13) recall the bridesmaids of the parable of the wise and foolish virgins (Matt. 25:1–13). In Lanyer's poem, the robes she invites the women to wear are not merely symbols of the "newnesse of life" that one must demonstrate if one answers God's invitation to grace, though this is the 1599 Geneva Bible's gloss on the wedding garment parable. Rather, they are Jesus the bridegroom's own priestly vestments and the spiritual merit they represent: "Let all your roabes be purple scarlet white, / Those perfit colours purest Virtue wore," the poet tells them ("To all," 15–16). As the marginal gloss informs them, these are *"The roabes that Christ wore before his death."*[44] The implication is clear: though the wise virgins of Jesus' parable are (on the literal level) mere attendants of the bridegroom, the women

Lanyer addresses are clothed in his garments because they are—both individually and as a group—his bride, for Christ "purchast *all* your loves / In bloody torments, when he di'd opprest" ("To all," 59–60; emphasis mine).[45] Because the bride is the body of the bridegroom who is her head, the vestments with which he clothes his body are—by extension—the vestments worn by each member of that body. In short, like the *"Maries"* clad in the "rich attires" of feminine virtue and presenting to their Lord "those oyntments he requires" (*SDRJ*, 1287, 1292, 1294), all of Lanyer's female readers are called to be priests, not (as in the traditional ecclesiology Ida Raming outlines) by serving as representatives of Christ, the church's head, but rather by living as beautiful earthly incarnations of his anointed, priestly body, his "faithfull Wife / The holy Church" (*SDRJ*, 1291–92).

4. LANYER'S CRITIQUE OF APOSTOLIC PRIESTHOOD

Lanyer approaches the idea of the church as Christ's spouse in a manner that stresses the gendered nature of the relationship. She defines the tie binding Ecclesia to Christ as the pure and constant love of a good woman who stands by her man when no *man* will, and her portrayal of Jesus' interactions with his disciples on the eve of the Crucifixion contrasts feminine loyalty with masculine faithlessness. The first and most prominent of the twelve apostles, Peter, is less loyal than a Petrarchan sonneteer: "his hot Love...proove[s] more cold than Ice" (*SDRJ*, 348) when he faces the threat of suffering and danger. The other apostles do no better; their promises to Christ prove as false as the vows that fickle male lovers swear to women: "Those deare Disciples that he most did love, / ...When triall of affliction came to prove, / They first left him, ... / For they were earth... / Though they protest they never will forsake him, / They do like men, when dangers overtake them" (625, 627–29, 631–32). Though to "do like men" is on one level merely to be human, made of "earth," the phrase's position in a poem that stresses the iniquities of human males and the long-suffering virtue of human

females makes clear that "men" is to be construed more specifically as referring to the apostles as examples of the male sex.[46]
It is the ultimate irony, from Lanyer's point of view, that these
cowardly and disloyal men are the very people recognized by the
institutional churches (both Roman Catholic and English) as the
first Christian priests and bishops.

But Jesus did choose them, Lanyer knows; she cannot avoid
dealing with the scriptural basis for their claim to the power
of the keys. As White points out, Lanyer's image of Margaret
Clifford as wielding the keys both "displaces" the apostles "and
invokes their authority"; in using the image, the poet reminds
her readers "that Christ explicitly empowered" the twelve
("Woman with Saint Peter's," 336–37). And that empowerment
is, of course, the point of origin for the apostolic succession,
according to which only those men ordained by the apostles,
and the priests they in turn ordained, and so on in a direct line
of orderly inheritance throughout the ages, are to be considered
duly anointed priests. But as Lanyer notes in her critique of secular aristocratic inheritance, "Titles of honour which the world
bestowes, / To none but to the virtuous doth belong" ("To the
Ladie *Anne*," 25–26). The "successors" of a worthy ancestor,

> although they beare his name,
> Possessing not the riches of his minde,
> How doe we know they spring out of the same
> True stocke of honour, beeing not of that kind?
> . . . .
> If he that much enjoyes, doth little good,
> We may suppose he comes not of that blood.
> ("To the Ladie *Anne*," 41–44, 47–48)

These lines, addressed to Lady Anne Clifford, introduce Lanyer's claim that Anne does worthily inherit the noble virtue of
her mother, the Countess of Cumberland. But the function of
that virtue is framed as a matter of Christian stewardship, and
it is precisely that function that many a titled wretch does not
fulfill:

> Nor is he fit for honour, or command,
> If base affections over-rules his mind;
> Or that selfe-will doth carry such a hand,
> As worldly pleasures have the powre to blind
> So as he cannot see, nor understand
> How to discharge that place to him assign'd:
>   God's Stewards must for all the poore provide,
>   If in Gods house they purpose to abide.
>
> ("To the Ladie *Anne*," 49–56)

This stanza is not explicitly about priesthood; it addresses the responsibility of every Christian, and in particular every Christian who has been endowed with wealth or status, to use what he or she has been given for the good of God's people, and especially for the relief of the poor. But as a glance at Milton's *Lycidas* confirms, Lanyer's critique of those nobles who do not carry on the virtues of their ancestors also applies to the decadent clergy, those the "Mitred" Peter of Milton's poem condemns as mere hirelings who, "for their bellies' sake, / Creep and intrude and climb into the fold" (*Lycidas,* 112, 114–15); their "scrambl[ing] at the shearers' feast" (117) clearly indicates that they care for nothing but earthly delights. As Lanyer complains (less eloquently, but no less indignantly than Milton), "worldly pleasures have the powre to blind" a man thus given to self-indulgence, "So as he cannot see, nor understand / How to discharge that place to him assign'd" ("To the Ladie *Anne*," 52, 53–54). He and his ilk are, as Milton's powerful mixed metaphor puts it, "Blind mouths! that scarce themselves know how to hold / A Sheep-hook, or have learn'd aught else the least / That to the faithful Herdsman's art belongs!" (*Lycidas,* 119–21). Unlike the travesties of nobility Lanyer decries, Anne Clifford is truly "Gods Steward," the heir to a mother who embodies Ecclesia and her ministry of "goodnesse, bountie, grace, love, pietie" ("To the Ladie *Anne*," 57, 66). And unlike the incompetent and power-hungry prelates of Milton's poem, who claim to represent the Good Shepherd himself, she is a "Faire Shepheardesse" whom Christ will "use / To feed his flocke, that trust in him alone" (133–34).

Jesus appointed Peter as the first to fulfill this priestly role when he commanded, "Fede my lambes" (John 21:15); and he designated Peter as the rock upon which he would build his church. But Lanyer believes that, in stressing their predecessor's commission, Peter's male successors tend to forget that Christ himself is the cornerstone. It is upon *him* that the church—defined not merely as a structure, but as a house made up of many living, active stones that are themselves called to be builders—establishes the kingdom of heaven: "He is the stone the builders did refuse, / Which you, sweet Lady, are to build upon; / He is the rocke that holy Church did chuse, / Among which number, you must needs be one" ("To the Ladie *Anne*," 129–32). In these lines, Lanyer alludes to the words of Peter himself in his first epistle; he tells all the faithful that they are priests, having come to the Lord "as vnto a liuing stone, disalowed of men, but chosen of God & precious. And ye as liuelie stones, be made a spiritual house, and holie Priesthode to offer vp spiritual sacrifices acceptable to God by Iesus Christ" (1 Pet. 2:4–5). Lanyer thus has Peter's own testimony on her side: however unbroken the institutionally sanctioned line of the apostolic succession with its inherited unction, every Christian is a priest, a true shepherd of the flock.

But he or she is so only if spiritually anointed. As George Herbert would insist in his poem "Aaron" (which is about ordained priesthood within the English church but is relevant also to the priesthood of all believers), it is not the mere physical application of holy oil or the imposition of hands that makes one a priest.[47] Rather, God's minister must be anointed with "Holinesse on the head, / Light and perfections on the breast."[48] Thus, when Lanyer urges her female readers to "Annoynt [their] haire with *Aarons* pretious oyle," the unction poured upon the hair is merely the outward sign of a virtuous mind: "Bring your palmes of vict'ry in your hands, / To overcome all thoughts that would defile / The earthly circuit of your soules faire lands" ("To all," 36, 37–39). These lines allude both to the welcome Christ received on his Palm Sunday entry into Jerusalem, and to the processional triumphs of imperial Rome (Christ's momentous donkey ride being a sacred parody and revision of such pagan ceremonies). Lanyer's female readers are thus anointed with Aaron's oil precisely insofar as they are both faithful disciples, greeting their savior with loud hosannas, and conquering heroes able to guarantee a spiritual *pax Romana* in their own minds through their devotion to the rule of virtue (see Seelig, "'To all vertuous Ladies,'" 54).

Similarly, the vestments of the true priest are not mere physical garments; in "Aaron," Herbert would affirm that "true Aarons," as opposed to mere imposters, "to the old man...rest, / And [are] in [Christ] new drest" (5, 19–20). He thus stresses the dictum of Colossians 3:9–10 ("ye haue put of the olde man with his workes, And haue put on the newe"). But for Lanyer, the apostolic priesthood was, from the start, mired in vices that prevented such a change of raiment. She stresses that even Jesus' "three deere friends" — "*Peter*, and the sonnes of *Zebed'us*" to whom "good *Jesus* opened all his woe" (374, 370, 371) — were utterly unable to divest themselves of Adam's carnality in order to attend their Lord in his hour of need. As Lanyer puts it, Christ himself knew that

> they had no powre to doe [him] good,
> But were the cause [he] must endure these blowes,
> Beeing the scorpions bred in *Adams* mud,
> Whose poys'ned sinnes did worke among [his] foes,
>   To re-ore-charge [his] over-burd'ned soule,
>   Although the sorowes now they doe condole.   (379–84)

The irony that Christ's friends are his enemies cannot be separated from their human patrimony; as sons of Adam, they are the cause of Jesus' suffering rather than his consolation. And the legacy is that of the Father rather than the mother: the "earth" of which they are made is "*Adams* mud," not Eve's (629, 381).

Their greatest faults, Lanyer insists, are their pride and ambition, vices that prevent them from realizing their essential fallenness. Alluding to Peter's hubristic claim that "Thogh that all

men shulde be offended by thee, yet wil I neuer be offended"
(Matt. 26:33), Lanyer shakes her head with a mixture of pity
and rebuke that diminishes his stature as the foremost apostle: "poore *Peter*, he was most too blame, / That thought above
them all, by Faith to clime" (*SDRJ*, 355–56). Peter's problem, she
observes, is that "No imperfection in himselfe he spies" (350).[49]
The female poet/priest, by contrast, is keenly aware of *her* weak-
nesses and thus relies upon God alone to keep her faithful to the
words of the Scripture. Before telling the story of the Passion,
including the shameful episode of Peter's denying the Lord, she
resolves to pray for God's "Grace" (297), which will ensure that

> in these Lines I may no further stray,
> Than his most holy Spirit shall give me Light:
>   That blindest Weaknesse be not over-bold,
>   The manner of his Passion to unfold
>
> In other Phrases than may well agree
> With his pure Doctrine, and most holy Writ.   (*SDRJ*, 301–06)

Woods's edition follows the 1611 text in placing a period after
"unfold," at the end of line 304; but I have emended that punctuation in the quotation above, for the stanzas are clearly meant to
be enjambed. Lanyer's sentence spans the white space that separates them even as she trusts that divine grace will bridge the
chasm between the Scriptures and her work.[50] The female poet
surrenders all authorial power to the deity whose Word is revealed
in the Bible; where Peter's "forward speech inflicted sinne and
shame" (357), she will make humble use of "plainest Words"
(311). Thus, while Peter—relying upon his own strength—does
not follow through on his vow of faithfulness to Jesus, the
poet—relying upon God's "most holy Spirit" (302)—can be confident that "That he will give me Power and Strength to Write, /
That what I have begun, so end I may" (298–99).

   In her fidelity to the Word, the poet resembles the faithful
women of the Gospels who, unlike Peter, never deny knowing
Jesus and never turn their backs on him. The women on the road
to Calvary, for example, rush in where apostles fear to tread:

When spightfull men with torments did oppresse
Th'afflicted body of this innocent Dove,
Poore women, seeing how much they did transgresse,
By teares, by sighes, by cries intreat, may prove,
What may be done among the thickest presse,
They labor still these tyrants hearts to move;
    In pitie and compassion to forbeare
    Their whipping, spurning, tearing of his haire.

                                          (*SDRJ*, 993–1000)

Wholly empathetic, the women share in Jesus' torments. In line
996, "may" seems to be a typesetter's error for an intensifying
"nay": the women not only "intreat" the torturers verbally;
they go so far as to "prove," to try physically whatever "may be
done" to stop the horror. They do not run from the scene, but
thrust their way into "the thickest presse" and "labor"—the
word always has a particular intensity when applied to the sex
that gives birth—to convert the wicked. Thus, though their
efforts are "all in vaine" (1001), they truly participate in Christ's
Passion and in his ministry.

Their counterapostolic successor in seventeenth century
England is the Countess of Cumberland, the incarnation of
Christ's "faithfull Wife, / The holy Church" (*SDRJ*, 1291–92),
whose vocation is to continue the sacerdotal work of the "*Maries*"
who "with pretious balmes attend" the entombed body of Christ
(1287; compare White, "Woman with Saint Peter's," 224). Margaret Clifford carries on with the same courage and devotion
as the women of Jerusalem who pressed forward on the road to
Calvary: "Oft times," Lanyer tells her, Jesus "hath...made triall
of your love,"

    And in your Faith hath tooke no small delight,
    By Crosses and Afflictions he doth prove,
    Yet still your heart remaineth firme and right;
    Your love so strong, as nothing can remove. (*SDRJ*, 1337–41)

This spiritual fidelity seals and confirms the countess's oneness
with her crucified Lord.

Only when they suffered their own Christ-like wounds, Lanyer believes, did the less than admirable apostles become martyrs, and thus enter into genuine priestly oneness with the suffering body of Christ. In the final chapter of John's gospel, immediately after appointing Peter to feed his flock, the resurrected Jesus tells the apostle that he will have to endure persecution, imprisonment, and worse: "When thou wast yong, thou girdedst thy self, & walkedst whither thou woldest: but when thou shalt be olde, thou shalt stretch forthe thine hands, & another shal girde thee, & lead thee whither thou woldest not" (John 21:18). Noting the allusion to crucifixion in the image of outstretched hands, the evangelist comments, "this spake [Jesus], signifying by what death [Peter] shulde glorifie God" (21:19). For Lanyer, Peter's experience of persecution, imprisonment, and martyrdom was the means by which the previously unworthy male apostle became a true priest; in her poem, the sufferings of Jesus' male followers endow them with the zeal and love they need in order to carry out their apostolic mission:

> what great sweetnesse did th'Apostles taste,
> Condemn'd by Counsell, when they did returne;
> Rejoycing that for him they di'd disgrac'd,
> Whose sweetnes made their hearts and soules so burne
> With holy zeale and love most pure and chaste.
>
> (*SDRJ*, 1793–97)

Lanyer clearly has in mind here the passage from the Acts of the Apostles in which Peter and the other apostles are jailed, interrogated, beaten, and finally released: "they departed from the Council, reioycing, that they were counted worthie to suffer rebuke for his Name. And daiely in the Temple, & from house to house they ceased not to teach, and preach Iesus Christ" (Acts 5:41–42). Lanyer's description of the "sweetnesse" that the apostles "taste" in their persecution continues the emphasis of her preceding stanzas on the martyrs Stephen and Laurence (both of whom were deacons rather than priests).[51] The delectable savor of Christ's body and blood is, for Lanyer, the

Eucharistic delight that entices men to give their lives for him. "Sweet Nectar and Ambrosia, food of Saints" flows from the crucified Lord (*SDRJ*, 1735), and "This hony dropping dew of holy love" (1737) is the motivation for martyrdom: "This love made Martyrs many deaths to prove, / To taste his sweetnesse, whom they so adored" (1741–42).

Swooning delight in Christ's unparalleled sweetness overcomes the poet herself near the end of *Salve Deus* in a series of stanzas on Christ's body and blood as Eucharistic food. This final course of Lanyer's poetic feast is a rapturous confection: from Christ's body flow "Sweet holy rivers, pure celestiall springs, / ... Swift sugred currents that salvation brings" (*SDRJ*, 1729, 1731); these "Faire floods" are "Sweet Nectar and Ambrosia, food of Saints, / ... hony dropping dew of holy love, / Sweet milke, wherewith we weaklings are restored" (1735, 1737–38). Christ expresses his love as a breastfeeding mother does, giving of his very substance.[52] But does Lanyer dwell too much on the sugar in his milk? From lines 1729 to 1802, the adjective "sweet" appears seven times, the noun "sweetness" eight times, and the participle "sweet'ned" twice, each time in the phrase "sweetnesse sweet'ned."

Men who "are Scholers, and by Art do write" ("To the Queenes," 149) would (and do) no doubt reject such cloying repetition. But what price sophistication? As Lanyer sees it, only men who surrender to Christ's "sweetnesse" and "bathe their snow-white wings" in the "sugred currents that salvation brings" can "flie to true eternall life" (*SDRJ*, 1733, 1731, 1734). The male martyrs were those who believed that Christ's blood can never cloy, who immersed themselves in the same sweet love that now enraptures the female poet and her female readers: "This love made Martyrs many deaths to prove, / To taste his sweetnesse, whom they so adored" (1741–42). Only in the countenance of such a man as Stephen, his "face repleat with Majestie and Sweetnesse" as he looks upon his persecutors, can Lanyer find the reflection of the new Adam rather than the old (1753). Only by sharing in Christ's suffering can a man be "Deckt in those colours which our Saviour chose" (1827) and enter into the priesthood that is, for Lanyer, a feminine office.

The martyrs are, to be sure, decidedly masculine in the courage they display as they evangelize; "these Champions" are Christian soldiers dedicated to the "glorious fight," not only "Suppressing evill" but "erecting good" (*SDRJ*, 1808, 1809, 1812). And yet they achieve perfect union with the Lord for whose "sweetness" they long only by submitting to "deaths that were most vile and base"; and in so doing, they—like the lactating Christ whose "Sweet milke" they drink—are feminized (1804, 1738): Stephen is "filled with the holy Ghost" as was the Blessed Virgin; Laurence's "holy teares" cool the "broyling gridyorne" where he "Yeeld[s] his naked body" like a virgin bride in order "To taste this sweetnesse, such was his desire"; and John the Baptist suffers a symbolic castration when he "Yeeld[s his head] joyfully unto the Sword, / To be cut off as [if] he"—the male *he*—"had never bin" (1761, 1790–92, 1818–19).

It is through the church the Countess of Cumberland embodies, moreover, that all people can "taste this sweetnesse" without suffering death. In Ecclesia's celebration of the Lord's Supper, Jesus

> Present[s] us the bread of life Eternall,
> His bruised body powrefull to revive
> Our sinking soules, out of the pit infernall;
> For by this blessed food he did contrive
> A worke of grace, by this his gift externall,
>   With heav'nly Manna, food of his elected,
>   To feed their soules, of whom he is respected.
>
> (*SDRJ*, 1778–84)

These lines clearly refer to the sacrament of the Eucharist, the outward sign or "gift externall" that feeds the faithful of both sexes. But "us" and "our" seem, in context, to refer most directly to women: the poet, the Countess of Cumberland, and the other female readers she has addressed from the start in her prefatory poems and essays. They are both the ministers and the most appreciative receivers of Christ's Eucharistic "gift

externall," which thus seems not so much the Lord's Supper as
it is celebrated in the liturgy of the English church, according to
the rubric of *The Book of Common Prayer*, as the sacrament of
Christ's presence in every exchange between charitable noblewomen and the lowly of the earth in whose humble faces they
see their Lord.

Taking seriously Jesus' assertion that "in as much as ye have
haue done it vnto one of the least of these my brethren, ye haue
done it to me" (Matt. 25:40), Lanyer represents an encounter
between the Countess of Cumberland and an unnamed male
peasant as the ultimate sacramental encounter between Margaret Clifford and Christ:

> Sometimes h'appeares to thee in Shepheards weed,
> And so presents himselfe before thine eyes,
> A good old man; that goes his flocke to feed;
> Thy colour changes, and thy heart doth rise;
> Thou call'st, he comes, thou find'st tis he indeed,
> Thy Soule conceaves that he is truely wise:
> > Nay more, desires that he may be the Booke,
> > Whereon thine eyes continually may looke.
>
> (*SDRJ*, 1345–52)

Lanyer's dramatic specificity in describing this moment makes
it sound like a script recreating a remembered scene, but the
realistic touches serve a symbolic purpose. The old shepherd is
here a visible and outward sign of Christ, one who manifests his
presence as both source of nourishment (feeder of the flock) and
incarnate Word of God ("the Booke" that reveals God's wisdom
to a discerning reader). The countess's response to him, which
is both physical and spiritual, shows her to be such a reader: she
flushes, she feels her "heart...rise," and she cries out to him.
They are outdoors, in some rural spot where the shepherd "goes
his flock to feed," not standing in a church before the Communion table; and yet the presence of Christ is palpable. It is this
sort of "heavenly Manna"—the bread of human compassion and
humility—that Lanyer wishes to distribute through her own
sacerdotal action as the author of *Salve Deus Rex Judaeorum*.

The title of the poem, in fact, provides a hint as to how Lanyer understands the relationship between womanly priesthood as a visible sign of the church's ministry and male apostolic priesthood. In a self-conscious play upon the sign that Pilate placed over the head of Jesus on the cross, her poem hails the crucified Christ as God and king of the Jews even though, as the 1599 Geneva Bible glosses Romans 10:19, "the Gospell was translated from [the Jews] to the Gentiles, because the Iewes neglected it," failing to recognize Jesus as their divine Messiah. "The hie Priests of the Iewes" object to Pilate's inscription, saying, "Write not, The King of the Iewes, but that he said, I am King of the Iewes" (John 19:21). But Jesus is still to be called "Rex Judaeorum," for the unbelief of Israel did not (as Paul stresses throughout Romans 10 and 11) invalidate God's covenant with the Jews: "all Israel shalbe saued, as it is written, The deliuerer shal come out of Sion, and shal turne away the vngodlines from Iacob" (Rom. 11:26; quoting Isa. 59:20). But their initial failure to acknowledge the Messiah has opened up the promise of salvation for the Gentiles, who, Paul says, "haue now obteined mercie through [the Jews'] vnbelefe" (Rom. 11:30). In Lanyer's work, women are to men as the Gentiles are to the Jews in Paul's epistle; the initial failure of the male apostles to fulfill their priestly function opens up the priesthood to women.[53] Yet, just as God's covenant with Israel is not ended and was not made in vain, so Christ's calling of the male apostles is neither invalidated nor canceled by the faithlessness and cowardice of those he called. On the contrary, some men (apostles like Peter and Andrew; John the Baptist, whom Lanyer ranks with Peter as one of the "Princes of th'Apostles" (SDRJ, 1801); and deacons like Stephen and Laurence) go on to live that vocation fully by becoming martyrs.[54] "Deckt in those colours which our Saviour chose; / The purest colours both of White and Red" (SDRJ, 1827–28), they are at last duly vested in the sacerdotal garments of Christ, who was himself both priest and sacrificial victim. They can, like Herbert's priestly speaker in the final line of "Aaron," stand up before the congregation and say, "Come people; Aaron's drest" (25).

Lanyer acknowledges the priestly precedent set by the male martyrs when, in the penultimate stanza of *Salve Deus Rex Judaeorum*, she turns from her account of them to address the Countess of Cumberland one last time: "Loe Madame, heere you take a view of those, / Whose worthy steps you doe desire to tread" (1825–26). Does the poet thus imply, as Su Fang Ng argues ("Aemilia Lanyer," 439), that "the standard for virtuous behavior is still man"? And has she thus "finally caved in to the pressures of patriarchy"?[55] Such a conclusion gives too little credit to the subtlety of Lanyer's thinking and to the ambiguity of her language. The martyrs predate Margaret Clifford, and thus she may be said to follow in their "worthy steps." But Lanyer stresses that the sweetness the male martyrs could taste only through death is amply poured out in this life upon the soul of woman, since it is she who remains faithful throughout the trials that life affords (compare Richey, *Politics of Revelation*, 82). And she need not be crucified or beheaded in order to wear the Christ-like vestments in which their bloody deaths clothe them, for she is a woman, and female experience as Lanyer represents it is in itself a martyrdom. Women, Lanyer stresses, are everywhere persecuted by the same "evill disposed men" who "dishonoured Christ his Apostles and Prophets, putting them to shamefull deaths" ("To the Vertuous Reader," 19, 25–26). The stanza in which Lanyer directs her patroness' gaze toward the male martyrs must be read in its entirety:

> Loe Madame, heere you take a view of those,
> Whose worthy steps you doe desire to tread,
> Deckt in those colours which our Saviour chose;
> The purest colours both of White and Red,
> Their freshest beauties would I faine disclose,
> By which our Saviour most was honoured:
>   But my weake Muse desireth now to rest,
>   Folding up all their Beauties in your breast.
>
>   (*SDRJ*, 1825–32)

The modifying phrase "Deckt in those colours" is here ambiguous; it may refer to "those" martyrs whom the countess emulates or to the countess herself, for Lanyer has made clear that her patroness, too, is "Deckt" in the colors of the Passion. Lanyer's role as the male martyrs' encomiast is, moreover, rendered superfluous by the countess's living example. All that they did and all that Lanyer could say—if her muse were not too weary to continue—is "Fold[ed] up" in the "breast" of Margaret Clifford.[56]

Thus, whatever the traditional claims for the establishment of the Christian priesthood at the Last Supper, Lanyer rethinks the apostolic succession; having abandoned and denied the Lord who ordained them, Jesus' male followers can share in the feminine communion that is the church as Lanyer envisions her, and wear her priestly garments only by vesting themselves in the colors of martyrdom. In *Salve Deus Rex Judaeorum*, man is not without hope, and the apostolic priesthood is not revoked; each man who feels himself called to ecclesiastical ministry may take up his cross and follow Jesus. But woman is Ecclesia incarnate, the gentle woman who heals the wounds in Jesus' body, feeds his flock, and proclaims his Word; she is the bride most faithful to her divine spouse.

5. Sacred Eros in *Salve Deus*

As living types of Christ's bride, virtuous women are—in Lanyer's view—incarnations of grace at work in the world. Their bodies, no less than their souls, are thus, like the Blessed Virgin, "full of grace." In Lanyer's poetry, the mother of Jesus is still alone of all her sex in that only she retains her virginity in becoming a mother and carries the Redeemer in her womb; but her relationship with the deity nevertheless transforms female sexuality in a way that has implications for all women. Before Mary, the sexual desire a woman experiences—at least insofar as it has a male object—implies her subjugation to the object of her desire; God punishes Eve by condemning her to painful childbearing, declaring that "thy desire shal be subiect to thine housband, and he shal rule ouer thee" (Gen. 3:16). The verse specifically says that the woman's "desire" (rather than her will or her understanding) "shal be subiect to [her] husband"; and though "desire" might be taken in a very general sense to mean "appetite" of any sort, the sexual connotations are inescapable in a Christian culture that strongly associates virtue—and particularly female virtue—with the containment or subjugation of sexual desire (compare Warner, *Alone of All Her Sex*, 57–63). Once Eve's desire is made "subiect to" Adam, however, she is—in her entirety—his subject, for "he shall rule ouer" her. As noted above, Lanyer argues through the voice of Pilate's wife that this patriarchal regime comes to an end when Pilate, condemning Jesus, commits a sin more heinous than Eve's; but in the poet's view, the idea that a woman's desire must be subject to her husband has already been exploded 33 years and nine months earlier by Mary, the second Eve. For the Virgin's "chaste desire" (*SDRJ*, 1079) is directed not toward her human fiancé, Joseph, but toward a divine Beloved who liberates rather than masters her. Her desire as Lanyer portrays it is not merely spiritual or emotional or intellectual (though it is all those); it is also a physically fertile eros that bears fruit in the flesh, bringing to birth the man/God who is not only the truest lover of every human soul, but, more specifically, the ultimate and most perfect object of *woman's* desire.

Lanyer privileges the relationship between the deity and souls housed in female bodies. Her point of departure in depicting the relationship between God and woman is the same scriptural language of heterosexual love and marriage upon which Donne draws. But the poetry that emerges from Lanyer's response to that language differs radically from Donne's divine poetry, in which the flesh is usually at odds with the spirit, the male body consumed with longing for human love lost, while the feminine soul struggles to surrender herself to God.[57] Lanyer does not entirely abandon such dichotomies. Her male martyrs' eagerness to die for love of Christ momentarily inspires her to generalize in the first-person plural about the bothersome weight of the flesh: Jesus' "Sweetnesse...makes our flesh a burthen to us, / Knowing it serves but onely to undoe us" (*SDRJ*, 1743–44). But it is no accident that Lanyer links this dualistic commonplace directly to images of dying males. Throughout *Salve Deus*, Lanyer implies that a woman's desiring Christian soul can be, and often is, in perfect harmony with her desiring body, and that union with Christ is the ultimate fulfillment of a woman's sexual longings. Woman as Lanyer portrays her needs no sonnet conceit—as Donne does in his "What yf this present were the worlds last night"—to see the "picture of Christ crucifyde" as a "bewteous forme" (*HSWhat*, 1, 3, 14). Nor is her relationship with him predicated, as Donne's is in "Batter my hart," upon being "enthrall[ed]" and "rauishe[d]"; for woman's God has already set her "free" and her desire for him is already "chast" (*HSBatter*, 13, 14).

Indeed, a woman's sexual desire as Lanyer defines it is not merely a metaphor for her spiritual aspiration; it is that desire directed toward its best object. As Michael Schoenfeldt puts it, Lanyer's Christ "functions…not as the negation but rather as the consummation of female heterosexual desire" ("Gender of Religious Devotion," 215).[58] Men, too, can experience this divinely oriented eros; the homoerotic ecstasy of mingled pain and pleasure in Lanyer's portrayal of the male martyrs makes bodily death the physical consummation of their spiritual longing for the "sweetness" of Christ. But Lanyer clearly sees these holy men as exceptions who prove the rule; they achieve sanctity only insofar as their bodily sufferings rid them of their male flesh, uniting them with the bridegroom through an experience of persecution and humiliation that mirrors the daily martyrdom of unjust subjugation endured by souls housed in female bodies.

Lanyer's work thus portrays Christ as the ultimate object of female desire. In the prefatory poem "To the Ladie *Susan*," she invites the Dowager Countess of Kent to welcome Christ not just as the Savior who died because he loved her, but also as the object of her own desiring gaze: "Receive your Love whom you have sought so farre, / Which heere presents himselfe within your view; /...Take this faire Bridegroome in your soules pure bed" ("To the Ladie *Susan*," 37–38, 42). And though erotic language is a commonplace of Christian spirituality, Lanyer pushes the boundaries of decorum. In her poem to Lucy, Countess of Bedford, feminine Virtue is the go-between who arranges a tryst between Christ and the countess's soul:

> Me thinkes I see faire Virtue readie stand,
> T'unlocke the closet of your lovely breast,
> Holding the key of Knowledge in her hand,
> Key of that Cabbine where your selfe doth rest,
> To let him in, by whom her youth was blest
>   The true-love of your soule, your hearts delight,
>   Fairer than all the world in your cleare sight.
>   ("To the Ladie *Lucie*," 1–7)[59]

Because Lucy, who was John Donne's principal patroness, was known for her learning, her "Virtue" is here described as "Holding the key of Knowledge"; and the well-read countess could not fail to miss an allusion encoded in Lanyer's prosody. Redirecting secular eroticism, Lanyer composes her poem to Lucy in rhyme royal, the verse form of Chaucer's *Troilus*. As a Christian Criseyde, Lucy is not carnal and faithless, but chaste and constant; she needs no Pandarus, no ordained male mediator, for her own "Virtue" is her priest.[60] She opens her chamber to a sacred lover even more faithful than Troilus, the truest of mortal paramours; but he is, nonetheless, a "true-love" and "lovely guest" (23) rather than a bridegroom. The countess's "lovely breast" is not merely the "Cabbine" of her own soul, but a chamber in which she—like Venus caressing the mortally wounded Adonis—may "entertaine" this "dying lover" ("To the Ladie *Lucie*," 2, 4, 16). His death is, moreover, the end result of his having taken an interest in humanity as a sinful text; thus, like many a literary lover (from Paolo and Francesca to Don Quixote), his reading of a morally questionable book motivates him to act in ways that lead to suffering for love's sake: his "heavenly wisdom read the earthly storie / Of fraile Humanity, which his godhead borrows," Lanyer explains, and in the "most pretious wounds" of his pierced body, Lucy's "soule may," in turn, "reade / Salvation" ("To the Ladie *Lucie*," 10–11, 13–14).

The countess's relationship with Christ is spiritual and intellectual, but the *locus* of that love is her "lovely breast." Perhaps Lanyer had in mind the anatomically correct female breastplate that Lucy wore when she appeared as the Amazon Penthisilea in the Christmas 1608 *Masque of Queens*, or the masque costume that the countess is modeling in John De Critz's portrait of her: an extremely low-cut gown with a wide open collar that reveals not only a great deal of cleavage, but an expanse of snow-white flesh extending from Lucy's ornate necklace to the point where her sleeves join the bodice.[61] The countess's "faire soule may sure and safely rest" in this anatomical locus, the poet explains, "When [Christ] is sweetly seated" there ("To the Ladie *Lucie*," 20–21). Indeed, Lucy's soul, these lines imply, is not fully at home in her own body until that body is a "bed of rest" for the Lord; it is he who makes it a "blessed bowre," adorning it with "Flowres of fresh comforts" and with "such rich beauties as may make it blest" (25, 24, 25, 26). Thus occupied, however, the countess's "brest"—her most obviously female body part—is the most sacred of dwelling places: "About this blessed Arke bright Angels hover" (19). The Litany of Loreto hails the Blessed Virgin as "Foederis arca," the "Ark of the Covenant" but Lanyer, assured that Nature and Grace were indeed united in the Virgin's womb, can joyfully bestow the same title upon the fair and very visible bosom of a contemporary lady.[62]

Near the beginning of *Salve Deus*, Lanyer again broaches the subject of the beautiful female body. This time, she does so negatively, in a passage (lines 185–248) identified by a marginal gloss as "*An Invective against outward beuty unaccompanied with virtue*"; but the point of this "invective" is not to condemn illicit sexual desire as something felt by outwardly lovely but inwardly corrupt women.[63] On the contrary, this section contributes to Lanyer's overall project of reclaiming eros for virtuous women by setting up an implicit contrast between women's grace-filled erotic desires and carnal lust of the sort men feel toward women in all the most famous tragic legends. In the stories Lanyer recounts, lust—*sinful* sexual desire—is something women experience as the objects of male concupiscence rather than as subjects who are themselves lustful. Thus, while the poet asserts that "That outward Beautie which the world commends, / Is not the subject I will write upon" (*SDRJ*, 185–86), she makes it clear that she rejects the female "Beautie" that is so often the focus of male-authored love poetry not only because it is ephemeral, falling victim to the masculine force of "tyrant Time," which "soone ends" it (187), but also because it is, by definition, an *object* rather than a *subject*. Defining physical beauty in Petrarchan language as "those matchlesse colours Red and White" (193), Lanyer insists that the object of the sonneteer's gaze—the "due proportion pleasing to the sight" (195)—is nothing but a target for male lust, "the White whereat [men] aime" (208). Lynette McGrath sums up eloquently Lanyer's subversive purpose in deploying traditional stories about fallen women:

> As they betrayed Christ's virtue, so men also seek to betray women's virtue.... Refuting the traditional argument which blames women's beauty for men's downfall..., Lanyer's poem chastises men for the fall of beautiful women. While men, contemplating women's beauty, formulate for themselves the limited, non-reciprocal goal of sexually possessing women's bodies, women, contemplating Christ, their true lover, are inspired by his beauty to a reciprocated desire for spiritual union with him. (*Subjectivity*, 218–19)

Throughout her "*Invective against outward beuty*," Lanyer condemns not women who act upon their sexual desire for men, but the beauty that makes women, whether chaste or unchaste, the objects and victims of corrupt masculine desire:

> Twas Beautie bred in *Troy* the ten yeares strife,
> And carried *Hellen* from her lawfull Lord;

> Twas Beautie made chaste *Lucrece* loose her life,
> For which prowd *Tarquins* fact was so abhorr'd.
>
> (*SDRJ*, 209–12)

Helen of Troy and Lucrece, two characters known in Lanyer's time partly through Shakespeare's portrayals of them as venal courtesan and chaste matron, have nothing in common except the fact that both were possessed of beauty that "bred" men's lust and aggression.[64] In these lines, Helen *does* nothing, but is passively "carried" away from legal subjugation into the tumult of war; and Lucrece's active choice of suicide as an alternative to ignominy is swallowed up in language that portrays "Beautie" as the malevolent force that "made" the heroine "loose her life." Considering the case of another Shakespearian beauty, Cleopatra, Lanyer again condemns not the woman's lustful desire, but female beauty as the object of illicit and violent male desire:

> Beautie the cause *Antonius* wrong'd his wife,
> Which could not be decided but by sword:
>> Great *Cleopatraes* Beautie and defects
>> Did worke *Octaviaes* wrongs, and his neglects.
>
> What fruit did yeeld that faire forbidden tree,
> But blood, dishonour, infamie, and shame?   (*SDRJ*, 213–18)

These lines do allude to some fault in Cleopatra, to her "defects" as well as her beauty, but they define the Egyptian queen as passive rather than active, as an imperfect object of desire rather than as a sinfully desiring subject.

Indeed, the idea of Cleopatra as a "faire forbidden tree" foreshadows the language of Pilate's wife later in the title poem, when she describes the original sin of Adam as an act arising from desire for a beautiful object: "The fruit beeing faire perswaded him to fall: / ...If he would eate it, who had powre to stay him?" (*SDRJ*, 798, 800).[65] In making this assertion, Lanyer hints at sexual duress: a woman is powerless to "stay" a man once he is intent upon satisfying the lust of his eyes. In the passage on Cleopatra, then, the queen's status as a "faire forbidden tree" marks her as the target of a man's uncontrollable lust for desirable objects; and Lanyer's language resonates with pity even as she castigates Cleopatra for freely consenting to be such an object:

> Poore blinded Queene, could'st thou no better see,
> But entertaine disgrace, in stead of fame?
> Doe these designes with Majestie agree?
> To staine thy blood, and blot thy royall name.
>   That heart that gave consent unto this ill,
>   Did give consent that thou thy selfe should'st kill.
>
> (219–24)

Yielding to male appetite is here tantamount to suicide; the woman who consents to the "ill" of a man's illicit desire has consented to her own destruction.

In her accounts of Rosamund and Matilda, the poet further explores the folly of surrendering—for whatever motive—to the objectifying and victimizing force of male desire. Lanyer's contention that "Beautie betraid her thoughts, aloft to clime, / To build strong castles in uncertaine aire" (227–28) evokes Rosamund's ambition, which provoked her to yield to King Henry's lust. Lanyer's reference to overblown aspirations as "strong castles" built "in uncertaine aire" is no mere cliché, for the proverbial phrasing recalls a key feature of Rosamond's story: the palace her lover built to hide her from his wife. As Lanyer sees it, the woman whose ambitions are constructed upon a foundation of masculine lust will find in her "strong castles" no real refuge; having enclosed herself within the role of desired beauty, she will inevitably be destroyed, for beauty itself is a traitor within the walls.[66]

Lanyer knew quite well from her own experience as the cast-off mistress of Lord Hunsdon that even a mutually satisfactory extramarital arrangement between a woman and a man who "hath Loved her well & kept her and did maintain her longe" might well lead, ultimately, to her disappointment and disempowerment.[67] But even this knowledge, interestingly enough, did not keep her from further indulging her own sexual desires when, 14 years before the publication of *Salve Deus*, Lanyer went to consult the astrologer and magician Simon Forman. In his diary, Forman portrays Aemilia as possessed of an appetite for heterosexual delights not wholly suppressed by her personal history. She has, he reports, pleasurable memories of life as the deceased Lord Hunsdon's mistress and mentions her previous life as his "pa[ra]mour" repeatedly. And when the astrologer himself makes sexual advances toward her, she agrees — according to his account in another of his notebooks — to an adulterous dalliance with him, though she carefully restricts it to activities that will not endanger or disempower her. According to his notes, Forman sent a messenger to Aemilia in September 1597 to inquire whether he might visit her, and she sent word back by the same servant "that if his mr came he should be welcom. & he wente and supped wth her and staid all night. and she was familiar & friendlie to him in all thinges. But only she wold not halek. Yet he tolde all parts of her body wilingly. & kyssed her often but she wold not doe in any wise." Lanyer's handling of her tryst with Forman as he recounts it here seems calculated to ensure her own pleasure while short-circuiting the force of male lust, so tellingly rejected in her poetry as victimizing the women that are its objects. By refusing to "halek" — Forman's idiosyncratic euphemism for the act of vaginal intercourse — Lanyer avoids becoming just another sexual conquest, underscores her prerogative to choose what she will and will not do, and avoids pregnancy, which had once already been the occasion of her disempowerment in that it necessitated her transition from a pleasurable life, unbound by any vow of obedient submission, as a nobleman's beloved "pa[ra]mour," to a state of deprivation and discontent as the unappreciated wife of a "minstrell."

Forman's account of his night with Lanyer may or may not be reliable,[68] but it does help to explain the approach Lanyer takes, even in an overtly religious poem addressed to an unexceptionally chaste widow, to the subject of predatory male lust. According to Lanyer's accounts of various chaste and unchaste female victims, such lust is problematic not because it taints a woman with impurity, but because it subjugates her and robs her of agency, reputation, and everything else worth having. Knowing this truth, Rosamund's wiser counterpart, Matilda, rejects not only a powerful man's lust, but all that it threatens and promises: her "noble minde did scorne the base *subjection* / Of Feares, or Favours, to impaire her Name" (243–44; emphasis added). Retaining her status as an active subject, she can joyfully pursue her own desire for "Honour" and salvation, "drink[ing] that poyson with a cheerefull heart, / That could all Heavenly grace to her impart" (246, 247–48).

Turning to Margaret Clifford, Lanyer asserts that the same grace Matilda found in death "possesse[s]" the countess's soul (*SDRJ*, 249); addressing Margaret directly, she testifies to her belief that "This Grace doth all imperfect Thoughts controule, / Directing thee to serve thy God aright; / Still reckoning him, the Husband of thy Soule" (251–53). These lines imply that the choice of God as spouse is an alternative to unchaste desires, modestly referred to as "imperfect Thoughts." But the prevailing characteristic of the countess is not chastity or celibacy per se, but agency, active choice. Whereas the human male's gaze is drawn to the passive physical beauty of woman as the object that it both desires and destroys, the divine male is attracted to the countess's beautiful soul, which is active—selecting its own objects—rather than passive: "most pretious in his glorious sight: / Because the Worlds delights shee doth denie / For him" (254–56). And the relationship between the countess's soul and her divine lover makes not her, but him, a victim, for it is he "who for her sake vouchsaf'd to die" (256).

Christ is thus to be preferred over human males not so much for the *prima facie* reason that he is divine while they are mere mortals, or because spiritual desire is superior to physical desire, but because God incarnate in the male body of Jesus is the best lover, the best object of female desire: spiritual, emotional, and erotic. He is both "The true-love of youre soule," Lanyer tells the Countess of Bedford, and "your hearts delight" ("To the Ladie *Lucie*," 6). "Loe here he coms," she continues, "all stucke with pale deaths arrows" (12). Lanyer's image eroticizes the Crucifixion by eliding Christ's piercing on the cross with the martyrdom of Saint Sebastian, often sensuously portrayed in Renaissance painting, and the result is an erotic appeal that reaches beyond any conventional allusion to the Song of Songs: "Vouchsafe to entertain this dying lover, / The Ocean of true grace, whose streames doe fill / All those with Joy, that can his love recover" (16–18). These passionate lines urge the addressee to direct all her erotic desire toward a God incarnate in flesh that is gloriously, specifically male, a God whose freely flowing blood is the ultimate ejaculation.

Wendy Wall argues, in light of Leo Steinberg's study of the sexuality of Christ in Renaissance art, that "Lanyer's portrayal of Christ as a lover and her focus on his body's 'rare' and eroticized parts" ought not to be considered sacrilegious, since it proceeds from a "mainstream theology concerned to show that Christ was fully human" and that he was "exempt from genital shame and could master his own (evident) sexual desire" (*Imprint of Gender*, 328, 327–28 n. 65). But the concerns of mainstream theology are not Lanyer's concerns; she eroticizes Christ's body not in order to confirm his humanity and his heroic continence but to emphasize the perfect continuity between heterosexual women's sublimated desires (including the "spiritual and textual desire" Wall herself stresses [329]) and their sexual desire for the consummate male lover. Her lines on the Countess of Cumberland's encounter with the "good old man" through whom Christ "appeares to [her] in Shepheards weed" are a subtle but significant example of this continuity: when she sees the man, Margaret Clifford's "colour changes, and [her] heart [does] rise" (*SDRJ*, 1347, 1345, 1348). Her response is corporal as well as emotional and spiritual. It is described in terms that evoke a first, exciting glimpse of a lover-to-be, rather than the familiar embrace of a spouse.

The infinitely desirable body of Christ was itself conceived, Lanyer's poem asserts, through the encounter between a woman filled with desire and the masculine God who smiled upon that longing. For the Virgin as Lanyer describes her is no passive receptacle; her chastity is not defined solely in negative terms as sexual abstinence. On the contrary, Lanyer insists that Mary's holiness is manifested in an active longing for the God who becomes the father of her child. The poet calls Mary's question to Gabriel "this thy chaste desire" (*SDRJ*, 1079), realigning the emphasis of Luke's account, in which Mary's acquiescence is paramount, to include a stronger sense of Mary as the subject as well as the object of desire. In fact, as Lanyer portrays her, Mary is "Above all other women highly blest" (1094) not only because she is favored by God, but also because she is beloved by the object of her *own* desire: she "find[s] such favour in his glorious sight, / In whom [her] heart and soule doe most delight" (1095–96).

The Blessed Virgin of *Salve Deus* even *initiates* the exchange that leads to her impregnation by the Holy Spirit:

> Thy lowly mind, and unstain'd Chastitie
> Did pleade for Love at great *Jehovaes* gate,
> Who sending swift-wing'd *Gabriel* unto thee,
> His holy will and pleasure to relate;
> > To thee most beauteous Queene of Woman-kind,
> > The Angell did unfold his Makers mind.
> > > (*SDRJ*, 1035–40)

In this passage, the piety of the Blessed Virgin is eroticized as a "plead[ing] for Love," an expression not only of her willingness to be the object of divine favor, but also of her status as the "active [subject] of [her] own religious experience" (McGrath, "Metaphoric Subversions," 109).[69] It is Mary's "mind," "lowly" though it is, that prompts Jehovah to "unfold" his own "mind" through Gabriel's message; and it is Mary's "unstain'd Chastitie"—potentially obedient but not at all silent—that clamors at God's "gate" and prompts him to convey to her "His holy will and pleasure" (*SDRJ*, 1035, 1040, 1035–36). Lanyer thus blurs the usual emphasis on the precedence and prerogative of the masculine divinity, refusing to accept the idea that the feminine soul's desire for God must remain studiously receptive and contingent. By comparison, Saint Bernard of Clairvaux, whose sermons on the *Song of Songs* are an ardent celebration of the bride's desire, sounds positively Protestant, for Bernard cautiously tells the monks to whom he preaches that "it is important for every soul...who is seeking God to realize that He was first in the field, and was seeking you, or ever you began to search for Him. For, if you do not acknowledge this, the great good may become the greatest evil" (*Saint Bernard on the Song of Songs*, 261).

Bernard's cautionary words proceed from his firm belief that feminine desire—including even the wholly spiritual desire of the soul for God—must always position itself as reactive rather than active, as passively responsive rather than generative. But such caution is misplaced, Lanyer believes, for God not only responds positively to Mary's clamoring at his gate (an image the poet borrows from Jesus' parable of the unjust judge [Luke 18:1–8]), thus defining her desire as something to which *he* must respond; God also defers to her choice, defining her consent to his will as something *not* automatically or legally due to him as her divine ruler. And Mary as Lanyer portrays her takes full advantage of that deference. Emphasizing the humble yet dignified way that Mary makes so bold as to "demand" that the angel answer her question (*SDRJ*, 1074) before she consents to God's will, the poet sets the Blessed Virgin up as a model of feminine circumspection, wisely cautious and modestly, effortlessly self-empowered in her dealings with the masculine deity who seeks her cooperation in the work of redemption.

In the scriptural account of the Annunciation, the angel's announcement of God's plan prompts a puzzled request for clarification: "How shal this be, seing, I know no man?" (Luke 1:34). For Lanyer, this verse makes clear that Mary's response to God's will, though humble and ultimately compliant, is not unquestioning:

> When on the knees of thy submissive heart
> Thou humbly didst demand, How that should be?
> Thy virgin thoughts did thinke, none could impart

This great good hap, and blessing unto thee;
Farre from desire of any man thou art,
Knowing not one, thou art from all men free:
    When he, to answere this thy chaste desire,
    Gives thee more cause to wonder and admire.

                                        (*SDRJ*, 1073–80)

Mary's "virgin thoughts" in this stanza are not naively confused;
rather, they are wise and lead her to "demand" clarification, thus
ensuring that nothing she agrees to will involve her subjugation.
Since Genesis 3:16 declares Eve's "desire...subject to" her husband, a woman who is "Farre from desire of any man"—feels no
desire *for* a man—is likewise set apart from any subjugation to
man. But the phrase "Farre from desire of any man" is ambiguous; it means not only that Mary does not want a human mate,
but also that she has removed herself from being the target of
men's desires (and thus has avoided being victimized in the way
that Rosamond will be). Since a woman cannot normally be
impregnated without being physically penetrated by a man, and
since Genesis 3:16 links heterosexual intercourse so firmly to
female subjugation, Lanyer's Mary wishes to be assured, before
she consents to bear a child, that such consent will not be construed as surrendering the freedom that she has guarded as carefully as her virginity itself. Her question is thus an expression
of "desire" for ongoing freedom that must be "answere[d]," and
God's response validates that desire (see also Schoenfeldt, "Gender of Religious Devotion," 217).

As Lanyer sees it, Mary's choice of the Almighty as the one
"In whom [her] heart and soule doe most delight" confirms her
freedom as a female human being enslaved neither to sin nor to
the will of her husband, nor even to the will of God, but rather
exalted by his "favour" (*SDRJ*, 1096, 1095). Of course, Mary's
own language in the Magnificat stresses her "poore degree" or
"base estate" (as the 1599 Geneva Bible renders and glosses
Luke 1:48). Lanyer paraphrases and then quotes directly from
this verse when she says that God "looked downe upon [Mary's]
meane estate" and "poore degree" (*SDRJ*, 1034, 1086). For the

poet is obliged to acknowledge the Virgin's submissive response to the Annunciation: "Beholde, the seruant of the Lord: be it vnto me according to thy worde" (Luke 1:38). But for Lanyer, the Virgin's becoming "Servant, Mother, Wife, and Nurse / To Heavens bright King" transforms those lowly female roles, making them royal appellations (*SDRJ,* 1087–88). The poet implies, moreover, that Mary's exaltation, far from making her an anomaly, exalts all women; thus, as if to replace with a more gynocentric title the eight royal designations the Litany of Loreto assigns Mary (Queen of Angels, of Patriarchs, of Prophets, of Apostles, of Martyrs, of Confessors, of Virgins; Queen of all Saints), Lanyer crowns the Blessed Virgin as the ruler and paragon of the sex she represents, calling her the "most beauteous Queene of Woman-kind" (1039).

Insofar as she is no less queen than handmaid, Mary's consent to be the mother of God's Son is not just acquiescence; it is ratification. Lanyer addresses her as a sovereign monarch affixing her seal to the Divine Word she loves and placing it carefully in the same cabinet that houses her peerless virtue: "Thus beeing crown'd with glory from above, / Grace and Perfection resting in thy breast, / Thy humble answer doth approove thy Love, / And all these sayings in thy heart doe rest" (1089–92). In line 1091, both "approove" and "Love" are richly ambiguous. On the one hand, Mary "confirm[s] authoritatively" or "sanction[s]" (*OED,* "approve," v.[1], def. 5) the intentions of the God who is her wooer and her "Love" in the sense of "beloved person" ("love," n.[1], def. 9a). In doing so, she also "pronounce[s]" him "to be good, commend[s]" him ("approve," v.[1], def. 6) and "experiences" him ("approve," v.[1], def. 9) *as* her "Love." At the same time, she "show[s] to be true, prove[s], demonstrate[s]" ("approve," v.[1], def. 1) the "Love" that she herself feels toward God, including love in the sense of "devotion" both religious and affectionate, and of "attachment" or "Amor" ["love," n.[1], defs. 2, 3, 4, 5a]). Through her consent, she also "approves" (that is, "demonstrate[s] practically, ... display[s], exhibit[s]" ["approve," v.[1], def. 3]) the depth of the love that motivates her and abides with her throughout her experience as the mother of the Word made flesh. Finally, Lanyer applies to the scene of the Annunciation Luke's assertion that when Mary heard the testimony of the shepherds sent by an angel to see her baby in the manger, she "kept all those sayings, & pondered them in her heart" (2:19). Lanyer's line "all these sayings in thy heart doe rest" (*SDRJ*, 1092) recalls both that moment and the rest of Luke's second chapter, in which old Simeon and Anna testify to the infant's messianic status, and the child Jesus himself tells Mary that he is doing his Father's business in the temple; she again, Luke says, "kept all these sayings in her heart" (Luke 2:51). In Lanyer's version of the Annunciation, Mary similarly makes her heart a resting place for the words of Gabriel, with the implication that she is an active listener, an auditor whose perfect reception of the angel's words fulfills their promise, and grants substance to their divine author's poetic intention. Only Milton will take one step further Luke's image of the "sayings" the Blessed Virgin keeps in her heart, for he will treat the Mary of *Paradise Regained* as a poet in her own right, assigning her a lengthy soliloquy in which she opens her sacred word-hoard, reflects on her experiences, and speaks in metaphorical language, saying, "My heart hath been a storehouse long of things / And sayings laid up" (*PR* 2:103–04).

Lanyer's Mary, while she speaks only the few words attributed to her in the Gospel of Luke, is nonetheless a powerful agent in the work of redemption. The high prerogative God grants to Mary in response to her active choice acknowledges her approval of his love not merely as spiritually fruitful, but also as an assisting efficient cause of the Incarnation (thus answering, in a sense, Donne's portrayal of Eve's sin in giving her husband the fruit as an assisting efficient cause of Adam's fall). And whereas Eve's punishment for her act was to be subjected to her mate, Mary is "crown'd with glory from above" (*SDRJ*, 1089) by her heavenly spouse and thus elevated rather than assigned to a subservient role. Lanyer even goes so far as to reverse the Virgin's own statement that her "soule magnifieth the Lord" (Luke 1:46), saying that "the Almightie magnified" Mary (*SDRJ*, 1033).

The liberated and proactive eros modeled perfectly by the Blessed Virgin is not just a good thing; it is the definitive characteristic of female virtue as Lanyer understands it. She is largely dismissive of the Old Testament heroine Susanna precisely because she deems the Hebrew matron's chastity too reactive and timorous.[70] Lanyer's widowed patroness, Margaret Clifford, models a contrasting kind of chastity, for her "chaste breast" is "guarded with strength of mind" that "prevents"—anticipates and wards off—any indecent proposals from "idle Lovers.../ Whose base abuses worthy minds prevents" (1545, 1552, 1551–52). The countess "Subdu[es] all affections that are base," conquering them actively rather than refraining from action due to "feare of Death" or disgust for "loathsome age" (1558, 1561, 1563), which Lanyer takes to be Susanna's reasons for rejecting the wicked elders.

But Margaret Clifford is characterized by active eros as well as by militant chastity. Like a heroine of a pastoral romance, she abandons life at court to seek her "love in lowly shepheards weed" (1714), knowing that Christ is, like so many pastoral characters, a royal personage in a humble disguise. Though by right he "weares th'imperiall crowne of heaven and earth" (1615), "Yet came he not in pompe or royaltie, / But in an humble habit, base dejected; / A King, a God, clad in mortalitie, /.../ A seeming Trades-mans sonne" (1706–08, 1715). And as Lanyer reminds Margaret Clifford's daughter, Anne, the God who thus became incarnate as a poor man cares nothing for earthly bloodlines or titles: he elevates to royal status all those "Whose virtuous deeds by his especially grace / Have gain'd his love, his kingdome, and his crowne" ("To the Ladie *Anne*," 22–23). It is not because she is the daughter of a lord and lady, then, but because she lives up to her noble title by practicing virtue that Anne is a fitting reader for a poem that presents to her Christ's "lovely love" (114). Given the tradition of the soul as feminine, of course, the poet could have used such language to present Christ to anyone, male or female. But Lanyer's final stanza to Anne Clifford specifically defines Christ's perfections in terms

of his attractiveness to *women:* "And if deserts a Ladies love
may gaine, / Then tell me who hath more deserv'd than he?"
(137–38).

The idea that Christ's perfections make him a particularly
perfect mate for the soul of the heterosexual woman is most provocatively advanced in Lanyer's prefatory poem "To the Ladie
Katherine Countesse of Suffolke," which declares Jesus the
embodiment of "all that Ladies can desire." Lanyer informs the
countess that, in *Salve Deus,* she "present[s] to [her] the King of
kings" and invites her to "take a perfit view" of the Savior who
wrote "the Covenant with his pretious blood, / That [her] faire
soule might bathe her in that flood" ("To the Ladie *Katherine*,"
85, 42, 43, 47–48). In the lines that follow, she recommends her
book as ideal reading for the countess's daughters, several of
whom had been married off at very tender ages in notoriously
politicized arranged marriages, and several of whom were as yet
unbetrothed:

> And let your noble daughters likewise reade
> This little Booke that I present to you;
> On heavenly food let them vouchsafe to feede;
> Heere they may see a Lover much more true
> > Than ever was since first the world began,
> > This poore rich King that di'd both God and man.
>
> Yea, let those Ladies which do represent
> All beauty, wisedome, zeale, and love,
> Receive this jewell from *Jehova* sent,
> This spotlesse Lambe, this perfit, patient Dove:
> > Of whom faire *Gabriel,* Gods bright *Mercury,*
> > Brought downe a message from the Deitie.
> > > ("To the Ladie *Katherine*," 49–60)

The daughters, the lines on Gabriel's embassage imply, ought to
take the Virgin Mother of Jesus as their model, receiving "the
Deitie" himself as the truest of lovers.

"Here may they see him," she continues, "in a flood of teares, /
Crowned with thornes, and bathing in his blood" ("To the Ladie
Katherine," 61–62); Christ, as a "Lover much more true" than

any Petrarch weeping for his Laura (52), will not just claim to be slain by love, but will *really* die for them, and in death his body will prove more beautiful than any lady blazoned in sonnets:

> No Dove, no Swan, nor Iv'rie could compare
> With this faire corps, when 'twas by death embrac'd;
> No rose, nor no vermillion halfe so faire
> As was that pretious blood that interlac'd
> His body, which bright Angels did attend,
> Waiting on him that must to Heaven ascend.
>
> ("To the Ladie *Katherine*," 79–84)

Next, in what appears to be a sacred parody of Ben Jonson's "Her Man Described by Her Own Dictamen" — one of the poems in *A Celebration of Charis in Ten Lyric Pieces*[71] — Lanyer lists the qualities women long for in a man and insists that Christ has them all. Jesus is he

> In whom is all that Ladies can desire;
> If Beauty, who hath bin more faire than he?
> If Wisedome, doth not all the world admire
> The depth of his, that cannot searched be?
> If wealth, if honour, fame, or Kingdoms store,
> Who ever liv'd that was possest of more?
>
> ("To the Ladie *Katherine*," 85–90)

Jesus meets or exceeds all the rather venal requirements of Jonson's Charis, who wants a man "Noble; or of greater blood," fashionable, with French manners, "Young...and fair" (possessing a whole catalog of specific physical beauties). In particular, Christ's deep Wisdom is of a "depth" more profound than any Charis imagines when she says she would fancy a man with "Venus and Minerva's eyes, / For he must look wanton-wise."[72]

To her credit (or Jonson's), Charis does go on to list a number of moral virtues that she would also seek in her man: he must be "Valiant" but not wrathful, "Bounteous as the clouds to earth, / And as honest as his birth," one who will "Nor do wrongs, nor wrongs receive."[73] Lanyer's Christ, for his part, possesses every godly virtue, including not only the masculine ones listed by Charis, but those considered requisite for women:

If zeale, if grace, if love, if pietie,
If constancie, if faith, if faire obedience,
If valour, patience, or sobrietie;
If chast behaviour, meekenesse, continence,
If justice, mercie, bountie, charitie,
Who can compare with his Divinitie?"
("To the Ladie *Katherine*," 91–96)

Jesus is—simply put—God's gift to women.

6. Envisioning Heterosexual Alternatives to Pauline Marriage

In her study of *Salve Deus* as a radical gospel, Achsah Guibbory argues that Aemilia Lanyer advocates a subversive Christianity in which rejecting marriage in favor of a passionate desire for Christ is a woman's only workable alternative to subjugation ("Gospel According to Aemilia," 202–04). Lanyer rejects marriage because her society's understanding of that "ordinance"—as it was called by English Protestants—was based upon Ephesians 5:

> Wiues, submit your selues vnto your housbands, as vnto the Lord. For the housband is the wiues head, euen as Christ is the head of the Church.... Therefore as the Church is in subiection to Christ, euen so let the wiues be to their housbands in euerie thing. Housbands, loue your wiues, euen as Christ loued the Church, & gaue him self for it.... So oght men to loue their wiues, as their owne bodies: he that loueth his wife, loueth him self. For no man euer yet hated his owne flesh, but nourisheth & cherisheth it, euen as the Lord doeth the Church. (Eph. 5:22–23, 24–25, 28–29)[74]

As Lanyer makes clear in the course of narrating Christ's Passion, she judges the teaching advanced in this passage to be faulty on several levels: it takes Genesis 3:16 as its premise; it relies upon the ability of mortal men to imitate Christ successfully; and its final analogy assumes the masculinity of the human subject that cherishes its own feminine flesh as an inferior though beloved possession. She cannot endorse these premises, given her strong belief that the sentence of Genesis 3:16 has been nullified by

Pilate's crime in condemning Jesus, that human females more
closely resemble Christ than human males do, and that the
female body is the feminine soul's equal partner—rather than
her beloved but definitively subordinate ward—in the work of
redemption.

All three of these beliefs are articulated, directly or indirectly,
in the episode of *Salve Deus* that tells of how Pilate's wife sought
to intervene in the Roman governor's judgment of Jesus. Her
subtly threatening plea—"Let not us Women glory in Mens fall, /
Who had power given to over-rule us all" (759–60)—concludes a
stanza; but in the next line, the reader realizes that the stanzas
are enjambed, that "Mens fall" is already a fait accompli, and
that the voice of Pilate's wife is also that of Lanyer, a Christian
woman who recognizes herself as liberated both spiritually and
politically by Christ's death: men "had power given to over-rule
us all. // Till now your indiscretion sets us free. / And makes our
former fault much lesse appeare" (760–62).[75] Since Eve's "sinne
was small" (818) compared to the crime of condemning Jesus,
men—both as rulers of church and society and as the so-called
lords of their wives—must recognize that their reign has come
to an end:

> Then let us have our Libertie againe,
> And challendge to your selves no Sov'raigntie;
> You came not in the world without our paine,
> Make that a barre against your crueltie;
> Your fault beeing greater, why should you disdaine
> Our beeing your equals, free from tyranny?   (825–30)

The fact that this speech is dramatically positioned as a wife's
speech to her husband resonates in crucial ways. Insofar as she
is challenging her husband's authority precisely because she
desires that he do something contrary to his imminent decision
to condemn Jesus, the speech itself is proof that Genesis 3:16
no longer holds force: woman's "desire" is longer "subiect to
[her] husband." Interpreting her message to Pilate as evidence
that she recognizes Christ as redeemer, moreover, Lanyer says

that Pilate's wife "sends...to beg her Saviours life" (752), demonstrating clearly that in this pagan marriage, as in so many Christian marriages (including the Countess of Cumberland's marriage to the worldly and unfaithful George Clifford), it is the wife, not the husband, who is more godly. The whole scene thus lends support to "Lanyer's generic representation of femininity as spiritually superior" (Mueller, "Feminist Poetics," 118) and undercuts the logic of Saint Paul's analogy between husbands and Christ.

But the poet's project extends beyond and below the realm of the spiritual; as Mueller notes, Lanyer seeks "to find and articulate transformative possibilities in gender relations" ("Feminist Poetics," 101). Though Pilate's wife says nothing about sexual desire specifically, her allusion to the pangs of childbirth—another of the punishments meted out by God to woman in Genesis 3—brings the female body and its sexual organs into the picture. The biological fact that giving birth involves pain is here represented not as a curse, but as evidence that man relies on woman and upon her willingness to suffer physically for his sake (since "if it were not by the means of women," Lanyer says in one of her prefatory pieces, "they would be quite extinguished out of the world, and a finall ende of them all" ("To the Vertuous Reader," 20–22). Woman's reproductive function is thus elided here with the function of Christ's sacrifice; he dies to save man's soul from hell, while woman endures something that hurts like hell to save him from extinction. Having thus reinterpreted woman's suffering in childbirth as a Christ-like sacrifice rather than as a punishment imposed upon her, Lanyer is prepared to argue that the other punishment imposed in Genesis 3:16 has been nullified and that a woman's sexual desire for a man no longer necessitates her subjection to him.

Pilate's wife, as Lanyer portrays her, desires justice. Lanyer herself "doth desire to doe / All services" to the Countess of Suffolk and to present her with "a perfit view" of Christ's suffering ("To the Ladie *Katherine*," 20, 43). She insists, moreover, that her poem is a "worke of Grace" sprung from the "desires" of the

Countess of Cumberland ("Cooke-ham," 12). Clearly, in seeking new ways to define and celebrate women's desire, Lanyer does not confine herself to the consideration of heterosexual longing. She is interested in "desire" in the broadest possible terms: as the defining characteristic of a human subject, and as that subject's movement toward a wide range of objects and aspirations.[76] But a significant aspect of this comprehensive interest is Lanyer's attempt to portray woman's desire for man as compatible with her desire for freedom and authority as well as with her Christian virtue. Lanyer does not, therefore, classify such desire as sinful or wrong. While she does glorify celibacy (praising in particular the chaste widowhood of her principal patroness), she does not condemn women who desire men. Rather, she rejects as fitting objects of desire two kinds of males: those who believe that the precepts advanced in Ephesians make them absolute monarchs of their wives, and those whose extramarital lust either victimizes or objectifies women: the seducer, the rapist, the adulterous paramour, and the violently vengeful would-be seducer. In short, Lanyer turns away from definitions of male/ female sexual relations that proceed from woman's status as the subject of man's rule or the object of his lust. But in doing so, she opens up an alternative definition of heterosexual love as the fulfillment of a woman's desire for the perfectly responsive man, who neither pursues her nor lords it over her, but mirrors and is mirrored by her desire.

The reader glimpses two such men in Lanyer's *Salve Deus Rex Judaeorum:* one in Lanyer's prefatory poem to Katherine Howard, Countess of Suffolk, and the other in the volume's title poem. In "To the Ladie *Katherine*," the addressee's husband is portrayed as being the greatest of many blessings that "concurre to make [her] fortunate" (24), and their marriage is cast as a study in mutuality rather than domination and submission. In the title poem, Lanyer sketches the Queen of Sheba as a woman whose irrepressible *eros* leads her to seek and "embrace" (*SDRJ,* 1594) that wisest and most amorous of kings, Solomon; this heroine's "Desire," Lanyer asserts, "worke[s] a strange effect" (1601), transporting her from her own country into a strange foreign realm and inspiring the female poet to celebrate an unfamiliar vision of heterosexual eroticism untainted by subjugation. The expression of that ideal is confined to three stanzas in the prefatory poem (after which Lanyer moves on to recommend that the Howards' daughters recognize Christ as the best lover) and a few more in the title work (after which Lanyer rethinks and devalues the ancient queen's choice of Solomon as compared to Margaret Clifford's "choyce" of Christ [*SDRJ*, 1673]); for the poet ultimately cannot present her seventeenth century audience with a practicable model of liberated female heterosexuality. Within the framework of the patriarchal Jacobean court as she and her readers know it, she must conclude that Jesus, the bridegroom of the Song of Songs, is the only husband and lover who will not dominate or degrade the woman who loves him. But the fleeting glimpses of heterosexual mutuality in Lanyer's portrayal of Solomon and Sheba and in her tribute to Katherine Howard's spouse are nonetheless significant; for they suggest that sexual relations between men and women *ought* to be determined by the free encounter of two desiring subjects, equal in power and beauty.

The Countess of Suffolk's husband as Lanyer represents him reflects on a human and secular plane the virtues of the heavenly bridegroom and thus merits praise in the same prefatory poem that defines Jesus as "all that Ladies can desire." In reality, neither the countess nor her husband, Thomas Howard, Earl of Suffolk, were particularly admirable individuals; but within the context of Lanyer's work, the love and fidelity Howard affords his wife are defined as exemplary. According to Lanyer, the earl displays many "noble virtues Fame can ne'r forget: / His hand being alwayes ready to afford / Help to the weak, to the unfortunate" ("To the Ladie *Katherine*," 26–28). The "noble deedes" for which the Howard line is known, she tells the countess, "Do now remaine in your most loyall Spouse, / On whom God powres all blessings from above" (33, 34–35). Indeed, Katherine Howard's husband is the most valuable asset (exceeding her

"beautie, wisedome, children, high estate") of the many that
"concurre to make [her] fortunate" (23, 24). Lanyer thus calls
him "your most honourable Lord" (25) not because Lady Katherine is his vassal or subordinate, but because he is *her* nobleman,
one of the many blessings she possesses. The possession is not
one-sided, however: he is a blessing to his wife precisely because
he recognizes her as *his* chief blessing: a "worthy Love" is a
blessing "more deare to him than all the rest," including even
such estimable assets as "Wealth, honour, children" (37, 36).
Indeed, Katherine is the "the loving Hinde and pleasant Roe, /
Wife of his youth, in whom his soule is blest, / Fountaine from
whence his chiefe delights do flow" (38–40).

   These lines draw on the book of Proverbs, in which the sage
advises his son, "Let thy fountaine be blessed, and reioyce with
the wife of thy youth. Let her be as the louing hinde and pleasant roe: let her breasts satisfie thee at all times, & delite in her
loue continually" (Prov. 5:18–19). The wife of a good husband is,
then, neither the object for which he lusts nor the subject over
whom he rules, but the cherished "Fountaine" whom he recognizes as the source of all his "delights": sexual and emotional,
intellectual and spiritual. In advancing this model of husbandly
devotion in the same poem that defines Jesus as the ideal man,
Lanyer tacitly embraces Saint Paul's exhortation to husbands at
Ephesians 5:25 ("Housbands, loue your wiues, euen as Christ
loued the Church"). And yet the *Salve Deus* as a whole vehe-
mently rejects the pronouncement of the previous verse: "as the
Church is in subiection to Christ, euen so let the wiues be to
their housbands in euerie thing." The poet finds it supremely
appropriate that a man should love his wife as Christ loves the
church, for she wholeheartedly believes that women are church-
like. But the second half of Saint Paul's analogy cannot hold,
Lanyer insists through her account of the Passion, for most men
are *not* Christ-like. They are at worst Christ-killers and at best
Christ-deniers, cowards who abandon the One they have sworn

to love. Self-sacrificing devotion is the furthest thing from their minds.

The poet thus leaves behind the commendation of Thomas Howard, admirable though the poet says he is, in order to introduce his wife to a royal lover who has done more for her than any human husband could:

> Heere I present to you the King of kings:
>
> Desiring you to take a perfit view,
> Of those great torments Patience did indure;
> And reap those Comforts that belongs to you,
> Which his most painfull death did then assure;
> Writing the Covenant with his pretious blood,
> That your faire soule might bathe her in that flood.
>
> ("To the Ladie *Katherine*," 42–48)

It is this same divine "Lover much more true / Than ever was since first the world began" who is presented to the Howards' daughters, in the next nine stanzas of the poem, as one "In whom is all that Ladies can desire" (52–53, 85).

The recommendation of Christ to these particular ladies — the daughters of Katherine and Thomas Howard — furthers Lanyer's overarching critique of "Christian" marriage as it was really experienced by Jacobean noblewomen; for, though the poet was, as she admits in the opening lines of the poem, a stranger to Katherine Howard, she certainly would have known (as pretty much everyone even casually acquainted with the English nobility did) how the Howards had been handling the selection of husbands for their daughters. Neither a young man's passionate delight in the "wife of [his] youth" nor his Christ-like love for her were, suffice it to say, primary considerations for the Earl and Countess of Suffolk as they brokered their daughters' marriages. On the contrary, the young women to whom Lanyer recommends Christ as an ideal lover had already been matched, while still of tender age, with husbands chosen for purely social and political reasons. And while arranged marriages were, of

course, the norm among the Jacobean nobility, the wedding of
Frances—the Howards' second daughter—had been showcased
at court in ways that would have made it, for Lanyer, a particularly vivid example of a contemporary aristocratic marriage
based on criteria that had nothing whatever to do with Christian faith, romantic love, or the sexual desires of the bride and
the groom.[77]

It *is* desire, however—her own desire—that leads Lanyer's
version of the Queen of Sheba to seek out Solomon. In the Christian exegetical tradition, the queen's journey, the difficult questions she asked the king, and her awed response to his wisdom
all prefigure the faithful's search for and response to Christ, of
whom Solomon is a type or foreshadowing (see Watson, "Queen
of Sheba," 116). Jesus himself is the source for this interpretation
of the queen's visit, for he rebukes the Pharisees by saying that
"The Quene of the South shal rise in iudgement, with the men
of this generacion, and shal condemne them: for she came from
the vtmost partes of the earthe to heare the wisdome of Solomon, and beholde, a greater then Solomon is here" (Luke 11:31).
As I have argued above, Lanyer interprets Christ's assertion as
granting the Queen of Sheba a position of authority on Judgment
Day; and as Lanyer understands the scriptural account of Solomon and Sheba, the queen is rewarded specifically because she
pursues her own, heartfelt desire so boldly. Lanyer does maintain that her patroness, Margaret Clifford, is superior to the Old
Testament heroine in that the countess seeks and desires Christ
himself rather than the type who foreshadowed him; but Lanyer
nevertheless portrays the "Ethyopian Queene" (*SDRJ*, 1569) as
heroic. Her virtue and heroism spring from an impulse that is
characterized not only by the thirst for holiness, wisdom, and
other transcendent ideals, but by erotic desire as well; Lanyer's
Queen of Sheba longs physically and emotionally, as well
as spiritually and intellectually, for a gloriously wise and beautiful man.

In Lanyer's account, the African monarch's journey "To heare
the Wisdom" of Solomon and the "many strange hard questions"

she frames for him are evidence that she, like the countess as
Lanyer describes her, spends her time wisely on intellectual
pursuits (*SDRJ*, 1578, 1581). The same phrase—"exercises of
the minde"—is used to describe the activities of both countess
and queen (1567, 1591).[78] Thus, Lanyer might have confined
her praises of Sheba to the realm of the spiritual and intellectual, which is precisely what Boccaccio does in his account of
the queen.[79] But she does not; in Lanyer's poem, the Queen of
Sheba's journey is a brave adventure motivated by unabashed
desire that is physical and emotional as well as intellectual and
spiritual:

> Spirits affect where they doe sympathize,
> Wisdom desires Wisdome to embrace,
> Virtue covets her like, and doth devize
> How she her friends may entertaine with grace;
> Beauty sometime is pleas'd to feed her eyes,
> With viewing Beautie in anothers face:
> > Both good and bad in this point doe agree,
> > That each desireth with his like to be.

> And this Desire did worke a strange effect,
> To drawe a Queene forth of her native Land,
> Not yeelding to the nicenesse and respect
> Of woman-kind; shee past both sea and land,
> All feare of dangers shee did quite neglect,
> Onely to see, to heare, and understand
> > That beauty, wisedom, majestie, and glorie,
> > That in her heart imprest his perfect storie.   (1593–1608)

Spirits *affect,* Wisdom *desires,* Virtue *covets,* Beauty is *pleased*
to *feed* her eyes, each *desireth,* This *desire* did work. The language of these stanzas stresses to the point of redundancy the
power and comeliness of well-directed female desire. Lanyer
includes the hunger for physical, visible beauty as well as the
longing for wisdom, and she envisions the meeting of Solomon
and Sheba as an "embrace." In asserting, moreover, that Virtue
"doth devize / How she her friends may entertaine with grace,"
she invites her noble readers to see in the words "friends" and

"grace" not only the innocuous meanings "companions" and "elegance" but the sexually charged definitions of "lovers" and "sexual favor." The queen's desire as Lanyer describes it is not exclusively or narrowly sexual; indeed, the line "Onely to see, to heare, and understand" allows a reader (should she "desire" to do so) to interpret the queen's "Desire" as fully sublimated into a longing for intellectual and spiritual enlightenment. But the association with female sexual desire remains, and it remains positive.

The "storie" of Solomon, his fame as a peerless king, is portrayed in emotionally and sexually charged language as penetrating his visitor's inmost being: Solomon's "beauty, wisedome, majestie, and glorie, /... in her heart imprest his perfect storie." But their union is a matter of her egress as well as of his ingress; the queen's longing for her royal equal "drawe[s]" her "forth" both from the land of Sheba and from the confines of she-virtue as mere "nicenesse and respect / Of woman-kind." Though one finds no record of her given name in the Scriptures, Lanyer stresses that she is honored by God in "that her memorable *Act* should be / Writ by the hand of true Eternitie" (*SDRJ,* 1687–88; emphasis mine). Her greatness is a function, not of a negatively defined chastity, a refusal to be tainted by illicit sexuality, but rather by the fact that she is the subject, not the object of the verb "desire," and that she puts her praiseworthy longings into action. As Michael Schoenfeldt puts it, "The relationship of Solomon and Sheba...exemplifies for Lanyer the possibility of heterosexual desire liberated from the patriarchal pressures that so frequently define it" ("Gender of Religious Devotion," 220).

Lanyer is but one in a long line—or in several different lines—of writers and storytellers who have been fascinated by the Queen of Sheba and have given her a crucial role in their myths and narratives. They have called her by many different names: Bilqis, Nicaula, Nikaulis, Makeda. And they have assigned her different adventures and physical characteristics. In Jewish and Islamic tradition, the queen is generally portrayed as subordinate to or dependent upon Solomon; in the Islamic versions, the story ends with Solomon's conversion of the queen to the worship of Allah and his insistence that, as a proper Muslim woman, she must have a husband. In most such accounts, Solomon makes her his own wife, while in others he insists that she marry a man of her own nation. In some renderings, he corrects a flaw in her beauty by inventing a depilatory that removes unsightly hair from her feet or legs.[80]

In Renaissance England, the most important application of the Queen of Sheba's story, and the one most relevant to Lanyer's reworking of it, is the use of the legend as a means of flattering royal personages. In Shakespeare's *Henry VIII*, Cranmer prophesies of the infant Elizabeth Tudor that "Saba was never / More covetous of wisdom and fair virtue / Than this pure soul shall be" (5.4.23–25). And Milton would praise Queen Christina of Sweden by comparing her to the Queen of Sheba.[81] But interestingly enough, the biblical heroine proved even more useful to English artists seeking to confirm the power of *kings*. In Hans Holbein's drawing of the queen's visit to Solomon, for example, "Solomon is squat, stocky, sprawling, and scowling...a thinly disguised portrait of Henry VIII"; Sheba, gesturing toward the tribute she presents to the more powerful male monarch, appears as "a wisely subservient woman" (Watson, "Queen of Sheba," 131).[82] The immediate context for Lanyer's literary portrait of Sheba was, moreover, the royal court of another pseudo-Solomon.[83] As the previous chapter observes, John Donne relies in his preface to *Pseudo-Martyr* upon King James's sense of himself as the English Solomon; but Donne alludes to the Queen of Sheba (fol. A3ᵛ) only in her capacity as the principal celebrator of Solomon's greatness, in order to stress the depth of James's Solomonic wisdom and declare what a privilege it is to enter into discourse with the monarch.

Nothing could be further from Lanyer's approach to the story; in her stanzas on Solomon and Sheba, she envisions a love that transcends hierarchy. The king and queen desire each other as equals, mirror images distinguished only by delightful differentiation in outward form and by the pleasurable tensions of intellectual exchange. This egalitarian conception of heterosexual attraction is reflected in the subtly varied spellings Lanyer uses in the stanzas on Sheba's meeting with Solomon, which begin with sets of identical words—"here Majestie with Majestie did meete, / Wisdome to Wisdome yeelded true content, / One Beauty did another Beauty greet" (*SDRJ*, 1585–87)—as if to train the reader's eye to seek those identities, and then move to a pattern of slightly varied spellings: "Bounty to Bountie" (1588), "Wisdom desires Wisdome" (1594), "Beauty sometime is pleas'd.../ With viewing Beautie" (1597–98).[84] Such variations in spelling may well be the accidental products of a typesetter's erratic practice; but if so, accident has beautifully underscored a vision that is clearly the poet's own: a vision of male/female love in which difference does not imply subjugation, in which sexual differentiation is a font of pleasure rather than a rigid foundation for tyranny.

It is only when she considers a more traditional version of Sheba's encounter with Solomon—a version in which the queen surrenders her sovereignty to a fellow creature—that the poet finds occasion to criticize the desiring woman:

> Yet this rare Phoenix of that worne-out age,
> This great majesticke Queene...
> ...to an earthly Prince did then ingage
> Her hearts desires, her love, her libertie,
> Acting her glorious part upon a Stage
> Of weaknesse, frailtie, and infirmity:
> > Giving all honour to a Creature, due
> > To her Creator, whom shee never knew. (*SDRJ*, 1689–96)

This stanza, which concludes Lanyer's description of Sheba, combines Christian and proto-feminist concerns: in her love for an "earthly Prince," her desire for a male, woman risks not only idolatry, but also a surrender to "weaknesse" and loss of "her libertie."

The problem is especially acute, Lanyer's imagery implies, in a culture where female submission to male rule is literally enacted "upon a Stage," as it was in the court of James I. Though the masques Queen Anne commissioned did deploy a number of subversive strategies that subtly undercut the king's authority, the most overt and explicit gestures of even these gynocentric masques venerated and all but deified "an earthly Prince" who equated monarchy and patriarchy.[85] Lanyer's final stanza on the inferiority of the Queen of Sheba as compared to a countess who avoids the court and its entertainments may even have a specific topical force, for one of the most decadent masques of the early Jacobean period involved a disastrous attempt to reenact Sheba's visit to Solomon. In a letter to a friend, John Harington describes the 1606 visit of Queen Anne's brother, King Christian IV of Denmark:

> One day, a great feast was held, and, after dinner, the represen-tation of Solomon his Temple and the coming of the Queen of Sheba was made, or (as I may better say) was meant to have been made, before their Majesties.... But, alass! as all earthly thinges do fail to poor mortals in enjoyment, so did prove our presentment hereof. The Lady who did play the Queens part, did carry most precious gifts to both their Majesties; but, for-getting the steppes arising to the canopy, overset her caskets into his Danish Majesties lap, and fell at his feet, tho I rather think it was in his face. Much was the hurry and confusion; cloths and napkins were at hand, to make all clean. His Maj-esty then got up and woud dance with the Queen of Sheba; but he fell down and humbled himself before her, and was carried to an inner chamber and laid on a bed of state; which was not a little defiled with the presents of the Queen which had been bestowed on his garments; such as wine, cream, jelly, bever-age, cakes, spices, and other good matters. (Ashton, *James I by His Contemporaries*, 243)

The description goes on, adding many more sordid details. Clearly, Harington is a witty observer with his own anti-Jaco-bean axe to grind; he specifically remarks on how little the court of James resembles that of his cousin and godmother, Queen Elizabeth. But however Harington may have embellished the

horrors of the Solomon and Sheba masque, any event even
vaguely resembling the debacle he describes would have made
it difficult for Lanyer, writing a few years later, to use the image
of Solomon and Sheba without evoking memories of a masque
that enhanced neither the honor of the ladies involved nor that
of the kings they attended. On the contrary, the "Stage / Of
weaknesse" on which the Queen of Sheba acts "her glorious
part" in Lanyer's poem is the pageant of sexuality played out
in a world where female desire presupposes male rule and both
are conflated with sinful idolatry and gluttony. In such a world,
Lanyer's lines suggest, the dignity of female desire is inevitably compromised, and with it the ideal of mutual love itself.
Lanyer thus briefly envisions an embrace beyond the imposi-
tions of power, a love in which male and female meet in mutual
"Majestie" (*SDRJ*, 1585), only to ground her portrait of Solomon
and Sheba in wary attention to the hierarchies that characterize
heterosexual relations in the fallen world generally and in the
court of James specifically.[86]

Things being what they are, God is the only king truly worthy of "perfect praises" (*SDRJ*, 1677). The only truly loving husband is a dead Husband, one whose death consoles all humanity
for the troubles caused by the first bad marriage. Lanyer praises
the widowed Countess of Cumberland for loving Christ as "the
Husband of thy Soule" (253),

> who for her sake vouchsaf'd to die.

> And dying made her Dowager of all;
> Nay more, Co-heire of that eternall blisse
> That Angels lost, and We by *Adams* fall.   (*SDRJ*, 256–59)

The idea of the human soul as Jesus' dowager queen works a sly
and genuinely witty change upon the traditional bride of Christ
image; it conflates the economic independence of a wealthy
widow—no longer answerable to any man—with the spiritual
liberty of a Christian soul. Lanyer revises Romans 7, which says
that the Christian soul is like a woman whose first husband, Sin,
has died, delivering her "from the law" which "bounde" her "in

subiection to" him and leaving her free to be married to "another,
euen vnto him that is raised vp from the dead" (Rom. 7:2, 4). For
Lanyer, too, Christ is the good spouse; but her dowager metaphor deemphasizes his resurrected life in order to stress that the
divine bridegroom, unlike many a human husband, can be relied
upon to leave everything to his wife when he dies. The poet thus
portrays Christian liberty and redemption as analogous not so
much to a happy second marriage, as to wealthy widowhood. In
drawing this analogy, Lanyer no doubt intends to appeal directly
to the poem's principal reader, Margaret Clifford; for, though
literally a dowager countess, Margaret found herself engaged in
exhausting legal battles to secure for herself and her daughter
certain properties that her late husband had willed away from
them before his death.[87] Another widow, Susan Bertie, Countess
Dowager of Kent, is included among those addressed in Lanyer's
dedicatory poems, and the idea of the soul as dowager may also
have appealed to Lanyer herself. Although her husband was still
alive (and acknowledged on the title page) when she published
her work in 1611, Lanyer portrays the paradoxical strength of
her own "weake Wit" (*SDRJ*, 287) and the "few humble Lines"
it produced (292) as the "Widowes Myte" of Mark 12:41–44 and
Luke 21:1–4. If this reference to the poor woman's coin is any
indication, Lanyer anticipated through the act of authorship the
relative "Myte" or power of widowhood.[88]

7. LANYER'S ARTFUL AND NATURAL HOMOEROTICS

While in Paul's epistle to the Romans, the soul's spiritual
widowhood frees her to marry a divine husband, Aemilia Lanyer's image of the Countess of Cumberland as "Dowager of all"
implies that God grants souls who love him a spiritual inheritance sufficient to make them independently wealthy; they
are thus free to direct their love and desire both toward him,
and toward a range of worthy creatures who reflect their maker's perfection. Lanyer feels that this freedom licenses her to
take not only spiritual and intellectual pleasure, but sensuous

delight, in all the beauties of Mother Nature and in those creatures favored by God and Nature alike: female human beings.
Since Nature is "That goodly Creature, Mother of Perfection, /
Whom *Joves* almighty hand at first did frame, / Taking both
her and hers in his protection," Lanyer is confident that this
indulgent matriarch will "in a Woman all defects excuse" ("To
the Queenes," 152–54, 156). Nature's blanket vindication of the
female sex ensures that the female poet's imperfect work of art
will be accepted as a spotless offering and that even her seemingly carnal desires will prove holy.

In addressing the Countess of Cumberland as the widowed
spouse of the crucified Jesus, Lanyer is even more confident, for
she knows, she says, that the godly Margaret Clifford approves
of her project:

> These high deserts invites my lowly Muse
> To write of Him, and pardon crave of thee,
> For Time so spent, I need make no excuse,
> Knowing it doth with thy faire Minde agree
> So well, as thou no Labour wilt refuse,
> That to thy holy Love may pleasing be:
>   His Death and Passion I desire to write,
>   And thee to reade, the blessed Soules delight.
>
> (*SDRJ*, 267–72)

In the closing lines of this stanza, the poet's longing is twofold:
she desires to write of Christ's death, which is the delight of all
redeemed souls; and she desires the Countess of Cumberland,
who is the delight of *her* blessed soul, as her reader. The apposi-
tive "the blessed Soules delight" modifies both the Passion of
Christ (in which Margaret Clifford, as a blessed soul, may take
renewed delight through Lanyer's poem) and "thee," Margaret
Clifford herself (who will delight Lanyer's soul if she consents
to read the work). Indeed, the stanza as a whole elides Lanyer's
desire to praise the Redeemer with her feelings about the countess. Following, as it does, one stanza on Clifford's godly self-
denial (which makes her "most pretious in [Christ's] glorious
sight" [*SDRJ*, 254]) and one stanza on Christ's sufferings (which

"Did gaine us Heaven when He did loose his breath" [264]), the opening phrase "These high deserts" is ambiguous. Lanyer feels her muse "invite[d]" both by Jesus' sacrifice and by Margaret Clifford's incomparable response to it. The poet responds to the crucified body of Christ, but also to the mortified flesh of a lady who will consent to whatever pleases her "holy Love." One cannot help but recall the pliant bride of Donne's "Show me deare Christ," but here that "Spouse, so bright and cleare" is "court[ed]" by the soul of a female poet. And while Donne makes his proposals to the Husband, Lanyer approaches the female spouse directly, telling her that she, no less than the "Death and Passion" of Christ, is "the blessed Soules delight" (272).

In fact, the Countess of Cumberland and a number of Lanyer's other female addressees are the objects of her "desire" as surely as is the feminized Christ of *Salve Deus*, who is sensuously described in the section of the poem identified by a marginal note as "A briefe description of his beautie upon the Canticles." In the Song of Songs, the bridegroom says to his bride, "Thy lippes are like a threde of skarlet & thy talke is comelie:...Thy lippes, my spouse, droppe as honie combes: honie and milke are vnder thy tongue" (4:3, 11). The bride in turn says, "His chekes are as a bed of spices and as swete flowres, & his lippes like lilies dropping downe pure myrrhe" (5:13). Lanyer applies to Christ both the bridegroom's description of the bride and the bride's images of the bridegroom:

> His lips like skarlet threeds, yet much more sweet
> Than is the sweetest hony dropping dew,
> Or hony combes, where all the Bees doe meet;
> Yea, he is constant, and his words are true,
> His cheekes are beds of spices, flowers sweet;
> His lips, like Lillies, dropping down pure mirrhe,
> Whose love, before all worlds we doe preferre.
>
> (1314–20)[89]

In this passage of Lanyer's poem, then, the bride and the bride-groom are one; for a woman to love Christ is thus not only to love God incarnate in male flesh, but also to love the feminine type which she and her fellow women embody.

In contemplating her ambitious plan to sing the praises of this bride/bridegroom, Lanyer thus turns to address a muse who is also, not surprisingly, androgynous. "My deare Muse," she asks, "now whither wouldst thou flie, / Above the pitch of thy appointed strain? / With *Icarus* thou seekest now to trie, / Not waxen wings, but thy poore barren Braine" (273–76). These lines begin by comparing the muse to a boy, but then liken his/her brain to an infertile womb. Judicious people will assume that he is doomed: "They'l thinke with *Phaeton*, thou canst neare recover, / But helplesse with that poore yong Lad to weepe: / The little World of thy weake Wit on fire, / Where thou wilt perish in thine owne desire" (285–88). Masculine ambition here mourns its own fiery demise by shedding the watery tears that are the hallmark of the putatively weaker sex. Or rather, Lanyer tells the ambitious muse, he/she *would* end by weeping this way, but will not because "the Weaker thou doest seeme to be / In Sexe or Sence" — whichever sex really *is* the weaker — "the more [God's] Glory shines, / That doth infuze such powerfull Grace in thee / To shew thy Love in these few humble Lines" (289–92). Boyish ambition meets feminine receptivity, and the result is the muse's ability to "shew" his/her "Love": which is not only Lanyer's love of a feminized Christ, but also, at least as vividly, her love of and desire for other women.

Some of the language the poet uses to praise female beauty and virtue is, of course, merely formulaic courtly compliment and has very little erotic impact; but Lanyer frequently makes a point of saying that her feelings toward the noble and royal ladies she addresses include not only admiration and reverence, but longing. She addresses Arabella Stuart as a "Great learned Ladie, whom I long have knowne, / And yet not knowne so much as I desired" ("To the Ladie *Arabella*," 1–2), thus expressing desire to become better acquainted with a prominent intellectual, but at the same time describing her desire for this "Rare *Phoenix*" as greater than her knowledge of her (3). In the poem to Queen Anne, Lanyer very decorously flatters the wife of James by praising her daughter, calling the Princess Elizabeth "the patterne of all Beautie, / The very modell of your Majestie" ("To the Queenes," 91–92). In the next line, however, she adds a provocatively equivocal modifying clause: "Whose rarest parts enforceth Love and Duty." The noun "parts" here no doubt refers primarily to "personal qualit[ies] or attribute[s], esp. of an intellectual kind; . . . abilit[ies], gift[s], or talent[s]" (*OED*, "part," n.¹ def. 15). But the verb "enforceth" can mean not only to "oblige," but also—with more physical and even sexual implications—"to force, ravish (a woman)" or "To compel, constrain" ("enforce," v. defs. 9, 10). And thus a reader so inclined may also read "parts" in fleshly terms, as referring to "portion[s] of" the princess's (or queen's) "body," or even—in light of one plural usage—"spec[ifically]. . . the genitals" ("part," n.¹ def. 4). Lanyer quickly chastens any hint of scandalous innuendo, for she returns to unambiguously chaste and reverent language in the final three lines of the stanza, in which she calls the princess "The perfect patterne of all Pietie" and begs, "O let my Booke by her faire eies be blest, / In whose pure thoughts all Innocency rests" ("To the Queenes," 94–96). Within the context of *Salve Deus* as a whole, however, these lines are not so much a guard against the carnal possibilities of the earlier line, as a way of insisting that Lanyer's sensuous compulsion to "Love" a royal lady's "rarest parts" is in no way incompatible with her desire to secure that princess's pious approval of her "Booke" in praise of God.

Lanyer knows, of course, that *idolatrous* love of any sort cannot be reconciled with Christian piety. In the poem "To all vertuous Ladies in generall," Lanyer stresses their association with virgin goddesses—Minerva, Cynthia, the Muses—and counsels them to follow only in the "paths" of such figures, "thogh faire *Venus* frown" ("To all," 26). The practice of virtue will, she stresses, liberate them from the realm of the physical altogether:

> Thus may you flie from dull and sensuall earth,
> Whereof at first your bodies formed were,

That new regen'rate in a second berth,
Your blessed soules may live without all feare,
Beeing immortall, subject to no death:
    But in the eie of heaven so highly placed,
    That others by your virtues may be graced.
                              ("To all," 64–70)

These ladies' souls are destined for a heaven in which their merits will, in very Roman Catholic–sounding terms, be applied to others by "the eie of heaven." But Lanyer does not specify what will become, in the meantime or in the long run, of the female bodies that were "at first...formed" out of "dull and sensuall earth."

To learn of that, we must turn to one of the dedicatory poems addressed to specific ladies "Whom Fame commends to be the very best" ("To all," 77). In the piece addressed "To the Ladie *Lucie,* Countesse of Bedford," Lanyer stresses that Lucy's body—her "lovely breast"—is the "blessed bowre" in which she trysts with "The true-love of [her] soule, [her] hearts delight" and is filled by the "streames" flowing from his "Ocean of true grace" ("To the Ladie *Lucie,*" 2, 24, 6, 17). The primary effect of the poem's passionate imagery is, as I argue above, to evoke the orgasmic bliss that arises from Lucy's spiritual union with Christ. But it also evokes Lanyer's own desire for Lucy. As Jonathan Goldberg points out, the poem portrays Jesus, Lucy, Lanyer, and Lanyer's book in terms that suggest "cross-gender identification" (*Desiring Women Writing,* 33); it thus presents itself as the private enclosure within which take place both Lucy's intimate encounter with Christ and Lanyer's intimate encounter with Lucy, her entry into Lucy's bosom. Languishing like the homoerotically arrow-pierced Saint Sebastian, the lovesick Christ of the poem is the model for male martyrs who, as Lanyer's title poem insists, die out of longing for his milky sweetness. But he also enters—admitted by "Virtue"—into the private "closet of [Lucy's] lovely breast." Thus, Goldberg observes, the "Christ of the poem" is both "penetrated, and penetrating"; he enters, but he is also a sacred container, a "blessed Arke..../

Where [Lucy's] faire soule may sure and safely rest, / When he is sweetly seated in [her] breast ("To the Ladie *Lucie*," 19–21). "As Woods's gloss reminds us," Goldberg adds, "the ark also figures Lanyer's poem, which contains the passion as its central narrative" (32, 33). As if these levels of ambiguity were not sufficient, the ark image also describes what Lucy's breast becomes once she has welcomed Lanyer's poem into the "Cabbine where [her] selfe doth rest" and thus admitted into her "bed of rest" the Christ Lanyer's poetry depicts. The poem to Lucy and the narrative poem it introduces are thus, as Lanyer portrays them, not only the means by which Christ may inhabit the countess and the means by which the countess may enter Christ, but also the female poet's means of intimate ingress, her keys to her reader's "lovely breast." As Goldberg sums it up, "Lanyer's humble self-effacement is also her self-propelling" (33).

Lanyer's description of Solomon and Sheba, too, vibrates with homoerotic undertones. The Queen of Sheba seeks out Solomon because "Wisdom desires Wisdome to embrace, / Virtue covets her like," and "each desireth with his like to be" (*SDRJ*, 1594–95, 1600). As Michael Morgan Holmes points out, despite the fact that these lines literally refer to a male-female relationship, "on a more symbolic level, Lanyer's Neoplatonic lexicon of sympathy and embraces contributes to the *Salve*'s investment in spiritual and physical sameness as the grounds of affection between women" ("Love of Other Women," 174). In fact, "affection" may be too pale a word for what Lanyer wishes to evoke in the stanzas on Solomon and Sheba; for, as I argue above, the poet takes pains to represent the queen as an embodiment of forthright, outward-traveling, and uninhibited female eros. And by portraying the male object of that erotic impulse as a person who is "like" the desiring woman, Lanyer implies that all such desire is on some level homoerotic. As Goldberg puts it, "Through the sovereign male figure, female-female desire is intimated" (*Desiring Women Writing*, 27).

In framing the homoerotic impulse as the essential ingredient of virtuous eros, Lanyer once again locks horns with Saint Paul, who, in Romans 1:24–27, defines any departure from the heterosexual norm as he and his readers understood it as degrading uncleanness. As Paul defines them, male same-sex desire and departures from "nature" in female sexual activity are not simply sinful, they are a consequence of sin. God punishes pagan idolaters for their misdirected religious devotion by allowing them to wallow in misdirected eros:

> [They] worshipped and serued the creature, forsaking the Creator.... For this cause God gaue them vp vnto vile affections: for euen their women did change the natural vse into that which is against nature. And likewise also the men left the natural vse of the woman, and burned in their luste one towarde another, and man with man wroght filthines, & receiued in them selues suche recompense of their errour, as was mete. (Rom. 1:25–27)

At the core of this passage is Saint Paul's concept of male heterosexuality and female sexual passivity as "natural," as fulfilling the reproductive function of the sexual organs and thus putting the female body to the "vse" it was meant to serve. Women making love to women (or in any other way departing from the passive role in a heterosexual relationship) are, in light of this approach to human sexuality, doing something "which is against nature," and men making love to men are producing only "filthines," rather than giving shape to new human beings by impregnating women.[90] But as Donne points out in his Holy Sonnet "O might those sighes and teares returne againe," any kind of sinful lust—including standard-issue Petrarchan "Idolatry" of the weeping and wailing variety—really is its own punishment: "long, yet vehement griefe hath beene / The effect and cause; the punishment and Sinne" (HSSighs, 1, 5, 13–14). Having wasted his "sighes and teares" on profane objects of desire, he cannot now piously "Mourne with some fruite, as [he has] mournd in vaine" (4).

In his "Sapho to Philænis," however, Donne imagines Sappho's passionate lesbian lovemaking with Philaenis as a sinless form of eros that is potentially fruitful rather than "vaine" or barren, and that involves not the abandonment or abuse of Nature, but the delightful union of Nature and Art.[91] Unlike "Menn," who "leaue behinde them that which their sin showes" — babies who resemble their fathers in appearance and in the original sin that they inherit from them — the "dalliance" of two women leaves no sinful trace; of it, "no more signes there are, / Then fishes leaue in streames, or birds in aire" (Donne, *Sappho*, 39, 41–42). Yet fish feel the water running over their fins, and birds ride blissfully on the wind. And since they are humans, not animals, the bliss of two women is not merely a matter of fluid or breath; "betweene [them] all sweetness may bee had; / All, all that nature yealds, or art cann adde" (*Sappho*, 43–44): the lines evoke both fleshly delights and invented pleasures that range from the prosthetic to the poetic.[92]

In her poem to the Countess of Pembroke, Lanyer also evokes — less explicitly, but no less ardently — a sensuous same-sex union that weds Art and Nature; the two feminine allegorical figures representing these concepts are, as Lanyer portrays them, joined in a universally beneficial marriage that is arranged when Mary Sidney and her female companions observe their "case" and decide the outcome of the two rivals' "antient quarrell." Their deliciously attractive contest, which takes place on the banks of a "sacred Spring" and "Add[s] fresh Beauty" to it, leads the "ravisht sences" of the observers to decide that the combatants "should for ever dwell, / In perfit unity by this matchlesse Spring" ("The Authors Dream," 86, 83, 81, 84, 87, 89–90). This scenario is a joyful revision of the scene near the end of book 2 of *The Faerie Queene* when Guyon, the stern and masculine embodiment of Temperance, is temporarily distracted by the alluring spectacle of "Two naked Damzelles" who "[seem] to contend, / And wrestle wantonly" in a pool of water at the heart of the Bower of Bliss (*FQ* 2.12.63:6, 7–8). Just before Guyon "espy[es]" these frolicsome maidens, Spenser's narrator describes the bower at length as "the most daintie Paradise on ground, / ...In which all pleasures plenteously abound"; but what makes it particularly beautiful is that "The art, which all that wrought, appeared in no place" (2.12.58:1, 3, 9). Indeed,

> One would haue thought, (so cunningly, the rude,
> And scorned parts were mingled with the fine,)
> That nature had for wantonesse ensude
> Art, and that Art at nature did repine;
> So striuing each th'other to vndermine,
> Each did the others worke more beautifie.   (2.12.59)

The beauty here is due to the mutual rivalry of Art and Nature; they cooperate in spite of their "diff'ring...willes" and their agreement is a matter of "sweete diuersitie." Or so it would seem; but the bower is, of course, not really so sweet. It is a foul nest of carnal incontinence, as becomes clearer in the next two stanzas, which describe "a fountaine" carved with "curious imageree /...and shapes of naked boyes, / Of which some seemd with liuely iollitee, / To fly about, playing their wanton toyes, / Whilest others did them selues embay in liquid ioyes." Trailing over the edges is "A trayle of yuie" made of gold that has been colored green to deceive the eyes of beholders; and it, too, is luxuriating in the font: "Low his lasciuious armes adown did creepe, /...themselues dipping in the siluer dew" (*FQ* 2.12.60–61). The *puti* immersing themselves in "liquid ioyes," the artificial ivy laving "his lasciuious armes" in something that looks like "siluer dew": all this excess is ripe for smashing by the Knight of Temperance. But then Guyon spies the two young damsels (2.12.63). They are engaged in vigorous homoerotic play, lifting each other out of the water, plunging each other under the surface, and engaging in all sorts of fetching aquatic maneuvers; but when they see Guyon, they stop and gaze at him. One hides herself in the water, while the other lifts herself higher "And her two lilly paps aloft display[s], / And all, that might his melting hart entise / To her delights, she vnto him bewray[s]: / The rest hid vnderneath, him more desirous ma[kes]" (2.12.66:6–9). The other, more bashful nymph competes with her companion for

Guyon's gaze; but while the first, like Nature, puts on a display of artless exhibitionism, the second plays the role of Art, cunningly releasing her knotted tresses and letting them fall so that she resembles a beautifully dressed statue, "th'yuorie in golden mantle gownd" (67:5).[93] Guyon slackens his pace and heads in their direction, but after being warned by his Palmer, he proceeds to save himself—and all the victims of Intemperance languishing under Acrasia's spell—by smashing the bower to smithereens. In Lanyer's poem, no such action is necessary or desirable, for the lovely female wrestlers stop their combat not to allure a man, but to join with each other "In perfit unity"; their amity is real, not dangerously illusory; their audience is female, not male; and "Since 'twas impossible either should excell, / Or her faire fellow in subjection bring," no one is victimized by their union. On the contrary, they are united "That unto others they might comfort give, / Rejoycing all with their sweet unitie" ("The Authors Dreame," 90, 91, 92, 95–96). The anti-Spenserian point is clear: art and nature *can* be in true harmony, and when they are, pleasure abounds for all. The homoerotic language Lanyer uses to describe that harmony works, moreover, on the literal as well as the figurative level; it reflects her sense that things are at their best when hierarchy is eliminated from relationships, and that the union of two female figures is the best image of love without hierarchy.

It is also an appropriate image for harmony between inner and outer self, the integration of body and soul that Lanyer believes every virtuous woman achieves. Gazing into the "Mirrour" of Lanyer's poem, the "faire eyes" of Anne Clifford will "view" not only her own spiritual and intellectual "virtues," but the harmonious union of lovely flesh and righteous soul; for "Virtue and Beautie both together run," Lanyer tells her, "When you were borne, within your breast to stay; / Their quarrell ceast, which long before begun, / They live in peace, and all doe them obey" ("To the Ladie *Anne*," 7, 8, 99–102). The woman in whom such a couple cohabits no longer experiences the dichotomy between flesh and spirit that Saint Paul describes in Romans:

> For I delite in the Law of God, concerning the inner man: But
> I se another law in my membres, rebelling against the law
> of my minde, & leading mee captiue vnto the law of sinne,
> which is in my membres. O wretched man that I am, who
> shal deliuer me from the bodie of this death!...I my self in my
> minde serue the Law of God, but in my flesh the law of sinne.
> (Rom. 7:22–25)

As Paul goes on to say, this warfare will come to an end for
those who live in Christ: "if Christ be in you, the bodie is dead,
because of sinne: but the Spirit is life for righteousnes sake. But
if the Spirit of him that raised vp Iesus from the dead, dwell in
you, he that raised vp Christ from the dead, shal also quicken
your mortal bodies, because that his Spirit dwelleth in you"
(Rom. 8:10–11). Paul's point, however, is to stress the need for
continued denial of the flesh, "For if ye liue after the flesh, ye
shal dye: but if ye mortifie the dedes of the bodie by the Spirit, ye
shal liue" (Rom. 8:13). The transfiguration of physical creation
will occur only in the future, at the final resurrection; in the
meantime, created matter suffers like a woman in labor: "the
creature also shalbe deliuered from the bondage of corruption
into the glorious libertie of ye sonnes of God. For we knowe
that euerie creature groneth with vs also, and trauaileth in paine
together vnto this present" (Rom. 8:21–22).

Lanyer cannot entirely disagree with Paul; she cannot claim
that the redemption of the body is fully accomplished as long as
human experience continues to involve physical suffering and
bodily death, including the agonies of childbirth. But for Lanyer,
there is no longer a war *within*; for "the erotic element" in her
spirituality, to quote McGrath, "marries woman's soul to her
body" (*Subjectivity*, 219); her inner woman and her female flesh
are, in short, joined in a blissful same-sex union. Donne, as I
point out above, briefly envisions such a marriage in a sermon on
the resurrection: "gladnesse shall my soul have, that this flesh,
(which she will no longer call her prison, nor her tempter, but
her friend, her companion, *her wife*), that this flesh, that is, I,
in the re-union...of both parts, shall see God" (*Sermons*, 3:112;

emphasis mine). For Donne, however, this is a fantasy projected into the not-yet-experienced future; for Lanyer, it is a present reality. Margaret Clifford has no need to die and go to heaven in order to see God both physically and spiritually, for the divinity is revealed to her in the terrestrial landscape. Recalling how the countess meditated on the Creator's power made manifest in the flora and fauna of Cookham, Lanyer says that her patroness "in their beauties did...plaine descrie, / His beauty, wisdome, grace, love, majestie" ("Cooke-ham," 79–80).

Clifford thus resembles the Elizabeth Drury of Donne's *Second Anniversarie*; both Elizabeth and Margaret are able to experience the "essential ioye" of the beatific vision even in this life, for both have "Here so much essentiall ioye, / As no chance [can] distract, much lesse destroy"; both are "with Gods presence...acquainted so, / (Hearing, and speaking to him) as to know / His face, in any naturall Stone, or Tree, / Better then when in Images they bee" (*SecAn*, 449–54). But while Donne feels the need to privilege things "naturall" as more capable of revealing God's face to Elizabeth Drury than any artificial "Images," Lanyer insists that the Countess of Cumberland can see God's image revealed just as perfectly in the book of poetry that the countess has inspired her to write. If the countess will use the eyes of her body to read it, Lanyer will "to the most perfect eyes of [her] understanding,...deliver the inestimable treasure of all elected soules, to bee perused at convenient times; as also, the mirrour of [her] most worthy minde, which may remaine in the world many yeares longer than [she], or [the poet] can live" ("To the Ladie *Margaret*," 28–32).

The poet's reference to *Salve Deus Rex Judaeorum* as a reflection in which Margaret Clifford may view herself links Lanyer's poetics to Donne's, for it hints that the countess has been to Lanyer's muse, as Elizabeth Drury was to Donne's, "a Father" (*SecAn* 35). She has bestowed her image upon the poem to which the writer gives birth. The God-revealing work Lanyer now "delivers" to Margaret Clifford began, she says in "The Description of Cooke-ham," as a gleam in the countess's eye: "From

[your] desires did spring this worke of Grace" (12).[94] Like most desires that, when satisfied, lead to procreation, Margaret Clifford's were transient, associated in the mother-poet's mind with "those pleasures past" that she and her baby's father-inspirer shared at Cookham. Those "fleeting worldly Joyes...could not last" ("Cooke-ham," 13, 14); but they were substantial enough to inseminate the poet's imagination, and the poem to which she has given birth may—as any couple's progeny often does—outlive both its parents. Unlike Elizabeth Drury in Donne's *Anniversaries*, however, the Countess of Cumberland has not been obliged to "refuse / The name of Mother" (*SecAn*, 33–34) in order to become a father. For her virtue is also apparent in Anne, the daughter she bore in her womb; Anne is, Lanyer asserts, "Heire apparant" to her mother's "Crowne / Of goodnesse, bountie, grace, love, pietie" ("To the Ladie *Anne*," 65–66).

Lanyer's feelings toward Margaret and Anne Clifford, her deep and abiding desire to be with them, and her longing for the pleasures she associates with their company, are ultimately frustrated. Her situation resembles that of Donne's Sappho, who stresses her female beloved's prelapsarian flawlessness and questions the right of any fallen Adam to plow her rich Edenic soil: "Thy body," Sappho tells Philaenis, "is a naturall Paradise, / In whose selfe, vnmanurd, all pleasure lies, / Nor needs perfection, why shouldst thou than / Admitt the tillage of a harsh rough Man?" (Donne, *Sappho*, 35–38). Philaenis is a paradise lost to Sappho, however, for she has in fact abandoned the passionate poetess for a man. Lanyer finds herself in a similar situation in "The Description of Cooke-ham," which describes the estate as an earthly paradise of "pleasures past" ("Cooke-ham," 13) and evokes the poet's deep nostalgia for the days before Margaret Clifford's daughter, Anne, was married. "That sweet Lady," Lanyer says, is "To honourable *Dorset* now espows'd." But the poet remembers the virginal Anne of the past,

> In whose faire breast true virtue then was hous'd:
> Oh what delight did my weake spirits find

In those pure parts of her well framed mind:
And yet it grieves me that I cannot be
Neere unto her, whose virtues did agree
With those faire ornaments of outward beauty,
Which did enforce from all both love and dutie.

. . . .

Therefore sweet Memorie doe thou retaine
Those pleasures past, which will not turne againe:
Remember beauteous *Dorsets* former sports,
So farre from being toucht by ill reports;
Wherein my selfe did alwaies beare a part,
While reverend Love presented my true heart:
Those recreations let me beare in mind,
Which her sweet youth and noble thoughts did finde:
Whereof depriv'd, I evermore must grieve.

("Cooke-ham," 93, 95–102, 117–25)

The lines on Princess Elizabeth in Lanyer's poem to Queen Anne
are ambiguous in their reference to the compelling power of her
"rarest parts" (which may be either physical or spiritual and intellectual); but this tribute to Anne Clifford makes explicit that,
while Lanyer's "weake spirits" found "delight.../ In those pure
parts of [Anne's] well framed mind," the "love and dutie" the
poet felt toward her were "enforce[d]" by her "faire ornaments of
outward beauty." The "sports" in which Lanyer remembers participating with the "beauteous" Dorset were, of course, wholly
virtuous—"farre from being toucht by ill reports"; for "true
virtue then was hous'd" in the virginal Anne's "faire breast"
(one wonders about the "then," which seems to imply that *now*,
as Dorset is a married woman out of touch with her old play-
mate, that breast has—like Cookham itself—been abandoned
by its former tenant). Whatever she thinks of her now too-dis-
tant beloved, however, Lanyer makes clear that, in her fondly
remembered interactions with Anne Clifford, she gave away her
"true heart." Taking part in the young lady's "recreations" was,
for her, an expression of "Love"; and being "depriv'd" of them
has left her disconsolate.[95]

Lanyer's contact with both Anne and her mother has been cut off—if it ever existed at all outside the realm of her poetry—by class distinctions, which she portrays as being enforced by "Unconstant Fortune,.../ Who casts us downe into so lowe a frame: / Where our great friends we cannot dayly see, / So great a difference is there in degree" ("Cooke-ham," 103–06). The whore Fortuna, Lanyer believes, serves the interests of men by leading noblewomen (whose marriages are always determined at least in part by their need to maintain what Fortune has bestowed on them by birth) to become "Parters in honour" ("Cooke-ham," 108)—those who part from their friends and family in order to maintain the honor of their house and create a new, partitioned coat of arms, joining their heraldic colors and devices with those of another noble family.[96] As one such parter, Anne Clifford has united herself with outward splendor while distancing herself from what really matters, the love of her humble admirer; she is now "Neerer in show, yet farther off in love, / In which, the lowest alwayes are above" ("Cooke-ham,"109–10).

The celibate widow Margaret Clifford will never again partition her noble escutcheon, but she, too, has parted from Lanyer, leaving the poet as desolate as the abandoned estate she describes. Lanyer insists that the bond uniting her with Margaret can never truly be broken. Cookham will live on in her poem; and though the countess has left that lovely house forever, her "virtues" will always dwell in Lanyer: they "lodge," she says, "in my unworthy breast, / And ever shall, so long as life remaines, / Tying my heart to her by those rich chaines" ("Cooke-ham," 208–10).[97] But the parallel these final lines draw between Cookham and Lanyer as places of lodging confirms what is implied throughout the poem through the use of pathetic fallacy: the emotions Lanyer projects onto the landscape of Cookham are her own, and Cookham is clearly devastated by the departure of the countess. The poem is structured around a series of reversals that illustrate the poet's pain: the "cristall Streames" of the estate are clear and sparkle in the sun's beams when Margaret Clifford comes to Cookham (27–28), but once she leaves, "those sweet Brookes that ranne so faire and cleare, / With griefe and trouble wrinckled [do] appeare" (183–84). The lady's presence causes "Each part" of the grounds "some new delight to frame"; but at her departure, "each thing d[oes] unto sorrow frame" (18, 132).[98] As long as Margaret and Anne are present, Cookham is a feminine paradise in which "all things" reflect the beauty of the female inhabitants and serve as malleable components for the poet's joyful "similies" (22). But once the Cliffords' "occasions" have "call'd [them] so away, / That nothing there had power to make [them] stay," Cookham—an image of Lanyer herself—is an Eden deprived of her Eve (147–48).

As Lanyer recalls the countess's departure, she remembers how Margaret took leave of the autumnal and wintery trees, whose falling leaves ("cast…away" in hopes of arousing the lady's pity) and "frozen tops like Ages hoarie haires" reflect the poet's distress:

> Yet did I see a noble gratefull minde,
> Requiting each according to their kind,
> Forgetting not to turne and take your leave
> Of these sad creatures, powrelesse to receive
> Your favour, when with griefe you did depart.
>
>   ("Cooke-ham," 141, 143, 149–53)

Woman's affinity with nature, so often stressed by Lanyer, here manifests itself in the countess's morally admirable consideration for the insensate "creatures" of Cookham, which she gently acknowledges for the joy they have afforded her. Yet when Margaret Clifford actually kisses her favorite tree goodbye, the appropriateness of her behavior comes under scrutiny. Though the poet praises the countess's action as "chaste" and "loving," she hastens to redirect the kiss according to her own sense of what is fitting:

> To this faire tree, taking me by the hand,
> You did repeat the pleasures which had past,
> Seeming to grieve they could no longer last.
> And with a chaste, yet loving kisse tooke leave,

> Of which sweet kisse I did it soone bereave:
> Scorning a sencelesse creature should possesse
> So rare a favour, so great happinesse.   (162–68)

Lanyer's situation as she portrays it in these lines is humiliating. Anne Baynes Coiro, stressing Lanyer's resentment of and resistance to the class distinctions that divide her from Margaret Clifford, points out the bitter humor implicit in the transition from 165 to 166.[99] Our expectation—that the countess has taken leave of the poet whose hand she is holding—is suddenly betrayed, and we learn that the kiss has been bestowed on a creature with only a vegetal soul. Lanyer thus trumps the resentment of male lovers like Sidney's Astrophil, who complain that pet birds and dogs are receiving the kisses due them; their rivals are at least sensate!

And yet, Lanyer's position in these lines is one of spiritual authority; the countess may not value the poet as she ought, but the poet herself knows the truth. She is an Eve who sins open-eyed in order to preach and prophesy through symbolic action. In purloining the kiss, she wrongs a creature placed below her in the Great Chain of Being, just as the countess—in bestowing the kiss on the tree rather than on Lanyer—wronged a creature placed below her in the false hierarchy of social class. The theft thus preaches a lesson: injustice breeds injustice; fickle "Fortune" betrays not only those who rely upon her, but innocent bystanders and innocent Nature as well:

> No other kisse it could receive from me,
> For feare to give backe what it tooke of thee:
> So I ingratefull Creature did deceive it,
> Of that which you vouchsaft in love to leave it.
> And though it oft had giv'n me much content,
> Yet this great wrong I never could repent:
> But of the happiest made it most forlorne,
> To shew that nothing's free from Fortunes scorne,
> While all the rest with this most beauteous tree,
> Made their sad consort Sorrowes harmony.

The floures that on the banks and walkes did grow,
Crept in the ground, the Grasse did weepe for woe.   (169–80)

As Milton will put it in his epic, "Earth felt the wound, and Nature from her seat / Sighing through all her Works gave signs of woe, / That all was lost" (*PL* 9.782–84). But as Patrick Cook points out, Lanyer's insistence that she cannot "repent" the "great wrong" she has committed "suggests that this is a Fortunate Fall" ("Aemilia Lanyer's 'Description,'" 115). Indeed, the poet's act here resembles Eve's as Lanyer defines it in the "Apologie" spoken by Pilate's wife. Eve's taking of the forbidden fruit is a forgivable error committed "for knowledge sake"; her "fault was onely too much love, / Which made her give this present to her Deare, / That what shee tasted, he likewise might prove, / Whereby his knowledge might become more cleare" (*SDRJ*, 797, 801–04). Lanyer, too, acts out of love, and in order to educate her putative superior. She knows that men will continue to oppress women, that they will not heed the prophetic voice of Pilate's wife. And she knows that "The Description of Cooke-ham" will not restore the female Eden she has lost. But the poet nevertheless plumbs the depths of postlapsarian existence, seeking—as Milton will on a far grander scale in *Paradise Lost*—not only to confront that existence's "desolation" ("Cooke-ham," 203) and "distance" from heaven (*PL* 9.9), but also to celebrate the "worke of Grace" that redeemed Nature can and must carry out ("Cooke-ham," 12).

MILTON

For all their boldness in poetically recasting the sacred feminine, neither John Donne nor Aemilia Lanyer was a revolutionary in the ordinary sense of the word. Donne did pose challenges to a wide variety of orthodoxies: to lyric conventions and outworn images, to both Roman Catholic and Calvinist definitions of grace, to established philosophies of love and received notions of gender; but he nearly always did so equivocally and indirectly, rather than blatantly. His genius was the genius of the "survivor," to quote Dennis Flynn's term: encoded, nuanced, oblique.[1] Lanyer, for her part, does not break free from her subservient place in the aristocracy she critiques; nor do the feminized Jesus of *Salve Deus* and his beheaded male disciples abolish the gender hierarchy that locates female strength in weakness, woman's goodness in her oppressed status. Lanyer conceives of a new theology and morality grounded in creative *ressentiment*, but it generates no Nietzschean shift in the values of her audience; her slave revolt remains confined within the covers of her book.[2]

John Milton, in contrast, was a genuine rebel; he not only entered the public arena, but also spoke out loudly, directly, and often shockingly therein, putting his life on the line to challenge political and religious orthodoxy. And his poems, no less than his polemical prose works, ring with devout, uncompromising heterodoxy; for Milton was, as John Rumrich puts it, "heretical to the core," never content to embrace a settled tradition in

215

matters religious, political, or poetic ("Radical Heterodoxy and Heresy," 156). Challenges to received opinion suffuse his poetic corpus. Milton's rejection of orthodoxy is less obvious to readers than it might otherwise be, however, because he is willing to make apparently conventional gestures, deploy traditional images, and evoke ancient formulas. He does not depend upon dissent for dissent's sake, and thus he feels no compulsion to reject such gestures, images, and formulas. Confident in his ability to detach them from their orthodox moorings, he puts them to work in pursuit of the never-yet-attained and always plural truths he seeks.

Milton's deployment of feminine archetypes is particularly subtle. His portraits of *mater ecclesia,* the virtuous soul, "advent'rous Eve," and Mary, the mother of Jesus, all reflect his conception of divine Sapientia and her human counterpart, the God-given created Wisdom that rejects folly and leads man to God.[3] Drawing upon the descriptions of Wisdom in the book of Proverbs and the additional passages on Wisdom in the Deuterocanonical Wisdom of Solomon and Ecclesiasticus, Milton forges a nonconformist Christian humanist version of the sacred feminine that is uniquely his own.[4] The divine Wisdom who declares herself God's partner in the work of creation (Prov. 8:30) and her created mirror, the wisdom that God "giueth...abundantly vnto them that loue him" (Ecclus. 1:10), are not, of course, the only avatars of the sacred feminine in Milton's poems. But he returns to these Wisdom figures again and again in portraying the character of the true church, the dynamics of redeemed spirituality, and the lineaments of virtuous discipleship in virginity, marriage, and maternity. In *Arcades,* Milton begins to formulate his own, highly distinctive approach to Wisdom as a "radiant" female figure whose "luster" is not merely allegorical, but rather shines forth in the living virtues of a godly woman. The Miltonic version of this ideal flowers in *A Mask Presented at Ludlow Castle,* bears fruit in *Paradise Lost,* and is pressed into a strong but mellow wine in *Paradise Regained.*

1. MATERNAL WISDOM AND PASTORAL MINISTRY IN *ARCADES*

The young Milton's idea of the sacred feminine was no doubt shaped by many influences, but the four most important of these were the Scriptures, and in particular the Wisdom books, both canonical and Deutero-canonical; his reading of Spenser, whom he would later call "our sage and serious Poet";[5] his Christian humanist approach to classical mythology, which helped to shape his interpretation of Scripture; and his evolving political stance, which inspired his resistance to what he would eventually define as a deadly mixture of political tyranny and false religion in the reign of Charles I. All four of these influences are operative in the aristocratic entertainments *Arcades* and *A Mask*, which he wrote in the early 1630s.

The first of these works is Milton's earliest exploration of a theme that was also central to the poetry of Donne and Lanyer: the flow of God's redeeming grace through a feminine channel. *Arcades*, which was "Part of an Entertainment" presented to the Dowager Countess of Derby, Alice Spencer Stanley Egerton, focuses on the dowager countess as a figure whose matriarchal dignity evokes that of the church, the great mother through whom flow the spiritual nurture, guidance, and healing that originate in divine Wisdom. But Milton's idea of the church is already—even at this early stage of his career—marked by a distinct anti-authoritarian quality. Whereas Donne struggles to define which version of the institutional church is "most trew, and pleasing to" God (*HSShow*, 13), the young Milton confidently points—much as Lanyer does in her *Salve Deus*—to the invisible church made visible in one good, Protestant lady. And like Lanyer, who praises the Countess of Cumberland for her rural withdrawal from the court of James, Milton defines his ideal noblewoman's goodness partly by placing it in opposition to the Stuart monarchy.

Arcades praises Alice Spencer Stanley Egerton as a reformed alternative to the Madonna-like figure of King Charles's French

Catholic consort, Henrietta Maria. As Barbara Lewalski demonstrates, building upon earlier work by Maryann Cale McGuire
and David Norbrook, *Arcades* reflects the youthful poet's
response to court masques commissioned by the king and queen:
lavish Whitehall productions (including several with texts by
Ben Jonson) that portrayed the royal marriage as a sublime union
of divine beauty and heroic love, holding up that nuptial ideal
as the source of virtue and heavenly perfection for all of Britain
(Lewalski, "Milton's *Comus*," 297–301).[6] As McGuire puts it,
"the queen, seated in state, was cast as the end of all quests,
the embodiment of Divine Beauty"; the spectators were led
"upward toward the apotheosized queen, and the visual journey culminate[d] with the theatrical image of the royal couple
united in love" (*Milton's Puritan Masque*, 74).

Such court productions, Lewalski observes, reflected Henrietta
Maria's Catholicism and her commitment to a Neoplatonic
doctrine that conceived of physical beauty as the outward and
visible sign of inward virtue ("Milton's *Comus*," 297). Both the
masques in which she performed and those written to be presented to her as the occupant of the throne of state thus involved
the deployment of Neoplatonic images within a context of
quasi-Catholic ritual and symbolism. They portrayed the queen
as an icon of chaste yet erotically engaged beauty and, at the
same time, as a divinely empowered madonna whose influence
reigned in heaven and on earth; she was always hailed by her second name as "Mary" or "Maria." In contrast, Milton's *Arcades*
hails a "rural Queen" (*Arcades*, 94, 108) who, though she appears
divine to those who encounter her, is firmly grounded in her
own humanity.

As John M. Wallace first pointed out in 1959 ("Milton's
Arcades"), Milton associates this "Queen," the Dowager
Countess of Derby, with the Judeo-Christian Sapientia, she by
whom "the waies of them which are vpon earth, are reformed,
& men are taught the things that are pleasant vnto [God], and
are preserued" (Wisd. of Sol. 9:18). This reading has not gone
unquestioned; Cedric Brown correctly points out that Wallace's

allegorical interpretation neglects "the range of significances" in the various pagan divinities to whom the dowager countess is compared and loses sight of *Arcades'* function, which is to praise the matriarch of a noble family not only for sapience, but for her "motherhood and regality." As Brown stresses, *Arcades* is a "familial tribute," not a theological allegory (*Milton's Aristocratic Entertainments*, 188 n. 4). But Wallace was nevertheless correct to single out the biblical image of Wisdom as central to the entertainment; for *Arcades'* three songs and the long speech by the Genius of the Wood all assert that the Dowager Countess of Derby is an ideal mother and queen—and thus a type of the church—precisely because she embodies the qualities of the created Wisdom that Augustine identifies as "the rational, intelligent mind of [God's] chaste city...on high [who] is our mother" (*Confessions*, 12.20). Milton applies to this mother all the qualities of God immanent attributed to Sapientia in the Wisdom of Solomon: her light illuminates and dignifies all that approach her; she is the matrix of good and the inspiration of eloquence; in her realm, fallen nature is healed and brought back into harmony with heaven. Vulgar "Fame" cannot convey her transcendent worth.

The date of *Arcades* is not certain, but according to Brown, whose study of the work has done most to clarify its historical context, the performance probably took place at Harefield, the estate of the dowager countess, in late summer or early fall of 1632. The 24-year-old Milton was clearly influenced, in composing the entertainment, by Edmund Spenser, whose *Teares of the Muses* was dedicated to the dowager countess when she was still the young Lady Strange, and whose "Hymne of Heavenly Beavtie" portrayed the biblical figure of Wisdom as a queen of "great powre and peerelesse maiestie" (*HHB*, 186; See Quitslund, "Spenser's Image of Sapience").[7] Caroline masques, however, provided the most important context for Milton's work. As Lewalski explains, several of the honoree's grandchildren—the children of her daughter Frances and her son-in-law and stepson, John Egerton—"had by this time danced in several Caroline masques" ("Milton's *Comus*," 298). These grandchildren included Penelope, who performed in the queen's Shrovetide 1631 masque, *Chloridia*, and four others who performed in the queen's Shrovetide 1632 masque, *Tempe Restored*: Katherine, Elizabeth, Alice (who would later perform as the Lady in *Comus*), and John (the elder brother in *Comus*).[8] As the titles *Chloridia* and *Tempe Restored* indicate, both of these court productions were pastoral in mode; in the first, Queen Henrietta Maria appeared as Chloris, the goddess of flowers; attended by 14 nymphs, she was heralded by Fame and presented to King Charles as "The ornament of bowers, / The top of paramours!" (Jonson, *Complete Masques*, 472). In the second, the enchantress Circe ceded her rule over the pastoral vale of Tempe to Divine Beauty in the person of the queen.

Thus, when the Genius of the Wood in *Arcades* welcomes "some noble persons of" the dowager countess's "Family, who appear on the Scene in pastoral habit, moving toward the seat of State" (*Arcades*, s.d., in *Complete Poems*, 77), he acknowledges that they are denizens "Of famous *Arcady*" (*Arcades*, 28), the royal court. As Lewalski points out, "Milton's entertainment...proposes to reclaim pastoral, intimating the superiority of the Harefield festivities and the virtues of the noble Protestant Countess and her household over the Queen and her courtly Arcadia" ("Milton's *Comus*," 300). The sense of Harefield as a better alternative to the court is clearest in the final song of the entertainment, in which the visitors are urged to "dance no more" in their old pastoral haunts, since now "A better soil shall give [them] thanks" (*Arcades*, 96, 101).[9] "Bring your Flocks," they are told, "and live with us":

> Here ye shall have greater grace,
> To serve the Lady of this place.
> > Though *Syrinx* your *Pan's* mistress were,
> > Yet *Syrinx* well might wait on her.
> > > Such a rural Queen
> > > All *Arcadia* hath not seen.   (103–09)

The reference to Pan and Syrinx—inserted into the Trinity manuscript at some point after the original composition of the text—may well recall Jonson's *Entertainment at Althorp*, which praised Queen Anne as Syrinx and lamented that her Pan, King James, was not present for the occasion. Here, the point is to insist that the current Stuart queen, Henrietta Maria, might more fittingly serve, rather than rule over, the dowager countess.[10] Charles's queen was the focal point for the 1631 and 1632 Twelfth Night masques, *Love's Triumph Through Callipolis* and *Albion's Triumph*, sitting in the chair of state toward which the masquers—Charles and his men—directed their movement. In Harefield, that place of honor is reserved, not for a fair, young, French Catholic queen, but rather for a venerable, elderly, English Protestant lady.

The "greater grace" afforded those who come to Harefield and serve its "rural Queen" is no doubt due partly to the impeccable Protestant credentials of the dowager countess, to whom Spenser had long ago dedicated *The Teares of the Muses*. It is also a matter of her role as a patroness of poets. In his dedication of that work, Spenser praises Alice Spencer Stanley as a *"Most braue and noble Ladie"* and thanks her for her *"particular bounties"* toward him (Spenser, *Poetical Works*, 480). In the first lament of the work, however, Clio, the muse of epic, complains that most persons of noble ancestry have turned their backs on learning and wisdom, and "now puft vp with sdeignfull insolence, / Despise the brood of blessed Sapience," failing to patronize heroic poetry and scorning both learning and noble deeds. Clio thus laments that "succeeding ages" shall "haue no light / Of things forepast, nor moniments of time, / And all that in this world is worthie hight, / Shall die in darknesse, and lie hid in slime" (*Teares* 71–72, 103–06). Only Spenser's patroness remains as a shining exception to this decadent rule. Years later, Milton would confirm his predecessor's judgment, hailing the dowager countess as a beacon of light. The opening song of *Arcades* stresses her luminescence:

Look Nymphs, and Shepherds look,
What sudden blaze of majesty
Is that which we from hence descry,
Too divine to be mistook:
    This, this is she
To whom our vows and wishes bend,
Here our solemn search hath end.

Fame that her high worth to raise,
Seem'd erst so lavish and profuse,
We may justly now accuse
Of detraction from her praise,
    Less than half we find exprest,
    Envy bid conceal the rest

Mark what radiant state she spreads,
In circle round her shining throne,
Shooting her beams like silver threads.
This, this is she alone,
    Sitting like a Goddess bright,
    In the center of her light.   (*Arcades*, 1–19)

The imagery of these stanzas, J. M. Wallace notes ("Milton's *Arcades*," 78–80), establishes the dowager countess as a type of Wisdom, the "blessed Sapience" to whom Spenser's Clio refers in her lament and of whom Spenser had later sung in "An Hymne of Heavenly Beavtie," which describes Wisdom as a figure

Clad like a Queene in royall robes, most fit
For so great powre and peerelesse maiestie.
And all with gemmes and iewels gorgeously
Adornd, that brighter then the starres appeare,
And make her natiue brightnes seem more cleare.

    (*HHB*, 185–89)

In Milton's text, no mention is made of jewels, and the dowager countess's own "radiant state" is thus even more heavily stressed, as it is in the scriptural source that both Spenser and Milton draw upon, the Wisdom of Solomon, which describes Wisdom as "the brightnes of the euerlasting light, the vndefiled mirroure of the maiestie of God, and the image of his goodnes.... For she is more beautiful then the sunne, and is aboue all the order of the starres, and the light is not to be compared vnto her" (Wisd. of Sol. 7:26, 29).

As Lewalski argues, Milton's directing such praise to a 73-year-old woman challenges "the Neoplatonic assumption" central to the Caroline court masques: "that [physical] beauty is the clear manifestation of inner virtue" ("Milton's *Comus*," 300; compare Wallace, "Milton's *Arcades*," 78). Milton praises not the loveliness of the aged noblewoman, but her dignity and spiritual luminosity. In Jonson's 1631 masque, *Loves Triumph Through Callipolis*, King Charles and his men journey to the throne of state and find there a queen whose light illuminates her entire realm. In *Arcades*, too, searchers undertake a pilgrimage toward an enthroned woman; but theirs is a "solemn search" very different from the erotic quest portrayed in the court masque. They gaze not upon the Neoplatonic ideal of chaste earthly beauty apotheosized, but upon Wisdom—the *Heavenly* Beauty Spenser had praised in the fourth of his *Fowre Hymnes*—embodied in a stately matriarch.[11] In Jonson's masque, Henrietta Maria's virtue is curiously braided together with her beauty in "interwoven lines of good and fair" that only the "mind's eye" can discern (*Complete Masques*, 456); but the goodness of the dowager countess in *Arcades* is plainly visible, "Too divine to be mistook" (*Arcades*, 4). Wallace argues that the Wisdom theme of *Arcades* is most clearly established by the fact that the dowager countess's worth, now witnessed after a long pilgrimage, exceeds what "Fame" had said of her. The Queen of Sheba traveled from afar to discover whether Solomon's reputation for wisdom was merited, and ended by admitting to the king that "the one halfe was not tolde me: for thou hast more wisdome and prosperitie, then I haue heard by reporte" (1 Kings 10:7).[12] In the same way, the visitors to Harefield find that the dowager countess exceeds all rumor and that they "may justly now accuse" Fame "Of detraction from her praise," since "Less than half [they] find exprest / *Envy* bid conceal the rest" (*Arcades*, 10,

11, 12–13). But *true* fame is, as Latona's son Apollo will tell the "uncouth Swain" of *Lycidas,* "no plant that grows on mortal soil" (*Lycidas,* 78). The Genius of *Arcades* will thus "lead" the Arcadian visitors to "where [they] may more near behold / What shallow-searching *Fame* hath left untold; / Which [the Genius] full oft amidst these shades alone / Ha[s] sat to wonder at, and gaze upon" (*Arcades,* 40–43).

Thus led, they will see a lady whose dignity brings to mind the greatest of the pagan mother goddesses:

> Might she the wise *Latona* be,
> Or the tow'red *Cybele,*
> Mother of a hundred gods;
> *Juno* dares not give her odds;
>   Who had thought this clime had held
>   A deity so unparallel'd?   (*Arcades,* 20–25)

This final stanza of the first song in *Arcades* stresses the dowager countess's likeness to Latona and Cybele, while elevating her above Juno. As Wallace points out, Latona, also known as Leto, was the mother of Apollo and Diana by Jupiter; she was known more for having been persecuted by the jealous Juno and for her own vengeful fury against Niobe than for her wisdom, but she is here called "wise," thus making the Wisdom theme of the work "wholly unambiguous" (Wallace, "Milton's *Arcades,*" 80). Wallace believes that "No amount of research into the history of Cybele and Latona" would associate them with *Sapientia;* the Dowager Countess's status as a Wisdom-figure relies, he insists, upon her own reputation and upon the allusion to Solomon and the Queen of Sheba earlier in the same song (85).

Research does, however, reveal a link between Latona and Wisdom; for Latona was the mother of Apollo, whose function as the "president" of the Muses the mythographer George Sandys describes in terms reminiscent of the Hebrew Bible's Wisdom; in the Wisdom of Solomon, Solomon says that when God granted him Wisdom, he received "true knowledge of the things that are, so that I knowe how the worlde was made, and the powers of the elements....For wisdome the worker of all things, hathe taught me it....She also reacheth from one end to another mightely, and comely doeth she order all things" (7:17, 21; 8:1). In Sandys, Apollo plays "harmoniously on the instrument of this world, moving in order and measure, and consorting with every part; so that by his meanes there is no dissonancy in nature." He is, moreover, a grandfather of sorts to the poets, for "*Jupiter* the divine mind, inspires *Apollo; Apollo* the Muses; and they their legitimate issue. Who are called by *Plato* the fathers of wisdome; and interpreters of the Gods" (Sandys, *Ovid's Metamorphosis*, 248, 249). Latona, as mother of Apollo, is thus the ultimate maternal source of divinely inspired poetic wisdom, great-grandmother of the Muses' children. By calling Latona "wise," Milton cements the association between this ancient mother goddess and the Wisdom that Solomon says was the "mother" of every good thing that he received (Wisd. of Sol. 7:12). The young poet could not have picked a more perfect classical type to complement a lady distinguished both by her patronage of the arts and by her motherhood.

But since Latona was the mother of only two divinities, Milton also compares the dowager countess—who was the mother, grandmother, and great-grandmother of many noble individuals—to Cybele, "Mother of a hundred gods," described by Sandys as a type of "the Earth which supporteth so many: said to be the mother of the Gods; or rather the general mother of all things" (Sandys, *Ovid's Metamorphosis*, 491). Juno—whose maternal role is subordinated to her function as the queen and consort of Jove and thus as "the President of marriage" and whose bird, the peacock, is "a proud and ambitious creature, affecting high places" (ibid., 298, 113)—thus seems in context to be the type of the Stuart queen consort, who cannot compete with the dowager countess as a matriarchal authority.

The web of imagery that links the dowager countess to the Wisdom of Scripture and to the mother goddesses of pagan antiquity also establishes her, I would argue, as a type of Ecclesia. For the church is a community of faith to whom God "giue[s]...

wisdome, and send[s his] holy Spirit from aboue" (Wisd. of Sol.
9:17), and "The children of wisdome are the Church of the righteous" (Ecclus. 3:1).[13] Like the Countess of Cumberland as a
type of Ecclesia in Lanyer's *Salve Deus,* Milton's "rural queen"
lives apart from the court, and the goodness of the rural estate
over which she presides depends upon the faithful ministry of a
pastoral caretaker, the Genius of the Wood. This local deity of
Harefield is a protective and healing "power" who cares for the
dowager countess's "fair wood." And just as the dowager countess is everything that Henrietta Maria is not, so the Genius
is everything the false Laudian shepherds of *Lycidas* fail to be.
The figure (whose gender is never specified) describes his or her
duties in terms that stress the healing of harms in a fallen world.
The Genius lives "in Oak'n bow'r," and has the skill

> To nurse the Saplings tall, and curl the grove
> With Ringlets quaint, and wanton windings wove.
> And all my Plants I save from nightly ill,
> Of noisome winds, and blasting vapors chill;
> And from the Boughs brush off the evil dew,
> And heal the harms of thwarting thunder blue,
> Or what the cross dire-looking Planet smites,
> Or hurtful Worm with canker'd venom bites.
> When Ev'ning gray doth rise, I fetch my round
> Over the mount, and all this hallow'd ground,
> And early ere the odorous breath of morn
> Awakes the slumb'ring leaves, or tassell'd horn
> Shakes the high thicket, haste I all about,
> Number my ranks, and visit every sprout
> With puissant words, and murmurs made to bless.
>
> (*Arcades,* 45–60)

In these lines, the Genius is a gentle, feminine gardener, an Eve-
like figure nursing her plants and weaving the wanton growth
of the estate; but the same figure is also a watchful, masculine
guard like Gabriel in *Paradise Lost,* patrolling his round and
numbering his ranks. As a poet, moreover, the Genius combines
the masculine force of "puissant words" with the preverbal,

feminine sound of "murmurs made to bless." Uniting male and female, as does the priest in Donne's poem "To Mr. Tilman," this spirit of nature thus demonstrates the essential harmony that rules in the dowager countess's beautifully Reformed domain, despite its fallen condition.

Indeed, the Genius provides an alternative to the Elysian fictions of Charles and Henrietta Maria, whose masques regularly represented their union as a blending of the French lily and the English rose and declared their reign a new golden age, their court a paradise. In place of the royal couple, Milton presents a quietly androgynous figure whose role is to nurture and mend the ills of a postlapsarian Eden, rather than to deny its diseases. As Brown observes, "the figure of healing, quietly but firmly, assumes the fallen nature of the world.... it is part of a large strategy of praise, that special protective powers ordained by God should be associated with the countess's estate. But a lesser poet than Milton would have *said* that it was because of her presence that such prosperous benediction reigned." Milton instead compliments the mistress of Harefield by assuming her ability to discern the unspoken implications of Genius's activities (*Milton's Aristocratic Entertainments,* 56). Harefield is no *papier-mâché* Eden, free of the "hurtful Worm" that "with canker'd venom bites"; rather, it is a true paradise regained, in which grace operates freely to heal the sickness the worm inflicts. And as the Wisdom of Solomon asserts, it is Wisdom herself who makes possible such healing: "the waies of them which are vpon earth, are reformed, & men are taught the things that are pleasant vnto [God], and are preserued thorow wisdome" (Wisd. of Sol. 9:18). Ruled over by an embodiment of Wisdom, Harefield is a true locus of grace.

The Genius's ministrations are tactile and verbal rather than visual and olefactory like the ceremonial "lustration" of Henrietta Maria's city in *Love's Triumph Through Callipolis.* As the masque begins, a speaker introduces an antimasque of profane lovers (a boaster, a balladeer, a jealous man, a melancholic, and other such "slaves to sense") who have invaded the sacred precincts of Callipolis (Jonson, *Complete Masques*, 457). Before Henrietta Maria's ideal Beauty can be joined to the ideal Love represented by Charles, the Chorus must purify the place, ceremonially *"walk[ing] about with their censers"* full of burning incense and driving out the unsuitably sensual and vice-ridden lovers (ibid., 457). This ritual (which must certainly have appeared to Milton to be outrageously Laudian and papistical) contrasts markedly with the homely household activities of the Harefield Genius, who nurses, brushes off, bustles quickly about, and then—without further ado—speaks the words and makes the sounds that the tender young plants need to hear.

In *Arcades*, such poetic sound enhances vision, providing a deeper understanding of and appreciation for that which the eyes gaze upon.[14] Even as it does so, however, it admits its own limitations: specifically, its inability to represent to mortal ears things that are beyond their ken. The Genius of the Wood explains that

> in deep of night, when drowsiness
> Hath lockt up mortal sense, then listen I
> To the celestial *Sirens'* harmony,
> That sit upon the nine infolded Spheres
> And sing to those that hold the vital shears
> And turn the Adamantine spindle round,
> On which the fate of gods and men is wound.
> Such sweet compulsion doth in music lie,
> To lull the daughters of *Necessity*,
> And keep unsteady Nature to her law,
> And the low world in measur'd motion draw
> After the heavenly tune, which none can hear
> Of human mold with gross unpurged ear.   (*Arcades*, 61–73)

As John Creaser observes, the Genius's insistence that heavenly music is beyond the audience's reach—inaudible even to the dowager countess herself—pointedly revises earlier aristocratic texts. "In Marston's entertainment for the same Countess of Derby years earlier," he notes, "the audience did hear what was said to be the music of the spheres. *Tempe Restored* paid its audience the same high compliment.... But Milton implies the common humanity of his hearers even after celebrating the Countess in conventional terms as 'a goddess bright'" ("'The present aid,'" 129–30). This gesture, like the plant-healing passage, is thus a gentle reminder that Harefield is part of a fallen world and at the same time a compliment to Harefield's mistress as one too good to desire undue flattery.

But, as the following lines make clear, she is also too good not to praise as highly as possible within the limits of piety. For the Genius of the Wood concludes his speech with deep reverence couched in the subjunctive mood, insisting that, though no mortal can hear the music of the spheres,

> yet such music worthiest were to blaze
> The peerless height of her immortal praise,
> Whose luster leads us, and for her most fit,
> If my inferior hand or voice could hit
> Inimitable sounds.   (*Arcades*, 74–78)

These lines reinforce the dowager countess's role as a Wisdom figure; for Wisdom, Solomon says, "shal lead [him] soberly in [his] workes" (Wisd. of Sol. 9:11), and the "rural Queen" of Harefield is she "Whose luster leads us" (*Arcades*, 94, 76). The line also recalls the church as reliable guide in Donne's "Annuntiation and Passion." Knowing that no one can adequately sing the "immortal praise" of such a figure, the Genius nevertheless expresses the desire to rise to the level that a great lady's goodness inspires and, in doing so, to transcend earthly limitations and enter into a music beyond this world, a music John Donne called "th'Extemporall song... / (Learn'd the first hower, that we see the King)" (*Sidney*, 51–52) and that Milton himself would call "the unexpressive nuptial Song" (*Lycidas*, 176) of heaven.

In "At a Solemn Music"—probably written not long after *Arcades*—Milton's concluding lines use a music image to evoke both the longing of the faithful on earth to join in that "nuptial Song" and the church's identity as the bride of Christ: "O may we soon again renew that Song, / And keep in tune with

Heav'n, till God ere long / To his celestial consort us unite, / To live with him, and sing in endless morn of light" ("At a Solemn Music," 25–28). Since "consort" means not only, as Carey's note observes, "a company of musicians," but also the wife of a ruler, the lines evoke both oneness with God's spouse and participation in the song she sings. The poet is praying to be made, like Elizabeth Drury in *The First Anniversarie*, "a part both of the Quire, and Song" (*FirAn*, 10). In *Arcades*, then, when the poet/minister directs the visitors toward a lady who is worthy of the spheres' music, that summons invites them to move toward union with the Church Triumphant.

The Genius is, moreover, determined to sing as they move toward her throne; despite the impossibility of reproducing the music of the spheres, "yet as we go, / Whate'er the skill of lesser gods can show, / I will assay, her worth to celebrate (*Arcades*, 78–80). He thus recalls the imperative of *The First Anniversarie* in which all who "vnderstood / Her worth" must "celebrate" a "Queene" and in which the poet himself refuses to be "deterre[d]" by her "incomprehensiblenesse" (*FirAn*, 72–73, 2, 7, 469). Having promised to sing and play after completing his speech, the Genius concludes with a final image of the luminous queen, vested in holiness, whom the visitors are bound to reverence: "And so attend ye toward her glittering state; / Where ye may all that are of noble stem / Approach, and kiss her sacred vesture's hem" (*Arcades*, 81–83). The text of *Arcades* ends with the Genius singing and playing the second song as he conducts the visitors to the dowager countess's chair, "where she sits / Clad in splendor as befits / Her deity" and the third song, the one urging them to "dance no more" in Arcady (*Arcades*, 91–93, 96).

The figure for whose sake the visitors are urged to reject Arcady and all its delights is, I would conclude, both transcendent and immanent, both heavenly and human. As the luminous queen and wise mother-goddess "Whose luster leads" all who turn their eyes to her, she is a reflection of divine Wisdom, God's "delite" (Prov. 8:30) who "comely doeth…order all things" (Wisd. of Sol. 8:1). She is also a type of divine Sapientia's created reflection, the wisdom that "filleth men with her frutes" (Ecclus. 1:20), and of the Church Triumphant, the heavenly consort of God in whose "Sphere-born" song ("At a Solemn Music," 2) all the faithful long to join. At the same time, however, she is a venerable queen mother in whose earthly realm a divinely called minister nurtures, heals, and cares for every tender shoot; and as such, Alice Spencer Stanley Egerton is a figure of the Reformed Church Militant, Milton's Protestant alternative both to the Roman Catholic madonna figure, Henrietta Maria, and to the English episcopacy whose faults he would criticize so bitterly only four years later in *Lycidas*.

Indeed, *Arcades* defines the dowager countess's estate in terms that evoke his later description of the church as a "family" under an "economicall"—that is, "domestick" and familial government.[15] The ultimate authority in such a family is not a human matriarch, but the divine Father: the "Jove" who has assigned the Genius of the Wood his powers and his duties. In *The Reason of Church Government*, that Father commissions the pastor of each congregation as "his spiritual deputy," entrusting the spiritual welfare of the faithful to a "minister" intimately familiar with his congregation and able to diagnose and treat "all [its] secretest diseases"; but the same father also expects every member of that congregation to ascend to the "hill top of sanctity and goodnesse" through participation in "holy duties" (YP 1:837, 842, 843). Thus, the Genius's long, central speech not only tells of how conscientiously he carries out the healing and nurturing duties assigned to him "by lot from *Jove*," but also invites all the shoots of the estate's "noble stem" to step forward into its Holy of Holies where they may advance to "greater grace" by "serv[ing]"—as he does—the "great Mistress of yon princely shrine" (*Arcades*, 44, 82, 104, 105, 36).

2. Ecclesiastical Discipline and Virginal Wisdom in *A Mask*

While *Arcades* celebrates a rural, decidedly Protestant alternative to Caroline court culture and religion, its religio-political implications remain relatively conservative; the queenly, maternal figure whose radiance guides the participants retains the authority and gravitas Donne affords the church as the third person of the feminine trinity in his "Annuntiation and Passion." Milton's prose treatises of the early 1640s make clear, however, that his evolving notion of Ecclesia would eventually lead him to define the Church Militant in far different terms: not as a radiant "starre" that guides souls toward heaven (*Annun*, 26), nor as a great queen mother ruling benevolently over her children, but as a pure, yet imperiled and fallible young virgin who is herself in need of guidance. The Lady of Milton's *Mask Presented at Ludlow Castle* is a figure of the pilgrim church thus defined; modeled on two traditional types of the Church Militant—the woman of Revelation 12, who wanders in the wilderness and is threatened by the Antichrist, and the bride of Canticles, who travels in search of her divine spouse—the Lady figures the pilgrim Ecclesia as a virginal daughter and sister who finds herself lost in the woods and who must in the end be rescued from captivity. And yet, from the mouth of that young virgin issues a discourse ringing with moral authority, theological self-assurance, and philosophical empowerment; and the minister of grace who ultimately frees her from bondage is a fellow virgin who responds to her virtue and her need by exercising a saving power that is not paternal, fraternal, *or* maternal, but sororal. In short, the Lady freed from Comus's chair by Sabrina is not the queenly, matriarchal "Goddess" of *Arcades*; she is neither the divine Wisdom of Proverbs 8 nor the created wisdom of the Deutero-canonical books who so closely resembles her divine counterpart and whom Augustine hails as "our mother...in heaven" whom "no change or variation affects" (*Confessions*, 12.20–21). Rather, she embodies the practical wisdom described in Ecclesiasticus: "she" who "goeth with the chosen women, and is knowen with the righteous and faithful," "the gift of the Lord" who "remaineth for the godlie" (Ecclus. 1:15, 11:17).

In Milton's portrayal, this wisdom is an intellectual virtue nearly indistinguishable from the moral virtue of chastity.[16]

The Lady defends herself valiantly and sagaciously against a figure representing moral decadence and ecclesiastical oppression but also opens herself to the aid of heaven, acknowledging her youthful limitations. She thus enacts the firmly Arminian theology of grace that distinguishes Milton's beliefs from those of Laud's Puritan adversaries and, at the same time, evokes the anti-authoritarian ecclesiology that would lead the poet to step forth, in *Lycidas* and the prose tracts of the 1640s, as prelacy's most formidable scourge.[17] The primary subjects of Milton's *Mask* are the virtue of chastity and, in particular, the powers and limitations of militantly chaste virginity; the work comments only indirectly and symbolically on the virtue of wisdom and on ecclesiastical matters. Yet, as Alice-Lyle Scoufos and Catherine I. Cox have shown, readers can learn much by studying the Lady as a type of the church. Doing so in light of the subtly shifting definitions of wisdom that emerge as the *Mask* unfolds leads to a new appreciation for the Lady's polyvalent significance: she exemplifies, I would argue, both the sapient "discipline" of a nonconformist Ecclesia and the wise mixture of valor and vulnerability that, according to Milton's Arminian theology of grace and works, preserves the spiritual virginity of the regenerate soul. This "sage / And serious" Lady is rescued from bondage, moreover, not by the direct intervention of a masculine deity, but by the ministrations of her fellow virgin, Sabrina, in whom are united grace and Edenic nature.

Milton's Lady may be interpreted as a type of the church most clearly near the end of the *Mask*, when the Attendant Spirit envisions the "Celestial *Cupid* ... / Hold[ing] his dear *Psyche* sweet entranc't / After her wand'ring labors long" (*Mask*, 1004–06) and celebrates the "blissful" offspring of their union, born "from her fair unspotted side" (*Mask*, 1010, 1009).[18] As John Leonard points out, the term "unspotted" evokes Ephesians 5:27, in which Christ is said to have given himself for the church in order to "make it vnto him self a glorious Church, not hauing spot or wrincle, or anie suche thing." "Milton," Leonard notes, thus "daringly imagines the consummation of the celestial marriage" ("'Good Things,'" 125); but even as he does so, he glances backward at the toil and trials of the Church Militant's sojourn in the wilderness, toils and trials that the audience of the *Mask* has just seen dramatized. The virtuous young daughter of the Earl of Bridgewater, as she wanders in the forest and endures Comus's attempts to seduce her, is thus a type both of the individual Christian *"Psyche"* and of the pilgrim church who will one day become the "eternal Bride" of "Celestial" Love in the person of Christ (*Mask*, 1005, 1008, 1004).

During her "wand'ring labors," however, neither the individual soul nor the church is perfect and infallible. As Scoufos demonstrates, the Lady of the *Mask* may be read as Milton's doctrinally nuanced Protestant response to centuries of tradition—from writings of the church fathers, through medieval mystery plays depicting the Antichrist's persecutions of Ecclesia, to Protestant allegorical dramas on the same subject—which interpreted the woman of Revelation 12 "as a symbol of the church in the Latter Days" (Scoufos, "Mysteries in Milton's Masque,"115).[19] As Scoufos explains, medieval and post-Reformation Catholic writings identify this wandering, persecuted woman as representing both the church and the Blessed Virgin Mary, and they insist on her virginal purity; both Donne and Lanyer work within this tradition. But many Protestant authors, including several who dramatized Revelation in Reformed versions of medieval mystery plays, rejected both the idea that the Virgin Mary was to be identified with Ecclesia and the notion that the church represented by the dragon-threatened woman of Revelation remains forever uncorrupted by the evils of the Antichrist (see Scoufos, 121–26). Such writers tended to distinguish between the faithfulness of the invisible and mystical body of Christ, and the errant ways of the visible church, much of which they believed to have been seduced by the Antichrist. Milton, Scoufos argues, draws upon this kind of distinction in the *Mask:* the Lady as a type of Ecclesia is thus "virginal, but she is not the Holy Virgin. Milton works softly but surely through the controverted ideas of the Reformation. His choice is of a pure, virtuous image, yet one which is vulnerable to ruin" (121).[20] More vulnerable, one might add, than Spenser's Una, perhaps the most famous Revelation-inspired figure of the virgin church-errant. Like Milton's Lady, Una wanders in the wilderness, is vulnerable to the deceptions of a magician, and resists the sexual assault of a captor; but Una never finds herself magically paralyzed, nor does she descend from the heights of her allegorical function as a type of truth in order to argue particulars with her enemies.[21]

The woman of Revelation is not the only biblical type of the church militant evoked by Milton's Lady; she also resembles — as does Una — the bride of Solomon's Song of Songs. As Cox points out, the bride, as she was "understood by Protestant translators, commentators and poets," is a type of the warfaring soul and the pilgrim Ecclesia of which that soul is a member; she is beautiful and chaste, yet subject to error and abuse ("The Garden Within," 24). In the biblical text, the bride "rise[s]" and "go[es] about in the citie, by the stretes & by the open places," and "seke[s] him that [her] soule loueth"; and she "commeth vp out of the wildernes" in her search (Song of Sol. 3:2, 6). She describes herself as both "blacke" and "comelie" (1:4).[22] Being neither unassailable nor invulnerable, she loses sight of her beloved, and is victimized by "watchmen" to whom she turns for help and direction (5:7); it is as a type of this fallible bride that Spenser's black-robed Una is capable of becoming lost with Redcrosse in the Wood of Errour and of failing to see through Archimago's deceptions. The Protestant writers on whom Cox focuses (including Antonio Brucioli, Francis Quarles, and George Gifford) stress even more heavily than does Spenser the bride's status "as a pilgrim or wandering woman"; they interpret her dark beauty as "paradoxically spotless and soiled" ("The Garden Within," 24, 29). Similarly, "While Milton's Lady remains chaste throughout the *Mask*, her enchantment and capture imply both persecution and spiritual error"; she is deceived and betrayed by Comus as the bride is by the "watchmen," whom Protestant interpreters identified as "false preachers..., tricksters, seducers, idolaters, and persecutors of the true church" (ibid., 30, 32).[23]

As Cox points out, moreover, Milton would later describe the ecclesiastical "discipline" by which Christ educates and perfects his virgin bride—makes her into the spotless Church Triumphant—in terms that recall the Lady of the *Mask* and thus retrospectively suggest her status as a type of Ecclesia. In *The Reason of Church Government* (which was published in 1642, a little over seven years after the *Mask* was first performed at Ludlow), Milton alludes again, as he had in the final song of the *Mask*, to Ephesians 5:27. Stressing that God is the father and Christ the betrothed husband of the church, Milton says that Christ, "expecting her to be presented before him a pure unspotted virgin...shew[s] his tender love to her" by "prescribing his owne wayes which he best" knows for "the improvement of her health and beauty," establishing specific means of instructing her and arranging the "discipline" according to which she is governed (YP 1:755; see Leonard, "'Good Things,'" 125). In the same work, Milton personifies ecclesiastical "discipline" in terms that recall the Lady's words at a memorable moment in the *Mask:* "'Discipline is not only the removall of disorder, but if any visible shape can be given to divine things, the very visible shape and image of vertue, whereby she is not only seene in the regular gestures and motions of her heavenly paces as she walkes, but also makes the harmony of her voice audible to mortall eares" (YP 1:751–52).[24] In her journey through this world, this passage asserts, both the church as a whole and each soul within her will see and be guided by the "visible shape" of divine virtue. In the *Mask*, just such a "form" comforts the perplexed and imperiled Lady, who declares, "O welcome pure-ey'd Faith, white-handed Hope, / Thou hov'ring Angel girt with golden wings, / And thou unblemish't form of Chastity, / I see ye visibly (*Mask*, 213–16). Reassured by what she sees, the Lady is emboldened to act as virtue incarnate, making the "harmony of her voice audible to mortal ears" (YP 1:752): "Such noise as I can make to be heard farthest / I'll venture, for my new enliv'n'd spirits / Prompt me" (*Mask*, 227–29).

The triad of virtues Milton's Lady envisions—faith, hope, and chastity—famously departs from the Pauline catalog of the theological virtues, displacing charity with chastity. Scholarly opinion is deeply divided on Milton's reason for making the shift; but one clear effect of his doing so, I would argue, is to emphasize that the Lady is a type, not of the Church Triumphant, nor of an episcopally governed (and governing) *mater ecclesia,* but of the Church Militant as Milton would portray her in *The Reason of Church Government:* a young virgin who, "though she be well instructed, yet is...still under a more strait tuition" (YP 1:755).[25] Later in the *Mask,* as many critics have observed, the Lady refers to the "doctrine of Virginity" using the same pair of modifiers—"sage / And serious"—that Milton would use in *Areopagitica* to praise Spenser as "a better teacher then *Scotus* or *Aquinas*" (YP 2:516). It is no surprise, then, that the virginal Lady's vision of the virtues owes much to Spenser, and specifically to his portrayal of the three theological virtues in book 1 of *The Faerie Queene,* where the Redcrosse Knight encounters the three sisters in the House of Holinesse.[26] Milton would no doubt have recalled Spenser's description of Charity as the only one of the three who is *not* a virgin:

> The eldest two most sober, chast, and wise,
> *Fidelia* and *Speranza* virgins were,
> Though spousd, yet wanting wedlocks solemnize;
> But faire *Charissa* to a lovely fere
> Was lincked, and by him had many pledges dere.
>
> (*FQ* 1.10.4.5–9)

Carissa is not present to greet Redcrosse and Una when they first arrive, since she has just given birth to a new baby; but when the repentant knight is at last introduced to her, he encounters a figure whose defining characteristic is maternal love: "Her neck and breasts were euer open bare, / That ay thereof her babes might sucke their fill"; and "A multitude of babes about her hong, / Playing their sports, that ioyd her to behold, / Whom still she fed, whiles they were weake and young" (*FQ* 1.10.30.7–8; 31.1–3). Though Carissa is still "a woman in her freshest age" who is "chast in worke and will" (*FQ* 1.10.30.1, 6), her nursing breasts identify her as one who has advanced from virgin minority (and the "strait tuition" it requires) to become a parental figure in her own right. As a fecund source of spiritual nurture, she resembles the *mater ecclesia* of medieval art and liturgy. But Milton's Lady has nothing to do with such a triumphantly nurturing and fully ripe Ecclesia; she is, on the contrary, a youthful virgin pilgrim who has not yet been united with her divine spouse. She is thus concerned less with *caritas*, the theological virtue of love selflessly dispensed, and more with *castitas*, the moral virtue of desire well directed or, as Saint Augustine puts it, "love well ordered" (Augustine, *On Lying*, 476). Chastity thus defined is, in Miltonic terms, love "under a more strait tuition," the version of *caritas* appropriate to a virgin.[27] In *The Reason of Church Government*, the same chapter in which Milton characterizes the church as a young virgin and defines "discipline" as virtue made visible also specifies more literally that ecclesiastical "discipline is the practick work of preaching directed and apply'd as is most requisite to *particular* duty" (YP 1:755–56; emphasis mine); the particular duty of the virgin Lady in the *Mask* is to find her way safely out of the woods, and the vision of Faith, Hope, and Chastity assures her that God will help her to do just that.

She is in error, however, in her belief "That he, the Supreme good . . . / Would send a glist'ring Guardian, if need were, / To keep [her] life and honor *unassail'd*" (*Mask*, 217, 219–20; emphasis mine). For God in fact allows them to be assailed; the "glist'ring Guardian" he sends does not prevent that. And though the Lady's faith, hope, and chastity preserve her from being seduced by the "lickerish baits" Comus offers (700), they cannot prevent him from imprisoning her before the Attendant Spirit arrives on the scene and—unable even then to help her himself—summons Sabrina to undo the spell of the "false enchanter" (814). Milton clearly intends us to see the gap between what the

Lady expects and what she experiences, for the Elder Brother's initial assertion that "A thousand liveried Angels lackey" the chaste soul, "Driving far off each thing of sin and guilt" (455–56) must be revised when he hears from the Attendant Spirit that his sister has been tricked by Comus; he must then concede that "Virtue may be assail'd" (589). Even then, the Elder Brother's insistence that it "may be assail'd, but never hurt, / Surpris'd by unjust force but not enthrall'd" (589–90) is soon shown to be only partially correct. The "false enchanter" (814) *is* able to hold the "corporal rind" of the Lady "immanacl'd" (664, 665) until Sabrina comes to her rescue.

The religio-political implications of her captivity become clear when one considers, as Leah Marcus does, that "The specifics of [Comus's] vocabulary, his festive attitudes, his charming cup...amount to a devastating portrait of clerics in the Church of England, the Mother Church" (*Politics of Mirth*, 86). Most specifically, as Marcus observes, Comus's *carpe diem* arguments resemble those of the Laudian apologists for holiday merrymaking; and when he insists that the Lady conform to "the canon laws of our foundation" (*Mask*, 808), he sounds positively prelatical, if not Roman Catholic. It is impossible to say for certain, Marcus adds, whether Comus's "foundation" is to be read as Roman Catholic, Anglican, or simply pagan: "But Milton's lack of specificity suggests that there is no significant difference....in any case [Comus's] call for a humble surrender to the cycle of the green world encourages a pre-Reformation stupor of ignorance leading to spiritual perdition" (195).[28]

But that it is specifically Archbishop Laud, and the institution of prelatical episcopacy that Milton has in mind is confirmed, I would argue, by the fact that Comus confines Milton's embodiment of the church militant in a "marble venom'd seat" (*Mask*, 916); that is, in a marble "chair set apart for the holder of some position of authority or dignity, the throne of a king or a bishop" (*OED*, "seat," n. def. 8a), and specifically one "Imbued with some virulent or malevolent quality; harmful or injurious in some way; noxious" (*OED*, "venomed," ppl. a. def. 3). The "*enchanted*

Chair" (*Mask*, in *Complete Poems*, s.d., 105) of Comus the false "Shepherd" (*Mask*, 321) is thus a nightmarish parody of a bishop's *kathedra*. Indeed, if one construes "marble venom'd" as a phrase meaning venomed with marble rather than as two separate modifiers (marble and venomed), then the marble — in all its opulence and Italianate antiquity — *is* the venom, the prelatical poison that refuses reformation and "In stony fetters fix[es]" the virginal church that is its victim (*Mask*, 819).

Comus immobilizes the Lady in his sinister marble chair in order to convince her, through the specious *carpe diem* philosophy he preaches, to drink from the "charmed Cup" he has inherited from Circe (*Mask*, 51). For as John Rumrich argues (*Milton Unbound*, 70–93), Comus's ability to imprison the Lady is not merely a function of his phallic aggression; it reflects the strong feminine and maternal associations of a figure who, though "Much like his Father" Bacchus, resembles "his Mother more" (*Mask*, 57).[29] In urging the Lady to drink from the "cordial Julep.../ That flames and dances" within the "crystal bounds" of his powerful mother's chalice, Comus insists that "one sip of this" both implies and attains wisdom: "Be wise, and taste" (*Mask*, 672–73, 811, 813). In *Arcades*, such an invitation to false epicurean/Laudian sapience could be parried by a "Goddess bright" possessed of maternal authority weightier than Circe's (*Arcades*, 18).[30] But in the *Mask*, no one could mistake the Lady for "the wise *Latona*" (*Arcades*, 20). Young, virginal, and conscious of her own "credulous innocence" (*Mask*, 697), she is not the scriptural Sapientia who provides Solomon with "All good things" and is "the autor thereof, & ... the mother of these things" (Wisd. of Sol. 7:11, 12). But she does know what "good things" are (*Mask*, 703) and is able to discern that they do not include the "treasonous offer" made her by someone who is not himself "good" (*Mask*, 702, 703).

The Lady refuses Comus's offer not because she cannot admit to her own desires, but because he is Comus — the embodiment of "*sensual Folly and Intemperance*" (*Mask*, 975) as well as the advocate of authoritarian "canon laws" (808). Her advocacy of "a well-govern'd and wise appetite" (705) is pivotal both in defining her virtue as an individual soul and in pointing to her function as a type of Ecclesia. The Lady's phrasing asserts not only that "appetite" must be "well-govern'd"—presumably by the higher faculties of will and reason, which take their cues from divine authority—but also that appetite can and should itself be "wise," that it has the wisdom to select the "good things" it will find really and substantially "delicious" (703, 704) rather than momentarily pleasing and ultimately cloying or destructive. And because appetite is gendered feminine in the Augustinian hierarchy of the soul, the idea that she is both "wise" in her own right and in need of governance or guidance from without points toward and helps to define the free yet feeble feminine "Virtue" in the Attendant Spirit's final song (1022). The Lady as she performs in *A Mask* is the visible embodiment of that virtue, which is "wise appetite": the will-to-ascent incarnate, who "alone is free" (1019). This free though feeble Virtue is the essence of Ecclesia as the poet conceives of her: no maternal avatar of divine Sapience, but a "Virgin wise and pure"—like the young lady thus addressed in one of Milton's sonnets, still "in the prime of earliest youth," and yet "Wisely...shunn[ing] the broad way and the green" in order to "labor up the Hill of Heav'nly Truth" (*Sonnet IX*, 14, 1–2, 4)

In the *Mask*, the Lady's eloquent defense of temperance and her powerful refusal to grace Comus's ears with a defense of virginity completes a multifaceted portrait initially sketched much earlier in the *Mask* of a youthful, feminine, and virginal wisdom. In order to appreciate the nature of the wisdom that the Lady articulates and embodies, we must first glance backward at that portrait. Doing so will clarify how the *Mask* defines Milton's idea of the Church Militant and the regenerate soul as possessing neither divine sapience, nor the maternal gravitas of wise maturity, but instead the emergent wisdom of a youthful maiden.

The *Mask*'s exploration of wisdom begins when the Elder Brother, confronted by the Second Brother's anxiety regarding their sister's exposed and vulnerable situation, insists that being alone in the dark woods will not disconcert her, since

> Virtue could see to do what virtue would
> By her own radiant light, though Sun and Moon
> Were in the flat Sea sunk. And Wisdom's self
> Oft seeks to sweet retired Solitude,
> Where with her best nurse Contemplation
> She plumes her feathers, and lets grow her wings
> That in the various bustle of resort
> Were all to-ruffl'd, and sometimes impair'd.   (*Mask*, 373–80)

The image of Wisdom here as a winged female creature subtly stresses her youth: she is accompanied (even in "retired Solitude") by the personification of "Contemplation," who functions as her "nurse," and she retreats from human society in order to let "grow her wings," which are not yet fully fledged. In this passage, then, we are encouraged to see the young and sexually unfledged Lady as an embodiment of Wisdom no less than of Virtue more generally.

The Second Brother responds negatively and pragmatically to his sibling's image of Wisdom preening her feathers in seclusion; he attempts to disassociate the idea of Wisdom thus defined from the person of his sister, insisting that the wilderness, though it may be a place of quiet retreat for a contemplative desert Father, is filled with dangers for a lovely young girl. Wisdom, for him, is a poor, old, male "Hermit" with "gray hairs," while the Lady is a type not of wisdom, but of "beauty," which

> like the fair Hesperian Tree
> Laden with blooming gold, had need the guard
> Of dragon watch with unenchanted eye,
> To save her blossoms, and defend her fruit
> From the rash hand of bold Incontinence.
>
> (*Mask*, 390, 392, 393–97)

This retort is largely valid; it reminds the audience of the very real danger in which the Lady—who did not seek "solitude," but had it imposed upon her as a "misfortune" (286)—finds herself. In the lines just preceding the brothers' entrance, she has told Comus that she could not be "In a place / Less warranted...or less secure" (326–27) than the isolated wilderness in which she has encountered him. One might even argue that the Second Brother's argument exposes the Elder Brother, with his belief in "retired," contemplative wisdom, as in fact "but a youngling in the contemplation of evill" (*Areopagitica*; YP 2:515).

But the Second Brother's comparison of his sister's "Beauty" to the golden apples of the Hesperides and to a "Miser's treasure" (*Mask*, 399) ignores the Lady's agency, regarding a "single help-less maiden" as neither wise nor foolish, but "unowned" (402, 407). This perspective is as inadequate as the Elder Brother's. Their sister's decision to trust in Comus's guidance is errone-ous, but it is a reasoned choice, made with the expectation that it may still lead to further "trial" and wisely supplemented by the Lady's prayer that "Providence" watch over her and "square" that "trial / To [her] proportion'd strength" (329–30). The prayer is essential, for it acknowledges the degree to which any human choice may lead to circumstances from which one cannot escape through the power of unassisted human virtue or wisdom, and that some such circumstances are *not* a matter of choice.[31]

In the dialogue between the Lady's precocious male siblings, however, the Second Brother's overly objectified and commodi-fied view of "beauty" in need of protection is answered not by the Lady's sense of her own "strength" and God's role in assist-ing it beyond its "proportion'd" limits, but rather by the Elder Brother's images of chastity as divinely self-sufficient. Defining his sister's virtue as more than capable of warding off any con-ceivable attack upon her virginal body, he invokes "the old Schools of *Greece* / To testify the arms of Chastity" (439–40). The weapons he recalls from ancient myth include the "dread bow" of "*Dian*..., / Fair silver-shafted Queen for ever chaste" and, even more interestingly, the aegis of Athena:

> What was that snaky-headed *Gorgon* shield
> That wise *Minerva* wore, unconquer'd Virgin,
> Wherewith she freez'd her foes to congeal'd stone,
> But rigid looks of chaste austerity
> And noble grace that dash't brute violence
> With sudden adoration, and blank awe?
>
> (*Mask*, 441–42, 447–52)

Athena is a wisdom goddess as well as a virgin; her aegis functions not only as protective armor, but also as a weapon with offensive capabilities. The image of "wise *Minerva*" wielding her "*Gorgon* shield" thus adds a new dimension to the Elder Brother's earlier image of sapience. Having previously imagined Wisdom as contemplative, picturing her as a feathered young female who withdraws from the "bustle of resort" in order to preen her wings in solitude, he now describes Minerva in terms that evoke both militant chastity and a more active and aggressive version of wisdom, essentially eliding the two. Indeed, though the Elder Brother is very confident that he can answer his own rhetorical question about the meaning of the aegis, a more traditional and perhaps more mature interpretation was readily available to Milton and his audience. As Carey observes in his note on the passage, Natale Conti's *Mythologiae* interprets the aegis as an allegory not of chastity, but of wisdom: "Gorgonis caput in pectore gestabat, quia nemo contra solis claritatem aut contra sapientiam aciem oculorum intendere impune potest" [She wore the Gorgon's head on her breast, because no one can turn his eyes against the light of the sun or against wisdom and remain unharmed] (Carey, *Milton*, 198). The Elder Brother may believe that Athena's principal characteristic—at least as concerns his sister—is chastity, and certainly we are repeatedly invited to admire that virtue in the Lady.[32] But while only she can "see…visibly" the "unblemish't form of Chastity" (*Mask*, 216, 215), the entire audience can see the Lady herself and hear the Athena-like wisdom she utters in her verbal battle with Comus. Through her performance, wisdom is—to paraphrase *Paradise Lost* 3.51—admitted to the audience members' minds at two entrances, that of the eye and that of the ear.

The Lady's wisdom is, if anything, amplified in the 1637 quarto version of the *Mask*; for, though readers can neither see nor hear Alice Egerton's original performance, they in a sense hear and see even more than the Ludlow audience did. Though the printed text gives the reader access to the Lady only through the visible words on the page, the lines on virginity that Milton added to her speech (779–99) and Comus's terrified response to those lines (800–806)—also added to the text in the first print edition—present a virgin's words of wisdom as earth-shaking ordnance. In reading these lines, one cannot help but recall Conti's interpretation of wisdom as a dangerous weapon:

> Shall I go on?
> Or have I said enough? To him that dares
> Arm his profane tongue with contemptuous words
> Against the Sun-clad power of Chastity
> Fain would I something say, yet to what end?
> Thou hast nor Ear nor Soul to apprehend
> The sublime notion and high mystery
> That must be utter'd to unfold the sage
> And serious doctrine of Virginity,
> And thou art worthy that thou shouldst not know
> More happiness than this thy present lot.
> Enjoy your dear Wit and gay Rhetoric
> That hath so well been taught her dazzling fence,
> Thou art not fit to hear thyself convinc't;
> Yet, should I try, the uncontrolled worth
> Of this pure cause would kindle my rapt spirits
> To such a flame of sacred vehemence,
> That dumb things would be mov'd to sympathize,
> And the brute Earth would lend her nerves, and shake,
> Till all thy magic structures rear'd so high,
> Were shatter'd into heaps o'er thy false head.   (779–99)

As William Shullenberger cheers, "You go, girl!" ("Profession of Virginity," 83). The "Sun-clad power of Chastity" as the lady envisions it is a force nearly identical to wisdom as Conti defines it: a light so bright that someone cannot "turn his eyes against" it without being injured. But it would not, according to the Lady, be chastity or virginity itself, but rather the "something" she would say, should she choose to "unfold" virginity's "sage / And serious doctrine" that would lay Comus's world in ruins. "Sage" being a particularly fragrant synonym of "wise," its enjamb-ment underscores the fact that articulate wisdom is the most potent weapon in the Lady's—and by extension the soul's and the Church Militant's—arsenal of virtues. The Lady is confi-dent that, should she "go on," the "dumb things" of the earth would "lend" support to her "sacred vehemence." She thus con-firms Solomon's assertion that "wisdome openeth the mouth of the domme, and maketh the tongues of babes eloquent" (Wisd. of Sol. 10:21).

Comus's terrified response makes clear that the Lady's speech is no idle threat; his reaction confirms that she does possess a power akin to that of the aegis as Conti describes it. "She fables not," Comus says,

> I feel that I do fear
> Her words set off by some superior power;
> And though not mortal, yet a cold shudd'ring dew
> Dips me all o'er, as when the wrath of *Jove*
> Speaks thunder and the chains of *Erebus*
> To some of *Saturn's* crew.   (800–805)

Chilled by the Lady's words, he cannot afford to face the full force of the wisdom she could utter should she choose to do so.

But he is not, as in the Elder Brother's fantasy of Minerva's aegis, "freez'd ... to congeal'd stone" by his fear; rather, he springs into action:

> I must dissemble,
> And try her yet more strongly. Come, no more,
> This is mere moral babble, and direct
> Against the canon laws of our foundation;
> I must not suffer this, yet 'tis but the lees
> And settlings of a melancholy blood;
> But this will cure all straight, one sip of this
> Will bathe the drooping spirits in delight
> Beyond the bliss of dreams. Be wise, and taste.   (805–13)

This "dissembl[ing]" speech, which masks Comus's fear and rouses him to the use of force, demonstrates the inadequacy of the Elder Brother's insistence that chastity automatically "dash[es] brute violence / With sudden adoration and blank awe" (451–52). Neither chastity *nor* wise eloquence is sufficient to protect against "brute" coercion, be it sexual or ecclesiastical. The Lady is thus saved from having Comus's libertine/prelatical cup forcibly pressed to her lips only by the entrance of her brothers, who "wrest [Comus's] Glass out of his hand, and break it against the ground," then drive the magician and "his rout" from the stage (s.d., 109).

The boys' victory is dependent, of course, upon their "hav[ing]...about" them the protective herb called "*Haemony*" (*Mask*, 647, 638), the significance of which is another of the *Mask*'s most heavily debated cruxes. The Attendant Spirit says that the plant he gives the brothers is "more med'cinal...than that *Moly* / That *Hermes* once to wise *Ulysses* gave" (636–37); he thus associates haemony with another kind of wisdom, the wily cunning and hermeneutic ability of Odysseus, while at the same time insisting that this "small unsightly root, /...of divine effect" (629–30) provides even more perfect protection than that afforded the decidedly *un*chaste Odysseus by the pagan god of eloquence. The root given to Thyrsis by "a certain Shepherd Lad" (619) may, as Hanford argues, represent the Platonic doctrine of virtue; it may, as Sears Jayne argues, be a Christian version of "philosophical knowledge" (Jayne, "Subject of Milton's Masque," 177), or, as John M. Steadman puts it, "Christian wisdom" ("Milton's Haemony," 206); it may, even, as Cedric Brown asserts, be "the word of God as ministered by the pastor" (*Milton's Aristocratic Entertainments*, 105). Certainly, Barbara Lewalski is right to stress that, in giving the brothers haemony, the Attendant Spirit acts as "a teacher, dispensing heaven's aid through human means, not miracles" ("Milton's *Comus*," 314). And, to some extent, all of these meanings are combined in Milton's ambiguous representation of the plant "of sovran use / 'Gainst all enchantments" (*Mask*, 639–40). As Maryann Cale McGuire asserts, haemony's meaning lies in the very multiplicity of readings it evokes. Comprehending the classical wisdom that Renaissance allegorists like Sandys and Golding found in Homer and Ovid, as well as Christian tenets, haemony with all its symbolic and etymological implications represents the weight of moral wisdom available in Milton's time. Unlike faith or virtue, two alternate readings given haemony, moral lore can be communicated by one individual to another, by the Shepherd Lad to Thyrsis and by Thyrsis to the brothers. Understood as wisdom, haemony can offer protection, as the Attendant Spirit claims, allowing its possessor a means of recognizing evil and even countering it. (*Milton's Puritan Masque*, 154–55)

The haemony-wielding male rescuers succeed, however, only in driving out Comus; they fail to capture him, and haemony has no power to reverse the spell he has cast upon the Lady. No earthly wisdom, even if heaven-sent, is enough to set the soul or Ecclesia free. In order to liberate her, the Attendant Spirit must call upon Sabrina, who functions as an agent of divine grace capable of releasing the Lady from Comus's "marble venom'd seat / Smear'd with gums of glutinous heat" (*Mask*, 916–17).

These famous lines stick fast in the minds of readers, for they describe in graphic terms the means by which Comus not only immobilizes the Lady but also—on some level—soils her. Despite the fact that her "ensnared chastity" remains unseduced by his "lickerish baits," the nether parts of her anatomy are placed in contact with a substance that reeks of concupiscence. She is thus compromised by her foe in a way that Spenser's Una never is, even when she finds herself in the clutches of the lustful Sansloy; Una need only shriek, and the fauns and satyrs appear to liberate her. No mysterious "gums" entangle her person. There is far more room for the reader of Milton's *Mask* to speculate about the nature of the Lady's gluey predicament, and the debate over its meaning has thus been long and sometimes angry. On one side are psychoanalytic readings, the best of which is that of William Kerrigan, who interprets the Lady as a surrogate for Milton and asserts that her "root-bound virtue...is not free. It is in bondage to the desire denied" (*Sacred Complex*, 55).[33] For Kerrigan, then, the image of Cupid and Psyche united in the final song "concedes that sexuality is, if not in the end, in the end of this work at least, the protean lord of our desire, and worlds we yearn for will be marked as desirable by erotic symbolism, all the more so if we must forfeit sexuality in order to reach them" (57). On the other extreme of critical opinion, as Ronald Corthell observes, are critics who "treat the Lady as a female victim (albeit a resourceful and resistant one) of sexual assault" ("Go Ask Alice," 112). Particularly vehement in this regard is John Leonard, who indicts Kerrigan's reading as an endorsement of Comus's point of view, which amounts to a psychoanalytic *apologia* for rape. Leonard argues persuasively that the masque does not portray chastity as involving the forfeiture of sexuality and that the Lady's "sage / And serious doctrine of Virginity" — especially when read in conjunction with the images of Cupid and Psyche in the Attendant Spirit's final song — is not a celibate creed, but rather a teaching very much in keeping with the Puritan notion of chaste marriage as a species of virginity.[34]

Still, a more recent reading of *Comus* by Debora Shuger, while not weighing in on the Kerrigan/Leonard debate, essentially confirms Kerrigan's reading within the framework of ancient, medieval, and early modern theology: neither the male poet nor the virtuous Lady of his masque is free from the unavoidable element of concupiscence in postlapsarian human nature. Stressing that Comus's "gums of glutinous heat" are described as a sticky birdlime that ensnares the Lady's chastity, Shuger cites Saint Augustine's anguished response to his own nocturnal emissions as evidence that he is not yet "wholly freed from that birdlime of concupiscence" and reads the *Mask* in light of related medieval texts dealing with the question of whether or not wet dreams are sinful. Initially stressing "the fact that the Lady preserves her moral freedom and purity despite being trapped on a 'venom'd seat'" (*Mask*, 916), Shuger argues that "*A Maske* divests the body's unwilling captivity of any moral significance, in the process drastically revising Spenser's Protestant ethic" ("'Gums of Glutinous Heat,'" 7). But she goes on to note that the "gums of glutinous heat" "problematize the Lady's distinction between corporeal bondage and mental freedom" (9). For Comus's chair is "a piece of magic furniture, but also, in French, the word for the flesh, *la chaire*.... The temptation scene grapples with the threat of an involuntary sexuality that mocks rational control, with the fearful power of diabolic inseminations, with the shame of being caught in the birdlime of fallen nature" (8, 9). Shuger's reading—which, like Kerrigan's, interprets the Lady as a surrogate for the male poet—does the most of any to explain how the Lady can be both "a true Virgin" (*Mask*, 905) with the wisdom to speak words that strike awe into the heart of concupiscence embodied, and at the same time, a soul helplessly "Root-bound" (*Mask*, 662) in the flesh and reliant upon exterior aid to release her from the snare in which that enemy—which is no less interior than exterior—entangles her.[35] The Lady is both of these things, just as the bride of Canticles is both "comelie" and "blacke" (Song of Sol. 1:4), and just as "Virtue" is both "free" and "feeble" (*Mask*, 1019, 1022).

Virtue as Milton defines her in his *Mask* thus combines valiant pursuit of the good with wise acknowledgment of her own vulnerability and insufficiency. On the religio-political level of meaning, the Lady's "sage / And serious doctrine of Virginity" points to her status as a type of the church who longs to be released from the carnal bondage of prelatical government precisely because she knows herself to be a virgin "under more strait tuition," rather than an ample and authoritative mother ruling over her children. Divine grace comes quickly, administered by Sabrina as the Attendant Spirit describes her, not simply to aid virgins in general, but to assist a virgin in trouble, one who has valiantly helped herself, but is at the limits of her power: "maid'nhood she loves, and will be swift / To aid a Virgin, such as was herself, / In hard-besetting need" (*Mask*, 855–57). Only when that need is met by Sabrina's "sprinkl[ing] on [her] breast / Drops that from [her] fountain pure, / [She has] kept of precious cure" (911–13), is the Lady is released from bondage; but she is then utterly free. As A. S. P. Woodhouse pointed out decades ago ("*Comus* Once More," 221–22), the process of purification by grace is symbolized in the *Mask* by Sabrina's use of her "chaste palms moist and cold" to anoint and release the Lady. It is this "infusion of divine grace" ("*Comus* Once More," 222) that makes the soul and the church into the immaculate bride of Ephesians 5:27. Milton's emphasis on Sabrina's own virginal status, I would add, makes her grace-full, healing touch that of a sister and fellow victim rather than the spell of an all-powerful mother figure.[36]

Still, as Cedric Brown objects, "The concept of grace will not do as the unique signature of Sabrina" (*Milton's Aristocratic Entertainments,* 123), and this is so not only because the Lady and her brothers encounter "repeated acts of providence" throughout their journey toward Ludlow (ibid., 124), but also because Sabrina is as much an embodiment of Nature as an agent of divine grace. Even more clearly than Lanyer's *Salve Deus,* Milton's *Mask* unites Nature and grace in one female figure.[37] While in Lanyer's poem the Countess of Cumberland uses an oak tree as a Bible stand ("Cooke-ham," 83–84), Sabrina is both the keeper of a divine "fountain pure" from which flow spiritually and physically efficacious "Drops...of precious cure" (*Mask,* 912–13) and a Welsh river into which grateful shepherds "throw sweet garland wreaths" (*Mask,* 850). As Diane McColley notes ("Milton and Ecology," 164), the Lady's "eloquent resistance prepares for her rescue from Comus, but the local genius of the river Severn effects it; grace works not through Platonic philosophy but through" a water deity who "with moist curb sways the smooth Severn stream" (*Mask,* 825). As a gentle force of Nature, Sabrina "oft at Eve / Visits the herds along the twilight meadows" (843–44), healing "with precious vial'd liquors" the damage done by supernatural beings like "the shrewd meddling Elf" (*Mask,* 847, 846). Thus, when the Attendant Spirit descends "from the starry threshold of *Jove's* Court" (1) to intervene in the Lady's captivity by summoning Sabrina, "Heav'n

itself...stoop[s] to" aid "Virtue" (1023, 1022) by making lowly
Nature herself an agent of grace.

Indeed, as "a Virgin pure" (*Mask*, 826) who is sensually and
playfully invoked "By all the *Nymphs* that nightly dance / Upon
[her] streams with wily glance" (883–84), Sabrina anticipates
prelapsarian Eden as Milton would describe it in *Paradise Lost*,
a landscape in which "Nature... / Wanton'd as in her prime, and
play'd at will / Her Virgin Fancies, pouring forth more sweet, /
Wild above Rule or Art" (*PL* 5.294–97). In the *Mask*, when the
Attendant Spirit begs Sabrina to "bridle in [her] headlong wave"
in order to answer his "summons" for aid (887, 888), the virgin
river goddess makes clear that her healing waters are "Wild above
Rule or Art"; they need not cease their "*stray[ing]*" motion (895)
in order for her to come to the aid of those on land:

> By the rushy-fringed bank,
> Where grows the Willow and the Osier dank,
>   My sliding Chariot stays,
> Thick set with Agate, and the azurn sheen
> Of Turquoise blue, and Em'rald green
>   That in the channel strays,
> Whilst from off the waters fleet
> Thus I set my printless feet.   (890–97)

As Brooks and Hardy point out in their gloss on these lines,
Sabrina's "'sliding chariot' is simply the water, and 'stays,' waits
for her, beside the bank, only in the paradoxical sense that there
is always the flowing water there" (*Poems of Mr. John Milton*,
225). The shady banks and gemstone hues of this distinctly
unbridled stream anticipate, moreover, the "crisped Brooks" of
paradise which flow from a "Sapphire Fount" in the midst of the
garden, "Rolling on Orient Pearl and sands of Gold, / With mazy
error under pendant shades" (*PL* 4.237–39). The Attendant Spirit
further acknowledges Sabrina's Edenic elision of Nature and
grace when he thanks her for her aid by praying that her "banks"
be blessed "With Groves of myrrh, and cinnamon" (*Mask*, 936,
937), trees Raphael encounters on his way to visit Adam and Eve

as he passes "through Groves of Myrrh, / And flow'ring Odors, Cassia, Nard, and Balm" (*PL* 5.292–93). And yet this Edenic nymph is also, as Shullenberger points out, "translat[ed] into a Christological type": "The 'cross-flowing course' of 'the flood' (831–32), which stays Sabrina's flight [from her stepmother] and initiates her apotheosis, the ritual preparation of her body and its anointment with spices, delicately evoke the passion and death of Jesus" ("Girl, Interrupted," 197, 196). Just as the body of the Savior is, in Lanyer's prose dedication to the Countess of Cumberland, the "excellent earth of the most blessed Paradice, wherein our second *Adam* had his restlesse habitation" ("To the Ladie *Margaret*," 12–14), and the "rivers of...grace" flowing out from it are "pure celestiall springs" (*SDRJ*, 1728, 1729), so Sabrina's Edenic waters flow with messianic power.

Once heaven has stooped to make Nature herself an agent of redemption, the redeemed soul/church she liberates not only rises from the earthly chains that imprison her, but also comes into her own as a teacher and guide for "Mortals" who desire to reach heaven: "She"—Virtue embodied in the Lady who is also a type of the virgin church—"can teach [them] how to climb / Higher than the sphery chime." But unlike Donne's Ecclesia in "The Annuntiation and Passion," who serves as "Gods Court of faculties," granting authoritative dispensations from on high and showing men the way by being herself "neerest to" God (*Annun*, 23, 29), the church as Milton envisions her is a youthful fellow climber. One should "Love" her and follow her because "she alone is free" (*Mask*, 1019), liberated by the power of a female figure who—like Lanyer's Margaret Clifford—unites Nature and grace. But Milton's virginal mountaineer is very different from Lanyer's matriarchal Ecclesia figure; for the Countess of Cumberland's virtue anticipates the Elder Brother's image of Athena as impenetrably strong in her own right: her "chaste breast, guarded with strength of mind" protects her from the "base abuses" of "idle Lovers" by "prevent[ing]" them (*SDRJ*, 1545, 1551, 1552), anticipating them and warding them off before they can make an objectionable move. Milton's Lady, by contrast, is a type of Virtue and of the virgin church precisely because she is both a bold, authoritative, and effective defender of the good *and* a "feeble" climber who relies upon the sisterly ministrations of divine grace to extricate her from the evil she cannot conquer on her own.

3. EVE AND WISDOM IN *PARADISE LOST*

When one studies *A Mask* in its Caroline context, the Lady's uncompromising defense of virginity resonates with the young Milton's disdain for the cult of married love promoted by King Charles and his queen. But the story of Milton and marriage does not end with *A Mask*. Moving past his distaste for the royal couple's inflated images of nuptial bliss and his own experience of a disappointing marriage, Milton would come to think of matrimony at its best as a holy and joyful state, subject to trials and marred by original sin, but potentially the greatest of blessings, a "Perpetual Fountain of Domestic sweets" (*PL* 4.760).[38] For the poet, whose divorce tracts imply that he believed the companionship of a good wife virtually essential to his own salvation,[39] and whose sonnet on his dead wife reveals the devastation he felt at being deprived of her, the marriage "bed" is the dwelling place and royal pleasure dome of sacred Eros: "Here Love his golden shafts imploys, here lights / His constant Lamp, and waves his purple wings, / Reigns here and revels" (*PL* 4.761, 763–65). Love's sweet dominion as it is evoked in these lines clearly revises the elaborate "revels" of Charles's reign on Milton's own terms, and they are interestingly revisionary terms. For though the imagery of the lines may be read as reflecting Milton's strong belief in gender hierarchy—the male god Cupid reigning over his female bride, Psyche—the revelous monarchy of the marriage bed in fact emerges from union rather than providing its hierarchical structure; love rules the loving soul, and those joined by love are mutually pierced by his "shafts," mutually illuminated by his "Lamp," mutually borne aloft by his "wings."

Man and woman thus united reflect the deity of Milton's opening invocation, who is both masculine and feminine, whose

Spirit incorporates both male and female functions, "brooding on the vast Abyss" and "ma[king] it pregnant" (*PL* 1.21, 22). As Fowler points out in his notes on these lines, "brooding" is Milton's rendering of "the Hebrew word in Genesis 1:2 that is translated in the Authorized Version as 'moved,' but in St. Basil and other patristic authors as *incubabat*." The combination of "brooding" and "mad'st it pregnant," Fowler adds, is "Not a mixed metaphor, but a deliberate allusion to the Hermetic doctrine that God is both masculine and feminine" (Fowler, *Paradise Lost*, 43; see also Grossman, "Genders of God"). Milton evokes this doctrine, I would contend, less in order to comment on the divine nature in its own right than to apply such images to the project of "justify[ing] the ways of God to men" (*PL* 1.26); for in attempting such a justification, Milton must deal first and foremost with the fact that the "men" with whom God has dealings are a group comprised of both male and female human beings, toward each of whom God's "ways" are dissimilar from the outset. According to Genesis 2, God forms man and woman using two different methods, he being molded out of earth and she, as a remedy for his aloneness, out of his rib. The interpretation of this particular way of proceeding plays a key part in the formulation of Judeo-Christian beliefs about the roles of man and woman in creation generally and in marriage particularly. Such exegesis is also, as we have seen in Donne's *Anniversaries* and Lanyer's *Salve Deus*, essential to any writer struggling to understand and ameliorate the vexed state of postlapsarian gender relations. But in *Paradise Lost*, probing the origins of gender trouble is an essential component of Milton's theodicy.[40] Why would a good and just God have created what has turned out to be such a deeply problematic differentiation? Might gender difference and even gender hierarchy—which Milton, unlike Lanyer, believes to have preceded the Fall—once have been a source of joy and pleasurably dynamic tension, rather than of anguish and enslavement? And how did it come to be otherwise? One of the goals of Milton's great epic is to answer these questions by exploring the relationship between man and woman; by imagining the particular excellences of unfallen woman as compared

with and joined to those of unfallen man; by attempting to imagine the perfect, yet beautifully various and ever-changing nature
of their prelapsarian union; and by analyzing the ways in which
original sin disrupts that union. In pursuing this project, Milton
again looks to the Wisdom books of the Bible, drawing upon
them for sage counsel on marriage and for images of Solomon
and Sapientia that inspire his portrayal of the unfallen Adam
and Eve. The first woman as he imagines her is thus a type of
Wisdom. She possesses, until she falls, a "Virgin Majesty" (*PL*
9.270) even more powerful than that of her wise descendant, the
Lady of *A Mask*; and after the Fall, her "demeanor meek" toward
Adam and "meek submission" to God (*PL* 11.162, 12.597) fore-
shadow the redemptive "Humiliation" of Wisdom incarnate,
Jesus, the "Son of God our Savior meek" (*PR* 1.160, 4.636).

Milton's understanding of Eve as a Wisdom figure begins with
his reading of the fourth and fifth chapters of Proverbs, in which
Solomon recounts two pieces of advice given to him by his father,
David: love Wisdom, love your wife. "Get wisdome," the father
tells his son, "Forsake her not, and she shal kepe thee: loue her,
and she shal preserue thee.... Exalt her, and she shal exalt thee:
she shal bring thee to honour, if thou embrace her.... kepe her,
for she is thy life" (Prov. 4:5–6, 8, 13). As the next chapter of
Proverbs makes clear, however, the bond between Wisdom and
the young husband does not preclude his loving and desiring his
wife; the exhortation in chapter 4 to embrace Wisdom is paral-
leled in chapter 5 when the father warns his son to reject the
temptations of the harlot and instead to drink from what Milton
calls the "Perpetual Fountain of Domestic sweets" (*PL* 4.760):
"Let thy fountaine be blessed, and reioyce with the wife of thy
youth. Let her be as the louing hinde and pleasant roe: let her
breasts satisfie thee at all times, & delite in her loue continually"
(Prov. 5:18–19). Presented in such close proximity, King David's
two directives to Solomon appear as two sides of the same coin:
the wise man should love Wisdom as a devoted husband loves
his wife, and the loving husband should love his wife as a wise
man loves Wisdom. Given Proverbs' function as a handbook of

practical ethics, moreover, chapter 5 clearly advocates conjugal love not merely as an image or trope for the love of Wisdom, but as its living manifestation. The wife is not a personification of Wisdom; rather, her husband's union with her is both an application of and testimony to his bond with Wisdom. As Lanyer had asserted in her poem to Katherine Howard through an allusion to the same verses from Proverbs 5, the wise man loves his wife, and the loving husband is a wise man. The adulterous fool, by contrast, embraces both the "strange woman" (Prov. 5:3) and Wisdom's nemesis, the harlot Folly.

These principles from the Proverbs of Solomon are particularly relevant to *Paradise Lost* because, as readers of the epic have long recognized, Milton clearly parallels Adam with Solomon, noting that the first man falls, as would "the Sapient King" of Israel (*PL* 9.442), when he turns away from Wisdom, "fondly overcome with Female charm" (9.999).[41] Solomon forsakes Wisdom, who could have kept him safe "from the strange woman, euen from the stranger that is smothe in her wordes" (Prov. 7:5), when he loves "many outlandish women" and they turn "his heart after other gods" (1 Kings 11:1, 4). Similarly, Adam disregards Raphael's exhortation to "Dismiss not [Wisdom], when most [he needs] her nigh" (*PL* 8.564); "attribúting overmuch to things / Less excellent" (565–66), Adam clings to a stranger who resembles the wife of his youth only in her fair "outside" (568).

Adam's analogical relation to Solomon evokes not only their parallel falls but a number of prelapsarian correlations as well. The unfallen Adam resembles David's son in wise blessedness just as his sinful folly is, in its turn, parallel with Solomon's. Yet despite the emphasis on paradisal goodness in studies by scholars such as Joseph Summers, Barbara Lewalski, and Diane McColley, the prelapsarian aspect of the Adam/Solomon analogy remains less than fully explored.[42] Milton evokes this analogy in a number of different ways, one of the most important being his portrayal of Adam and Eve's "connubial Love" (*PL* 4.743). The couple's prelapsarian state reflects not only Solomon's first marriage to "Pharaohs daughter" (1 Kings 7:8), whom Milton alludes to as "the Sapient King['s] /...fair *Egyptian* Spouse" (*PL* 9.442–43), but also Solomon's union with Wisdom, whom he "loued...and soght...from [his] youth...[and] desired to marye her, suche loue had [he] vnto her beautie" (Wisd. of Sol. 8:2). As Adam before his fall may be likened to Solomon in all his glory, so Eve—whom he calls "Heav'n's last best gift" to him (*PL* 5.19)—resembles the Wisdom Solomon receives as God's "gifte" (Wisd. of Sol. 8:21).

Milton embeds in the discourse of prelapsarian Eden numerous parallels between Eve and Wisdom. Describing Eve and her effects on Adam, Milton draws again, as he had in describing the mother-goddess of *Arcades,* upon Scriptures in which Wisdom is personified as a woman. And when the characters of *Paradise Lost* refer to "Wisdom," their language implies that the unfallen Eve resembles and reflects her. By thus establishing Eve's likeness to Sapientia, Milton underscores Eve's dignity and helps to define the ways in which she, though fashioned out of Adam's rib rather than made directly in the image of God, also possesses God-like qualities: "for in *thir* looks Divine / The image of thir glorious Maker shone, / Truth, Wisdom, Sanctitude" (*PL* 4.291–93; emphasis mine).[43] Even more importantly, the Eve/Wisdom parallel allows Milton to articulate two essential aspects of the Fall as he conceives it. First, he evokes his sense of what the Fall does to woman, not simply as a human being, but specifically *as woman;* he explores the particular consequences of Eve's sin for her and "her Daughters" (*PL* 4.324). Second, Milton defines the nature of Adam's sin, portraying it as a rejection of Wisdom that is, at the same time, a lapse in his true love for Eve. In each case, "loss of *Eden*" (*PL* 1.4) involves a violation of the link between woman and Wisdom, for that likeness—the fact that Eve resembles Sapientia—is, as Milton sees it, an essential component of paradisal experience for both man and woman. The poet's parallel between Eve and Wisdom is, then, neither a lapse into naive allegory nor a reduction of Eve to type or symbol. It is, on the contrary, a thoroughly Miltonic analogy that helps to delineate the poet's sense of human experience both before and after the Fall.[44]

Eve's resemblance to Wisdom is most subtly suggested in *Paradise Lost* through the newly created Adam's conversation with God in book 8. This colloquy has no explicit source in the opening chapters of Genesis.[45] A similar exchange does take place, however, between God and the son of David in the Wisdom of Solomon. In the ninth chapter of this book, Solomon recounts his prayer—described more briefly in the canonical 1 Kings 3— that God grant him Wisdom. In its references to man's rule over the animals and in its profound humility, Solomon's petition provides a model for Adam's prayer in book 8 of *Paradise Lost:*

> O God of fathers, and Lord of mercie, *which hast made all things* with thy worde, And ordeined man thorow thy wis-dome, that he shulde haue *dominion ouer the creatures* which thou hast made, ...Giue me that wisdome, which sitteth by thy throne, ...For I thy seruant...am a feble persone.... Send her out of thine holy heauens, & send her from the throne of thy maiestie *that she may be with me, & labour.* (Wisd. of Sol. 9:1–2, 4–5, 10; emphasis mine)

Adam's request, like Solomon's, is addressed to God as Creator of "all things" (Wisd. of Sol. 9:1); the deity is, in Adam's speech, "Author of this Universe" who has "provided all things" (*PL* 8.360, 363). Both requests include grateful reference to man's God-given sovereignty "ouer the creatures" (Wisd. of Sol. 9:2), those "inferior far beneath [him] set" (*PL* 8.382). Most impor-tantly, both requests are for a "consort" (*PL* 8.392) who will dwell "with" the petitioner (Wisd. of Sol. 9:10) and serve "to help, / Or solace his defects" (*PL* 8.418–19). Solomon desires Wisdom, he explains in the chapter that introduces his prayer, as a companion: "When I come home, I shal rest with her: for her companie hathe no bitternes, and her felowshippe hathe no tediousnes, but mirthe and ioye" (Wisd. of Sol. 8:16). Similarly, Milton's Adam seeks "fellowship" and "rational delight" (*PL* 8.389, 391), and he finds them in Eve, whose company would make even "toilsome" labor "sweet" (*PL* 4.439).

In *Tetrachordon,* Milton explains that Adam's appreciation for the gift of Eve is attributable to his prior possession of the gift of wisdom: "*Adam* who had the wisdom giv'n him to know all creatures...no doubt but had the gift to discern perfectly, that which concern'd him...; and to apprehend at first sight the true fitnes of that consort which God provided him" (YP 2:602). In *Paradise Lost,* Adam's discernment is underscored even more heavily; it precedes Eve's creation and—in effect—calls for it. Adam desires a truly fitting companion, one who shares in God's "Image, not imparted to the Brute" (*PL* 8.441). Thus, commending Adam for his "knowing not of Beasts alone, /...but of...[himself]" (8.438–39), the Lord creates Eve as the embodiment of Adam's wise longing: "Thy wish, exactly to thy heart's desire" (8.451). Solomon has the wisdom to ask for the Wisdom he receives; but in choosing his wives, he behaves foolishly. In contrast, Adam has the wisdom to ask God for the very mate he is meant to have, the wife God designs as a "helpe mete" for him.[46]

When he sees the mate God fashions in answer to his prayer, however, Adam is overwhelmed. He describes her effect upon him in terms that, as John Reichert points out, initially recall the goddesslike Wisdom figure Spenser celebrates in his "Hymne of Heavenly Beavtie" (*Milton's Wisdom,* 13–14). In Spenser's poem—which had provided the young Milton with a point of departure for the "goddess bright" of his *Arcades*—those who achieve the heights of Neoplatonic vision gaze adoringly on Sapience (*HHB,* 183) and scorn thereafter all lesser beauties. Compared to her "All other sights but fayned shadowes bee" (*HHB,* 273); worldly honor seems "basenesse, and all riches drosse" (279). Similarly, Adam's first sight of Eve prompts him to declare that she is "so lovely fair, / That what seem'd fair in all the World, seem'd now / Mean" (*PL* 8.471–73).

But for Milton, Reichert points out, such a response is flawed; in *Paradise Lost,* it is Satan who tells Eve she is a goddess resembling Spenser's Sapience, and it is the fallen Eve who describes the effects of the "Wisdom-giving" forbidden fruit (*PL* 9.679) as making all former sweetness seem "flat...and harsh" (*PL* 9.987, discussed by Reichert, *Milton's Wisdom,* 9, 10–11). Hence,

Reichert explains (13–14), the unfallen Adam immediately modifies his initial description of Eve's beauty: he begins by saying that she makes all else seem "Mean," but immediately revises: "Mean, or in her summ'd up, in her contain'd / And...her looks... / into all things from her Air inspir'd / The spirit of love and amorous delight" (*PL* 8.473–74, 476–77). In *Paradise Lost*, Reichert concludes, the attainment of wisdom depends upon the rejection of the Spenserian goddess figure and the Neoplatonic "philosophy of renunciation" symbolized by her in favor of an experiential and conversational ideal: "Milton's Wisdom, embodied in the Son, Raphael, and Michael..., is accessible and sociable. 'She' condescends to Adam and Eve for conversation and friendship, just as Urania, who is Milton's muse and Wisdom's sister, descends from heaven nightly to visit the poet" (Reichert, *Milton's Wisdom*, 11, 15).

Milton's Wisdom is, indeed, characterized by her sweet intimacy with man. But Milton's portrayal of her in the poem does not call for the use of quotation marks around the word "she"; for Eve—no less than the Son or the angels who visit Eden—embodies that distinctly Miltonic conception of Wisdom as active, dialogic, defined by Becoming rather than by static Being. In the beautiful aubade that opens book 5, Adam—echoing the language of Solomon in the Song of Songs—addresses his spouse as "my ever new delight" (*PL* 5.19). The delight she gives is "ever new" because she does not sit enthroned, inspiring rapt admiration as does Spenser's Wisdom goddess, but instead stimulates Adam's perceptions, repeatedly expanding his field of vision.

As Barbara Lewalski points out, Eve "'invents' and anticipates Adam in using such literary forms as the autobiographical narrative and the love sonnet" and "also makes the first foray into the realm of astronomical speculation when...she poses a question about the stars" (Paradise Lost *and the Rhetoric*, 189). In fact, Eve's inquiry about celestial lights (*PL* 4.657–58) provides a point of departure for her husband's questions to Raphael in book 8. And when Adam asks Eve to fetch fruit from her "stores" for the angel's visit (*PL* 5.313–20), she clarifies his understanding of Eden's domestic economy, pointing out how "small store will serve, where store, / All seasons, ripe for use hangs on the stalk" (5.322–23). In none of these circumstances does Eve explicitly teach Adam, and yet he learns from her; and in following her lead, he is putting into action the wisdom she resembles: his own wisdom. As Solomon says of the wisdom God bestows upon him, "All good things therefore came to me together with her," though he "knewe not that she was the mother of these things" (Wisd. of Sol. 7:11, 12).

It is as mother that Raphael greets Eve, and in doing so, he draws a Wisdom-related analogy between her fruitfulness and that of the garden:

> Hail Mother of Mankind, whose fruitful Womb
> Shall fill the World more numerous with thy Sons
> Than with these various fruits the Trees of God
> Have heap'd this Table.   (*PL* 5.388–91)

These lines combine two tropes: the trees of the garden are personified as having "heaped" the table with their fruit, while Eve — who literally gathers "fruit of all kinds" and "on the board / Heaps with unsparing hand" (*PL* 5.341, 343–44) — is defined as the most fruitful tree of all. Satan later calls the forbidden tree "Mother of Science" (9.680), and it is as such a tree and such a mother that the fallen Eve offers the fruit of knowledge to her husband, who finds her bearing "in her hand / A bough of fairest fruit" (9.850–51). But as Raphael's greeting makes clear, the unfallen Eve's "fruitful Womb" makes her an unforbidden tree of life rather than a forbidden tree of knowledge, the "Mother of Mankind" rather than of "Science." In this, she resembles the divine Wisdom of Proverbs: "Her waies are waies of pleasure, and all her paths prosperitie. She is a tre of life to them that laie holde on her, and blessed is he that reteineth her" (Prov. 3:17–18).[47]

In the same scene of *Paradise Lost*, Eve is also linked to the Wisdom of Proverbs through her activities as the hostess of the feast. In Proverbs, Wisdom "hath killed her vitailes, drawen her wine, and prepared her table" (9:2). Eve is a prelapsarian embodiment of this figure "on hospitable thoughts intent" (*PL* 5.332): "for drink the Grape / She crushes, inoffensive must, and meaths / From many a berry, and from sweet kernels prest / She tempers dulcet creams" (5.344–47). Before the Fall, as Milton often demonstrates in *Paradise Lost*, the richest images and experiences we know as fallen beings were subtly different and subtly purer. As the woman who enacts unfallen humanity's reflection of divine Wisdom, Eve "gathers" fruit (5.343) rather than "kill[s] her vitailes" (though her hand is, no less than Wisdom's, "unsparing" [5.344]); and the beverages she mixes can delight without inebriating. In Scripture, the meal is allegorical; in Milton's poem, it is a real dinner in which "real hunger"—both physical and intellectual—is satisfied (*PL* 5.437). But Eve presides, as Wisdom does in Proverbs, at the meal that occasions man's enlightenment. In short, Eve becomes the stranger, the seducer, only when she ceases to be, in her own right, the sapiential "kinswoman" whose companionship is recommended in Proverbs 7:4–5. Until she sins, she is the mate "who sees when [Adam is] seen least wise" (*PL* 8.578), the woman whose very presence strengthens him against temptation, as he himself testifies when he tells her that he finds himself, when accompanied and beheld by her, "More wise" (9.311).

Eve becomes Adam's spouse and the embodiment of Milton's interactive and experiential idea of Wisdom only after she, like Adam, briefly indulges and then rejects a conception of Wisdom as an all-absorbing female beauty upon which the beholder's "ioy, ... comfort, ... desire, ... [and] gaine / Is fixed" (*HHB*, 271–72). Renaissance illustrations of this Neoplatonic Sapientia often portray her as a fair virgin gazing upon her reflection in a mirror, and Eve's first memory of herself is as such a virgin. Her version of the Neoplatonic speculum is "the clear / Smooth Lake" (*PL* 4.458–59) in which she sees and loves her own beauty. When she turns away from her reflection to embrace Adam, Milton dramatizes the rejection of one conception of Wisdom in favor of another. For Eve and for Adam, as for Milton himself, the relation of human to human is the speculum that makes wisdom and thus true self-knowledge possible; one can see oneself fully only when one looks at someone who is not precisely one's self, but rather one's "*other* self" (*PL* 8.450; emphasis mine).

The autobiographical speech in which Eve describes her initial attraction to the "smooth wat'ry image" (*PL* 4.480) ends with her humble testimony to the supremacy of a Wisdom whose beauty she beheld only when she came to know Adam. Even in these seemingly submissive lines, however, Eve preserves her own majesty and prerogative, stressing her capacity for insight and intimating the sapiential nature of her own character: "I yielded, and from that time see / How beauty is excell'd by manly grace / And wisdom, which alone is truly fair" (*PL* 4.489–91). Kerrigan and Braden argue that it is a mistake to neglect the enjambment of these lines and to assume that "manly" modifies "wisdom" as well as "grace." Eve's first assertion, they note, merely confirms her sexual preference: to say that "beauty is excelled by manly grace" is to say that "the male body is preferable as a love object to the more beautiful female body, . . . that she is, in other words, heterosexual." But according to Kerrigan and Braden, the verb "see" is here meant in its "intellectual sense," and wisdom is "linguistic and invisible, conceptual rather than perceptible"; it is "a higher-order beauty, alone *truly* fair, because truth is not an image but a knowing" ("Milton's Coy Eve," 41). This logocentric reading is plausible but not exhaustive. For the "seeing" of which Eve speaks is, by the critics' own explanation, not exclusively intellectual; the vision by which Eve judges Adam's "manly grace" preferable to her own beauty is physical, even sensual sight. And though truth may be "not an image but a knowing," the two are not entirely separable for Eve. Indeed, as Kerrigan and Braden go on to note, Eve's version of knowing "was first of all a knowing of a beautiful image," her own reflection in the pool (41). But how appropriate is it to speak of "knowing," of *scientia*, in this context where Eve herself is making a point about the fairness of "wisdom," of *sapientia*? We must note that in describing wisdom she does not desert visual and aesthetic language in favor of abstract intellectual terms; she does not say that wisdom "alone is truly true" but that it "alone is truly fair." Her ongoing stress upon the aesthetic qualifies the absoluteness of Eve's tribute to "manly grace" as a thing more excellent than beauty. Furthermore, Milton himself personifies Wisdom as female in the invocation of book 7 when he refers to her as Urania's "sister"; thus, whether consciously or not, Eve's declaration that "wisdom...alone is truly fair" defers not to the male but to a feminine principle more beautiful than any one female body, even her own.

In the invocation of Urania at the beginning of book 7, Milton calls his muse the sister of Wisdom: "Before the Hills appear'd, or Fountain flow'd," he says, addressing Urania in words that recall Wisdom's self-description in Proverbs 8, "Thou with Eternal Wisdom didst converse, / Wisdom thy Sister, and with her didst play / In presence of th' Almighty Father, pleas'd / With thy Celestial Song" (*PL* 7.8–12). The "Eternal Wisdom" evoked here is divine—identified in traditional exegesis as a type of the second person of the Trinity, the "Son both of God and Man" (*PL* 3.316) whom the Father refers to as "my wisdom" (*PL* 3.170).[48] The wisdom Solomon sought and received from God is the created mirror of that uncreated, divine Sapientia; and it is this created wisdom that the prelapsarian Adam, as the perfect type of Solomon, possesses. As the "Daughter of God and Man" (*PL* 4.660, 9.291), Eve is the earthly portrait of both the heavenly Wisdom and the earthly. She is the "Best Image of" wise Adam (*PL* 5.95) as the Son is the "Divine Similitude" (*PL* 3.384); and, like the "Eternal Wisdom" who plays in the presence of the Father, Eve is the beloved daughter of the one for whom she sings. Thus, when "our first Father" responds "in delight" to Eve's lyrical autobiography by smiling "with superior Love" (4.495, 497, 499), he foreshadows the heavenly scene Milton evokes at the start of book 7, in which "th' Almighty Father" is "pleas'd" by the music of his daughters.[49]

The language describing Adam's response to Eve's speech is, moreover, delicately ambiguous. In saying that Adam is delighted by Eve's "submissive Charms" (*PL* 4.498), Milton would seem to underscore the pliant acquiescence displayed in Eve's lyrical story of her "yield[ing]" to Adam; but "submissive Charms," no less than "obsequious Majesty" (*PL* 8.509), "coy submission," or "modest pride" (4.310), is a telling oxymoron. The word "charm" evokes not only an alluring feminine grace or sweetness, but—as Milton recalls when he says, "Song charms the Sense" (*PL* 2.556)—a powerful incantatory verse.[50] Considering that Adam will eventually be "overcome by" the power of Eve's "Female charm" (*PL* 9.999), and taking into account Milton's particular sensitivity to etymological echoes, one cannot help but hear such echoes reverberating in Eve's "submissive Charms." The phrase suggests that Adam's pleasure derives not only from Eve's meek compliance, but also from her use of ambiguous, lyrical language—including the subtle enjambment of "manly grace / And wisdom"—that delicately qualifies that compliance.

The power of Eve's "submissive charms"—the half-hidden strength in her poetry of submission—is partly due to her use of the word "alone"; in speaking of "wisdom, which alone is truly fair" Eve implies that wisdom's "fair[ness]" is a *function* of wisdom's solitude, that the Elder Brother of the *Mask* was correct when he said that "Wisdom's self / Oft seeks to sweet retired Solitude" (375–76). And by so implying, Eve gently reinforces the association between her own female beauty and the fairness of Wisdom; for she, unlike Adam, takes pleasure in being alone, as is clear from her account of her creation, her retreat from the conversation in book 8, and her desire to work alone in book 9. Indeed, Adam's sense of Eve's perfection is in part a response to these solitary inclinations: despite his failure to appreciate for himself the pleasures of being alone, Eve's husband links her beauty to the fact that she is "Not obvious, not obtrusive, but retir'd" (*PL* 8.504), that she is a person who retreats from company rather than seeks it, who "would...not unsought be won" (*PL* 8.503). It is this singleness and apartness in her, no less than her chastity, that maintains "the Virgin Majesty of *Eve*" (9.270) even within a sexually consummated marriage.[51]

But Eve, like Wisdom, is no "proud fair"; and Adam is no "starv'd Lover...best quitted with disdain" (*PL* 4.769–70). Eve yields to him, becomes his spouse; and the language Adam uses to describe her implies that, in doing so, she becomes his Eden. As Milton calls paradise "the blissful Seat" (*PL* 1.5), "the happy seat of Man" (3.632), and "A happy rural seat of various view" (4.247), so Adam speaks of Eve as the seat—the home or dwelling place—of his own best qualities: "Greatness of mind and nobleness thir seat / Build in her loveliest, and create an awe / About her, as a guard Angelic plac't" (*PL* 8.557–59). The awe "create[d]" by "Greatness of mind and nobleness" protects Eve as Gabriel and his "guard Angelic" protect the garden.[52] This awe is not, however, the rapt adoration of a devotee; it is not even, strictly speaking, Adam's emotion. Rather, it is a power "About" Eve that gently yet firmly shapes Adam's approach to her. As Raphael explains, it ensures that the pleasure he derives from Eve's loveliness is tempered by reverence: she is "Made so adorn for [his] delight the more," but awe-inspiring to remind him of her sapiential capacities: "So awful, that with honor thou may'st love / Thy mate, who sees when thou art seen least wise" (8.576, 577–78). As long as Eve retains her likeness to divine Wisdom, Adam's reverence for her is fully in keeping with his obedience to God, for Wisdom is "a pure influence that floweth from the glorie of the Almightie: therefore can no defiled thing come vnto her" (Wisd. of Sol. 7:25), and as Adam testifies, no evil can "harbor" in Eve, "Created pure" (*PL* 5.99, 100). Indeed, Raphael's assertion that Adam's "mate...sees when [he is] seen least wise" implies that the acuity of her vision would be sufficient to supplement any deficiency or lapse in his own created wisdom. But once she has fallen, following in her footsteps means abandoning Wisdom.

The idea of Eve as Wisdom's rival is not unthinkable to Adam even before the Fall; in his conversation with Raphael, he expresses his troubled observation that neither he, the rational and authoritative first father, nor the heavenly sister Sapientia has the slightest chance of victory in a contest with mother Eve:

> All higher knowledge in her presence falls
> Degraded, Wisdom in discourse with her
> Loses discount'nanc't, and like folly shows;
> Authority and Reason on her wait.   (*PL* 8.551–54)[53]

This kind of talk, while not sinful, strikes Raphael as dangerous, and he responds by correcting Adam's underestimation of
Wisdom. Like the sage of Proverbs, who insists that Wisdom
"shal preserue thee" (Prov. 4:6), Raphael stresses that Wisdom is
Adam's best defense in moments when he is tempted to subordinate himself to the allure of mere outward female beauty:

>   be not diffident
> Of Wisdom, she deserts thee not, if thou
> Dismiss not her, when most thou need'st her nigh,
> By attribúting overmuch to things
> Less excellent, as thou thyself perceiv'st.
> For what admir'st thou, what transports thee so,
> An outside?   (*PL* 8.562–68)

In interpreting these lines, it is important to note that Raphael
does not label Eve as a thing "less excellent"; rather, he stresses
that Adam will undervalue his own wisdom if he responds only
to Eve's outward appearance. To do so is, on one level, to fail
in "self-esteem" (*PL* 8.572); on another level, it is to reduce
"Heav'n's last best gift" (*PL* 5.19) to a mere "outside." Of course,
that "outside" is in no way pernicious as long as it is the dwelling of Eve's pure and unfallen soul; Raphael's advice anticipates
the circumstances Adam will face when the fallen Eve's alluring beauty clashes with her new identity as "the stranger" who
uses "flattering lippes" to lure a man into sin (Prov. 7:5, 21). It
is against this Eve, this woman "with an impudent face" whose
"house is the waie vnto the graue" (Prov. 7:13, 27), that Wisdom
would have been Adam's best defense: "Saie vnto wisdome,
Thou art my sister: and call vnderstanding thy kinswoman, That
they maie kepe thee from the strange woman" (Prov. 7:4–5).

  The lesson taught by the sage of Proverbs and by Raphael
is as nuanced and precise as the angel's distinction between a

healthy appetite for knowledge and an intemperate "Surfeit" which "turns / Wisdom to Folly, as Nourishment to Wind" (*PL* 7.129–30). "Knowledge is as food" (*PL* 7.126), except when it is the knowledge conveyed by forbidden fruit; and embracing Eve is as an embrace of Wisdom until Eve has become the strange woman, the harlot who tempts young men away from the ways of Wisdom. Until she falls, however, Eve is not the stranger against whom Wisdom must guard; on the contrary, to love and cherish her—along with paradise itself—is to be wise as an earthly creature should be: "joy thou / In what he gives to thee," Raphael advises Adam, "this Paradise / And thy fair *Eve:* Heav'n is for thee too high / To know what passes there; be lowly wise" (8.170–73). Like the sage of Proverbs, Raphael here makes love of Wisdom analogous with love of one's wife. To rejoice in the garden and in his unfallen spouse is, for the unfallen Adam, to live a life of Wisdom commensurate with his human capacities.

In *Tetrachordon,* Milton constructs a fascinating parallel and contrast between divine Wisdom as the recreational companion of God and woman as man's delightful relief from his labors:

> No mortall nature can endure either in the actions of Religion, or study of wisdome, without somtime slackning the cords of intense thought and labour: which lest we should think faulty, God himself conceals us not his own recreations before the world was built; *I was,* saith the eternall wisdome, *dayly his delight, playing always before him.* And to him indeed wisdom is as a high towr of pleasure, but to us a steep hill, and we toyling ever about the bottom: he executes with ease the exploits of his omnipotence, as easie as with us it is to will: but no worthy enterprise can be don by us without continuall plodding and wearisomnes to our faint and sensitive abilities. We cannot therefore alwayes be contemplative, or pragmaticall abroad, but have need of som delightfull intermissions, wherin the enlarg'd soul may leav off a while her severe schooling; and like a glad youth in wandring vacancy, may keep her hollidaies to joy and harmles pastime: which as she cannot well doe without company, so in no company so well as where the different sexe in most resembling unlikenes,

and most unlike resemblance cannot but please best, and be
pleas'd in the aptitude of that variety. Wherof lest we should
be too timorous, in the aw that our flat sages would form us
and dresse us, wisest *Salomon* among his gravest Proverbs
countenances a kinde of ravishment and erring fondnes in the
entertainment of wedded leisures. (YP 2:596–97)

A wife is here both like and unlike Sapientia: on the one hand,
she is her "mortall" husband's leisuretime alternative to the
pursuit of created wisdom, his relief from the rigors of action
and study. On the other, her relationship with her spouse is the
earthly reflection of the deity's own relationship with "eternall
wisdome." And for the unfallen Adam in *Paradise Lost*, whose
"nature" is not yet "mortall," the reflection is more perfect;
as long as he acknowledges his own creaturely limitations and
remains "lowly wise," there is no clear-cut distinction between
his labor and his leisure, between his pursuit of Wisdom — divine
or created — and his embrace of Eve.

As the narrator explains when Adam's "studious thoughts
abstruse" lead him to ask Raphael about cosmology and astron-
omy (*PL* 8.40), Eve leaves their company not because she dislikes
such intellectual discussions, and not because she is incapable
of appreciating the angel's lofty discourse, but because "such
pleasure she reserv'd, / *Adam* relating, she sole Auditress" (*PL*
8.50–51). Adam, she knows, will "intermix / Grateful digressions, and solve high dispute / With conjugal Caresses, from his
Lip / Not Words alone pleas'd her" (*PL* 8.54–57). While these
lines may be read as condescending toward Eve, as implying her
preference for sensuous "digressions," they say at least as much
about Adam and about the relationship of intellectual labor
to nuptial leisure in paradise. In mentioning that Adam will
"intermix /... digressions" when he relates the angel's astron-
omy lesson, Milton playfully alludes to the astronomical definition of the term "digresssion" — "Deviation from a particular
line, or from the mean position; deflexion; e.g. of the sun from
the equator, or of an inferior planet from the sun" (*OED*, n. def.

3)—thus eliding the substance of the husband's lecture with his playful departures from the subject at hand. His "digressions" are thus "Grateful" not only because they are, to Eve, "Pleasing to the mind or the senses, agreeable, acceptable, welcome" (*OED*, adj. def. 1); but also because, by transferred epithet, they demonstrate Adam and Eve's thankfulness for the marvelous cosmos that is the subject of their inquiry, a gratitude without which such inquiry is vain. Nor are the couple's "conjugal Caresses" merely an alternative to the "high dispute" that they "solve" (*PL* 8.56, 55). The *OED* cites *Paradise Lost* 8.55–56 as illustrating the definition of "solve" as "To dissolve, put an end to, settle"; but to "solve" can also be "To explain, clear up, resolve, answer" (*OED*, v. def. 3), and surely that meaning applies here as well. The "youthful dalliance" of the "Fair couple, linkt in happy nuptial League" (*PL* 4.338, 339) does not so much put an end to the formidable deliberations in which Adam and Eve engage, as resolve and answer the questions those discussions raise.

Adam confirms his grasp of the essential link between loving Eve and being "lowly wise" when he observes that the human "Mind or Fancy" must be

> warn'd, or by experience taught...
> That not to know at large of things remote
> From use, obscure and subtle, but to know
> That which before us lies in daily life,
> Is the prime Wisdom.   (*PL* 8.188, 190–94)

Eve is herself the most beautifully familiar presence that "before [Adam] lies in daily life"; his delight in her, he tells Raphael in words with the same quotidian and domestic stress, is a response to "Those thousand decencies that daily flow / From all her words and actions" (*PL* 8.601–02). Like the Wisdom of Proverbs 8:30, who "was daily [God's] delite," Eve's presence is the definitively joyful feature of Adam's quotidian "experience" (*PL* 8.190).

Adam's testimony about the lesson his "experience" teaches conflates the guidance provided by experiential knowledge with the instruction he has just received from Raphael, the "pure / Intelligence of Heav'n" by whom he is "taught to live, / The easiest way, nor with perplexing thoughts / To interrupt the sweet of Life" (*PL* 8.180–81, 182–84). Unlike Chaucer's Wife of Bath, Adam feels no tension between *auctoritee* and experience; both teach the same curriculum.[54] But in speaking of the need for experience's teachings, he genders the "Mind or Fancy," asserting that "she" (like the Wife of Bath) is a traveling woman, "apt...to rove / Uncheckt, and of her roving is no end; / Till warn'd, or by experience taught, she learn" (*PL* 8.188–90).

The Eve of book 9 proves to be an incarnation of the roving fancy Adam describes in his speech; and she sins when she allows herself to be taught by an experience that contradicts rather than reinforces authority: the alleged experience of the serpent. This is not the experience that teaches "to know / That which before us lies in daily life, / Is the prime Wisdom" (*PL* 8.192–94). On the contrary, it is such a teacher's opposite, for the serpent claims to have found wisdom in a fruit set so "high from ground" as "would require / [Eve's] utmost reach or *Adam's*" (9.590–91). The serpent insists that it has "wound" its way up (9.589) to an otherwise inaccessible wisdom, and Eve's trust in his account of such experience leads her to violate the pronouncement of divine authority, the command she herself personifies as a woman, calling it "Sole Daughter of [God's] voice" (9.653).[55] When she follows the serpent's lead and breaks God's command, Eve essentially redefines experience as a force that assaults God's female offspring: both the prohibition that is the daughter of his voice, and Eve herself, the "Daughter of God and Man" (*PL* 4.660, 9.291). She thus violates her own sapiential identity, gloating over the conquest of Wisdom and abandoning the prerogative she maintained for herself when she asserted that "wisdom...alone is truly fair" (4.491):

> Experience, next to thee I owe,
> Best guide; not following thee, I had remain'd

> In ignorance, thou op'n'st Wisdom's way,
> And giv'st access, though secret she retire. (*PL* 9.807–10)

In light of earlier passages that describe how Eve "yielded" to Adam's wooing, the specter of sexual coercion arises from these lines.[56] When Eve initially rejects Adam in favor of her own reflection, the Creator intervenes, leading her to her spouse; but the choice to yield herself to him, both sexually and emotionally, remains her own. "Experience" as Eve describes it affords "Wisdom" no such choice. Though she, like "retir'd" Eve (*PL* 8:504), would "retire" from those who pursue her, Experience "op[ens] Wisdom's way"—the passage to her most "secret" self—and "giv[es] access" to any who would enter it.

Given Milton's conception of experience as a teacher in harmony with authority, and of created wisdom as essentially experiential, Eve's description of "Experience" as an invader or violator of Wisdom reveals the depths of her fallenness. "Experience" acts as a particularly insidious procurer, resembling the wicked old bawd in Shakespeare's *Pericles*, who wants to make the virginal Marina into her most profitable commodity, or the whorehouse servant—Boult—assigned to "Crack the glass of [Marina's] virginity" so that future customers may find her "malleable" (*Pericles*, 4.4.142–43). What has Eve to do with such figures? She once had all the modesty and all the majesty of Marina herself; though living in an uncorrupted paradise, she guarded her right to be "retir'd" (as Adam puts it in book 8), to deflect—through "sweet reluctant amorous delay"—any direct "access" to her person, even by the man she acknowledges as her "Guide / And Head" (*PL* 4.311, 442–43).[57] But now she praises the importunate aggression of Experience as a "guide" who does not defer to female prerogative.

In eating the fruit, she has followed the same false "guide" who lured her skyward in her dream. But he no longer flatters as he did in that nighttime visit; in the dream, she almost mistakes him for Adam, and he does behave similarly as he courts and woos and offers "pleaded" reason. But Experience as she now perceives it does none of these; rather, it behaves quite aggressively;

and there is something quite threatening about this force which lays bare the feminine personification of Wisdom, which gives the persistent suitor an access she would otherwise resist. As the retired proponent of "sweet reluctant amorous delay," Eve ought to be on her guard. But she is not; rather, she exults in Wisdom's helplessness. In book 4, she tells Adam that "wisdom...alone is truly fair," but she makes no explicit reference to Wisdom's gender; if anything, she allows her spouse to hear a masculine adjective carry across two words and a line ending to modify both "grace / And wisdom" as "manly." As Adam puts it, more accurately than he realizes, the unfallen Eve is "not obvious"; her language keeps one crucial dimension of Wisdom's fairness—its gender—just outside Adam's range of vision. In so doing, Eve preserves both Wisdom's secrecy and her own prerogative to veil or unveil female beauty—and femininity itself—before her husband's eyes. In book 9, by contrast, Eve quite explicitly identifies Wisdom as a "she" even as she sacrifices her own status as "not obvious, not obtrusive," to become one of Wisdom's most impatient suitors. In following the aggressive lead of Experience as the guide who overrules Wisdom's secrecy and retirement, Eve begins to reshape the world and to make it into a universe devoid of "coy submission," a world in which Elizabeth Drury can remain "Cloath'd in her Virgin white integrity" (*FunEl*, 75) only by dying, a starkly pragmatic place in which people pursue their desires—sexual, intellectual, political—without regard for the wise ambiguities and sweet ceremonies that characterized unfallen existence. At the same time, she destroys the prelapsarian definition of woman as presider over ambiguity and ceremony; she surrenders the prerogative that allows her to decide when and how female beauty—whether it be her own, or that of Wisdom personified—will become visible to Adam.

The change in Eve's status is immediately apparent in the scene where she gloats over Experience's conquest of Wisdom. Taking comfort in the remoteness of heaven, she moves directly from the image of Wisdom's penetration to an absurdly furtive posture of her own:

> thou op'n'st Wisdom's way,
> ...though secret she retire.
> And I perhaps am secret; Heav'n is high,
> High and remote to see from thence distinct
> Each thing on Earth.   (9.809–13)

In these lines, Eve's hope of escaping God's notice, of remaining "secret," is prompted by her idea of Wisdom as a "secret" feminine being hiding herself from prying eyes. Ironically, however, the sin she has committed invades her own sweet privacy—her own integrity, in the original sense of the word— even as Experience violates and exposes the sanctified secrecy of Wisdom.

Indeed, before she fell, Eve desired to spend some time outside of Adam's company: her attraction to solitude recalled her original joy in her own reflection and her time alone tending the flowers while Adam spoke with Raphael. This desire was dangerous, as it turns out; but it was pure and it helped to define "woman" in terms not wholly contingent.[58] In Milton's Eden, the love of solitude is a gender-specific trait, and it belongs to the female, not the male. All that changes with the Fall. Eve becomes desperate to keep Adam with her; resolving that she would rather lead him to his death than think of him living on without her, she returns to him and declares that she will never again put herself through the "pain of absence from [his] sight" (*PL* 9.861); eating the forbidden fruit is, in short, the first step to defining woman as a stiflingly clinging vine. She becomes more psychologically dependent on her husband even as she is sentenced to a more complete subjection to him. When the divine judge declares, "to thy Husband's will / Thine shall submit, hee over thee shall rule" (10.195–96), he introduces coercive authority into the blissful gradations of prelapsarian gender hierarchy; the husband will have access to the wife, as Experience has to Wisdom, "though secret she retire."

Appalled by the tyrannical aspirations of Nimrod, Adam declares that God has sanctioned man's rule only over the beasts and "human left from human free" (*PL* 12.71), but Michael explains that the Fall has introduced enthrallment into human politics: "Since thy original lapse, true Liberty / Is lost, which always with right Reason dwells / Twinn'd, and from her hath no dividual being" (12.83–85). The aggressive image Eve uses to praise Experience in book 9 suggests that for woman, this loss of freedom has very specific implications, not only political and social, but psychological and erotic: the Fall impairs female sexual freedom.

There are bawdy versions of this philosophy; one can find it in Carew's "A Rapture" and Lovelace's ingenious "Love Made in the First Age," which tells of a sexual golden age "When cursed No stain'd no maid's bliss" (line 10). These cavalier rakes use the idea of paradisal free love in order to seduce or otherwise control their female addressees, and they stress that—in the time before honor was invented—women were free to "just say yes." But in Milton's treatment, freedom involves a more complicated right to privacy, to a selfhood that chooses when and how to let the Other cross its boundaries. It is just such a right and prerogative that is destroyed by Eve's sin against Wisdom. Like freedom as Michael defines it, which "dwells / Twinn'd" with a female personification of reason, the free, unfallen Eve is twinned with a feminine personification of Wisdom "and from her hath no dividual being." As long as she was loyal to her sister-in-coyness, retired Wisdom, Eve maintained her own integrity. But in dividing her own interests from those of Wisdom, exposing Wisdom to the rough characters clamoring at her gate, and becoming one of those who would despoil her, Eve "[exposes] a Matron"—herself—only to find that in doing so, she does not "avoid worse rape" (*PL* 1.505). Rather, she introduces into human sexuality and into her own marriage a previously unknown mixture of "lust and violence" (1.496), desire and duress, which Milton identifies as the work of Belial and evokes in his book 1 allusion to the sins of Sodom and Gibeah.[59]

The debasement and devaluation of female sexuality is, as Milton perceives it, one of the most sadly familiar aspects of postlapsarian life; the poet's perspective is perhaps most subtly indicated, however, not in the horrifying physical violence of Gibeah — where a woman is brutally gang-raped and her dead body cut into pieces — nor even in the much-discussed carnivorousness of Adam and Eve's postlapsarian coitus (which is anticipated in Lanyer's sardonic question, "If he would eate it, who had powre to stay him?" [*SDRJ*, 800]), but in Adam's vision of the "Bevy of fair Women, richly gay / In Gems and wanton dress" whom Michael identifies as Cain's "beauteous offspring" (*PL* 11.582–83, 613). Though the "fair female Troop" Adam observes seems to be a collection "Of Goddesses, so blithe, so smooth, so gay" (*PL* 11.614–15), and though they are brides who "light the Nuptial Torch" (11.590), not prostitutes or concubines, they are hollow shells, drained of substance and dignity in order to cater to the appetites of the fallen male:

> empty of all good wherein consists
> Woman's domestic honor and chief praise;
> Bred only and completed to the taste
> Of lustful appetence, to sing, to dance,
> To dress, and troll the Tongue, and roll the Eye.
>
> (*PL* 11.616–20)

These degraded parodies of Eve's "sweet attractive Grace" (*PL* 4.298) are "Bred" out of their father Cain's sinfulness; but the reduction of human sexuality to mere carnivorous "taste" and "lustful appetence," the loss of man's reverence toward woman, has its origin in the loss of reverence toward Wisdom. In the scene following his fall, Adam begins his lustful "dalliance" with a self-consciously witty pun that reduces "Sapience" — literally knowledge acquired by tasting — to aesthetic and gastronomic "taste" (*PL* 9.1016, 1018, 1017). He compliments Eve's "elegant" choice of foods, praising her discriminating "Palate" even as he hungrily eyes her body as another dainty he can "enjoy" (9.1018, 1020, 1032).[60]

In response to the vision of Cain's daughters, Adam smugly assumes (*PL* 11.632–33) that "the tenor of Man's woe" is always "from Woman to begin," but Michael corrects him: "From Man's effeminate slackness it begins, / ...who should better hold his place / By wisdom, and superior gifts receiv'd" (*PL* 11.634–36). Michael's words are ambiguous. On one level, they hold the male to a more rigorous standard than the female, alluding to Adam's "place" as Eve's superior in the hierarchy of prelapsarian Eden. But they do so in the same spirit that inspires Lanyer when she says that "*Adam* can not be excusde," since "What Weaknesse offerd, Strength might have refusde, / Being Lord of all, the greater was his shame" (*SDRJ*, 777, 779–80). Even more interestingly, however, Michael's rebuke subtly reverses the terms Eve used to praise Adam in book 4, when she claimed to "enjoy / So far the happier Lot, enjoying [Adam] / Preëminent by so much odds" (4.445–47). According to her words, it was she — in receiving Adam — who a "superior [gift] receiv'd." In confirming the opposite, at the very point when Adam's misogynous remarks seek to blame woman for man's misery, Michael alludes obliquely to Adam's own prelapsarian perception that, of all his "gifts receiv'd," Eve was the most definitively superior, "Heav'n's last best gift" (*PL* 5.19).

Michael's stern chastening of Adam recalls, moreover, the warning Raphael gives him in book 8 when, reflecting on the way Eve's presence affects him, he wonders if "Nature" somehow impaired his strength by taking Eve from his side (*PL* 8.534–37). Often, "what she wills to do or say, / Seems wisest, virtuousest, discreetest, best," Adam declares; more disturbingly, he feels that "Wisdom in discourse with [Eve] / Loses discount'nanc't, and like folly shows" (8.549–50, 552–53). As noted earlier, Raphael answers these admissions not with an attack on Eve but with a defense of the female personifications — Natura and Sapientia — whom Adam impugns in his speech:

> Accuse not Nature, she hath done her part;
> Do thou but thine, and be not diffident
> Of Wisdom, she deserts thee not, if thou
> Dismiss not her, when most thou need'st her nigh.
>
> (*PL* 8.561–64)

It is Adam's failure to follow Raphael's advice that Michael is rebuking when he says man should have held "his place / By wisdom, and superior gifts receiv'd" (*PL* 11.635–36). In light of Raphael's image of accompaniment, of Wisdom as a female figure whom Adam needs "nigh," Michael's preposition "By" takes on a spatial dimension. Man is not only to hold his position *by means of* wisdom, the God-given human faculty, but also *by the side of* Wisdom, the female personification of God's sapience. In recalling Raphael's speech, then, Michael indicts Adam for failing to "hold his place" both in his relationship with Wisdom, identified as one of the "superior gifts receiv'd" by man, and in his relationship with Eve, whom the unfallen Adam recognizes as "Heav'n's last best gift" (*PL* 5.19). Adam's sin sunders the bond that unites him with Wisdom even as it warps and adulterates the bond that unites him with Eve.

After the fact, he tells the divine judge that he committed this sin because he was unable to make the distinction between the fallen Eve and the Wisdom she once resembled. He claims that he "could suspect no ill" from the woman God gave him as His "perfet gift" and that "Her doing seem'd to justify the deed" (*PL* 10.140, 138, 142). These words recall Adam's prelapsarian admission to Raphael that whatever the unfallen Eve "wills to do or say, / Seems wisest, virtuousest, discreetest, best" (8.549–50). But as Adam went on to explain in that speech, he was not "foil'd" by such feelings; on the contrary, he remained "still free" to "Approve the best, and follow what [he] approve[d]" (8.608, 610–11). In book 9, then, when Adam discovers that Eve has eaten the fruit, he is—as Milton stresses—"not deceiv'd" (9.998). He knows that his wife has been "beguil'd," led into the sinful folly that is wisdom's opposite. Indeed, when he says that Eve is "Defac't," he acknowledges how perceptibly her sapiential beauty has been marred; he recognizes that she no longer resembles "wisdom, which alone is truly fair" (9.905, 901; 4.491).

The yet-unfallen Adam thus speaks "to himself," not to the "ruin'd" creature who stands before him (9.895, 906) when he makes his heartbroken and hyperbolic apostrophe to Eve as God's perfect creature: "O fairest of Creation, last and best / Of all God's Works... / How art thou lost, how on a sudden lost" (9.896–97, 900). But these words, with which Adam his "inward silence" breaks (9.895), also begin to break his ties to Wisdom. By insisting that Eve was "fairest...last and best" — not of God's "gifts" to him, but "Of all God's Works" — he undervalues himself, "whose perfection," as the divine judge later reminds him, "far excell'd / Hers in all real dignity" (10.150–51). He also slights the Wisdom whose beauty the unfallen Eve herself praised as more perfect than her own. Having thus suppressed both his sense of Wisdom's preeminence and the "self-esteem" Raphael warned him to maintain (8.572), he makes his own existence contingent upon that of the fallen woman: "to lose thee were to lose myself," he says to her (9.959). Though "not deceiv'd," he is "fondly overcome with Female charm" (9.998, 999).

The language of this crucial line emphasizes that, like "the unwiser Son / Of *Japhet*" who was "ensnar'd" by Pandora (*PL* 4.716–17), Adam has been seduced away from Wisdom; but it also suggests that in abandoning Wisdom, Adam compromises his love for Eve. He behaves "fondly," which means "foolishly" (*OED*, def. 1); his submission to Eve's "charm" is thus Wisdom's opposite, Folly. But he does not abandon Wisdom for *love* of Eve. Indeed, the very adverb that defines his action as foolish subtly invalidates Eve's flattering tribute to his decision as "Illustrious evidence" of "exceeding Love" (*PL* 9.962, 961): to behave "fondly" — "with self-pleasing or affectionate credulity" (*OED*, def. 2) — is not to behave lovingly. Adam does not speak of his love for Eve; instead, he says, "I feel / The Bond of Nature draw me to my own" (9.955–56). This natural affinity is *fondness:* "Instinctive or unreasoning liking or partiality; strong inclination, propensity or desire" (*OED*, def. 4); and such fondness is not love.[61]

Love, as Dennis Danielson points out in an article on "What Adam Should Have Done," is the self-sacrificial impulse of the Son, the Father's own "wisdom" (*PL* 3.170).[62] In the Son of God's offering of himself for fallen man's sake, the reader can see the clear alternative to Adam's disobedience; the Son's "meek aspéct / ... breath'd immortal love / To mortal men, above which only shone / Filial obedience" (3.266–69). As long as he remained unfallen and immortal, Adam had the ability to intercede for Eve, to offer to die *for* her rather than to sin and die *with* her. But only "Filial obedience" (3.269) would have made such an offer possible; Adam chooses instead to disobey.[63] Without obedience, there is neither wisdom nor love, only the "Link of Nature" or "Bond of Nature" that "draw[s]" him to behave "fondly" (9.914, 956, 914, 999)—instinctively, irrationally, foolishly.

Woman, in the eyes of the man thus fallen, is reduced to a "fair defect / Of Nature" (*PL* 10.891–92); the hopeless Adam foresees history as an endless pageant of woe in which all ills are due to "Female snares" (10.897). And as long as man remains trapped in such misogyny, he remains unredeemed, despairingly certain that he is "miserable / Beyond all past example and futúre, / To *Satan* only like both crime and doom" (10.839–41). His "mysterious reverence" for "the genial Bed" (8.599, 598) turns to a bitter prediction that, from this time forward, man "never shall find out fit Mate" (10.899); and toward Eve, whom he refers to as "that bad Woman" (10.837), he feels only rage and resentment. Indeed, when she approaches him, he equates her with the devil: "Out of my sight, thou Serpent, that name best / Befits thee with him leagu'd, thyself as false / And hateful" (10.867–69).

But Eve, though scorned and rejected, answers hate with love: "Forsake me not thus, *Adam*, witness Heav'n / What love sincere, and reverence in my heart / I bear thee" (*PL* 10.914–16). As many readers of *Paradise Lost* have acknowledged, these words of Eve are the first break in the destructive cycle of mutual blame that has enveloped the fallen pair. They demonstrate that, far from being "leagu'd" with Satan, Eve longs to renew the "nuptial League" (4.339) that she and Adam share as husband and wife. And while he may equate her with the "Serpent" (10.867) and himself with Satan in "both crime and doom" (10.841), Eve urges their reconciliation precisely on the basis of their "one enmity" toward that "Foe..., / That cruel Serpent" (10.925, 926–27). She recognizes in Adam not the Adversary, but her own spouse and best ally, her "only strength and stay" (10.921). Thus, she does not stop with the expression of love; rather, as Danielson points out, Eve tries to do as a fallen wife what Adam ought to have done as an unfallen husband. She tells Adam that she will "importune Heaven, that all / The sentence from thy head remov'd may light / On me" (10.933–35). This is a "hopelessly heroic gesture," for "their fallenness precludes either Adam's or Eve's now taking 'all' upon his or her own head"; but it is also "genuinely exemplary" (Danielson, "Through the Telescope," 123). As Joseph Summers explains (Muse's Method, 178), Eve's words echo the genuinely redemptive self-offering of the Son—who is God's own "word, ...wisdom, and effectual might" (3.170).

Only divine Wisdom can save Adam and Eve from damnation; but in Paradise Lost, redemption cannot take place until the rift between the sexes has been healed, and this healing is brought about through the regeneration of Eve's sapiential character. A "remnant of [Eve's] supple prelapsarian nature remains for prevenient grace to work on" (McColley, Milton's Eve, 210); thus, the effect of grace is to restore some part of her original resemblance to Wisdom. And this effect appears when Eve, Wisdom's "Defac't" likeness, echoes—however imperfectly and unwittingly—the love and humility of God's own "wisdom," the Son. As in the days before the Fall, Adam learns from the example set by his sapiential spouse: in response to Eve's prostration at his feet, Adam relents and becomes penitent, proposing that they both humble themselves before God in the same way.

In Scripture, it is Wisdom herself who redeems Adam: "She preserued the first father of the worlde...and brought him out of his offence" (Wisd. of Sol. 10:1). The postlapsarian Eve is not this female savior; she cannot, of herself, bring Adam "out of his offence." But Milton's parallels between Eve and Sapientia find their ultimate significance in Eve's echoes of divine Wisdom's self-sacrificial love and in her place as the type of "*Mary* second *Eve*," in whose womb that Wisdom will become incarnate (*PL* 10.183). As Adam's vision in book 11 confirms, fallen history will too often be a sordid affair: man's love reduced to the lustful gaze of "eyes" that "Rove without rein" and woman's grace reduced to the "amorous Net" cast by a gem-bedecked "female Troop" (11.585–86, 614). But salvation history begins only when the dignity of both man and woman is restored; as Raphael puts it, "two great Sexes animate the World" (8.151). Thus, Adam is saved only by renewing his love for his spouse, whose "Seed" (10.180) will be the savior. He receives the gift of God's grace only through his reconciliation with Eve, "Heav'n's last best gift"; he cannot love Wisdom without loving his wife.

4. JESUS AS SON AND STUDENT OF MARY IN *PARADISE REGAINED*

The stark contrast between the prelapsarian Eden of *Paradise Lost* and the sinful world of *Paradise Regained* is nowhere clearer than in the gender shift divine Wisdom undergoes when she becomes incarnate as the world's redeemer. As an unmarried male invulnerable to woman's charms, Milton's Jesus initially seems to be a type of Wisdom utterly detached from the sacred feminine. He neither embodies Sapientia in a beautiful female form (as does the unfallen Eve), nor models man's love for her (as does the unfallen Adam). Nor does the Savior combat Satan by tapping directly into the divine Wisdom that is his birthright, and—according to the Father's language at *Paradise Lost* 3.170—his preincarnate identity. Rather, Jesus exemplifies perfect use of the created, human wisdom that is God's gift to fallen humanity, and he does so in ways that contrast his masculine strength with Eve's feminine weakness. For Milton, however, even Jesus' perfect human wisdom has feminine associations, for in *Paradise Regained,* the Savior's teacher and his wisest disciple is a woman, his mother, and the virtue that she cultivates in him incorporates both masculine potency and feminine meekness.

Near the end of *Paradise Lost,* Adam speaks as a regenerate soul, declaring humbly to Michael all that he has learned from his glimpses of the future and in particular from what Michael has told him about the saving deeds of the Redeemer to come, whom he calls "The Woman's seed, . . . thy Saviour and thy Lord" (*PL* 12.543–44). Michael has stressed that the Messiah will defeat Satan not through force of arms, but through obedient suffering and love, and though Adam many times fails to grasp his angelic teacher's lessons, the essential points finally become clear to him:

> Henceforth I learn, that to obey is best,
> And love with fear the only God, to walk
> As in his presence, ever to observe
> His providence, and on him sole depend,
> Merciful over all his works, with good
> Still overcoming evil, and by small
> Accomplishing great things, by things deem'd weak
> Subverting worldly strong, and worldly wise
> By simply meek; that suffering for Truth's sake
> Is fortitude to highest victory,
> And to the faithful Death the Gate of Life;
> Taught this by his example whom I now
> Acknowledge my Redeemer ever blest.   (*PL* 12.561–73)

Michael responds approvingly, "This having learnt, thou hast attain'd the sum / Of wisdom" (*PL* 12.575–76), and he goes on to assure Adam that the man whose "Deeds," "Faith," and "Virtue" put such wisdom into practice will "possess / A paradise within [him], happier far" than the garden lost by sin (*PL* 12.582, 583, 586–87). *Paradise Regained,* as John Shawcross points out, "is about . . . the ways in which Michael's counsel can be internalized and made available for action" (*Paradise Regain'd,* 81).

But what does it mean for postlapsarian man to reach the ultimate wisdom? Michael commends Adam for attaining "the sum" of human wisdom that is God's gift to regenerate humanity, but that wisdom is linked to divine Sapientia. As Saint Augustine points out, "there is a certain supreme wisdom of

God, by participation in which every soul...constituted truly wise acquires its wisdom" (*Harmony of the Gospels*, 1.23.35). Augustine goes on to explain the relationship between divine and human wisdom in terms that serve as an excellent gloss to Milton's Christology in *Paradise Regained:*

> seeing that Christ Himself is that Wisdom of God by whom all things were created, and considering that no rational intelligences...receive wisdom except by participation in this Wisdom.... Divine Providence, having respect to the interests of mortal men whose time-bound life was held engaged in things which rise into being and die, decreed that this same Wisdom of God, assuming into the unity of His person the (nature of) man, in which He might be born according to the conditions of time, ...should utter and perform and bear and sustain things congruous to our salvation; and thus, in exemplary fashion, show at once to men on earth the way for a return to heaven. (*Harmony*, 1.35.53)[64]

Augustine is arguing here that divine Wisdom becomes human partly in order to model for human beings the God-given *created* wisdom that regains paradise. It is human wisdom in its most perfect form that the Jesus of *Paradise Regained* deploys in his battle with Satan, which the heavenly choir celebrates as "his great duel, not of arms, / But to vanquish by wisdom hellish wiles" (*PR* 1.174–75). As John Carey points out in his edition, Milton follows in "a long line of theologians from Ambrose on" when he adopts "the view that Christ underwent temptation only as a man, and hence did not use divine power to drive the devil away" (*Milton*, 417; see also Lewalski, *Milton's Brief Epic*, 163). And it is, in turn, human wisdom—given by God, but not divine—that each man and woman is called to exercise within the particular circumstances of his or her life.[65]

The perfection of the Messiah's human wisdom is, however, a reflection of his identity as divine Wisdom incarnate; even the wisest of men cannot compare to him (see Lewalski, ibid., 301–02). When the voluptuary devil Belial suggests that Satan attempt to ensnare Jesus in "Amorous Nets," he reminds the

Adversary that "Women, when nothing else, beguil'd the heart /
Of wisest *Solomon*" (*PR* 2.162, 169–70). But Satan rejects the
plan, pointing out that "he whom we attempt is wiser far /
Than *Solomon*, of more exalted mind, / Made and set wholly on
th'accomplishment / Of greatest things"; no woman, no matter
how beautiful or seductive, could inspire "fond desire" in him
(*PR* 2.205–08, 211). Nor could any woman's captivating charms
remain effective in his presence:

> should she confident,
> As sitting Queen ador'd on Beauty's Throne,
> Descend with all her winning charms begirt
> To enamor, . . .
>
> . . . .
>
> How would one look from his Majestic brow,
> Seated as on the top of Virtue's hill,
> Discount'nance her despis'd, and put to rout
> All her array; her female pride deject,
> Or turn to reverent awe!   (*PR* 2.211–14, 216–20)

These lines recall and reverse Adam's ill-advised tribute to
Eve: "All higher knowledge in her presence falls / Degraded,
Wisdom in discourse with her / Loses discount'nanc't, and like
folly shows" (*PL* 8.551–53). In a contest with Wisdom incarnate, Satan knows, the "Plumes" of postlapsarian female beauty
would "Fall flat and shrink into a trivial toy" (*PR* 2.222–23).

He is right, of course, but Satan's tone of disparagement in
dismissing "female pride" reveals in him the same misogyny
for which Michael rebuked Adam when he reacted with sexist
self-righteousness to the vision of Cain's goddesslike daughters.
Like that "Bevy of fair Women" (*PL* 11.582), the seductresses
that Belial recommends and Satan dismisses are fallen parodies
of Eve's "Virgin Modesty" (*PL* 8.501) in all its innocent subtlety;
they are, in Belial's words,

> graceful and discreet,
> Expert in amorous Arts, enchanting tongues
> Persuasive, Virgin majesty with mild

> And sweet allay'd, yet terrible to approach,
> Skill'd to retire, and in retiring draw
> Hearts after them tangl'd in Amorous Nets.   (*PR* 2.157–62)

One cannot read these lines without recalling Adam's description of the prelapsarian Eve: "Not obvious, not obtrusive, but, retir'd" (*PL* 8.504), possessed of qualities that "create an awe / About her, as a guard Angelic plac't" (8.558–59). In particular, Belial's admiration for the persuasive power of "Virgin majesty" recalls and contrasts with the prelude to the Fall, when Adam is persuaded by Eve's "Virgin Majesty" (9.270)—not yet sinful, though overconfident—to allow the separation that leads to disaster. The implications are frightening; in the *fallen* world, even the undeflowered maiden is "Expert" and "Skill'd" in the ways of sin. It will take a better man than Adam—"one greater Man" (*PL* 1.4), in fact—to resist such "Virgin majesty."

The Jesus of *Paradise Regained* is precisely that man, and Satan knows it. He thus assails the "glorious Eremite" (*PR* 1.8) with cunning arguments rather than with what Belial calls "amorous Arts" (*PR* 2.158). The effect of this choice is to set up a contrast, not so much between Jesus and Adam (since Satan does not even try to make Jesus fall in the way that Adam did) as between the son of Mary and Adam's "facile consort *Eve*" (*PR* 1.51), who was led into sin by the brilliant sophistry of the serpent. In *Paradise Lost,* the opening gambit of the false but persuasive argument that convinces Eve to eat of the forbidden fruit recalls the effective techniques of classical rhetors:

> As when of old some Orator renown'd
> In *Athens* or free *Rome,* where Eloquence
> Flourish'd, since mute, to some great cause addresst,
> Stood in himself collected, while each part,
> Motion, each act won audience ere the tongue,
> Sometimes in highth began, as no delay
> Of Preface brooking through his Zeal of Right.
> So standing, moving, or to highth upgrown
> The Tempter all impassion'd thus began.   (*PL* 9.670–78)

The speech that follows begins with an impressive apostrophe—
"O Sacred, Wise, and Wisdom-giving Plant" (9.679)—that mis-
represents the tree of knowledge as the source of sapience and
"Mother of Science" (9.680). But because this eloquence is false,
the orator Satan resembles is the sophist, not the noble states-
man or the true philosopher. Speaking as if motivated by "his
Zeal of Right," he in fact uses the art of rhetoric only for his
own profit.

In *Paradise Regained*, Milton carefully sets up a contrast
between Eve's failure in the face of such seductive grandilo-
quence and Jesus' victory when confronted with similar rhetorical deceptions. After the failure of his initial attempts in book
3 to seduce the Savior with the promise of worldly power and
glory, and before he continues to tempt him in book 4, Satan
finds himself stymied:

> Perplex'd and troubl'd at his bad success
> The Tempter stood, nor had what to reply,
> Discover'd in his fraud, thrown from his hope,
> So oft, and the persuasive Rhetoric
> That sleek't his tongue, and won so much on *Eve*,
> So little here, nay lost; but *Eve* was *Eve*,
> This far his over-match.   (PR 4.1–7)

This figure who outmatches his enemy so easily is the divine
Wisdom that Eve only reflects, and he puts into practice the
God-given human wisdom that Eve ultimately rejects. Where
Eve fails, Jesus stands firm.

He does so despite the fact that Satan tries on him a stronger
and more cleverly couched version of the strategy he used on Eve;
the devil attempts to convince Jesus that he will never be ready
to put his wisdom to use as long as he remains untouched by
the hand of experiential knowledge: "The wisest, unexperienc't,
will be ever / Timorous and loth, with novice modesty / (As
he who seeking Asses found a Kingdom) / Irresolute, unhardy,
unadvent'rous" (PR 3.240–43). Satan here alludes to the young
Saul (described in 1 Sam. 9:1–10:1), who went in search of his

father's lost livestock and returned as an anointed king, endowed with majesty. But many words in the passage also recall the Eve of *Paradise Lost* whose "Virgin *Modesty*" yields to Adam with "obsequious Majesty" and who moves from "*unexperienc't* thought" to sinless sexual experience with "*modest* pride, / And sweet, reluctant, amorous delay" (*PL* 8.501, 509; 4.457, 310–11; emphases mine). Eve's delectably assenting reluctance could be interpreted as "Timorous and loth, ... / Irresolute, unhardy, unadvent'rous" (*PR* 3.241, 242) only from the warped perspective of the fallen world in which the "Bold deed" of "*advent'rous Eve*" sets a sinful precedent for Adam, and in which woman is "nothing *loath*" in response to man's carnivorous advances (*PL* 9.921, 1039; emphases mine). But it is the inventor of sinful experience who tempts Jesus, as he did Eve, by impugning inexperience, and the adjectives Satan uses recall (even as they misrepresent) the unfallen Eve. Eve was sweetly "Irresolute" in her initial retreat from and return to Adam, and yet the energy and frankness of her prelapsarian enterprise and curiosity disprove Satan's claim that the inexperienced are always "Timorous and loth" or "unadvent'rous."

Still, recently uncloistered virtue will find it difficult to contradict such a claim; even Jesus himself ventures no immediate response to Satan's assertion. Before he answers, he lets pass over 140 lines in which he consents to survey things that ostensibly may "inform" his inexperience in "regal Arts, / And regal Mysteries" (*PR* 3.247, 248–49); he even lets Satan lecture him on the manly subject of establishing and extending empire.[66] But when at last he answers, he is—of course—"unmov'd" (*PR* 3.386) by all that Satan has set "Before [his] eyes" (*PR* 3.390). The contrast with Eve is vivid, and vividly gendered. Her heart is a feminine receptacle into which the tempter's "words replete with guile / ...too easy entrance w[i]n" (*PL* 9.733–34), and her "ears" ring with the sound of his "persuasive words, impregn'd / With Reason, to her seeming" (*PL* 9.736, 737–38). Jesus is, however, unimpressed by what Satan has "in [his] ear / Vented" (*PR* 3.390–91). Sapientia has become incarnate as a he rather than a she, a definitively male hero who is as impregnable by aggressive argument and virile spectacle as he is impervious to female charm.

The feminine personification of Wisdom does not entirely disappear in the presence of her messianic incarnation, however; in discourse with Satan, the Son of God alludes both to her and to the harlot who impersonates her. Rebuking the devil for commending pagan philosophers, Jesus insists that such thinkers can never lead men to Sophia: "Who... seeks in these / True wisdom finds her not, or by delusion / Far worse, her false resemblance only meets, / An empty cloud" (PR 4.318–21). The spectral figure of false wisdom is clearly a type of the adulterous Folly of Proverbs, who beckons to foolish young men and leads them astray; for, Jesus asserts, the Greeks and Romans achieve the appearance of sapience through mere rhetorical cunning, "swelling Epithets, thick laid / As varnish on a Harlot's cheek" (PR 4.343–44).[67]

Nevertheless, as Jesus' eloquence makes clear, Milton does not think skillful rhetoric itself is false wisdom. In *The Reason of Church Government*, the author goes so far as to imagine the establishment of civic festivals featuring

> wise and artfull recitations sweetned with eloquent and graceful inticements to the love and practice of justice, temperance, and fortitude, instructing and bettering the Nation at all opportunities, that the call of wisdom and vertu may be heard every where, as *Salomon* saith [Prov. 8:1–3], *She crieth without, she uttereth her voice in the streets, in the top of high places, in the chief concours, and in the openings of the Gates.* (YP 1:819)

Milton here uses the scriptural figure of Sapientia to signify the eloquence of skilled rhetors who advance masculine *vertu* in general and, in particular, the virtues Milton deems essential to a well-ordered commonwealth. The Jesus of *Paradise Regained* has not yet entered into his public ministry; he has gone into the desert "the better to converse / With solitude" (PR 1.190–91), the "sweet retired" state which the Elder Brother of the *Mask* identifies as one often sought by "Wisdom's self" (*Mask,* 376, 375). But when his privacy is invaded by Satan, he proves himself a brilliant orator whose words even his opponent cannot help but admire, and the insincere compliment the devil gives Jesus again associates him with female personifications of the divine.

Satan's compliment is not strictly false; rather, Satan illustrates the beauty of truth through mellifluous verse that is authentic in substance even as it is falsely flattering in purpose. He admits that, though the "ways of truth" are "rough to walk," they are "Smooth on the tongue discourst, pleasing to th' ear, / And tunable as Silvan Pipe or Song" (*PR* 1.478–80). The innocent and valiant younger brother declares no less in *A Mask* when he exclaims, "How charming is divine Philosophy! / Not harsh, and crabbed as dull fools suppose, / But musical as is *Apollo's* lute" (*Mask,* 476–78). But Satan, of course, tells the truth for falsehood's sake, and a lie is embedded in the rhetorical question, assertion, and petition that follow his description of Truth's discourses; for though in reality Jesus' rebukes have left him "inly stung with anger and disdain" (*PR* 1.466), he claims to be delighted by the "ways of truth" as they are eloquently expounded by Jesus: "What wonder then if I delight to hear / Her dictates from thy mouth? most men admire / Virtue, who follow not her lore: permit me / To hear thee when I come" (*PR* 1.481–84). The devil here praises Jesus as a mere spokesman for Truth and Virtue, each of which he personifies as feminine; but, as Jesus has observed (*PR* 1.356), Satan knows, at least in part, the true identity of the man he flatters. Jesus is not a mouthpiece for an allegorical lady whose ways are "Hard" (*PR* 1.478); as divine Wisdom incarnate, he is himself "the Way, and the Trueth, & the Life" (John 14:6). The subject of his ponderings in the desert is, after all, "How best the mighty work he might begin / Of Savior to mankind, and which way first / Publish his Godlike office now mature" (*PR* 1.186–88).

The "Godlike" nature of this redemptive mission notwithstanding, however, Jesus must carry it out as "one greater Man"

(*PL* 1.4); to atone for humanity's sin, he must be human. Thus, in responding to Satan's enticements, Jesus does not speak as the divine Son. Rather, he answers as a man who has—as Michael put it to Adam—"attain'd the sum / Of wisdom" (*PL* 12.575–76). He puts to use the gift of created wisdom, rather than manifesting his power as the uncreated, begotten Wisdom of God, even though the first temptation he faces is an invitation to act in his divine capacity, to show that he is "the Son of God" and "Command / That out of these hard stones be made thee bread" (*PR* 1.342–43). Jesus knows that to do so would be to "distrust" God (*PR* 1.355), and so he refuses, rebuking the tempter with the wisdom of Deuteronomy 8:3: "is it not written / ...Man lives not by Bread only, but each Word / Proceeding from the mouth of God, who fed / Our Fathers here with Manna" (*PR* 1.347, 349–51). He speaks these words not through his capacity as Wisdom incarnate, but rather as a wise human being, an Israelite who looks to the deeds of the God of Israel as recorded in the Scriptures so as to "observe / His providence, and on him sole depend" (*PL* 12.563–64). In doing so, he shows himself to be the "Redeemer ever blest" from whose "example" the future-schooled Adam of *Paradise Lost* learns true *human* wisdom (12.573, 572).

But from whose instruction and example did Jesus the human being learn? The nature of Jesus' intellectual development had, of course, been a much-discussed theological question from the patristic period onward; Calvin's ideas on the subject provide a helpful point of reference, since the Thirty-Nine Articles of the English church and the Puritan theology against which Milton defined his own idiosyncratic mixture of Arian and Arminian theology both take their cue from Calvin. In discussing Luke 2:40, which says that the child Jesus "grewe, and waxed strong in Spirit, and was filled with wisdome," Calvin explains: "we infer that this progress, or advancement, relates to his human nature: for the Divine nature could receive no increase" (*Commentary on a Harmony*, 1:166).[68] It was not, Calvin stresses, that "knowledge lay concealed in Christ, and made its appearance in him in progress of time" (1:167). Rather, his human "soul was subject to ignorance" and "so far as was necessary for our salvation, the Son of God kept his divine power concealed" (1:166, 167). Calvin believes, however, that the human Christ's only teacher was God himself; his evidence for this view is John 7:15–16, where Jesus' listeners are dumbfounded by his ability to teach the Scriptures and wonder, "How knoweth this man the Scriptures, seing that he neuer learned?" Jesus answers, "My doctrine is not mine, but his that sent me." For Calvin, this passage provides "an astonishing proof of the power and grace of God, that Christ, who had not been taught by any master, was yet eminently distinguished by his knowledge of the Scriptures; and that he, who had never been a scholar, should be a most excellent teacher and instructor" (*Commentary on the Gospel*, 1:289). Calvin interprets Jesus' response as saying, in essence, "When you see a teacher not trained in the school of men, know that I have been taught by God" (1:289).

The same view of Christ as divinely instructed underlies Calvin's reading of the incident in Luke when the child Jesus interacts with the doctors of the law in the temple. Luke says that Jesus sat "in the middes of the doctours, bothe hearing them, and asking them questions. And all who heard him, were astonied at his vnderstanding, and answers" (Luke 2:46–47); Calvin interprets the evangelist's reference to the doctors' *hearing* Christ as implying that they "acted the part rather of scholars than of teachers." The 12-year-old boy is already their instructor rather than their pupil. Calvin explains,

> He had not yet been called by the Father, to avow himself a public teacher of the Church, and therefore satisfied himself with putting modest questions to the doctors. Yet there is no room to doubt that, in this first attempt, he already began to tax their perverse way of teaching: for what Luke afterwards says about answers, I consider as denoting, agreeably to the Hebrew idiom, any kind of discourse. (*Commentary on a Harmony*, 1:169–70)

In *Paradise Regained*, however, Jesus' recollections about the same incident imply that he entered into conversation with the doctors as both a teacher *and* a scholar:

> The Law of God I read, and found it sweet,
> Made it my whole delight, and in it grew
> To such perfection that, ere my age
> Had measur'd twice six years, at our great Feast
> I went into the Temple, there to hear
> The Teachers of our Law, and to propose
> What might improve my knowledge or their own;
> And was admir'd by all.   (*PR* 1.207–14)

The verb "propose" here means "put forward or present for consideration, discussion... set forth, propound" (*OED* v. def. 2a). Jesus himself thus introduces the questions that will help him to "improve [his] knowledge," but he clearly feels himself able to learn through his encounter with the "Teachers."

Still, there are things that neither the Torah nor any man can teach him. His source for knowledge of the word of God concerning his own conception and birth—the narrative that will be recorded in the opening chapters of Matthew's and Luke's Gospels—is a woman, his mother. In 30 lines directly quoting her words to him as a youth, Jesus recalls what Mary told him about the Annunciation, his birth, and all that followed (*PR* 1.229–58); the effect is remarkable. In the best of the surprisingly few scholarly works that discuss the Mary of *Paradise Regained*, Dayton Haskin points out that,

> as Milton gives his readers access to the Son's memory of his mother's words, he has Mary giving a unified account of what the evangelists will give only piecemeal. The point here is not that Milton draws this from Matthew and Luke and puts it into the mouth of Mary; it is rather that Milton implies that Mary was the source of these materials for the evangelists, that before anyone recorded what happened, Mary had been the bearer of the scriptural word, first to her Son at the time when he needed to know it and then to those who were the

sacred penmen writing it down for aftertimes. ("Matthew, Mary," 82)[69]

In *Paradise Regained*, Haskin stresses, Mary not only bears in her womb God's Word incarnate, but bears *to* him "the scriptural word" that proclaims his identity and mission.

In so doing, I would add, she conveys the highest *human* wisdom to the man who is divine Sapientia incarnate. For Milton, of course, there is no Immaculate Conception, and thus Mary cannot be all that Eve was before she sinned; Jesus, not she, is the embodiment of divine Wisdom. But as the second Eve, Mary is that Wisdom's mother and teacher.[70] While the prelapsarian Eve is an earthly image of both the uncreated divine Wisdom who plays in the presence of the Almighty Father and the created wisdom Solomon sought as his consort, Mary simply lives out in her own life the practical wisdom God bestows on those he redeems. She makes clear through her words and actions that she, who bore divine Wisdom in her womb, has also received from God the created wisdom that shows "to men on earth the way for a return to heaven" (Augustine, *Harmony*, 1.35.53). Milton has clearly taken to heart Calvin's exhortation in reflecting on the Annunciation: "let us not be ashamed to receive instruction from her who carried in her womb Christ the eternal 'wisdom of God' [1 Cor. 1:24]" (*Commentary on a Harmony*, 1:32).

The poet goes much farther than Calvin, however, for he portrays Mary as instructing her son about his identity, whereas Calvin stresses Mary's failure to understand that identity.[71] Commenting on Mary and Joseph's incomprehension of the young Jesus' explanation that he must be about his Father's business (Luke 2:49), Calvin asks,

> is it not astonishing, that Joseph and Mary *did not understand* this answer, who had been instructed by many proofs, that Jesus is the Son of God? I reply: Though they were not wholly unacquainted with Christ's heavenly origin, yet they did not comprehend, in every respect, how he was intent on executing his heavenly Father's commands: for his calling had not yet been expressly revealed to them. Mary *kept in her heart* those

things which she did not fully understand. Let us learn from this, to receive with reverence, and *to lay up* in our minds, (like the seed, which is allowed to remain for some time under grounds) those mysteries of God which exceed our capacity. (*Commentary on a Harmony*, 1:171)

For Calvin, Mary is thus in the position of instructor only as we may learn from her example; in relation to her son, she is only a pupil.

But in Milton's poem, as is clear in Jesus' account of why he went to converse with the temple doctors, the line between teaching and learning is not so clear-cut; rather, students instruct their teachers, and teachers learn from their students. Milton's Mary is able, once the "seed" of which Calvin speaks has matured in her mind, to serve as her son's teacher. Recalling her finding of the young Jesus in the temple and his assertion that he must be about his Father's business, Mary says, "what he meant I mus'd, / Since understand" (*PR* 2.99–100); that understanding, in turn, gives her strength in the face of Jesus' current unexplained absence: "I to wait with patience am inur'd; / My heart hath been a storehouse long of things / And sayings laid up, portending strange events" (*PR* 2.102–04). The scriptural prompts for these lines of *Paradise Regained* are Luke 2:19 (following the shepherds' visit to the manger, "Marie kept all those sayings & and pondered them in her heart") and Luke 2:51 (following the finding of the child Jesus among the temple doctors, "his mother kept all these sayings in her heart"). As Haskin explains, "Just what Mary did 'in her heart' is not immediately clear from Luke's word *symballousa*...rendered *conferens* in the Vulgate and 'pondered' in the English versions" ("Milton's Portrait," 177).

Calvin himself stresses that such musing is a sign of godly wisdom:

Mary's diligence in contemplating the works of God is laid before us for two reasons; first, to inform us, that this treasure was laid up in her heart, for the purpose of being published to others at the proper time; and, secondly, to afford to all the godly an example for imitation. For, if we are wise, it will be the chief employment, and the great object of our life, to consider with attention those works of God which build up our faith. *Mary kept all these things.* This relates to her memory. Συμβάλλειν signifies to throw together,—to collect the several events which agreed in proving the glory of Christ, so that they might form one body. For Mary could not wisely estimate the collective value of all those occurrences, except by comparing them with each other. (*Commentary on a Harmony*, 1:124–25)

Milton clearly agrees, for the portrayal of Mary in *Paradise Regained* implies a similar idea of the role Mary plays. She is a "portrait of the responsible reader" (Haskin, "Milton's Portrait," 180), modeling what Calvin calls contemplation of the "works of God." And since she stores up what she has seen and heard in order to publish it "to others at the proper time" (Calvin, *Commentary on a Harmony*), she also becomes the oral storyteller who provides Luke with the narratives recounted in his Gospel. In doing so, Haskin stresses, Milton's Mary models the devout poet's own creative process as he works to "collect, compare, and recombine texts in a continuing search for meanings that cannot be permanently fixed" ("Milton's Portrait," 180). Indeed, if John Shawcross's detailed and persuasive argument for an early date of composition is correct, the parallel between the poet and Mary is all the stronger. Shawcross contends, on the basis of prosody, orthography, and bibliographic context that books 1, 2, and 4 of *Paradise Regained* were first composed in dramatic form as early as 1642–44, with book 3 being added between 1646 and 1649 and the whole being revised as an epic after 1665. If Milton did compose the work in this manner, his mind, like Mary's heart, was "a storehouse long of things / And sayings laid up" and only later brought forth.

While the poet's words teach only his readers, however, Milton's Mary teaches the Redeemer himself. Her instruction of him, Jesus' recollection makes clear, springs from her practice of careful listening and study, for things Mary hears from her son's lips make her aware of his desire to liberate Israel and abolish tyranny, and that awareness motivates her to teach him about himself. "[My] growing thoughts," Jesus recalls, "my Mother soon perceiv[ed] / By words at times cast forth" (*PR* 1.227–28). Responding to those "words," Mary urges him to "nourish" his "High...thoughts" (230, 229), informs him of his divine parentage (233–37), and recounts what had been foretold of his kingly, messianic destiny (240–58). At the time she does this, moreover, she has clearly meditated long on what Jesus told her years before when she found him in the temple and he said that he must attend to his Father's business. It is in light of that meditation and of the "High...thoughts" his later words reveal that she decides she must tell him more about the unique way in which God is a father to him.[72] As she does so, she still does not fully understand his mission, for she (like Jesus himself at this point) still thinks of his role in largely political terms; but she is nonetheless an effective teacher. For her words propel Jesus to further study of God's Word (*PR* 1.259–67), and the Scriptures in turn reveal to him that he is called to bear the weight of men's sins rather than to liberate them politically.

The action of *Paradise Regained* takes place at a point in time when Jesus has yet to begin his redemptive work; indeed, he has gone to the desert "Musing and much revolving in his breast, / How best the mighty work he might begin / Of Savior to mankind, and which way first / Publish his Godlike office now mature" (*PR* 1.185–88). Before he can begin, he must undergo a trial of obedience not unlike the one his mother successfully endured many years before. In conversation with Gabriel, the Father recalls the Annunciation, reminding the angel of how he informed "the Virgin pure" that she would bear a son and responded to her "doubting how these things could be" (*PR* 1.134, 137). The "reference to Mary's testing" here, Haskin argues, "serves as background and establishes a continuity between the obedience once displayed by Mary and that in which Jesus is now to be schooled." The obedience involved is not blind; it is *wise*, for "Far from precluding questioning and doubting on the part of the tested, this testing necessitates active exploration in a spirit of openness to God" (Haskin, "Matthew, Mary,"

81). Such a spirit of openness is what the Hebrew scriptures call "fear of the Lord"; it is what Abraham demonstrates when he does not hesitate to obey the command to sacrifice Isaac, and as Wisdom herself declares in Proverbs 9:10: "The beginning of wisdome is ye feare of the Lord."[73]

But fear of the Lord does not banish all fear; and Milton acknowledges this fact as he chooses to depict Mary in a moment of anxiousness. Jesus has not returned with the others who went to be baptized by John, and she has heard "tidings of him none" (*PR* 2.62). Thus, "Within her breast, though calm, her breast though pure, / Motherly cares and fears got head, and rais'd / Some troubl'd thoughts" (*PR* 2.63–65). The cares and fears to which mothers are prone here stage a rebel uprising, prompting "troubl'd thoughts" to disturb the peace. But they are unsuccessful, for Mary's breast remains "calm" and "pure"; and as a mother, she gets the "troubl'd thoughts" properly "clad" in "sighs" before she lets them out. Mary recalls all the hardships and fears that she suffered "by the birth [she] bore" (*PR* 2.71) during that ill-timed winter trip to Bethlehem, conveying a sense of the delivery not as miraculously painless (as in medieval legend), but burdensome and difficult. She recalls, too, the flight into Egypt (*PR* 2.75–78) and the moment in the temple when Simeon prophesied "that through [her] very Soul / A sword [should] pierce" (*PR* 2.90–91). Thinking that such pain may now be very near, Mary remarks on the irony of Gabriel's having hailed her as "highly favor'd": "this is my favor'd lot, / My Exaltation to Afflictions high" (*PR* 2.91–92). At first blush, these somewhat bitter-sounding words recall the moment in *Paradise Lost* when Satan alleges that his "highest place" in hell "condemns [him] to greatest share / Of endless pain" (*PL* 2.27, 29–30); but while Satan's claim to unenviable precedence leads him deeper and deeper into damnation, Mary turns her ironic observation into a profession of faith: "Afflicted I may be, it seems, and blest; / I will not argue that, nor will repine" (*PR* 2.93–94).[74] Rejecting the hellish trap of self-pity, Mary here declares in brief the same paradoxical creed that Adam embraces when he acknowledges "that suffering for Truth's sake / Is fortitude to highest victory, /

And to the faithful Death the Gate of Life" (*PL* 12.569–71). She, like Adam, attains the "sum / Of wisdom" (*PL* 12.575–76) when she realizes that affliction and blessing are one.

Milton's depiction of Mary breaks off as she, "pondering oft, and oft to mind / Recalling what remarkably had pass'd / Since first her Salutation heard, with thoughts / Meekly compos'd await[s] the fulfilling" (*PR* 2.105–08). The reader is very much aware of what that "fulfilling" will be: Jesus' death and resurrection. *Paradise Regained* ends, however, with the completion of the Savior's mission still in the distant future. Though the angels celebrate his victory as having "aveng'd / Supplanted *Adam*" (*PR* 4.606–07), it is clear that "by vanquishing / Temptation," he has "regain'd lost Paradise" (*PR* 4.607–08) only as vacant territory in which human beings will *some day* live again:

> A fairer Paradise is founded now
> For *Adam* and his chosen Sons, whom thou
> A Savior art come down to reinstall,
> Where they shall dwell secure, when time shall be
> Of Tempter and Temptation without fear.   (*PR* 4.613–17)

The work of "reinstall[ing]" man in paradise is the suffering and death Jesus has yet to undergo; it is not even started yet, as the conclusion of the angels' hymn acknowledges in its exhortation: "on thy glorious work / Now enter, and begin to save mankind" (*PR* 4.634–35). Why, then, most readers have wondered, does Milton end the work by deferring Jesus' public ministry yet again? In the notorious closing lines of *Paradise Regained*, Jesus continues on a private path: "hee unobserv'd / Home to his Mother's house private return'd" (*PR* 4.638–39).

This return to the womb of domestic comfort tempers Milton's heroic portrait of the Messiah as masculine victor, "True image of the Father" (*PR* 4.596) "with Godlike force endu'd / Against the Attempter of [his] Father's Throne" (4.602–03). Indeed, as Marjorie O'Rourke Boyle explains in a recent study of the poem, it introduces into Milton's brief epic a nonscriptural Marian detail found in the medieval Franciscan *Meditationes vitae Christi*, a widely circulated text, some English translations of which were still popular even with Protestant readers in Milton's time. But why does Milton devote the concluding emphasis of his brief epic to this feminizing, quasi-Catholic image?[75] As Haskin reads it, the conclusion of *Paradise Regained* implies Jesus' need to continue the pondering, collation, and interpretation that are the defining activities of his mother's experience; his return to Mary's house may even imply the need for further instruction, for

> if we were to make a harmony of the four gospels (as Milton no doubt did), the next event to take place would be the wedding feast at Cana (John 2). There Mary will break through, we might say, the newly acquired lessons in detachment that her son has learned as he spurned Satan's various offers. She will teach Jesus a new lesson about timing when she prods him to act in response to human needs. For John, this is a way of introducing his guiding notion of the *kairos*, the right time, a notion that informs Milton's poem at virtually every turn. For Milton, who sends his hero home to his mother's house in private after the temptations, this is a way of suggesting how waiting itself needs to be done *at* the right time, rather than simply *for* the right time. (Haskin, "Matthew, Mary," 83)

In short, Jesus' return to Mary's sphere of influence will foster his continued growth in wisdom.

Haskin's reading of *Paradise Regained* in light of the miracle at Cana helps clarify just how different Milton's Mary and Jesus are from Calvin's. For Calvin had interpreted Christ's initial response to Mary at Cana—"Woman, what haue I to do with thee? mine houre is not yet come" (John 2:4)—as a rebuke calculated to prevent anyone from overestimating his mother's power. "Christ," Calvin says, "meets the danger, that no improper use may be made of what his mother...said"; Jesus wants to be sure no one thinks it is "in obedience to her command that he afterwards perform[s] the miracle" (*Commentary on the Gospel*, 1:84). But Calvin does not go on to explain why, harsh words notwithstanding, Jesus does immediately proceed to remedy the problem his mother has pointed out. As Calvin sees it, the "hour" that has "not yet come" when Mary speaks to her Son must be the precise moment at which Jesus, by changing the water to wine, does see fit to employ his miraculous powers. That moment has technically "not yet come" when he replies to Mary; but it is certainly immanent. Only by breaking Jesus' "hour" down into minutes can Calvin insist that, "As he reproves his mother for unseasonable haste, so, on the other hand, he gives reason to expect a miracle." To support his conclusion, Calvin digs for supporting evidence in Mary's response to Jesus: "The holy Virgin acknowledges both [the rebuke and the fact that he has given her reason to expect a miracle], for she abstains from addressing him any farther; and when she advises the servants to do whatever he commands, she shows that she expects something now" (*Commentary on the Gospel*, 1:85). But perhaps the fact that she says nothing more to Jesus is merely a good teacher's tactic, a silence that allows her student to find his own best response to the situation. It seems strained to claim that Mary has acted with "unseasonable haste" in quietly pointing out that their hosts have run out of wine (John 2:3). Such a claim is belied by the fact that, once Mary has drawn his attention to the situation, Jesus does indeed act "now" (to use Calvin's term) rather than allowing his hosts to be humiliated. The text does not exclude the possibility that he acts in response to his mother's prompting, choosing to reveal himself *before* his hour rather than ignore her charitable observation. Milton does not portray the Cana episode; but in ending *Paradise Regained* with the image of Jesus' return to Mary's house, he creates a similar impression, hinting at Mary's ongoing role in her son's spiritual education.

Boyle objects to the idea that Jesus' return to his mother has to do with her role as his teacher: "for if the Son has vanquished Satan by the correct responses to the temptations, the right readings of the diabolical script, why must he return home to her? Surely not for further lessons" ("Home to Mother," 500). But the use of terms like "correct responses" and "lessons" seriously conflicts with Milton's concept of wisdom as a matter of ongoing growth, fluid interpretation, and indeterminate teacher/student status. In *Paradise Lost,* Adam's teacher, Raphael, explains his ignorance concerning the specifics of man's creation and humbly confirms that he can learn something by listening to Adam (*PL* 8.217–48); as Milton portrays her, Mary, too, has taught and will continue to teach her teacher. The story of the finding in the temple concludes with Jesus' return to the home of Mary and Joseph, where he "increased in wisdome, & stature, and in fauour with God and men" (Luke 2:52). As Milton sees it, the time for such growth is never past, even for Wisdom incarnate; a grown man can still learn much from a wise mother.

Indeed, in portraying Mary as Jesus' teacher, Milton highlights the female, human contribution to Jesus' mission as the Messiah and advances a vision of redemption as a process of reconciling not only the divine and the human, but also the masculine and the feminine. As Shawcross explains, *Paradise Regained* depicts in Jesus' response to temptation

> a blending of the conscious and the unconscious, of the animus and the anima, of the male principle with the female principle, of the Self with the godly. Jesus combines in his ministry the strength of the eagle and the gentleness of the dove, the power of the lion and the meekness of the lamb. He represents the oneness of Man and Woman, and *Paradise Regain'd* proclaims that Mankind's place of rest will be attained only by the symbolic Adam and Eve within us all going forth hand in hand. (Shawcross, *Paradise Regain'd,* 69)

Shawcross's eagle/dove imagery may at first seem more Donnean than Miltonic in spirit, given that no eagles are featured in *Paradise Regained,* and that the only dove to appear is not directly associated with Jesus' mother, but is rather the Spirit of God, who descends upon Jesus "in likeness of a Dove / ...while the Father's voice" speaks from heaven to declare him that Father's "beloved Son" (*PR* 1.30–31, 32). But Milton's Jesus does in fact unite the eagle and the dove in a manner no less "Mysterious," though very different from that employed in

Donne's "The Canonization." He does so through the practice of what his Father calls "consummate virtue" (*PR* 1.165), a virtue that unites masculine and feminine goodness. This perfected, comprehensive virtue raises his thought to "soar" (*PR* 1.230) like an eagle toward the Father, but also directs those thoughts back to the meek mother who first urged him to give his thoughts eagle's wings. Nor are the two entirely distinct in his mind: in a fascinating acknowledgment of the feminine dimension of the sacred realm in which his Father dwells, the Son of God and Mary even goes so far as to assert that the spirit of God who descends upon him in the form of a dove after his baptism—that same "Holy Ghost" who "on [his mother]...come[s]" at the moment of his conception (*PR* 1.138)—emerges from a feminine dwelling place: "Heaven open'd her eternal doors," he recalls,

> from whence
> The Spirit descended on me like a Dove;
> And...my Father's voice,
> Audibly heard from Heav'n, pronounc'd me his,
> Mee his beloved Son.   (*PR* 1.281–85)

The paternal voice, like the divine spirit, here issues from the open portals of a celestial matrix.

But what Shawcross recognizes as the "blending of the...male principle with the female principle" in *Paradise Regained* shines most clearly in what "the eternal Father" (*PR* 1.168) himself says of Jesus' "consummate virtue" (1.165). Speaking to Gabriel—the angel he had sent 30 years earlier as his messenger "to the Virgin pure / In *Galilee*"—"the most High" stresses not only Jesus' status as "the Son of God; / of...birth divine," but also his identity as "a man" produced "Of female Seed" (*PL* 1.134–35, 128, 136, 141, 150, 151). As the Father's speech continues, he insists upon the paradox of "strong Sufferance," of active "o'ercom[ing]" through passive "Humiliation." Jesus will

> conquer Sin and Death the two grand foes,
> By Humiliation and strong Sufferance:
> His weakness shall o'ercome Satanic strength

> And all the world, and mass of sinful flesh;
> That all the Angels and Ethereal Powers,
> They now, and men hereafter, may discern
> From what consummate virtue I have chose
> This perfect Man, by merit call'd my Son,
> To earn Salvation for the Sons of men.   (*PR* 1.159–67)

This passage says nothing directly of Mary's role in her son's life. It is Jesus' virtue, not his mother's, that will overcome the world, the flesh, and the devil to "earn Salvation for the Sons of men."[76] And yet, as John Rumrich points out, Milton makes an unprecedented narrative choice in *Paradise Regained* when he includes Jesus' mother in his account of the temptation in the wilderness: "Even Matthew and Luke, who begin their gospels with the Nativity, do not refer to it in their relation of the temptation nor do they inventory Jesus' youthful aspirations. But Milton, as the human Son approaches the critical stage of his life, chooses to stress the birth and development of 'this man born and now up-grown' (*PR* 1:140)" ("Milton's *Theanthropos*," 61). In stressing that development, Rumrich observes, Milton strongly intimates that Mary serves as "the medium for much of Jesus' self-consciousness, especially his grand ambition.... She is evidently the single most influential person in his psyche" (62).

More specifically, the portrayal of Mary and her role in Jesus' upbringing provides Milton with a gender-specific way of introducing into *Paradise Regained* the Arminian notion of virtue as contributing to the work of redemption. As in *A Mask*, with its image of Virtue teaching mortals to climb heavenward, paradise is regained in Milton's brief epic not simply or exclusively through the sacrifice of the Redeemer but also through the virtuous life he lives, the life to which all Christians are called. And Jesus' virtue, as *Paradise Regained* portrays it, is cultivated by the mother who both spurs him to masculine heroism and models feminine meekness and patience.

Mary's teaching of the masculine lesson is most clearly evident in Jesus' recollection of how his mother informed him of his special relationship with God, told him to "let [his thoughts] soar / To what height sacred virtue and true worth / [Could] raise them" (*PR* 1.230–32), and urged him to the performance of "matchless Deeds" through which he might "express [his] matchless Sire" (*PR* 1.233). By encouraging her son in this way, Mary acts as an educator who grasps the purpose of learning as Milton defines it in *Of Education:* "to repair the ruins of our first parents by regaining to know God aright, and out of that knowledge to love him, to imitate him, to be like him, as we may the neerest by possessing our souls of true vertue, which being united to the heavenly grace of faith makes up the highest perfection" (YP 2:366–67). Because the boy she is teaching is the Messiah and the Son of God, moreover, Mary as Milton imagines her makes a uniquely important contribution to this educational program; her pupil will apply what he learns from her directly to his messianic mission, and will thus succeed more fully than any other student in "regaining" what Adam and Eve lost: paradisal intimacy with and likeness to God. Thus, the Attendant Spirit's promise that Virtue "can teach ye how to climb / Higher than the Sphery chime" (*Mask*, 1020–21) finds its fulfillment first in the virtuous Mary's teaching her son to "let [his thoughts] soar / To what height sacred virtue and true worth / Can raise them" (*PR* 1.230–32) and subsequently in Jesus' own educational work as the "living Oracle" whom God sends "Into the World to teach his final will" (*PR* 1.460–61).

As the words of the Father testify, this "living Oracle" is not exclusively masculine in character. Rather, he takes the form of a "man" whom God himself has "produce[d] ... / Of female Seed" (*PR* 1.150–51), and his "consummate virtue" is made manifest through "strong Sufferance" — which is to say, not only "Patient endurance, forbearance, long-suffering" (*OED*, "sufferance," n. def. 1), but also the distinctly feminine strength of "Passivity, receptivity" (*OED*, "sufferance," n. def. 3).[77] As Regina Schwartz puts it, Jesus will redeem man "through his suffering and death. But Milton understands this willingness on Christ's part as a radical passivity. It is achieved only by refusing" all the other means of redemption offered by Satan. For Milton, Schwartz observes, the "essence" of redemption is "obedience" ("Redemption," 39) and its corollary, silence:

> Having silenced [Satan's] idolatrous concepts of salvation, Jesus does not propose a new one; he does not say that now that he has rejected the satanic options for redemption, he will offer divine ones. While his adversary falls silent, Jesus stands silent, silent because he has submitted himself to the mystery of divine will, to the mystery of divine grace, to the mystery of redemption. (42)

Jesus' silence and obedience, along with his unassailable chastity—which makes a mockery of Belial's suggestions for sexual temptation in book 1 of *Paradise Regained*—combine to define his "consummate virtue" as no less feminine than masculine.

This element of Jesus' virtue does not emerge only outside the frame of *Paradise Regained,* in the humiliation and agony of the Passion that he will undergo in the future; rather, the feminine dimension of the Savior's character emerges repeatedly during the temptation that is the poem's focus: he rejects—in lines that would have delighted Aemilia Lanyer had she lived to read them—not only the masculine military strength of mail-clad men and horses, which he dismisses as "ostentation vain of fleshly arm" (*PR* 3.387), but also the learned male philosophers of Greece and Rome, whom Satan recommends for his study. These thinkers' various definitions of virtue, Jesus explains, are all deficient. Particularly problematic are the teachings of "The Stoic," who invests himself "in Philosophic pride, / By him call'd virtue; and" deems "his virtuous man, / Wise, perfect in himself, and all possessing / Equal to God" (*PR* 4.300–303). But all the pagan philosophers are fatally handicapped in their attempts to define virtue, for they lack the truth that is revealed only through the Scriptures and, the narrator of *Paradise Lost* would no doubt add, through the prophetic voice of a blind prophet chosen by God to dilate the Scriptures:

> Alas! what can they teach, and not mislead;
> Ignorant of themselves, of God much more,
> And how the world began, and how man fell

> Degraded by himself, on grace depending?
> Much of the Soul they talk, but all awry,
> And in themselves seek virtue, and to themselves
> All glory arrogate, to God give none,
> Rather accuse him under usual names,
> Fortune and Fate, as one regardless quite
> Of mortal things.   (*PR* 4.309–18)

These lines make clear that the "virtuous man" of the pagan philosophers (*PR* 4.301) fails to grasp the justness of God's ways in part because the belief that man can be "perfect in *himself*" (*PR* 4.302; emphasis mine) involves a definition of human merit that relies too heavily on the masculine reflexive pronoun and on the Latin roots of the word "virtue." For the ancient Greeks and Romans, who knew nothing of the Fall or of how grace intervenes to repair its effects, *virtus* consisted of manliness, of those qualities of valor and active strength displayed by the worthy *vir*. The pagans thus fail—despite what Donne hailed as the prophetic accuracy of their grammar, which enabled them to call "vertues by the name of shee" (*FirAn*, 176)—to grasp what the divine Father conveys when he says that the "consummate virtue" of the "perfect Man" will manifest itself in "Humiliation and strong Sufferance" (*PR* 1.165, 166, 160). They have no way of comprehending the feminine virtues Mary inculcates in her son.

Even in the speech in which she urges him "By matchless Deeds" to "express [his] matchless Sire" (*PR* 1.233), Mary begins by counseling Jesus to perform a nurturing, maternal function. Having overheard remarks that reveal his "High...thoughts," she advises him, "but *nourish* them and let them soar / To what height sacred virtue and true worth / Can raise them" (*PR* 1.229, 230–32; emphasis mine). She thus includes a feminine imperative in her lesson, even as she herself "nourish[es]" Jesus' aspiration to "victorious deeds" of a distinctly masculine sort, "heroic acts" of virtue resembling those he performed before his incarnation when he "subdue[d] and quell[ed]" the forces of "Brute violence and proud Tyrannic pow'r" (*PR* 1.215, 216, 218, 219) by defeating Satan and his minions during the war in heaven.[78] But as the more direct and intimate portrait of Mary in book 2 of *Paradise Regained* makes clear, the nourishment that Jesus' mother provides for his masculine "thoughts" in their "soar[ing]" upward motion is not her only contribution to the formation of his character as the redeemer. Perhaps even more important is the way that she models "strong Sufferance" through all the trials she endures. Steeling herself for the agonizing penetration that Simeon foresees when he tells her that "through [her] very Soul / A sword shall pierce" (*PR* 2.90–91), she accepts the irony that her own "Exaltation" is only "to Afflictions high" (*PR* 2.92). And when she "with thoughts / Meekly compos'd await[s] the fulfilling" of Gabriel's promise and Simeon's dire prophecy (2.107–08), she establishes meekness as the very essence of the "sacred virtue and true worth" (1.231) toward which she has propelled her son, "the Son of God our Savior meek" (4.636).[79] He may not seem particularly "meek" during the course of the poem as he answers every satanic argument with crushing coolness and certainty, but it is his meek obedience to his Father, an obedience he has seen his mother practice in every aspect of her life, that frees him to speak and act with such clarity of purpose. And it is to that meek "Mother's house" that he—his trial completed— "private return[s]" (*PR* 4.639).

CODA: MARIAN POETICS

John Donne, Aemilia Lanyer, and John Milton challenge their readers to rethink, from a variety of post-Reformation perspectives, the relationship between the practice of human virtue and the unique achievement of Christ as Redeemer. All three define their own poems as good works that may contribute to the ongoing renovation of fallen humanity and all three celebrate, through those works, various female figures who embody the sacred feminine at work in the world: the feminine trinity of Donne's "The Annunciation and Passion," the "shee" he praises in his *Anniversaries*, and the good wife he mourns in "Since She whome I lovd"; the Queen Elizabeth of Lanyer's poem to Princess Elizabeth, the perfectly liberated Virgin Mary of her *Salve Deus*, and the priestly Ecclesia of the same work; the "goddess bright" of Milton's *Arcades*, the valiant Lady of *Comus*, and the eloquent Mary of *Paradise Regained*.

Each poet is capable of inscribing the redemptive function of woman and of the feminine in terms the other two might barely recognize, much less endorse. The figure of woman as priest, so essential to Lanyer's vision, would make no sense to Donne, for whom woman is a sacrament—perhaps the most important sacrament—rather than the sacerdotal figure who administers it. For Milton, neither priestly ministry nor outward signs of grace are so important as the inward promptings of divine Wisdom who—like her sister, Urania, and like virtue herself—leads human beings heavenward. Similarly, the figure

of church as guide, beloved, bride, and mother, a figure whom
Lanyer and Donne imagine vividly and whom they both link
very closely with exalted images of the Blessed Virgin, is gradually revised and reworked in the poetry of Milton, who imagines
Ecclesia first as a wise and elderly avatar of the pagan mother-
goddesses Latona and Cybele, then as a Virgin Lady wandering
in the woods and freed from bondage by a sister virgin. Despite
their differences, however, and in a variety of ways that reflect
those differences, all three poets find in Mary, the mother of
Jesus, an inspiration for their literary practice.

For Donne, Mary's function as *Theotokos*, God-bearer, makes
her a model for divine poetry as Donne wishes it to function: as
a work of human hands that proves sacramentally efficacious for
the devout receiver. In Donne's *La Corona*, the miracle of the
incarnation has very specific metapoetic implications; because
the pregnant Virgin is her "Makers maker," she inspires the poet
to believe that his sonnets, "Weav'd in" a "low devout melan-
cholie" (*La Corona*, 2) that emulates Mary's humility, may likewise house Christ "in little roome" (27), making him present to
readers who would partake of him in a poetic Eucharist. In "The
Annunntiation and Passion," Mary's status as the paradoxical
object of the speaker's gaze, a sacred oxymoron "seen" by him
and by his reader, is but one of several subtle parallels between
the Blessed Virgin and the deeply oxymoronic literary work in
which she appears. Like Mary, "The Annunntiation and Passion"
is both "Sad and rejoyc'd"; as a manuscript poem that is to be
read only by a coterie audience, but is nonetheless in circulation,
it is—like Mary—both "Reclus'd" and "Publique" (*Annun*,
13, 12). And Mary is seen—in line 14 of a 46-line poem—"At
almost fiftie, and at scarce fifteene," two ages that are reflected
by the line's own position at a point just shy of line 15 in a
work that will end just short of line 50. Finally, as Mary is "At
once receiver and the legacie" (*Annun*, 18), so the poem is both
the receptacle into which the poet pours his meditations and
the gift he offers to his readers for their pious delectation. The
Anniversaries, too, focus upon "the Idea of a Woman," defining

sacramentality itself as feminine. But as we have seen, the Mary of *The Second Anniversarie*—"exalted more for being good, / Then for her interest, of mother-hood" (*SecAn*, 343–44)—helps Donne to shift from the sacramental poetics of *The First Anniversarie*, in which the poet-speaker invites readers to participate in and embody the virtue of the dead Elizabeth Drury, to a heavenly poetics that directs the reader's gaze away from all earthly vessels of divinity, even the Blessed Virgin's own Eucharistic motherhood. By rejoicing that she is not that which men have said, moreover, Donne's Mary celebrates her capacity to transcend clumsy misreadings by those who do not appreciate her real meaning; she thus serves once again as a model for the poem in which she appears: a work that is—to use a term Donne used to describe his *Biathanatos*—highly "misinterpretable" (*Letters*, 21).

Lanyer, too, takes the Virgin of Nazareth as her inspiration for a Eucharistic poetics, but she thinks of Mary less as a figure upon whom she may model her text and more as a model for her own activity as a female poet. In presenting her poem as a sacred feast wherein her readers may receive the "Paschal Lambe" she has "prepar'd" for them to "feed upon," she claims for herself the Marian labor of presenting the Body of Christ to the world ("To the Queenes," 85, 89). Being herself—like Jesus' mother—a base-born woman of "meane estate" (*SDRJ*, 1034), Lanyer finds in Mary, as Achsah Guibbory notes, "a precedent for female priesthood, for woman's worthiness to contain and offer up God for human salvation" ("Gospel According to Aemilia," 206). And while Donne's poems never quote the words attributed to Mary in the Gospels, Lanyer's "beauteous Queene of Woman-kind" is as remarkable for the utterances that emerge from her lips as for the child that emerges from her womb. The poet praises Mary using language drawn from her Magnificat, presents Gabriel's visit as God's response to the Virgin's "plead[ing] for Love at great *Jehovaes* gate" (*SDRJ*, 1036), and paraphrases her response to the angel ("be it vnto me according to thy worde" [Luke 1:38]) in terms that realign the emphasis of the scriptural source, presenting Mary's answer as the verbal signifier of her own blessed state and of the love she feels, rather than of her consent to God's word or the angel's: "Thus beeing crown'd with glory from above, / Grace and Perfection resting in thy breast, / Thy humble answer doth approove thy Love" (*SDRJ*, 1089–91). Perhaps most remarkably of all, Lanyer devotes a full eight-line stanza to Mary's question, "How shal this be, seing, I know no man?" (Luke 1:34), framing that inquiry so as to present the Virgin as a reverent but relentless questioner who "humbly [did] demand, How that should be?" (*SDRJ*, 1074). Mary thus sets an example for the female poet, whose art is devoted to humbly but insistently demanding explanations for all that she finds questionable and problematic, from gender hierarchy to class distinctions.

Milton is also interested in Mary's verbal self-expression; he digs beneath the few utterances ascribed to her in Scripture to imagine her at one point exhorting her Son and at another reflecting in a quiet yet undeniably pointed soliloquy on her unenviably "favor'd lot," which has turned out to be an "Exaltation to Afflictions high" (*PR* 2.91, 92). Like Lanyer, who analyzes the Virgin's response to Gabriel, Milton attends to Mary's inner life, her thoughts, her ways of processing what she sees, hears, and feels. Inspired by Luke's references to the way the Virgin pondered things she experienced and sayings she heard, both Lanyer and Milton present Mary as thoughtful; but Milton goes so far as to portray Jesus' mother as meta-thoughtful, as reflecting on her own reflectiveness and conjuring a metaphor to describe it: "My heart hath been a storehouse long of things / And sayings laid up" (*PR* 2.103–04).

The containment imagery of these lines notwithstanding, Milton is far less interested than either Donne or Lanyer in Mary's status as a vessel. *Paradise Regained* is designed to educate readers in the ways of Christ's "consummate virtue" rather than to serve as a sacramental dwelling place through which the poet may present him. But since Mary is herself an educator, as the brief epic portrays her, Milton, no less than

Donne or Lanyer, can still associate Mary's maternal *opus* with his own work as a literary artist. His way of doing so is perhaps even more daring than that of either of his predecessors, since his Mary not only bears Jesus in her womb, but speaks at length in words not found in the Gospels, nurturing, educating, and encouraging her son through the words she utters. Her speeches live in the young Savior's memory as he, emulating his mother's "pondering oft" in his own "Musing and much revolving in his breast," ponders "How best the mighty work he might begin / Of Savior to mankind" (*PR* 2.105, 1.185, 186–87). Jesus has clearly taken to heart Mary's teachings. And the poet himself, given his desire to present Jesus "as one man whose rite of passage has shown how to live one's life" (Shawcross, *Paradise Regain'd*, 83), seems also to have internalized Mary's exhortations and to have understood them as encouraging him in his *own* endeavor. For the opening lines of the work in which Jesus recalls Mary's inspiring speech to him ring with many of the same words and images that Mary uses in that speech. She urges her Son to perform "matchless *Deeds*" that will fulfill the aspirations of his "High...thoughts," letting them "*soar* / To what *height* sacred virtue and true worth / Can raise them, though *above* example high" (*PR* 1. 229, 230–32; emphases mine). Milton, for his part, begs the spirit of God to let his poem soar, to carry his song "through *height* or depth of nature's bounds / With prosperous wing full summ'd to tell of *deeds* / *Above* Heroic," that is, to recount the very deeds "above example high" toward which he will imagine Mary spurring her son (*PR* 1.13–15, 232; emphases mine). And just as "our Savior meek" (*PR* 4.636) applies to his redemptive mission his female parent's most characteristic virtue, so the poet, in pursuit of his poetic mission, activates and dramatizes Mary's "thoughts / Meekly compos'd" (2.107–08), which is to say thoughts not merely "Made calm or tranquil; properly adjusted" (*OED*, "composed," ppl. a. def. 4) by the exercise of meekness, but also—by her and by the poet—humbly and unassumingly "construct[ed] (in words)," "ma[d]e or produce[d] in literary form" (*OED*, "compose," v. def. 5).

Donne, Lanyer, and Milton were three very different poets, three very different kinds of seventeenth century Protestant, three human beings with very different ideas of woman. But they nevertheless have in common their metapoetic reliance upon Mary, their practice of a poesy that springs from and insists upon reverence for the sacred feminine, their filial attentiveness to the wisdom of the Mother.

Notes

NOTES TO INTRODUCTION

1. These figures are particularly prominent—and often elided—in the iconography and liturgy of the Middle Ages and Counter-Reformation. An excellent example of the latter is the Office of the Blessed Virgin Mary, a popular Roman Catholic psalter that originated in the ninth or tenth century and was standardized by Pope Pius V in 1585; it was issued in a facing page Latin/English edition in 1599 under the title *The Primer; or, Office of the Blessed Virgin Marie, in Latin and English.* This Marian version of the Liturgy of the Hours was reprinted many times throughout the seventeenth century; it is mentioned in several lists of Roman Catholic books confiscated or targeted for confiscation by agents of the English government (see Rostenberg, 36, 120, and illustration 13). *The Primer* includes Marian prayers, antiphons, and hymns, as well as readings from Ecclesiasticus (in which Wisdom speaks in the first person) and from the Song of Solomon (selections featuring the bride). See also the traditional Latin lyrics for Marian feasts in the *Gradualia* of William Byrd (published in two books, 1607 and 1610). On early Christian and medieval visual representations of Ecclesia and of Mary as type of Ecclesia or mother of the church, see Thérel, *Les Symboles,* 78–202, and Neff, "The Pain of *Compassio.*" On the medieval elision of created Wisdom and the Virgin Mary, see Bouyer, *The Seat of Wisdom.*

2. The Hebrew scriptures portray both Jerusalem and God's people as his daughter or spouse; see especially Zechariah 9:9, Song of Solomon 3–7, and Hosea 1–4. As the Geneva Bible marginal glosses attest, Solomon's marriage to the daughter of the pharaoh in Psalm 45 is also interpreted as a type of Christ's union with the church. New Testament texts describing the church as Christ's spouse

include Ephesians 5:22–33 and Revelation 19:7–8, 21:1–22:21. See also Romans 7:1–6 on the soul's marital union with Christ.

3. See Ruether's chapter 10, "Mary and the Protestants" (*Mary*, 70–75) as well as Graef's overview (*Mary*, 2:6–17) of sixteenth century Protestant commentary on Mary.

4. On Spenser and the feminine, see Quitslund, "Spenser's Image of Sapience"; Davies, *The Feminine Reclaimed*; Philippa Berry, *Of Chastity and Power*; Cavanagh, *Wanton Eyes and Chaste Desires*; Walker, *Medusa's Mirrors*; and Eggert, *Showing Like a Queen*. Scholars sensitive to gender in Herbert's poetry include Asals, *Equivocal Predication*; Schoenfeldt, *Prayer and Power*; and Rubin, "The Mourner in the Flesh." On Quarles's use of the Song of Solomon, see Hill, "The Parable of the Absent Lover"; on aspects of gender in the translations of Mary Sidney Herbert, see Fisken, "Mary Sidney's *Psalmes*"; Waller, "The Countess of Pembroke"; Hannay, "'House-Confinèd'"; and Clarke, "'Lovers' Songs'"; on gender in Vaughan's poetry, see Nelson, "Gender and Politics." Wilcox, "Exploring the Language of Devotion," argues that, in the period 1630–60, English "devotional writing...draws closer to a 'female aesthetic'" (86).

5. Here and throughout, Donne's *Satyres* are quoted from Shawcross, *The Complete Poetry of John Donne*, and cited parenthetically by abbreviated title and line number.

6. For a brief survey of these divisions, see Shell and Hunt, "Donne's Religious World," 69–73.

7. English Protestantism is not, of course, a monolithic discourse. Defining precisely how Donne's theology, ecclesiology, and politics fit into the complex landscape of the English Reformation is an ongoing effort, and scholars differ widely in their assessments of how Donne defined his own positions, even after he became dean of St. Paul's. I would confirm Doerksen's assertion that, "in his sermons and other late prose writings, Donne identifies in his own way with the conformist Calvinist piety that prevailed in the leadership of the Jacobean Church of England (as it had done in the later Elizabethan Church)" ("Polemist or Pastor?" 12). But as I have demonstrated in my discussion of Donne's position on a particularly controversial aspect of Eucharistic doctrine, it is important to underscore Doerksen's phrase "in his own way" (see my *Literature and Sacrament*, 9–14, 252–59). For a helpful overview of the complexities underlying various denominational labels in Elizabethan and Jacobean England, see Shell and Hunt, "Donne's Religious World," 73–78.

8. The only previous book-length study to consider Lanyer's poetry in relation to that of both Donne and Milton is Susanne

Woods's *Lanyer: A Renaissance Woman Poet*, which brings Donne, Milton, and other Renaissance writers into play specifically in order to illuminate Lanyer's contribution to seventeenth century English literature. Other scholarly works offering comparative studies of Donne and Lanyer or Lanyer and Milton are rare; the most significant are Schoenfeldt, "Gender"; Holmes; McBride and Ulreich, "'Eves Apologie'" and "Answerable Styles"; and Josephine A. Roberts, "Diabolic Dreamscape." Not surprisingly, a larger number of scholarly efforts compare or contrast the poetry of Donne and Milton; see especially Potter, "Milton's Early Poems"; Tillyard, *The Metaphysicals*; Grierson, *Criticism and Creation*; Low, "Eve's Additions," and *The Reinvention of Love*); Stull ("'Why are not Sonnets'" and "Sonnets Courtly and Christian"); Pollock, "'The Object, and the Wit'"; Fogle, "'Such a Rural Queen'"; Turner, *One Flesh*; Jordan, *The Quiet Hero*; Holstun, "'Will you rent'"; Guibbory, "Donne, Milton"; Frontain, "Law"; and Hadfield, "Literary Contexts," 61–62.

9. Fish, "Why Milton Matters," 10.

10. Particularly useful in tracing the history of Marian doctrine and devotion is Graef, *Mary*. Warner's popular feminist study of Mary, *Alone of All Her Sex*, is also helpful, though less theologically sophisticated. Ruether provides a clear and succinct explanation of how and why the Reformation not only deemphasized Mary and discouraged devotion to her, but "diminishe[d] the role of the 'feminine' as a symbol of the human nature of the church in relation to God" (*Mary*, 72); Clarke, "The Iconography of the Blush," discusses the resurgence of Marian literature as reflecting Queen Henrietta Maria's influence in Caroline England, and Albrecht, *The Virgin Mary*, approaches Marian themes and images in Donne's writing through an overview of Mary's significance within hermetic, kabbalistic, and Lullian discourse. For an ecumenical overview of twentieth century scripture scholarship relevant to Marian theology, see Brown et al., *Mary in the New Testament*. On the development of the idea of the church as Christ's bride, see Chavasse, *The Bride of Christ*. On Mary, Ecclesia, and Beatrice in Dante's *Paradiso*, see Pelikan, *Eternal Feminines*. On feminine elements in medieval Christianity, see also Bynum, *Jesus as Mother*, "'And Woman His Humanity,'" and *Fragmentation and Redemption*; and Newman, *Sister of Wisdom* and *God and the Goddesses*. Rice, *The Renaissance Idea of Wisdom*, surveys Christian and classical ideas of Wisdom as they were understood during the Renaissance; Quitslund, "Spenser's Image of Sapience," surveys the Christian, Neoplatonic, and kabbalistic sources on which Spenser may have drawn in composing his "Hymne of Heavenly Beautie"; and

Manley, *John Donne*, applies a similar survey to the interpretation of Donne's *Anniversaries*. For feminist perspectives on the Pauline and Deutero-Pauline epistles—foundational texts for any Christian writer dealing with the church as Christ's bride, with marriage, or with gender—see Levine and Blickenstaff, *A Feminist Companion to Paul*, and Polaski, *A Feminist Introduction to Paul*.

11. The sermon, on Proverbs 8:17, was preached before Queen Anne on December 14, 1617, a few months after the death of Donne's wife: "*Salomon*, whose disposition was amorous, and excessive in the love of women, when he turn'd to God, he departed not utterly from his old phrase and language, but... conveyes all his loving approaches and applications to God, and all Gods gracious answers to his amorous soul, into songs, and Epithalamions, and meditations upon contracts, and marriages between God and his Church, and between God and his soul" (*Sermons*, 1:237). For more on the sermon as it casts light on "Since She whome I lovd," see chapter 1, part 3, below. On sacralized, sacramental sexuality in Donne's love poetry, compare Hester, "'Let me love'"; Guibbory, "Donne, Milton," "Fear of 'loving more,'" and "'The Relique'"; and Sabine, "No Marriage in Heaven."

12. In his conversations with Drummond of Hawthornden, Ben Jonson said "that Dones Anniversarie was profane and full of Blasphemies that he told Mr Donne, if it had been written of ye Virgin Marie it had been something to which he answered that he described the Idea of a Woman and not as she was" (Jonson, "Ben Jonson's Conversations," 133; qtd. in the Donne *Variorum* 6:240).

Notes to "Donne"

1. The intersection of sacred and profane in Donne's works is a critical commonplace; for my perspective on the particulars of theological debate as they apply to Donne's poetics, see my *Literature and Sacrament*.

2. All that is known for certain about the date of "Show me deare Christ" is that it is one of "the three late poems unique to" the Westmoreland manuscript ("General Textual Introduction," *Variorum* 7:1.ci). For an overview of the arguments dating it to 1620, see *Variorum* 7:1.456–58. See also Cain, "Donne's Political World," 95, who believes the sonnet was written circa 1622 and reflects Donne's religio-political concerns that year.

3. For feminist indictments of the elegies, see Guibbory, "'Oh, Let'"; Docherty, *John Donne Undone*, 51–87; and Fish, "Masculine Persuasive Force." For a critique of the term "misogynist" as it is

used in feminist Donne criticism, see Stewart, *"Renaissance" Talk*, 153–98.

4. See also Hester, "'Let me love,'" and DiPasquale, "Donne's *Epigrams*."

5. "Oh let not me serve so," 9–10, in *Variorum* 2:110–11. All subsequent quotations from Donne's elegies are taken from volume 2 of the *Variorum* and cited parenthetically by short title and line number.

6. On the elegies generally and "To his Mistress going to bed" in particular as Donne's satirical response to the cult of Elizabeth, see Hester, "Donne's (Re)Annunciation"; Young, "'O My America'"; Guibbory, "'Oh, Let'"; and Labriola, "Painting and Poetry." On the cult of the virgin queen as displacing the cult of the Blessed Virgin, see Yates, *Astraea*; Strong, *The Cult of Elizabeth*; and the useful modifications of their thesis in Philippa Berry, *Of Chastity and Power*. Hackett, *Virgin Mother, Maiden Queen*, argues that Elizabeth was never seriously set up as a Protestant alternative to the Virgin but acknowledges that poems like Spenser's April eclogue were "reappropriating" the biblical myth "of the holy virgin-bride-mother,...purifying it of Marian and Catholic connotations" (111–12). Hackett does not acknowledge how distasteful and ripe for satirical attack such "reappropriating" would have been to Elizabethan recusants and to any poet sympathizing with them, but she does chronicle the emergence in the 1590s of the iconoclastic portrayals of Elizabeth further explored in Walker, *Dissing Elizabeth*.

7. Curle's witticism was recorded by his fellow student, John Manningham in an April 1603 diary entry (*The Diary*, 221); a garbled version of Donne's epigram "A Lame Begger" is transcribed on the leaf just preceding the one that includes Curle's remark. On the possibility that "A Lame Begger" satirizes the queen's favorites (Essex and/or Ralegh), see DiPasquale, "Donne's *Epigrams*."

8. *Sorrowes Ioy* (Cambridge: John Legat, 1603) is reprinted in Nichols, *The Progresses*, 1:1–24.

9. I do not disagree with Cain, "Donne's Political World," who argues that the "new monarch" was one "with whom [Donne] shared many values" and whose "reign marked a period in which Donne could subscribe to the ruler's principles without compromising his own" (90–91). But I would qualify, in light of the strong emphasis on the sacred feminine in Donne's early Jacobean poetry, Cain's assertion that "the patriarchal authority over church and state that James represented...seemed [to Donne] the best defence against religious violence of the kind seen in France" (91).

10. See Hackett, *Virgin Mother, Maiden Queen*, 217–18.

11. John Harington, in Nichols, *The Progresses*, 49.

12. *Triplici nodo*, 20. Though the title page of the anonymous first edition is dated 1607, it appeared in February 1608. Healy notes, "There seems to have been little doubt about the identity of the author" (*Ignatius His Conclave*, xxi). I quote from a facsimile edition that reproduces the king's personal copy of the anonymous first edition, complete with James's own corrections for the second edition, many of which involve shifting from third person to first person. All subsequent quotations from *Triplici nodo* and from the Roman Catholic documents to which James was responding, which were reproduced within *Triplici nodo*, are taken from this edition.

13. As Sommerville explains, James's Latin title is a carpentry metaphor: the king's triple wedge will cut through a triple knot in a piece of wood (James I, *Political Writings*, 284 n. 497). For the dates and circumstances of the two *breves*, Bellarmine's letter, and the king's treatise, see *Catholic Encyclopedia*, s.v. "English Post-Reformation Oaths." The dates cited are Gregorian style; in England, which was still using the Julian calendar, the date of each document was ten days ahead of the Gregorian date.

14. Augustine, *The Trinity*, book 9, section 2, p. 272. Subsequent quotations from *De Trinitate* are taken from this translation and cited parenthetically as *The Trinity* by book and section number.

15. Donne would have grown up with the Roman Catholic Church's designation of Good Friday as a fast day. Post-Reformation citizens still observed such dietary restrictions, being required by civil rather than ecclesiastical law to fast and abstain throughout Lent. See Frere, *The English Church*, 101; Hooker's defense of fasting as a religious practice (*Laws* 5.72 in Hooker, *Of the Laws*, 2:407–27); and the Elizabethan "Homily on Good Works: And First, of Fasting," (*Certaine Sermons*, 2:81–94).

16. Compare Albrecht, *Virgin Mary as Alchemical*, 98–105, on the ouroboros—alchemical symbol of "the unity of matter"—as the poem's "organizing principle," and Kirkpatrick, "Donne's 'Upon the Annunciation.'"

17. Though he does not discuss Mary's presence in the poem, Whalen, *Poetry of Immanence*, 77–78, comments on how *Annun* evokes a relationship between the soul and the church.

18. Compare A. B. Chambers, "*La Corona*," 150–52; and Malpezzi, "Donne's Transcendent," 149–50.

19. Johnson, *Theology of John Donne*, 139. As Whalen, *Poetry of Immanence*, puts it, "The body silenced at the outset...is reasserted in the flesh and blood messianic sacrifice." Whalen goes on to note the ways in which the poem evokes Donne's struggle to articulate an English Protestant version of Real Presence (78). See

below, sections 3 and 5–7 on the Eucharist and woman in Donne's poetry.

20. See Gardner, *Divine Poems of John Donne*, 154–55, on the date of "A Litanie." Donne's preoccupations in the wake of the oath of allegiance controversy are reflected in lines 170–71, which pray for guidance about when equivocation is acceptable.

21. See Albrecht, *Virgin Mary as Alchemical*, on Mary's "*active* role in the making of the Christ child" (154–56).

22. See Shell and Hunt, "Donne's Religious World," on the issue of patristic authority in "A Litanie": "filial respect is praiseworthy, but one can only abide by paternal authority if one's forefathers are right" (72).

23. I am indebted to Anne Lake Prescott, "Refusing Translation," for pointing out the implications of the Julian versus Gregorian discrepancy in interpreting Donne's "Annuntiation and Passion." Prescott observes that, whatever the poet's attitude toward King James I, the king would surely have welcomed "Donne's calendrical assumptions" (120).

24. Compare *Sermons*, 9:399, in which Donne stresses the conjugal nature of the baptismal "contract" and calls the Eucharist the "consummation" of the marriage which took place in baptism. In another sermon, he refers to the Eucharist as the soul's marriage to Christ (6:85).

25. I quote throughout the texts of the Holy Sonnets as they appear in the Westmoreland Sequence (*Variorum* 7:1.11–20).

26. The prayer book notes that this idea of a wife's role is taken from one of the Petrine epistles; the source is 1 Peter 3:1–2.

27. Moloney, *John Donne*, detects in the poem a "Dantesque" sacramentalism and says that its "reverence for womanhood" is atypical for Donne (144). See also Malpezzi, "Love's Liquidity," who reads the poem as an unconflicted "tribute to Anne's intimate relationship to her earthly and to her divine spouse as well as a celebration of God's love flowing freely through the world" (202).

28. See *Sermons*, 2:340. Augustine, Donne notes, finds various kinds of good in marriage.

29. The psalm, which is used in the marriage rite of the English church, promises that the two kinds of labor introduced after the Fall will bear fruit in the virtuous man's marriage: "thou shalt eat the labor of thy hands... / Thy wife shall be as the fruitful vine: upon the walls of thy house" (*BCP*, 294).

30. Compare Gardner, *Divine Poems of John Donne*, 154, and Grenander's response ("Holy Sonnets," 100–105). The sonnet has been misread by critics who stress only the poet's negative emotions; see Harry Morris, "John Donne's Terrifying Pun," 134, and

Carey, *John Donne*, who equates Anne with the "World, fleshe, yea Deuill" of the final line (59).

31. Compare Calvin, who emphasizes the idea of a sacrament as God's means of assisting feeble human faith (*Institution of Christian Religion*, 4.14.1).

32. For a discussion of Donne's engagement with this text, see Sabine, "No Marriage in Heaven," 232, 239, 248–50.

33. The Latin phrase puns on the popular epitaph *cara conjux*, "beloved wife." Compare *Sermons*, 3:77, where Donne alludes to Augustine's interpretation of Job's wife: "This flesh, this sensuall part of ours, is our wife: and when these temporall things by any occasion are taken from us, that wife, that flesh, that sensuality is left to murmure and repine at Gods corrections."

34. It seems likely that Donne's feelings on this score influenced his decision never to remarry. In his 1620 sermon for the wedding of Sir Francis Nethersole, he quotes Matthew 19:12 and explains, "the better to un-entangle themselves from those impediments, which hinder them in the way to heaven, [some men] abstaine from marriage" (*Sermons*, 2:339). For a feminist reading of this sermon, see Meakin, *John Donne's Articulations*, 140, 142, 165–81.

35. In his sermons, Donne regularly attributes to Saint Paul all the epistles now classified by many Scripture scholars as Deutero-Pauline or Pseudo-Pauline, including 2 Thessalonians, Colossians, Ephesians, 1 and 2 Timothy, Titus, and Hebrews.

36. See Stachniewski, "Despair of the Holy Sonnets," 687.

37. As is clear from context in the *Sermons*, Donne did not distinguish between John the Evangelist and John of Patmos; see esp. *Sermons*, 7:438.

38. See the 1560 Geneva Bible gloss: "this is the seconde time that he suffered him self to be caried away with the excellencie of ye persone."

39. See Lewalski, *Protestant Poetics*, who feels that this sonnet "especially its conclusion, seems less unified and effective than is usual in Donne" (273).

40. Compare Grenander, "Holy Sonnets," 105, and Low, *Reinvention*, who says line 10 may be read as implying that God "switch[es] roles, playing the conventional woman's part and passively 'offring' himself in place of Donne's wife"; "In the rest of the sestet," Low notes, "the sexual roles become entirely uncertain....nothing is clear or easy for Donne in this new love relationship. The marriage trope fragments and breaks into confusing pieces" (75).

41. Donne prays for a newly married couple that "if they may not die together,...he that died for them both, will bring them together again in his everlastingnesse" (*Sermons*, 3:244).

42. See *Sermons*, 3:254, in which Donne says that, in heaven, "I shall see all the beauty, and all the glory of all the Saints of God, and love them all, and know that the Lamb loves them too, without jealousie, on his part, or theirs, or mine."

43. See Low, *Reinvention:* "he is consumed with unsatisfied desire [and]...engaged in an endless and possibly hopeless quest. In this regard, he...resembles the disappointed lover of the Petrarchan tradition" (76).

44. The poem may commemorate Tilman's becoming a deacon on December 20, 1618, or his ordination to the priesthood on March 12, 1620; see Novarr, *The Disinterred Muse*, 113.

45. See Malpezzi, "Adam, Christ, and Mr. Tilman," on sacred hermaphroditism.

46. See also Albrecht, *Virgin Mary as Alchemical*, 168–69.

47. See a letter to Henry Goodyer in which Donne says, "You know I never fettered nor imprisoned the word Religion; not...immuring it in a *Rome*, or a *Wittemberg*, or a *Geneva*; they are all virtuall beams of one Sun...connaturall pieces of one circle" (*Letters*, 29). See also Shell and Hunt, "Donne's Religious World," 75–80.

48. On Donne's reinvention of patristic sources, and of Augustine in particular, in his sermons, see Stanwood, "Donne's Reinvention," 197.

49. Augustine, *Expositions of the Psalms*, 16:27. The passage appears in Exposition 2 of Psalm 33, section 6, which discusses verse 4 of the psalm. Subsequent quotations from the *Expositions* are taken from this translation and cited parenthetically by Exposition number, psalm number, and section number.

50. See Hooker, *Of the Laws* 5.62.11, and Donne, *Sermons*, 5:101.

51. Ilona Bell answered my paper on "Show me deare Christ" with this counterreading at the annual conference of the John Donne Society in Gulfport, Miss., February 13, 2004. I am indebted to her for providing me with an alternative perspective on the sonnet.

52. The title page of the 1611 edition of *An Anatomy of the World* identifies the subject of the poem in these words. The title page is reproduced in facsimile in the *Variorum*, 6:1. All subsequent quotations from the *Anniversaries* and "A Funerall Elegie" are taken from this edition and cited parenthetically by abbreviated title and line number.

53. See DiPasquale, *Literature and Sacrament*, 7–26; see also Martin, "Unmeete Contraryes," on how Donne "'triangulates' between Calvinist iconoclasm and Counter-Reformation neosacramentalism" (197).

54. On references to the sacraments in Donne's *Anniversaries* and on the poems as serving a sacramental function, see Kremen,

Imagination of the Resurrection, 116, 122; Fielding, "John Donne," 199; Milgate, *John Donne,* xxxv–xxxvi; Stanwood, "'Essential Joye,'" 387; and Martin, "Unmeete Contraryes," 196.

55. For an overview of criticism focusing on "The Poet and His Audience," see the *Variorum* commentary on the *Anniversaries* (Parrish, 6:317–25). In particular, note Quinn, "Donne's *Anniversaries* as Celebration," 369, who stresses that the poems perform a "public act" of celebration, and Parrish, who argues that their ideal audience is a "congregation of God's elect...who come prepared to accept, believe, and be uplifted through the word of the poet-priest" ("Poet, Audience," 112). See also Lewalski on the poems as "public exercises" (*Donne's* Anniversaries, 90, 91) and Frontain on the poet as prophet ("Law, Song, and Memory") and preacher ("Donne's Protestant *Paradiso,*" 133).

56. See also the *Variorum* commentary on the words "forme and frame" in line 37 (Parrish, 6:377–78).

57. Aquinas's understanding of the relation between word and sign in a sacrament is based on his reading of Ephesians 5:25–26 and of Augustine ("The word is added to the elemental substance, and it becomes a sacrament" [*Tractates on the Gospel of John,* tractate 80, section 3 on John 15:1–3]). Subsequent quotations from Augustine's *Tractates* are taken from this translation and cited parenthetically by tractate and section number.

58. The English Protestant doctrine of the Eucharist is sometimes dubbed "virtualism" because its defenders think of the essence of the sacrament, its "inward form," in dynamic terms, stressing efficacy rather than substance. They speak of the essential "forme" of both baptism and the Lord's Supper as a participation in the "vertue" of Christ's Crucifixion. See Hooker, *Of the Laws,* 5.67.7, 5.67.12; and Donne, *Sermons,* 5:108–09.

59. The quotation Donne modifies here is taken from Augustine's Tractate 80, section 3 on John 15:1–3. See also Aquinas, who quotes Augustine verbatim—adding his own explanations—in *Summa Theologica* 3.60.7: "the word operates in the sacraments 'not because it is spoken,' i.e. not by the outward sound of the voice, 'but because it is believed' in accordance with the sense of the words which is held by faith."

60. See especially Nicolson, *Breaking of the Circle,* 69–88, who is well refuted by Martz, *Poetry of Meditation,* 354–56. Other critics who discuss this theory are listed in the *Variorum* commentary (Parrish, 6:296).

61. See Mann, "Typology of Woman," on how "This retort, which is often dismissed, underscores the exemplary and hortatory intention of the poems" (338).

62. The *OED*'s first example of "just" in the sense "No more than; only, merely; barely" as used to qualify a verb or adjective dates from 1665; the earliest example of the word being used in that sense with a noun dates from 1785 (adv. def. 5a, b). Donne's primary sense in the phrase "just truth[s]" depends upon the older adjectival definition of "just" as modifying something "that is such properly, fully, or in all respects" (adj. def. 11), but he seems also to be anticipating the later adverbial definition and another adjectival definition that, according to the *OED*, first appeared in 1753: "Characterized by or involving exact correspondence." Compare Donne's letter to Henry Goodyer from around the same period (*Letters*, 74); Lewalski, *Donne's* Anniversaries, 193; and Hardison, *Enduring Monument*, 166–69.

63. For other interpretations of Elizabeth Drury as symbolic, see Coffin, *John Donne*, 270, 276–77; Martz, *Poetry of Meditation*, 233; Richard E. Hughes, "Woman in Donne's *Anniversaries*"; Manley, *John Donne*, 13–50; and Lewalski, *Donne's* Anniversaries, who proposes "that Elizabeth Drury functions in these poems as a poetic symbol." Lewalski discounts the significance of Elizabeth's gender, for she reads the "Reality" that Elizabeth Drury symbolizes as broadly human and Christian—a "regenerate Christian bearing the image of God restored by grace"—rather than specifically female or feminine (143, 163). Manley, by contrast, highlights Donne's concern to represent a specifically *feminine* "Idea" (18).

64. See also Hardison, *Enduring Monument*, 170, 186, and Stanwood, "'Essential Joye,'" 388–89.

65. According to this usage, "idea" is a synonym for "form" in its Aristotelian sense; see Tayler, *Donne's Idea of a Woman*, 27–31, 153–54 n. 27) and the discussion of the word "forme" above.

66. Tayler finds all symbolic readings of the *Anniversaries* untenable and, in particular, attacks Lewalski's interpretation of the term "Idea" as Donne used it in defending his work against Jonson's objections. Lewalski, *Donne's* Anniversaries, begins with a Neoplatonic definition of "Idea" as "pattern" and argues that "the 'shee' of the poem" embodies God's "idea" insofar as she is "at once image (of God) and Platonic archetype" (112, 113). Tayler, *Donne's Idea of a Woman*, retorts that "The proposed sense of the word 'idea' can be the principle by which God wrote the poem of the world; because it is divine, it cannot be the principle by which Donne wrote The Anniversaries" (15); he bases his own reading of the poems on a detailed etymology of the word "idea," arguing that "Donne's answer to Jonson...depends on the meanings acquired by *idea* in its relation to *species* during the second half of the sixteenth century" (27). I have followed Tayler in relying upon the

"Aristotelean-Thomist" definition of the word "idea" (ibid., 29) as the key to what Donne meant when he spoke of "the Idea of a Woman."

67. The poem finds fault with the whole Christian world, considering both Protestant and Roman Catholic perspectives. Compare Young, *Doctrine and Devotion,* who argues that Donne's stance in his sacred poems is "typical of the English devotional poets of the seventeenth century, who, though mostly Protestants, are not, *in their poetry,* so much militant proponents of the Reformation doctrine of grace as Christians... seeking to articulate the experience of grace (or its absence) in their lives" (32).

68. Lucy, Countess of Bedford, served as godmother to Donne's daughter Lucy some three years before he wrote these lines. In a letter dated August 6, 1608, Donne mentions his preparations for the following Monday (August 8), when the countess was to do him the "favour... of giving her name to [his] daughter" (*Letters,* 119); there is no evidence, however, that the ceremony was delayed to suit the schedule of the child's noble godmother.

69. See Lewalski, *Donne's* Anniversaries, on Donne's interest in Luther's typological method, "in which the words of scripture, regarded as God's promises, are seen to refer to the three advents of Christ—in the flesh, in our souls by grace, and in glory" (163).

70. In reading Elizabeth Drury as a Wisdom figure informed by the Hebrew concept of the Shekinah, Manley, *John Donne,* also suggests that the "shee" of the poem, though not God, is a manifestation or agent of God's immanence, his sacramental presence or "indwelling" (29).

71. On the Virgin Mary as the "organizing principle throughout the *Anniversaries,*" see Albrecht, *Virgin Mary as Alchemical,* 118–31.

72. I am indebted to Graham Roebuck for pointing out an interesting shift in Donne's use of pronouns here. Most readers would no doubt interpret the *we*'s of lines 94–95 ("we are neuer well, nor can be so"; "We are borne ruinous") as referring to the fallenness of humanity in general. But if, in lines 107–08, women are the *they* who kill *us;* that *us* must be the male *we* who spend our vital substance in the act of intercourse; and if so, it is possible to conclude that the earlier *we*'s refer to males as well: it is they who are born ruinous, their state observed and mourned, but not necessarily shared, by the "poore mothers" who give birth to them. Compare June Morris on humorous caricature and hyperbole in the *Anniversaries.*

73. On Christian applications of alchemical terminology, see Gareth Roberts, *Mirror of Alchemy,* 78–82, and Albrecht, *Virgin Mary as Alchemical.*

74. Edward Tayler, *Donne's Idea of a Woman*, 30; see also Rudnytsky, "'Sight of God,'" 187, and Pollock, "'The Object, and the Wit,'" 307, 311.

75. Roman Catholic Church, *Canons and Decrees*, 72. The passage is taken from the thirteenth session's "Decree Concerning the most Holy Sacrament of the Eucharist."

76. "Except thou feed (not banquet) on / The supernaturall food, Religion, / Thy better Grouth growes withered, and scant" (*FirAn* 187–89); the rift between the concrete verb phrase "feed on" and the vague generality of its object seems, from a Roman Catholic perspective, to be the gap opened up by the Protestant declaration that "The body of Christ is geuen, taken, and eaten in the Supper, only after an heauenly and spirituall maner" (*Thirty-Nine Articles*, Article 28). From a Protestant perspective, the lines might rebuke the Catholic laity's tendency to be "gazers" rather than "eaters" (*Certaine Sermons*, 2:197), to "banquet" only on "Religion," on the passive piety of Eucharistic adoration, and to leave the sacramental elements untasted. Compare Fielding, "John Donne and the New Christianity," 199.

77. See Lewalski, *Donne's* Anniversaries, 259–60, and my discussion of "virtualism" in note 58 above.

78. Manley, *John Donne*, 1–4, argues that the poems were composed in the same order as in the 1612 edition: the *Anatomie* first, then "A Funerall Elegie," and then *The Second Anniversarie*. Most scholars have thought otherwise: E. K. Chambers, *Poems of John Donne*, 2:235–36; Grierson, *Criticism and Creation*, 2:178; Bald, *Donne and the Drurys*, 69–98; and Lewalski, *Donne's* Anniversaries, 221–24 all believe that "A Funerall Elegie" was composed first. Parrish argues that the poem ought to be read in the way its textual position suggests, as a transition from *The First Anniversarie* to the *Second Anniversarie*; but he, too, concludes that it was most likely the first written.

79. See section 3 above for my discussion of this sermon passage in relation to "Since She whome I lovd." On Elizabeth's body, see Love, "Argument," 360, and McDuffie, *To Our Bodies*, 105–10.

80. See Frontain, "Donne's Imperfect Resurrection," and Frost, "*Magnus Pan Mortuus Est.*"

81. Biblical scholars today are divided on whether or not Saint Paul wrote the epistle to the Colossians, but it is attributed to him in the Geneva Bible.

82. See also the Geneva Bible gloss on John 20:17, and Calvin, *Institution of Christian Religion*, 4.17.29.

83. See also Albrecht's discussion of how Donne "create[s] associations between his Idea of Virtue, represented by Elizabeth

Drury, and specific attributes of the Virgin" Mary (*Virgin Mary as Alchemical,* 121).

84. Compare Meakin's feminist analysis of the *Anniversaries* as distinguishing between the "Protestant virgin" destined for marriage and the Catholic ideal of a "virgin *in perpetua*" (*John Donne's Articulations,* 205).

85. The Litany of Loreto was not available in print in early-seventeenth-century England, but Donne would almost certainly have known the prayer. Devotion to Our Lady of Loreto was a major element of Counter-Reformation spirituality on the Continent, and English Catholics of Donne's day would also have known and used the version of the Litany approved by Sixtus V in 1587.

86. See the many glosses in the *Variorum* commentary note on lines 341–42 (Parrish, 513). But see also Klawitter, "John Donne's Attitude": "the lines... could very well mean that her freedom from all sin ['being good'] merits her more adulation in heaven than her motherhood does" (128).

87. Donne's beliefs about the Immaculate Conception may have changed over time. Compare "A Litanie," which is also ambiguous in this regard; the speaker says that Mary "made / One claime for innocence, and disseiz'd sinne" (*Lit* 39–40). Gardner, *Divine Poems of John Donne,* 84, interprets these lines as implying rejection of the Immaculate Conception; Klawitter, "John Donne's Attitude," 133, 135, disagrees but notes that Donne did reject the doctrine in a 1618 sermon (*Sermons,* 1:307).

88. I quote the Latin text of the epitaph from volume 8 of the Donne *Variorum* (182). Wesley Milgate's English translation (printed in his edition of *The Epithalamions, Anniversaries, and Epicedes,* 213–14) is quoted in full in the *Variorum* commentary (8:432–33).

NOTES TO "LANYER"

1. Richey, "'To Undo,'" argues that Lanyer knew Cornelius Agrippa's 1529 *De nobilitate & praecellentia foeminei sexus.* There is no definitive evidence that Lanyer read Boccaccio's *Concerning Famous Women* (ca. 1361–62), Christine de Pizan's *Book of the City of Ladies* (1405), or any of the early modern English contributions to the *querelle des femmes,* but it is difficult to imagine the author of *Salve Deus* passing up the opportunity to purchase and read such provocatively titled works as *Jane Anger Her Protection for Women* (1589), Anthony Gibson's *A Womans Woorth, defended against all the men in the world* (1599), the 1605 *An Apologie for*

Women-Kinde (by "I. G."), and William Heale's *An Apologie for Women* (1609).

2. See Alan Stewart, *The Cradle King,* 176; Lee, *Great Britain's Solomon,* 148; Robert Ashton, *James I,* 10, 229; and Michael B. Young, *King James.*

3. On the coronation incident and other evidence relevant to the unresolved question of Anne's religious loyalties, see Barroll, *Anna of Denmark,* 162–72.

4. I quote the poem, citing line numbers parenthetically, from James VI and I, *Selected Writings,* 138–40.

5. See Woods, *Lanyer,* 48–54, on Lanyer's tributes to Elizabeth as compared to Spenser's.

6. See Rienstra, "Dreaming Authorship," 95–97, and, for evidence that James's irenic policies were seen by his contemporaries as evidence that he lacked virility, Michael B. Young, *King James,* 69–101.

7. Prince Henry had long been a factor in the tensions between Anne and James. A little over a year after the prince's birth in 1594, the queen had objected to the king's sending Henry to be raised in the household of the Earl of Mar. Her request that her son be returned to her began a battle of wills between Anne and James that was the talk of England and Scotland. See Barroll, *Anna of Denmark,* 20–25, 28–37, 120; Bergeron, *Royal Family, Royal Lovers,* 54–58, 62, 88; Lee, *Great Britain's Solomon,* 108, 142; and Alan Stewart, *The Cradle King,* 140–41, 143.

8. See also Milton's "Methought I saw my late espoused saint" (*Complete Poems,* 170–71), which similarly stresses the redeemed status of a wife who died as a result of giving birth.

9. Lanyer uses exact rhyme-royal in another prefatory poem, "To the Ladie *Arabella.*" Her prosodic choice here seems especially pointed, as Arabella Stuart had "a strong claim to the throne" and had fallen out of favor when, in 1610, King James felt threatened by her decision to marry a man with royal blood (Woods, *Poems of Aemilia Lanyer,* 17n). Ironically, the rhyme scheme was known as "royal" because it had been invented by James's medieval ancestor, James I of Scotland.

10. See also Exodus 23:16, 19, and 34:22, 26, and Leviticus 2: 12–14.

11. The lamb to be included among the first fruits (Lev. 23:12) and the Passover lamb (Exod. 12:5) were both to be unblemished males; Christians interpret both as types of Christ.

12. See Woods, *Poems of Aemilia Lanyer,* 11n.

13. Compare Woods, *Lanyer,* 52.

14. For an overview of biblical, patristic, and medieval commentary on the book of Nature and the book of Scripture as the two texts in which Wisdom reveals God to humankind, and for an interpretation of *Paradise Lost* in light of this traditional idea, see Reichert, *Milton's Wisdom.*

15. See Schnell, "'So Great a Difference,'" who "conjecture[s] that the only relationship Lanyer had with any patroness occurred in the realm of wish-fulfillment fantasy" (34). But see also McBride, "Remembering Orpheus," 91.

16. On Lanyer's "displac[ing] Mary Sidney," see McBride, "Remembering Orpheus," 94–97.

17. On Lanyer's poetry as Eucharistic, see especially McGrath, *Subjectivity*, 226–44, and "Metaphoric Subversions." See also Wall, *Imprint of Gender*, 324–26; Guibbory, "The Gospel According to Aemilia," 192, 206–07; and McBride, "Sacred Celebration," 61, 64–66, 78–79. On Lanyer and the "virtualism" of English Protestant Eucharistic theology, see Patrick Cook, "Aemilia Lanyer's "Description,'" 116–18.

18. On art and nature in Lanyer, see Beilin, *Redeeming Eve.* 185, 189, 201–04; Woods, "Vocation and Authority," 87–91; Holmes, "Love of Other Women," 175–76; Rienstra, "Dreaming Authorship," 88–89; and Loughlin, "'Fast ti'd unto them,'" 145–50, who analyzes "The Authors Dreame." On Nature as "maternal Muse," see McGrath, *Subjectivity*, 96, 226; and on "the limits of masculine knowledge" in Lanyer's poem, see Richey, *Politics of Revelation*, 74–76. Lanyer's reference to learned male writers conjures the image of Ben Jonson, her self-consciously scholarly contemporary; see Woods, "Aemilia Lanyer and Ben Jonson," 15–30.

19. On maternal language in Lanyer, see Miller, "(M)other Tongues."

20. Compare the discussion of this passage in Richey, *Politics of Revelation*, 69–70.

21. See the 1560 Geneva Bible gloss on the word "tre" in Proverbs 3:18. See also Ecclesiasticus 14:26 and 24:15, 20, 22, in which Wisdom is gendered feminine and described as a tree, mother, and object of desire. On tree imagery in Lanyer, see Beilin, *Redeeming Eve*, 323–24 n. 27; Patrick Cook, "Aemilia Lanyer's 'Description,'" 110–11, 114–15; and Loughlin, "'Fast ti'd unto them,'" 171–72.

22. Calvin, *Commentary on a Harmony*, 1:33. On the angel's calling Mary *"blessed among women,"* Calvin says, *"Blessing* is here put down as the result and proof of the Divine kindness. The word *Blessed* does not…mean, Worthy of praise; but rather…Happy." Compare Aquinas, *Summa Theologica*, 3.27.5. For a discussion of

twentieth century debate and consensus on this passage from Luke, see Brown, *Mary in the New Testament*, 126–34.

23. The translators of the King James Bible (published in the same year as Lanyer's book) do not mention at all that Mary herself is "full of" something; they render the verse, "Hail, *thou that are highly favored.*"

24. See also the line "Mary that mother art of grace" in the traditional hymn "Memento salutis auctor," which is included in the *The Primer, or Office of the Blessed Virgin Marie* (107). On Lanyer's adaptation of Catholic spirituality, see Holmes, "Love of Other Women," 177–78, 188 n. 38; and Guibbory, "Gospel According to Aemilia," 198, 209–10 n. 17.

25. As Boss, *Empress and Handmaid*, 133, stresses, the emphasis of the doctrine as originally formulated fell not on Mary's uniqueness, but rather on her fulfillment of the potential blessedness inherent in all human flesh and—more radically—in all human sexuality.

26. As Boss, *Empress and Handmaid*, notes in summarizing the defense of the Immaculate Conception by John Duns Scotus (1266–1308), "to claim that Mary was preserved from contracting original sin is to say not that she did not need to be redeemed, but on the contrary, that she was the object of Christ's most perfectly redemptive action" (129). Belief in the Immaculate Conception would thus not prevent one from calling Jesus Mary's "Saviour," as Donne—a reader of Scotus—knew perfectly well, despite his implying otherwise in the 1618 Whitehall sermon. Indeed, his reference to Jesus' dying "for her, when she needed not that hell" is something of a homage to Scotus, who stresses that God acts outside the range of any temporal "when" and hints at the idea that the sorrows of the Passion were the only "hell" that could threaten his already redeemed mother. On Donne's (private) poetic versus (public) homiletic stance on the Virgin, see Klawitter, "John Donne's Attitude."

27. Without any other copytext than the 1611 edition, one cannot reconstruct the text, which seems to reflect authorial confusion rather than a simple compositor's error, since the simplest emendation (flipping the order of the phrasing in line 1019) destroys the stanza's rhyme scheme.

28. As Micheline White, "Woman with Saint Peter's Keys?" points out, this allusion to Mary Magdalene in Lanyer's prefatory epistle "To the Vertuous Reader" draws upon a traditional idea of Magdalene as apostle to the apostles and type of the church. As White notes (335), Donne draws upon the same tradition in "To the Lady Magdalen Herbert, of St. Mary Magdalen," which says

that "An active faith so highly did advance" the saint, "That she once knew, more than the Church did know, / The *Resurrection*" (*MHMary* 3–4). See DiPasquale, *Literature and Sacrament*, 97–100; and Asals, *Equivocal Predication*, 94–101.

29. On Lanyer's use of biblical typology as a means of bridging the gap between spiritual and worldly concerns, see Loughlin, "'Fast ti'd unto them.'"

30. The traditional notions Raming, *Exclusion of Women*, outlines are clearly established in one of the earliest nonscriptural texts to deal with the subject, the *Apostolic Constitutions*, a "fourth-century pseudo-Apostolic collection, . . . of . . . treatises on Christian discipline, worship, and doctrine" (*Catholic Encyclopedia*, s.v. "Apostolic Constitutions"). Like the Pauline texts, the *Apostolic Constitutions* exclude women from administering the sacrament of baptism on the grounds of the subordinate status assigned them as punishment for Eve's sin; they also use the argument, still frequently cited today, that Jesus did not comission women to baptize (see Raming, *Exclusion of Women*, 18). For more recent feminist perspectives on the Pauline and Deutero-Pauline epistles, see Levine and Blickenstaff, *A Feminist Companion to Paul*, and Polaski, *A Feminist Introduction to Paul*.

31. England had probably seen some debate over women's fitness for the priesthood during the late Middle Ages, as Catholic accusations against the heretics known as Lollards often cited their approval of women as preachers and even as administrators of the sacraments; see Aston, *Lollards and Reformers*, 49–70. English Puritans of Lanyer's time, however, objected to the administration of sacraments by women; they were particularly alarmed by midwives' administration of baptism in situations when a baby might otherwise die unbaptized. See the responses to this controversy in Hooker, *Laws* 5.62.3, and in the rulings of King James at the 1604 Hampton Court Conference (Barlow, *Svmme and Svbstance*, 17–18).

32. See also Guibbory, "Gospel According to Aemilia," 200–201.

33. On the degree to which Christ is "feminized" in Lanyer's poetry, see Krontiris, *Oppositional Voices*, 116–18; McGrath, *Subjectivity*, 230–31; Wall, *Imprint of Gender*. 322, 328–29; Mueller, "Feminist Poetics," 112–17; Schoenfeldt, "Gender of Religious Devotion," 215; Goldberg, *Desiring Women Writing*, 33–35; Holmes, Love of Other Women, 178–79; Berry, "'Pardon,'" 213–15; and Rogers, "Passion of a Female Literary," 437–40, 446.

34. Beilin, *Redeeming Eve*, 198, notes the parallel between the countess and the Blessed Virgin Mary; Woods, "Vocation and

Authority," remarks that the church is "explicitly represented by the Countess of Cumberland" in Lanyer's work (92); Keohane, "'That blindest Weaknesse," also notes the parallel with the Virgin and the countess's status "as a figure for the Church" (365–66, 381).

35. The Gospel of Mark identifies the women as Mary Magdalene, Mary the mother of James, and Salome (16:1). Matthew mentions only "Marie Magdalene, and the other Marie" (28:1). Luke refers more broadly to "the women...which came with him from Galile" (23:55).

36. Beilin, *Redeeming Eve*, points out that this part of Lanyer's poem stresses "the female imagery attached to the Church" and underscores the idea that "the Church and the ideal woman possess many of the same qualities" (198–99). See also Phillippy, "Sisters of Magdalen," 82, 98, 105.

37. On traditional interpretations of Mary Magdalene, see Haskins, *Mary Magdalen*; Asals, *Equivocal Predication*; and Good, *Mariam*.

38. The Vestriarian Controversy reached its climax at Easter 1560, almost a decade before Lanyer was born; but the question of ministerial garb remained a bone of contention throughout the reigns of Elizabeth and James. See Hooker, *Laws*, 5.29.1–7, and Barlow, *Svmme and Svbstance*, 99–102.

39. The use of consecrated oil in Baptism was one of the Roman Catholic ceremonies originally retained in the 1549 *Book of Common Prayer* but excised in 1552. See Cressy, *Birth, Marriage, and Death*, 136–37.

40. Keohane, "'That blindest Weaknesse,'" argues that Lanyer refers to Peter "as the rock of the Roman Catholic Church, the Pope. Transferring the keys therefore empowers the Countess...and at the same time suggests a wrenching of control away from the patriarchal Catholic Church" (380) But this conclusion is forced, for Lanyer sees little need to fight battles against Rome; her Protestant addressees have already triumphed in their resolve to live "unsubjected" to "*Romes* ridiculous prier and tyranny" ("To the Ladie Susan," 24, 25). Moreover, as Keohane also points out, Lanyer seems aware that Catholic spirituality is more open to the power of the feminine than is Protestantism (366). Matthew 16:19 had, as White observes, "a complex history in Protestant countries, for while Protestants argued that the passage did not provide a basis for Papal supremacy, they still believed that it provided a blueprint for the responsibilities of priests" ("Woman with Saint Peter's," 193). Lanyer's reference to Peter's keys thus establishes the Countess of Cumberland as a type of the church in its pastoral ministry, not as a

female replacement for the pope. See also the marginal commentary on Matthew 16:19 in the 1599 Geneva Bible; Calvin, *Institution*, 3.4.12–24; and Hooker, *Laws*, 6.4.1–2.

41. Richey, *Politics of Revelation*, 64–68, 75–76, documents a precedent and likely source for Lanyer's reinterpretation of Scripture, including her handling of the Queen of Sheba, in Henry Cornelius Agrippa's *Of the Nobilitie and Excellencie of Womankinde* (1542), a work widely read in England throughout the reign of Queen Elizabeth. On Lanyer's use of arguments similar to Agrippa's, see also Turner, *One Flesh*, 109–13, and McBride and Ulreich, "'Eve's Apologie.'" On the Queen of Sheba's role as a judge, see Loughlin, "'Fast ti'd unto them,'" 143–44.

42. See also Seelig, "'To all vertuous Ladies,'" 56, and Pearson, "Women Writers and Women Readers," 46.

43. Compare White, "Woman with Saint Peter's," 329–30.

44. In the title poem, the suffering Jesus is clad in "Pure white, to shew his great Integritie, / His innocency," along with "Purple and Scarlet" that "well might him beseeme, / Whose pretious blood must all the world redeeme" (*SDRJ*, 891–92, 895–96).

45. Compare Loughlin, "'Fast ti'd unto them,'" 153, 154–55.

46. See Beilin, *Redeeming Eve*, 195; White, "Woman with Saint Peter's," 205–20; and Woods, *Lanyer*, 136–40, and "Lanyer and Southwell," 81–83.

47. For the use of oil in ordination ceremonies, see *The Catholic Encyclopedia*, "Holy Orders."

48. George Herbert, "Aaron," lines 1–2, in Herbert, *Works*, 174. Subsequent quotations from Herbert's "Aaron" are taken from this edition and cited parenthetically by line number. White, "Woman with Saint Peter's," also cites Herbert's "Aaron" as a literary exploration of priesthood (340 n. 21).

49. The Jewish priesthood of Jesus' time is, for Lanyer, an even more extreme example of men's failure to fulfill the sacerdotal role. Compare Mueller, "Feminist Poetics," 117.

50. Compare Herz, "Aemilia Lanyer," who silently changes the period to a comma and observes, "Something interesting happens over the stanza break: with 'unfold' she safely and properly occupies the role of exegete; with 'In other phrases,' she becomes a Gospel writer herself" (130). See also Guibbory, "Gospel According to Aemilia"; Powell, "'Witnesse thy wife'"; McBride and Ulreich, "Answerable Styles"; and Rienstra, "Dreaming Authorship," 87.

51. Lanyer probably had several reasons for singling out Saint Laurence (d. 258 AD) as the only nonbiblical, post-apostolic martyr she mentions. He was one of the most popular saints of the Roman church from the fourth century onward, and hundreds of English

churches were dedicated to him before the Reformation (*Catholic Encyclopedia*, s.v. "St. Lawrence" and "Patron Saints"). He was known not only for his courage in the face of the horrible death devised for him by the Emperor Decius (being roasted on a gridiron) but also for his charitable care of the poor and for his wit. See also *The Golden Legend*, 4:211, 213, 215.

52. See also Lanyer's description of the garden of Gethsemane as the place where Jesus goes "to meete his long nurst woe" (336). On Jesus as mother in medieval literature, see Bynum, "'And Woman His Humanity'" and *Jesus as Mother*. See also McGrath, *Subjectivity*, 230, 234.

53. Compare McBride, "Gender and Judaism," 35, and Mueller, "Feminist Poetics," 118.

54. The list, of course, excludes Lanyer's principal scriptural adversary, Paul, who preached female subordination on the basis of Eve's transgression but was never martyred.

55. See also Krontiris, *Oppositional Voices*, 119.

56. See also Goldberg, *Desiring Women Writing*, who stresses that Lanyer portrays Margaret Clifford as "a woman identified with female-identified (suffering, beheaded men)" (39), and Loughlin, "'Fast ti'd unto them,'" 163–65.

57. Some of Donne's *Songs and Sonets*, by contrast, embrace a pre-Christian idea of human love as "utterly 'transforming,' providing access to the divine" (Guibbory, "'The Relique,'" 35).

58. See also Beilin, *Redeeming Eve*, 190, 199; McGrath, *Subjectivity*, 218–19, 221, 229–30; Wall, *Imprint of Gender*, 325–29; Woods, "Vocation and Authority," 92–96; Keohane, "'That blindest Weaknesse,'" 371–75; and DiPasquale, "Woman's Desire," 61–64, 376.

59. McBride, "Sacred Celebration," calls this poem "a little gem, perhaps the most polished and accomplished single piece of Lanyer's work" (78); see also Goldberg, *Desiring Women Writing*, 27–33.

60. Schoenfeldt, "Gender of Religious Devotion," observes that, in the Bedford poem and elsewhere throughout her volume, "Lanyer finds herself functioning as a kind of divine procuress, arranging relationships between these noble ladies and her heavenly lord" (216). See also Benson, "To Play the Man," who argues that in the Bedford poem, "virtue is Lanyer's poetry, which will allow Christ into the closet of Bedford's breast" (256). Lanyer's conception of Virtue is also discussed by McGrath, *Subjectivity*, 216, 224–25; McBride, "Sacred Celebration," 70–78; and Seelig, "'To all vertuous Ladies,'" 50–56.

61. Compare Donne's verse epistle to Lucy, "Honour is so sublime perfection," in which he says of the countess's body: "This,

as an Amber drop enwraps a Bee, / Covering discovers your quicke
Soule; that we / May in your though-shine front your hearts thoughts
see" (*BedfHon*, 25–27). Maurer observes that, considered in relation
to "the sketch of what [Lucy] wore as Penthesileia in *The Masque of
Queens*, the line conveys Donne's appreciation for . . . a disguise that
makes its wearer's intentions plainer than common decency would
allow" ("Real Presence," 225).

62. "This blessed Arke," which is very ambiguously positioned,
may also be read as referring to Christ or to Lanyer's poem. See
Goldberg, *Desiring Women Writing*, 32–33.

63. See Woods, *Lanyer*, 42, 54–61, on Lanyer's response, in this
section and throughout *Salve Deus*, to Spenser's *Fowre Hymns*,
which were dedicated to the Countess of Warwick and to her sister,
the Countess of Cumberland, whom Lanyer chose as her own principal dedicatee.

64. See Mueller, "Feminist Poetics," on Lanyer's response to
"evil-doing" female protagonists in works by her male contemporaries (214–15).

65. Lanyer here interprets Genesis 3:6 with brilliant selectivity,
mounting a direct rebuttal to the Geneva Bible gloss that claims
Adam was "moued by ambicion at [Eve's] persuasion." The scriptural verse says that "the woman (seing that the tre was good for
meat, and that it was pleasant to the eyes, & a tre to be desired to
get knowledge) toke of the frute thereof, and did eat, and gaue also
to her housband with her, and he did eat." Lanyer does not deny
that Eve had fleshly motivations, but she ignores these as negligi-
ble and stresses the intellectual rationalization that the text assigns
only to Eve: "If *Eve* did erre, it was for knowledge sake" (*SDRJ*,
797). Then, since the Bible says nothing about why Adam did what
he did, Lanyer is free to assert that one of the two other reasons
Eve had for eating (the fact that the tree's fruit was "pleasant to the
eyes") must have been the deciding factor for the man.

66. On Lanyer's approach to the figures of Lucrece, Cleopatra,
Octavia, Rosamund, and Matilda as responses to the treatment of
those figures in the poetry of Shakespeare, Daniel, and Drayton, see
Mueller, "Feminist Poetics," and Woods, *Lanyer*, 33–41, 83–90. See
also Pearson, "Women Writers and Women Readers," 49.

67. This and the other passages quoted in this paragraph appear
in the manuscript records of Simon Forman, quoted in Woods,
introduction to *Poems of Aemilia Lanyer*, xviii, xxii–xxiii.

68. As Goldberg, *Desiring Women Writing*, 24–25, points out,
it makes little sense to assume that Forman was lying in his own
diary about his failure to get what he wanted from Lanyer.

69. McGrath, "Metaphoric Subversions," 109, applies this phrase to Lanyer's female readers.

70. See the detailed analysis of Lanyer's Susanna in DiPasquale, "Woman's Desire," 365–68.

71. The *Celebration* was not published in its entirety until it appeared in the posthumous 1640 edition of Jonson's *Works*. However, a portion of one of the ten "pieces," "Her Triumph" was included in a 1616 performance of Jonson's *The Devil Is an Ass*; it is possible that other lyrics from this grouping were circulating in manuscript at a date early enough for Lanyer to have seen them before writing her poem for the Countess of Suffolk.

72. *A Celebration of Charis in Ten Lyric Pieces*, no. 9: "Her Man Described by Her own Dictamen," 15–16 (Jonson, *Complete Poems*, 134).

73. Ibid., lines 41, 43–44, 49.

74. On Lanyer's resistance to Saint Paul's interpretation of Genesis, see Richey, "To Undo the Booke." For twenty-first century feminist perspectives on Ephesians, see Levine and Blickenstaff, *Feminist Companion to Paul*.

75. See Mueller, "Feminist Poetics," on these lines as an "ominous pragmatic warning…based on the status quo of gender politics" (119).

76. See, for example, Lanyer's allusion to the spiritual aspirations of Katherine Knevet as "those sweet desires, / That from your perfect thoughts doe daily spring" ("To the Ladie *Katherine*," 103) and to her own authorial ambition as a Phaeton-like overreacher that may "perish in [his] own desire" (*SDRJ*, 288).

77. In 1606, Frances Howard (age 13) wed Robert Devereux, Earl of Essex (age 14), the son and heir of Queen Elizabeth's ill-starred favorite. Their wedding—January 5, 1606—was celebrated at court with great fanfare, the text for the wedding masque being provided by Ben Jonson. But Frances and Robert were considered too young to consummate their marriage directly following the wedding, and so the couple were separated while the young husband completed his education on the Continent. The marriage failed, obviously and scandalously, not long after his return in 1609. The marriages of Frances' sisters were also quite obviously politically strategic. In 1605, the eldest Howard daughter, Elizabeth (age 18), was married to the 58-year-old widower William, Lord Knollys. And in December 1608, Catherine Howard (still in her early teens) wed William Cecil, the son of the Howards' powerful political rival, Robert Cecil; they, too, were separated for some time before they were considered old enough to consummate the marriage. David Lindley notes that

Lord Howard "was behaving somewhat unusually" in arranging for Frances and Catherine to marry at so young an age, for the "average age" at which even aristocratic unions were contracted "had crept up between the late sixteenth and early seventeenth centuries" (*Trials of Frances Howard*, 14).

78. On the Queen of Sheba's desires, see Hutson, "Why the Lady's Eyes," 34, and McGrath, *Subjectivity*, 222.

79. See Boccaccio, "Nicaula, Queen of Ethiopia," *Concerning Famous Women*, 93–94.

80. For more complete accounts of these traditions, and of the Queen of Sheba's status in Ethiopian Christianity and in medieval typology and legend, see Pritchard, *Solomon and Sheba*, and Philby, *Queen of Sheba*.

81. *Second Defence of the English People* (YP 4:605–06).

82. Watson, "Queen of Sheba," describes the scriptural verses inscribed around the king's throne in the engraving as making "perfect sense as allusions to the political state of England, and the supremacy of the monarch. The traditional interpretation of the Queen of Sheba as the Church would not be an inappropriate reference to Henry's ecclesiastical policy" (131).

83. See Parry, *Golden Age Restor'd*, 21, 24–26, 29–35, on James's encouragement of imagery that identified him as the English Solomon, a king of great wisdom and learning, and a man of peace.

84. Compare Richey, "'To Undo the Booke,'" 125, on Lanyer's "artful doubling of subject and object" in this passage.

85. In his accession speech to Parliament, James declared that "I am the Husband, and all the whole Isle is my lawfull Wife; I am the Head, and it is my Body" (*Political Works*, 272). On James's theory of kingship and its relationship to Jonson's masques, see chapter 2 of Goldberg, *James I*.

86. See Guibbory, "Gospel According to Aemilia," 192–93, for a discussion of Lanyer's work in the context of Jacobean patriarchy.

87. George Clifford had willed to his brother portions of his estate that would otherwise have been inherited by his and Margaret's daughter, Anne, Countess of Dorset. See Lewalski, "Re-Writing Patriarchy and Patronage," 89–97.

88. On early modern attitudes toward the sexual needs of widows and their relatively unrestricted lives, see McGrath, *Subjectivity*, 45–46.

89. See Woods's note on line 1314 (*Poems of Aemilia Lanyer*, 107).

90. Twenty-first century Scripture scholarship challenges the idea that Romans 1:26 includes a condemnation of lesbianism; see

Swancutt, "Sexy Stoics," 63–64, and Polaski, *Feminist Introduction to Paul*, 23.

91. Contemporary scholars are divided in their assessments of the poem; some argue that it evokes Sappho's desire only to contain it within hetero-normative bounds, while others assert that the poem genuinely celebrates same-sex love. See the overview of scholarship in Meakin, *John Donne's Articulations*, 91–94. Most persuasive is Paula Blank's reading of the poem as Donne's exploration of his own "homopoetics." See also Mueller, "Lesbian Erotics"; Holstun, "'Will you rent'"; Revard, "Sapphic Voice"; Infante, "Donne's Incarnate Muse"; Harvey, "Ventriloquizing Sappho"; Correll, "Symbolic Economies"; Prescott, "Male Lesbian Voices"; Meakin, *John Donne's Articulations*, 85–138; and Bell, "Gender Matters." Whatever Donne's intentions and whatever the effect of "Sapho to Philænis" as a whole, several passages in the poem harmonize with the homoerotic undertones of Lanyer's *Salve Deus*; see Holmes, "Love of Other Women," 169.

92. Some critics interpret Sappho's remark about lesbian intercourse leaving "no...signes" as an indication that Donne's real intent is to represent Sapphic love as radically insignficant, and thus essentially meaningless. I disagree, for the speaker's point is that there are no *sinful* traces left by women's lovemaking, no tracks that indicate a robbery; though we are left to wonder whether Sappho succeeds in winning Philaenis back, her words — regardless of their rhetorical success or lack thereof — movingly represent what used to happen between Sappho and her lover. And the fish-in-water–birds-in-sky images evoke natural locomotion that, though it leaves no print, is not without significant grace. I am reminded of the English Protestant doctrine that states that the Eucharistic signs are neither empty nor significant in and of themselves, but rather evoke real presence through the active participation of the communicant; when the act of receiving ceases, so does the signification. As Prescott points out in discussing "Sapho to Philænis," "if he *is* commenting on" the signifying power versus insignificance of "language, then what he says is relevant to post-Reformation arguments over the Eucharist and over how signs relate to the things they point at" ("Male Lesbian Voices," 112).

93. See MacLure, "Nature and Art," on "the natural and the artificial" in the Bower of Bliss as "imaged in the behavior of" the "naked Damzelles" (10).

94. While the "desires" from which the poem "springs" might also be interpreted as womb or matrix, I would argue that Lanyer

intends to evoke the countess's fatherly function; for in describing Anne Clifford later in "Cooke-ham," she calls her "that sweet Lady sprung from *Cliffords* race, / Of noble *Bedfords* blood" (93–94). As Woods's note explains, her father's family were "the Cliffords, earls of Cumberland," while her mother's were "the Russells, earls of Bedford." The child springs from the father's line and is formed from the maternal blood.

95. On Anne Clifford's homoerotic relationship with her cousin Frances Bouchier and on Lanyer's evocation of same-sex desire, see McGrath, *Subjectivity*, 67, 215–17.

96. Compare Helena's rebuke to Hermia in Shakespeare, "A Midsummer Night's Dream," 3.2.210–14.

97. See Patrick Cook, "Aemilia Lanyer's 'Description,'" 116–18, on the ways in which these concluding lines complete the movement of Margaret Clifford's virtue "from the estate...to the poet's breast" and contribute to the Eucharistic poetics of *Salve Deus*.

98. See Duerden, "Crossings," on the chiastic structure of "The Description of Cooke-ham."

99. See Coiro, "Writing in Service," 372, 373, 374. On class and patronage issues in Lanyer's work, see also McBride, "Sacred Celebration," 64; McBride and Ulreich, "Answerable Styles"; Schnell, "'So Great a Difference'" and "Breaking"; Duerden, "Crossings"; Schoenfeldt, "Gender of Religious Devotion," 212–14; McGrath, *Subjectivity*, 214–17; Lamb, "Patronage and Class"; and Loughlin, "'Fast ti'd unto them.'"

NOTES TO "MILTON"

1. See Flynn, "Donne the Survivor," who applies to Donne's Elizabethan recusant experience the psychology of survivorship as defined by Bruno Bettelheim.

2. Compare Herz, "Aemilia Lanyer": "There is...no evidence that anyone ever read [Lanyer's] little book"; the volume's "culminating gesture of farewell is ultimately both a textual and historical fact. Lanyer disappears from her book and into her book" (129, 127).

3. *Sapientia increata* is the Wisdom of Proverbs 8, traditionally identified with the second person of the Trinity; *sapientia creata* is the Wisdom of Ecclesiasticus 1:4 ("Wisdome hathe bene created before all things"). See Augustine, *Confessions:* "created wisdom...[is] the intellectual order of being which by contemplating the Light becomes light itself" (12.20). Created wisdom, he goes on to explain, "derives its being from" God and "shin[es] with [God's] light" (*Confessions*, 12.21). See also Aquinas, *Summa Theologica*,

1.41.3. Many passages on Wisdom in the Wisdom of Solomon and Ecclesiasticus may be read as applying either to the uncreated, begotten Wisdom who *is* God or to the created Wisdom that mirrors God. For an overview of Christian ideas of divine and created Wisdom, their relation to Neoplatonic and kabbalistic ideas of Wisdom, and the relevance of both to Spenser's "Hymne of Heavenly Beavtie," see Quitslund, "Spenser's Image of Sapience."

4. Protestant scholars exclude from the canon of Scripture some books included in the Vulgate and Roman Catholic translations thereof and designated by the Council of Trent as "Deutero-canonical" — "constituting a second Canon, accepted later than the first, but now of equal authority" (*OED*): among them, the Wisdom of Solomon, Ecclesiasticus (also called Sirach), and the chapters on Susanna in the book of Daniel. Given the importance of these books in the exegetical tradition, however, the translators of the Geneva and King James versions did translate them and print them under the label "Apocrypha." For a sense of the standard English Protestant attitude toward these books, see the introductory note on them in the 1560 Geneva Bible (386). On Milton's respect for and frequent references to the Apocrypha, see Mollenkott, "The Pervasive Influence."

5. Milton uses the phrase in *Areopagitica* (YP 2:516).

6. Lewalski's discussion of specific Caroline masques as points of reference for Milton enhances earlier scholarly analysis of *Arcades* and *Comus* as reformed masques. See especially McGuire, *Milton's Puritan Masque*; Norbrook, "Reformation of the Masque"; and Cedric Brown, *Milton's Aristocratic Entertainments*.

7. This and subsequent quotations from Spenser's *Foure Hymnes* and *Teares of the Muses* are taken from *The Poetical Works* and cited parenthetically by line number.

8. Lewalski's assertion that the dowager countess had herself danced in Queen Anne's masques during the previous reign is inaccurate; see Barroll, *Anna of Denmark*, 51–52.

9. See Brown, *Milton's Aristocratic Entertainments*, 46. In answer to Dubrow's argument that "it is by no means clear that the text [of *Arcades*] presents the praise of this noble lady as an alternative rather than a supplement to that of the king" ("Masquing of Genre," 66), I would argue that the imperative to "dance no more" in Arcady strongly stresses that Harefield and its lady are a *replacement* for the court and its queen.

10. See Brown, *Milton's Aristocratic Entertainments*, 46–47, and Lewalski, "Milton's *Comus*," 301.

11. Compare Lewalski, "Milton's *Comus*," 303. The version of Neoplatonism at work in *Love's Triumph Through Callipolis* is, I would argue, the doctrine of the first two hymns in Spenser's

Fowre Hymnes, "An Hymne in Honovr of Love" and "An Hymne in Honovr of Beavtie." Spenser scholars are divided on how to understand the distinctions between these two poems and the third and fourth hymns, which celebrate Heavenly Love and Heavenly Beauty. See Quitslund, "Spenser's Image of Sapience," 183–84. See Woods, *Lanyer,* 54–61, on *Salve Deus* as "perhaps...extending or correcting" Spenser's *Fowre Hymnes.*

12. Wallace, "Milton's *Arcades,*" 79, quotes the King James Version: "the half was not told me: thy wisdom and prosperity exceedeth the fame which I heard."

13. Compare *Paradise Lost,* book 12, in which Adam asks "what will betide the few / His faithful," after the Messiah "reascend[s]." Michael tells Adam of the "Comforter...who shall dwell / [God's] Spirit within them" (480–81, 486, 487–88). This Spirit is no doubt the same divine Spirit invoked at *Paradise Lost* 1.17 in terms that associate it with the "Heav'nly Muse" first mentioned at *PL* 1.6, and said in the opening invocation of book 7 to be the sister of Wisdom (*PL* 7.9–10). See Fowler's notes, 41, 43, 356.

14. Vision remains an important component of *Arcades;* the first song's emphasis on light imagery, its invitations to "Look," "descry," and "Mark" (*Arcades,* 1, 3, 14) the great lady, and the Genius's description of himself as often "gaz[ing] upon" the Dowager Countess (43) all make it necessary to qualify Lewalski's contention that "good art" in Milton's entertainment is "not the Neoplatonic arts of vision given priority in [Henrietta Maria's 1632 masque] *Tempe Restored*" ("Milton's *Comus,*" 301).

15. These terms come from a passage in *The Reason of Church Government:* "the government of the Gospell being economicall and paternall, that is, of such a family where there be no servants, but all sons in obedience, not in servility,...how can the Prelates justifie to have turn'd the fatherly orders of Christs household, the blessed meeknesse of his lowly roof, those ever open and inviting dores of his dwelling house which delight to be frequented with only filiall accesses, how can they justifie to have turn'd these domestick priveleges into the barre of a proud judiciall court" (YP 1:848–49).

16. Compare Aquinas, who calls created wisdom the greatest of the "intellectual virtues" because its object, that which it "considers," is God, "the Supreme Cause" (*Summa Theologica,* 2.1.66.5). Milton would have agreed that "Wisdom is called an intellectual virtue, so far as it proceeds from the judgment of reason: but it is called a gift, according as its work proceeds from the Divine prompting" (2.1.68.1).

17. On the Arminian theology underlying the *Mask* and on the degree to which that theology was compatible with opposition to Laud's authoritarian ecclesiology, see Martin, "Non-Puritan Ethics."

18. These lines were not spoken during the Ludlow Castle performance of the *Mask* in 1634. They were added in the first print edition of the work, which contains passages (including both the one containing the image of Cupid and Psyche and the Lady's lines on the "sage / And serious doctrine of Virginity" [786–87]) that are missing from the performance script as represented by the Bridgewater manuscript. See King, "Milton and the Bishops," 283–86, on the "paleographical evidence...that Milton inserted the most radical satiric attacks on ecclesiastical affairs" when he revised the performance text of the work for publication in 1637. See also Tillyard, "The Action of *Comus*," 53–55.

19. This figure, "clothed with the sunne," is threatened by a "great red dragon," gives birth to "a man childe" destined to "rule all nations with a rod of yron," and then flees into the "wildernes where she hathe a place prepared of God" (Rev. 12:1, 3, 5, 6). See also King, "Milton and the Bishops," who asserts that "we may regard *Comus* in many respects as a very free elaboration on the Book of Revelation" (286).

20. Scoufos, "Mysteries in Milton's Masque," reads not only the *Mask*, but also *De Doctrina Christiana* and Milton's antiprelatical writings, as stressing the church's vulnerability and inability to "achieve perfection in this life"; the poet defined "perfect happiness," she concludes, as reserved for "the Bride of Christ in eternity" (122). Honeygosky, *Milton's House of God*, disagrees, arguing that there is no such dichotomy between the visible and invisible church in Milton's thought (4, 44).

21. Una does fill Sansloy's ears with "piteous plaints" when he captures her, "But he enrag'd with rancor, nothing heares" (*FQ* 1.3.44:2, 5). When next we see them, and he "With fawning wordes" attempts to court her, she gives no verbal reply, but remains "As rocke of Diamond stedfast euermore." When Sansloy tears off her veil and begins to "assayle" her physically, Una screams, attracting the attention of the satyrs who frighten Sansloy away (*FQ* 1.6.4.1, 5; 5.3; 6.1–2). Shullenberger ("Girl, Interrupted," 187), notes the parallel between Una and the Lady.

22. According to the Geneva Bible gloss on chapter 1, verse 4, "The Church confesseth her spots & sinne, but hathe confidence in ye fauour of Christ."

23. The idea of the Lady as an imperfect church-in-training rather than a venerable icon is compatible with Heather Dubrow's

argument that Milton's *Comus* is "a draft for a reformed masque, not its polished realization" ("Masquing of Genre," 79). Just as, for Milton, the Reformed church is a work in progress, so no single work can represent the perfected state of a genre.

24. Though Cox cites both this passage on "discipline" as virtue made visible and the passage on the education of a virgin (quoted above), she does not discuss the ways in which the Lady's vision and subsequent song demonstrate her responsiveness to divine discipline. Barker, *Milton and the Puritan Dilemma,* 16, also notes but does not comment on the "echo of *Comus*" in *The Reason of Church Government.*

25. Christopher argues that Milton's choice to displace charity with chastity reflects the Reformed emphasis on faith over works; she reduces the "sage / And serious doctrine of Virginity" to the doctrine of *sola fide.* But as Martin, "Non-Puritan Ethics," has shown, the theology underlying the *Mask* is in fact Arminian. Obertino, "Milton's Use of Aquinas," inverting Christopher's reading, interprets chastity in the *Mask* "as a pervasive metonymy for charity" (21). McMichaels, "The Lady Rises," rejects both Christopher's and Obertino's arguments but replaces them with an equally strained attempt to demonstrate that, "If chastity has a metonymic value in the poem, it is a metonymy for...temperance" (153).

26. Spenser's influence on Milton in his composition of the *Mask* is a critical commonplace based on the Spensarian Neoplatonism of the Elder Brother and on Milton's use of Spenser's *Faerie Queene* as his source for the legend of Sabrina. See Hughes's note on line 822 of *A Mask.*

27. Compare Kerrigan, *Sacred Complex,* who quotes Spenser's description of Charissa as a suckling mother in support of his psychoanalytic reading of the *Mask* (50–53).

28. Scoufos, "Mysteries in Milton's Masque," compares *A Mask* to John Foxe's militantly Protestant *Christus Triumphans: Comoedia Apocalyptica* (1556): "By the third act of the *Comoedia,* Foxe's Antichrist (Pseudamnus, the Pope) has seduced the whole world with his 'Circean cups of luxury.'" He then attempts to claim Ecclesia as his bride, but she rejects him (119).

29. Rumrich, *Milton Unbound,* stresses Comus's fascination with Mother Nature's "excessive fertility" as a sinister manifestation of his strongly maternal identity (74).

30. On Comus as an Epicurean and the Lady as a Stoic, see McMichaels, "The Lady Rises."

31. See ibid., 156–59, on the limits of human virtue in the *Mask.*

32. See also Shullenberger, "Profession of Virginity," 85–87, on other passages from Sandys's interpretation of Ovid's Medusa as they apply to the Lady's chastity.

33. See Corthell, "Go Ask Alice," on Kerrigan's argument as "a strong psychoanalytic version of a rather long tradition of suspicious, if not prurient, commentary on the possibility of the Lady's complicity" (112).

34. Leonard, "Saying 'No' to Freud," argues that the Lady's "doctrine of virginity" is not a commitment to life-long celibacy: "It is precisely because her doctrine does include the possibility of a lawful 'unfolding' of virginity that the Lady declines to 'unfold' it to Comus" (136).

35. See also Broaddus, "'Gums of Glutinous Heat,'" 207, who interprets the "gums" in light of Renaissance medical treatises on female nocturnal emissions, and McMichaels, "The Lady Rises," 156–58, who compares the Lady's situation to that of the besieged castle of Alma in book 2 of *The Faerie Queene* and interprets her captivity as dramatizing the "inner struggle between her reason and her appetites."

36. Some of the nymphs whose names the Attendant Spirit invokes in summoning her do, as Revard, *Milton and the Tangles,* 132, demonstrates, have maternal attributes and functions; but Shullenberger, "Girl, Interrupted," 198, overemphasizes these slender maternal associations. I would note, with Rumrich, *Milton Unbound,* that "The pattern followed by the good characters in *Comus* . . . is to reject scornfully the maternal dependence represented by Circe's son," and that Sabrina is particularly well suited to rescue the Lady from the magic Comus learned from his mother since she "was herself the victim of a menacing maternal figure" (91).

37. Woodhouse, "The Argument," asserts that Milton, unlike many of his Puritan contemporaries, denied the complete separation of Nature and grace; but in "*Comus* Once More," he argues that the *Mask* maps a progression from purely natural virtue, to Nature operating in cooperation with grace (in the brothers' use of haemony), to the operation of grace alone in the person of Sabrina. Christopher's Calvinist reading (*Milton and the Science*) imposes on the *Mask* a Puritan divorce between Nature and grace, while other scholars build on or modify Woodhouse's argument that Nature and grace are compatible or cooperative in the work. See especially Brown, *Milton's Aristocratic Entertainments;* McMichael, "The Lady Rises"; and Martin, "Non-Puritan Ethics."

38. On Milton's ideas about married love and divorce as reflecting and bringing to its logical conclusion the doctrine of marriage

that Puritan preachers and writers were promoting throughout the early seventeenth century, see Haller, " 'Hail Wedded Love.' "

39. See especially the passage in chapter 5 of the *Doctrine and Discipline of Divorce* on how an unhappy marriage may lead a man to "dispair in vertue, and mutin against divine providence" (YP 2:254).

40. On *Paradise Lost* as "expos[ing] the intrinsically unstable foundation of Eden's hierarchical society," see John Rogers, "Transported Touch." The *OED* definition of "theodicy" quotes, without attribution, Milton's phrase "justify the ways of God to men" (*PL* 1.26).

41. In his note on *PL* 9:439–43, Fowler cites Ricks's discussion (*Milton's Grand Style*, 133–35) of the Adam/Solomon analogy, and notes that Augustine makes use of this analogy in book 14 of *City of God*.

42. See Summers, *The Muse's Method*; Lewalski, *Paradise Lost and the Rhetoric*; and McColley, *Milton's Eve* and *Gust for Paradise*.

43. In *Tetrachordon*, Milton stresses the use of the pronoun "him" in the phrase "in the image of God created he him" (Gen. 1:27), arguing—with 1 Corinthians 11 as support—that "woman is not primarily and immediatly the image of God, but in reference to the man" (YP 2:589). In *Paradise Lost*, too, Adam and Eve are "Not equal" (4.296) since he is made "for God only, shee for God in him" (4.299); but the poetry nonetheless modifies the emphasis of the divorce tract in order to emphasize Eve's share in the *imago dei*. "Had the Image of God bin equally common to them both," Milton explains in *Tetrachordon*, "it had no doubt bin said, In the image of God created he them" (YP 2:589). The poet comes suggestively close to just such a revision in book 4 of *Paradise Lost* when he makes double use of "their" in lines 291–92 ("in thir looks Divine / The image of their glorious Maker shone"). In book 7, however, Raphael stays closer to Genesis and to Milton's *Tetrachordon* reading when he says to Adam, "in his own Image hee / Created thee, in the Image of God / Express.... / Male he created thee, but thy consort / Female for Race" (*PL* 7.526–30). Compare Donne's cheeky opening line in a verse epistle to the Countess of Huntingdon, "Man to Gods image, *Eve* to mans was made." For readings of Milton's subtle revisions or redefinitions of gender hierarchy in *Paradise Lost*, see Aers and Hodge," 'Rational Burning,' " and Martin, "Demystifying Disguises."

44. Ferry, *Milton's Epic Voice*, calls *Paradise Lost* "antiallegorical" and argues that Milton "limit[s] his allegory to parts of the poem relating only to fallen experience" (131); Quilligan, *Language*

of Allegory, 181–82, and Madsen, *From Shadowy Types*, build upon
this theory. But Shawcross, "Allegory, Typology," argues that such
readings perpetuate eighteenth century critics' un-Miltonic insistence on a clear distinction between the mimetic and the allegorical; in *Paradise Lost*, Shawcross argues, Adam and Eve's status as
"real" characters does not preclude their functioning allegorically
"as representatives of humankind whose experiences figure forth
the experiences of the world" (65).

45. Sims, *Bible in Milton's Epics*, notes scriptural analogues for
a few lines of this passage; the most significant is Genesis 18:30,
Abraham's colloquy with God over the fate of Sodom.

46. For a contrasting argument, which reduces Eve to the
embodiment of Beauty and Adam to the embodiment of Wisdom,
see Startzman, "Wisdom and Beauty."

47. Interpreting Proverbs 3:18, Augustine says that "Wisdom—
which is the same as Christ himself—is...the tree of life in the
spiritual paradise...; but the tree of life was also created in the
bodily paradise [of Eden] (to signify Wisdom, indeed)....the tree
of life was both some kind of real tree and yet was also a figure
of Wisdom" (*The Literal Meaning of Genesis* VIII.9(5)–10; in *On
Genesis*, 352–53). See chapter 2 in this volume on Lanyer's use of
biblical tree of life images.

48. In *De Doctrina Christiana*, the Wisdom of Proverbs is defined
as "a poetical personification of wisdom" rather than a representation of God's Son. But the point in that treatise is to argue that
the female figure who speaks in Proverbs 8 represents the Father's
wisdom rather than a distinct divine person, and that, therefore,
one cannot make claims about the coeternity of the Son on the
basis of Proverbs 8. But in *Paradise Lost* 3.170, the Father unequivo-
cally calls the Son "My word, my wisdom, and effectual might."
Thus, the Son as he exists and acts within the unfolding events
of *Paradise Lost* truly *is* what the female Wisdom of Proverbs represents. See also Davies and Hunter, "Milton's Urania," 38. The
link between Wisdom and the Son underscores Eve's likeness to
Wisdom; for as Joseph Summers, *The Muse's Method*, chapter 7,
and McColley, *Milton's Eve*, 51–57, both argue, Milton frequently
draws parallels between Eve and the Son. For detailed discussions
of Milton's Christology, see Lewalski, *Milton's Brief Epic*, 133–63,
and Rumrich, "Milton's *Theanthropos*." On Milton's address to
his muse as Wisdom's sister, see also Steadman, *Milton's Biblical*,
112–13.

49. Both scenarios of fatherly approval are linked to accounts
of Creation: Eve's description of her own awakening, and Milton's
hexameral book 7.

50. According to the *OED*, the verb "charm" is derived from the noun, which in turn is derived from Latin *"carmen* song, verse, oracular response, incantation." The primary sense of "charms" at *Paradise Lost* 4.498 is clearly that of noun definition 3a: "Any quality, attribute, trait feature, etc., which exerts a fascinating or attractive influence, exciting love or admiration. In *pl.*, esp. of female beauty, great personal attractions." The *OED* notes, however, that this meaning is "figurative"; the noun's primary meaning (def. 1a) is "The chanting or recitation of a verse supposed to possess magic power or occult influence; incantation, enchantment; hence, any action, process, verse, sentence, word or material thing, credited with such properties." Compare Sidney's comments on the etymology of "charm" in *The Defense of Poesy* (*Sir Philip Sidney*, 214, 215).

51. See Leonard, "Saying 'No' to Freud," 125, on Calvin's notion of virginity as extending to chaste marriage and on the use Milton makes of this idea of virginity both at *Paradise Lost* 9.270 and in *An Apology Against a Pamphlet* (YP 1:892–93), where he discusses the 144,000 virgins of Revelation 14:4. See also Long, "Contextualizing Eve's and Milton's Solitudes."

52. See also the suggestive language Milton uses to describe the mount of paradise in book 4: "delicious Paradise" is a *hortus conclusus* that protects "her enclosure" (132, 133) and ensures with "thicket overgrown" that "Access [is] deni'd" (136, 137) to all but "her" rightful inhabitants.

53. On this passage as demonstrating "that [Adam] is capable of falling, and that he knows it," see Reichert, "'Against His Better Knowledge,'" 87.

54. Chaucer's Wife of Bath begins her Prologue with words that must have had great resonance for Milton: "Experience, though noon auctoritee / Were in this world, is right ynogh for me / To speke of wo that is in mariage" (1–3). See the discussion of wisdom and experience in Rice, *Renaissance Idea of Wisdom*, chapter 4. Particularly interesting is Thomas Elyot's translation of some verses by the early sixteenth century German humanist Conrad Celtis: "Memorye hyght my mother, my father experience. / Grekes calle me Sophi, but ye name me Sapience" (*The Boke named the Gouernour* 2:367; quoted in Rice, 99).

55. The phrase is an English rendering of the Hebrew "Bath Kol," a voice sent from heaven; see Hunter, "Prophetic Dreams," 280. Merritt Hughes's note on the line sums up Hunter's conclusion: Eve is using a term that refers to "a revelation of God's will of less weight than an absolute command" and, in so doing, "is softening the divine prohibition" (*Complete Poems*, 393). From another

perspective, however, Eve's choice of words strengthens the bond between her and God's law by reflecting Scripture's portrayal of a father's precepts or the Law as female: "Let thine heart holde fast my wordes: kepe my commandements, and thou shalt liue. Get wisdome:...neither decline from the wordes of my mouth. Forsake her not, and she shal kepe thee: loue her and she shal preserue thee" (Prov. 4:4–5).

56. On the "sense of sexual violation" in this passage, see Eleanor Cook, "Melos versus Logos," 202.

57. Eve's memories of her own "experience" would, if she had recalled them, have protected her just as Abdiel's memory of his own experience protects him: "by experience taught we know how good, / And of our good, and of our dignity / How provident [God] is, how far from thought / To make us less, bent rather to exalt / Our happy state" (PL 5.826–30). Instead of recalling her own positive experience of God's beneficence, Eve endorses the serpent's insinuation (PL 9.729–30) that God envies humans and wants "to keep [them] low and ignorant" (9.704).

58. On the scene in book 9 where Eve persuades Adam to allow her to work on her own, see Reichert, "'Against His Better Knowledge,'" who argues "that during the scene both Eve and Adam grow in knowledge and hence in virtue" (88).

59. These stories—Genesis 19 and Judges 19—involve the sacrifice of a woman's body in order to placate attackers who intend homosexual rape. Compare Turner, One Flesh, who discusses Jean-Baptiste von Helmont's reading of the Fall in his 1648 Ortus Medicinus as proceeding from Adam's rape of Eve, who was originally created to be his superior but who is debased by the rape and later "becomes an accomplice" in his sin when she gives him "the aphrodisiac fruit" (152–54).

60. On the sapience/taste pun, see Ricks, Milton's Grand Style, 133–35.

61. Adam does use the word "love" once in his internal monologue but only in reference to what he fears he will lose in losing Eve: "How can I live without thee, how forgo / Thy sweet Converse and Love so dearly join'd" (PL 9.908–09). In his spoken address to Eve (921–59), he does not use the word at all.

62. As Danielson, "Through the Telescope," 124, notes, Ephesians 5:25 calls husbands to Christ-like, self-sacrificial love: "Housbands, loue your wiues, euen as Christ loued the Church, & gaue him self for it."

63. See Leonard, Naming in Paradise, 213–32, on the nature of Adam's sin: "Adam dies with Eve, for his own sake. He might have died for her, for her sake" (217). As Shawcross, "Allegory, Typology,"

notes, Eve's praise of Adam—"O glorious trial of exceeding Love, /
Illustrious evidence, example high!" (*PL* 9.961–62) offers Adam not
"as a type of the Christ but as what (*we* recognize) would become
under positive circumstances the antitype....But Adam puts self,
a narcissistic self, first and does not maintain faith" (62). See also
Champagne, "Adam and His 'Other.'"

64. Milton rejects the idea, central to Augustine's theology and
to orthodox Christianity, of Christ's place as the coeternal second
person of the Trinity; but he nevertheless portrays the Son as the
Father's "word, [His] wisdom, and effectual might," and in book 7
of *Paradise Lost*, that "Word, the Filial Godhead" effects the work
of Creation, thus demonstrating "Majesty Divine, Sapience, and
Love" (*PL* 3.170, 7.175, 194, 195).

65. Christians are to imitate the Son of God only in their mode
of self-governance, not in the specifics of action. See Shawcross,
Paradise Regain'd, 82–83, on why the Jesus of *Paradise Regained* is
not an *exemplum* in the ordinary sense of the word.

66. On the silence of Jesus in *Paradise Regained*, see Ken
Simpson, "Lingering Voices."

67. For an explanation of Jesus' response here in relation to
his earlier commendation of Socrates (*PR* 3.96–99), see Lewalski,
Milton's Brief Epic: the book 3 passage reflects "a tradition of commentary pointing to Socrates' death for truth's sake...as foreshadowing Christ's death." But in book 4, Milton's Jesus assumes "a radical
distinction between knowledge (*scientia*), which derives from the
study of the things of the world, and wisdom (*sapientia*), which
comes only from above,...a Christian commonplace prevalent
from Augustine's time through the seventeenth century....Christ's
vehement rejection of knowledge offered in place of wisdom is
firmly grounded in the tradition which identifies God as the substance and source of wisdom" (240, 291, 298).

68. In this case, Calvin's opinion resembles that of Aquinas,
who also asserts that Christ possessed empirical, acquired knowledge (*Summa Theologica*, 3.9.4).

69. See also Haskin on the traditional "joining" of "Luke and
Mary...in the imaginations of Christians" ("Milton's Portrait,"
171).

70. On Milton's handling of the Eve/Mary typology in *Paradise
Lost* and *Paradise Regained*, see Petit, "The Second Eve"; Pecheux,
"Concept of the Second Eve"; and Carolyn Smith, "Virgin Mary."

71. Milton's portrayal of Mary might be construed as countering both Calvin's insistence that Christ had no human teacher
and Aquinas's explicit denial that Mary was a teacher (*Summa
Theologica*, 3.27.5).

72. Compare Kerrigan, *The Sacred Complex*, 106–08: "Milton reveals a psychological aspect to the theological contention that Mary supplies the humanity of Christ. The hero has assimilated his mother, grieved, and identified. She is an internal presence, contributing from within to his work of salvation.... This mother removes from the life of her heroic son any possibility of duplicating the tragedy of Oedipus...; when Christ returns home, he knows who he is.... On the pinnacle he will do no more than what Mary has urged. She initiates his separation from her, a mother who does not tempt or retard, but rather propels her son to the paternal identification that resolves the Oedipus complex and organizes his autonomy."

73. See Genesis 22:12: "Then [the angel of the Lord] said, Lay not thine hand vpon the childe, nether do anie thing vnto him: for now I knowe that thou fearest God, seing for my sake thou has not spared thine onely sonne." Abraham's attitude of trust and openness is captured in his prophetic response to his son a few verses earlier; Isaac asks, "where is the lambe for the burnt offring?" and he answers, "My sonne, God wil prouide him a lambe" (Gen. 22:7, 8).

74. Rumrich, *Milton Unbound*, locates a possible source for this passage in Spenser's portrayal of Marinell's mother (*FQ* 3.4.36:1–5) and characterizes Mary's speech as expressing the "injured, almost bitter, consciousness that she has been misled by the promise of exaltation and favor" (83).

75. Boyle, "Home to Mother," argues that Milton intends the reader to recall another, later scene in the *Meditationes* in which Jesus visits his mother after the Resurrection; Milton thus achieves, she believes, "a closure so subtle and suggestive that it has eluded modern criticism" (517).

76. In his prose, Milton goes so far as to brand Saint Irenaeus "the Patron of Idolatry" for his assertion that Mary's "obedience... was the cause of salvation to her selfe, and all mankind." The point here actually has little to do with Mary, however; Milton wishes to discredit Irenaeus because defenders of prelacy have invoked him as an early "Patron of *Episcopacy*" (YP 1:642).

77. As the *OED* points out, the noun "sufferance" is related to the verb "suffer," which may be defined in distinctly feminine terms: "To be the object of an action, be acted upon, be passive" (v. def. 4). This definition includes as an example Satan's lines from *Paradise Lost* 1.157–58: "Fall'n Cherub, to be weak is miserable / Doing or Suffering."

78. Before his incarnation, the Son's "virtue" is not so clearly his "voluntary observance of the recognized moral laws or standards of right conduct" (*OED*, "virtue," n. def. 2a) or his "merit" ("virtue," n. def. 5a) as it is when God speaks of Jesus' "consummate

virtue" at *Paradise Regained* 1.165. Rather, it is the divine "power or operative influence" ("virtue," n. def. 1a) that the Father bestows on him as he sends him into battle: "Into thee such Virtue and Grace / Immense I have transfus'd, that all may know / In Heav'n and Hell thy Power above compare" (*PL* 6.703–05). In heaven and on earth, though, virtuous action "manifest[s] him worthiest to be Heir /... and to be King" not just by inheritance, but "By Sacred Unction, [his] deserved right" (*PL* 6.707–09).

79. Compare Shawcross, *Paradise Regain'd*: "The concept of meekness... is specifically associated with the mother and the return to the mother's house" (63). On Milton's belief that "obedience is not a function of servility but rather the highest form of ethical autonomy," see Schoenfeldt, "Obedience and Autonomy," 366.

Bibliography

Aers, David, and Bob Hodge. "'Rational Burning': Milton on Sex and Marriage." In *Milton Studies,* vol. 13, edited by James D. Simmonds, 3–33. Pittsburgh: University of Pittsburgh Press, 1979.

Agrippa, Henry Cornelius. *De nobilitate & praecellentia foeminei sexus.* Antwerp, 1529. Translated by Edward Fleetwood as *The Glory of Women; or, A Treatise Declaring the Excellency and Preheminence of Women Above Men.* London, 1652.

Albrecht, Roberta. *The Virgin Mary as Alchemical and Lullian Reference in John Donne.* Selinscourt, Pa.: Susquehanna University Press, 2005.

Anger, Jane. *Jane Anger her protection for women.* London: Richard Jones and Thomas Orwin, 1589. Facsimile rpt., *Defences of Women: Jane Anger, Rachel Speght, Ester Sowernam, and Constantia Munda.* Introduction by Susan Gushee O'Malley. Aldershot: Scolar Press, 1996.

The Apocrypha or Non-Canonical Books of the Bible: The King James Version. Edited by Manuel Komroff. New York: Tudor Publishing, 1936.

Aquinas, Saint Thomas. *The Summa Theologica of St. Thomas Aquinas.* Trans. Fathers of the English Dominican Province. 2nd and rev. ed. [London: Burns, Oates, and Washburne], 1920[–1942]. Available at www.newadvent.org/summa.

Arminius, Jacobus. *The Works of James Arminius.* 3 vols. Translated by James Nichols and William Nichols. Grand Rapids, Mich.: Baker Book House, 1991.

Asals, Heather. *Equivocal Predication: George Herbert's Way to God.* Toronto: University of Toronto Press, 1981.

Ashton, Robert, ed. *James I by His Contemporaries: An Account of His Career and Character as Seen by Some of His Contemporaries.* London: Hutchinson, 1969.

Aston, Margaret. *Lollards and Reformers: Images and Literacy in Late Medieval Religion*. London: Hambledon Press, 1984.

Augustine, Saint, Bishop of Hippo. *The City of God Against the Pagans*. 6 vols. Translated by G. E. McCracken, W. M. Green, D. S. Wiesen, P. Levine, E. M. Sanford, and W. C. Greene. Cambridge, Mass.: Harvard University Press, 1957–72.

———. *The Harmony of the Gospels*. Translated by S. D. F. Salmond, edited by M. B. Riddle. In *A Select Library of the Nicene and Post-Nicene Fathers of the Christian Church*, vol. 6, edited by Philip Schaff, 65–236. Grand Rapids, Mich.: W. B. Eerdmans, 1979.

———. *On Lying*. Translated by H. Browne. *A Select Library of the Nicene and Post-Nicene Fathers of the Christian Church*, vol. 3, edited by Philip Schaff, 457–77. Grand Rapids, Mich.: W. B. Eerdmans, 1979.

———. *Tractates on the Gospel of John*. 5 vols. Translated by John W. Rettig. In *The Fathers of the Church: A New Translation*, vols. 78, 79, 88, 90, 92, edited by Thomas P. Halton et al. Washington, D.C.: Catholic University of America Press, 1988–95.

———. *Sermons*. 11 vols. Translated by Edmund Hill, edited by John E. Rotelle. *The Works of Saint Augustine: A Translation for the Twenty-First Century*, part 3, vols. 1–11. Brooklyn, N.Y.: New City Press, 1990–97.

———. *The Trinity*. Translated by Edmund Hill, edited by John E. Rotelle. *The Works of Saint Augustine: A Translation for the Twenty-First Century*, part 1, vol. 5. Brooklyn, N.Y.: New City Press, 1991.

———. *The Confessions*. Translated by Maria Boulding, edited by John E. Rotelle. *The Works of Saint Augustine: A Translation for the Twenty-First Century*, part 1, vol. 1. Hyde Park, N.Y.: New City Press, 1997.

———. *Expositions of the Psalms*. 5 vols. Translated by Maria Boulding, edited by John E. Rotelle. *The Works of Saint Augustine: A Translation for the Twenty-First Century*, part 3, vols. 15–19. Brooklyn, N.Y.: New City Press, 1999–2004.

———. *On Genesis*. Translated by Edmund Hill, edited by John E. Rotelle. *The Works of Saint Augustine: A Translation for the Twenty-First Century*, part 1, vol. 13. Hyde Park, N.Y.: New City Press, 2002.

Baker-Smith, Dominic. "John Donne's *Critique of True Religion*." In Smith, *John Donne: Essays*, 404–32.

Bald, R. C. *Donne and the Drurys*. Cambridge: Cambridge University Press, 1959.

————. *John Donne: A Life*. Edited by Wesley Milgate. New York: Oxford University Press, 1970.

Bale, John. *A mysterye of inyquyte contained within the heretycall genealogye of P. Pantabolus*. Geneva: M. Woode, 1545.

Barker, Arthur E. *Milton and the Puritan Dilemma, 1641–1660*. Toronto: University of Toronto Press, 1942.

Barlow, William. *The Svmme and Svbstance of the Conference...at Hampton Court*. London: Iohn Windet, for Mathew Law, 1604.

Barroll, Leeds. "Looking for Patrons." In Grossman, *Aemilia Lanyer*, 29–48.

————. *Anna of Denmark, Queen of England: A Cultural Biography*. Philadelphia: University of Pennsylvania Press, 2001.

Beilin, Elaine. *Redeeming Eve: Women Writers of the English Renaissance*. Princeton, N.J.: Princeton University Press, 1987.

Bell, Ilona. "Gender Matters: The Women in Donne's Poems." In Guibbory, *Cambridge Companion to John Donne*, 201–16.

Benson, Pamela Joseph. "To Play the Man: Aemilia Lanyer and the Acquisition of Patronage." In *Opening the Borders: Inclusivity in Early Modern Studies: Essays in Honor of James V. Mirollo*, edited by Peter C. Herman, 243–64. Newark: University of Delaware Press, 1999.

Bergeron, David M. *Royal Family, Royal Lovers: King James of England and Scotland*. Columbia: University of Missouri Press, 1991.

Bernard of Clairvaux, Saint. *Saint Bernard on the Song of Songs: Sermones in Cantica Canticorum*. Translated and edited by a religious of C. S. M. V. London: A. R. Mowbray, 1952.

————. *Homilies in Praise of the Virgin Mary*. Translated by Marie-Bernard Saïd. Kalamazoo, Mich.: Cistercian Publications, 1993.

Berry, Boyd. "'Pardon...though I have digrest': Digression as Style in 'Salve Deus Rex Judaeorum.'" In Grossman, *Aemilia Lanyer*, 212–33.

Berry, Philippa. *Of Chastity and Power: Elizabethan Literature and the Unmarried Queen*. London: Routledge, 1989.

Bewley, Marius. "Religious Cynicism in Donne's Poetry." *Kenyon Review* 14 (1952): 619–46.

Blamires, Alcuin, Karen Pratt, and C. W. Marx, eds. *Woman Defamed and Woman Defended*. Oxford: Clarendon Press, 1992.

Blank, Paula. "Comparing Sappho to Philaenis: John Donne's 'Homopoetics.'" *PMLA* 110, no. 3 (1995): 358–68.

Boccaccio, Giovanni. *Concerning Famous Women*. Translated by Guido A. Guarino. New Brunswick, N.J.: Rutgers University Press, 1963.

Boss, Sarah Jane. *Empress and Handmaid: On Nature and Gender in the Cult of the Virgin Mary*. London: Cassell, 2000.

Bouyer, Louis. *The Seat of Wisdom: An Essay on the Place of the Virgin Mary in Christian Theology*. Translated by A. V. Littledale. New York: Pantheon Books, 1962.

Boyle, Marjorie O'Rourke. "Home to Mother: Regaining Milton's Paradise." *Modern Philology* 97, no. 3 (2000): 499–527.

Bradburie, Thomas. "On the Death of Our Late Queene." In *The Progresses, Processions, and Magnificent Festivities, of King James the First, his Royal Consort, Family, and Court; Collected from Original Manuscripts*, vol. 1, edited by John Nichols, 9. New York: Burt Franklin, 1965.

Broaddus, James W. "'Gums of Glutinous Heat' in Milton's Mask and Spenser's *Faerie Queene*." *Milton Quarterly* 37, no. 4 (2003): 205–14.

Brooks, Cleanth, and John Edward Hardy, eds. *Poems of Mr. John Milton: The 1645 Edition with Essays in Analysis*. New York: Harcourt, Brace, 1951.

Brown, Cedric. *John Milton's Aristocratic Entertainments*. Cambridge: Cambridge University Press, 1985.

Brown, Raymond E., Karl P. Donfried, Joseph A. Fitzmyer, and John Reumann, eds. *Mary in the New Testament: A Collaborative Assessment by Protestant and Roman Catholic Scholars*. Philadelphia: Fortress Press, 1978.

Byng, Tho[mas]. "You Orphane Muses..." In *The Progresses, Processions, and Magnificent Festivities, of King James the First, his Royal Consort, Family, and Court; Collected from Original Manuscripts*, vol. 1, edited by John Nichols, 8–9. New York: Burt Franklin, 1965.

Bynum, Carolyn Walker. *Jesus as Mother: Studies in the Spirituality of the High Middle Ages*. Berkeley and Los Angeles: University of California Press, 1982.

———. "'And Woman His Humanity': Female Imagery in the Religious Writings of the Later Middle Ages." In *Gender and Religion: On the Complexity of Symbols*, edited by Caroline Walker Bynum, Steven Harrell, and Paula Richman, 257–88. Boston: Beacon Press, 1986.

———. *Fragmentation and Redemption: Essays on Gender and the Human Body in Medieval Religion*. New York: Zone Books, 1991.

Byrd, William. *Gradualia: Books I and II*. Edited by P. C. Buck et al. New York: Broude Brothers, 1963.

Cain, Tom. "Donne's Political World." In Guibbory, *Cambridge Companion to John Donne*, 83–99.

Calvin, John. *The Institution of Christian Religion.* Translated by Thomas Norton. London: Arnold Hatfield for Bonham Norton, 1599.

———. *Commentary on the Gospel According to John.* 2 vols. Translated by William Pringle. Grand Rapids, Mich.: W. B. Eerdmans, 1956. *Calvin's Commentaries.* Available at www.ccel.org/ccel/calvin/calcom34.i.html.

———. *Commentary on a Harmony of the Evangelists, Matthew, Mark, and Luke.* 3 vols. Translated by William Pringle Grand Rapids, Mich.: W. B. Eerdmans, 1956–57. *Calvin's Commentaries.* Available at www.ccel.org/ccel/calvin/calcom31.i.html.

Carew, Thomas. *The Poems of Thomas Carew.* Edited by Rhodes Dunlap. Oxford: Clarendon, 1949.

Carey, John. *John Donne: Life, Mind, and Art.* New York: Oxford University Press, 1981.

Carey, John, ed. *Milton: The Complete Shorter Poems.* London: Longman, 1971.

Carpenter, Nan Cooke. "Milton and Music: Henry Lawes, Dante, and Casella." *English Literary Renaissance* 2 (1972): 237–42.

The Catholic Encyclopedia. 15 vols. Edited by Charles G. Herbermann et al. New York: Robert Appleton Company, 1907–22. Available at www.newadvent.org/cathen/index.html.

Cavanagh, Sheila T. *Wanton Eyes and Chaste Desires: Female Sexuality in* The Faerie Queene. Bloomington: Indiana University Press, 1994.

Chambers, A. B. "*La Corona:* Philosophic, Sacred, and Poetic Uses of Time." In *New Essays on Donne,* edited by Gary A. Stringer, 140–72. Salzburg: Institut für Englische Sprache unde Literature, 1977.

Chambers, E. K., ed. *The Poems of John Donne.* 2 vols. London: Lawrence & Bullen, 1896.

Champagne, Claudia M. "Adam and His 'Other Self' in *Paradise Lost:* A Lacanian Study in Psychic Development." *Milton Quarterly* 25, no. 2 (1991): 48–59.

Chaucer, Geoffrey. *Chaucer's Major Poetry.* Edited by Albert C. Baugh. Englewood Cliffs, N.J.: Prentice-Hall, 1963.

Chavasse, Claude. *The Bride of Christ: An Enquiry into the Nuptial Element in Early Christianity.* London: The Religious Book Club, [1939?].

Christine de Pizan. *The Book of the City of Ladies.* Translated by Earl Jeffrey Richards. New York: Persea Books, 1982.

Christopher, Georgia B. *Milton and the Science of the Saints.* Princeton, N.J.: Princeton University Press, 1982.

Church of England. *Articles whereupon it was agreed by the Archbishoppes and Bishoppes ... 1562.* London: Richard Jugge and John Cawood, 1571.

————. *Certaine Sermons or Homilies Appointed to be Read in Churches In the Time of Queen Elizabeth I (1547–1571). A Facsimile Reproduction of the Edition of 1623*. 2 vols. in 1. Introduction by Mary Ellen Rickey and Thomas B. Stroup. Gainseville, Fla : Scholars' Facsimiles and Reprints, 1968.

————. *The Book of Common Prayer 1559. The Elizabethan Prayer Book*. Edited by John E. Booty. Charlottesville: University Press of Virginia, 1976.

Clarke, Danielle. "The Iconography of the Blush: Marian Literature of the 1630s." In *Voicing Women: Gender and Sexuality in Early Modern Writing*, edited by Kate Chedgzoy, Melanie Hansen, and Suzanne Trill, 111–28. Pittsburgh: Duquesne University Press, 1997.

————. " 'Lovers' Songs Shall Turne to Holy Psalmes': Mary Sidney and the Transformation of Petrarch." *Modern Language Review* 92, no. 2 (1997): 282–94.

Coffin, Charles Monroe. *John Donne and the New Philosophy*. Morningside Heights, N.Y.: Columbia University Press, 1937.

Coiro, Ann Baynes. "Writing in Service: Sexual Politics and Class Position in the Poetry of Aemilia Lanyer." *Criticism* 35 (1993): 357–76.

Cook, Eleanor. "Melos versus Logos, or Why Doesn't God Sing: Some Thoughts on Milton's Wisdom." In *Re-membering Milton: Essays on the Texts and Traditions*, edited by Mary Nyquist and Margaret W. Ferguson, 197–210. New York: Methuen, 1987.

Cook, Patrick. "Aemilia Lanyer's 'Description of Cooke-ham' as Devotional Lyric." In Cunnar and Johnson, *Discovering and (Re)covering*, 104–18.

Corns, Thomas N., ed. *A Companion to Milton*. Malden, Mass.: Blackwell, 2003.

Correll, Barbara. "Symbolic Economies and Zero-Sum Erotics: Donne's 'Sapho to Philaenis.'" *ELH* 62, no. 3 (1995): 487–507.

Corthell, Ronald. "The Obscure Object of Desire: Donne's *Anniversaries* and the Cultural Production of Elizabeth Drury." In *Critical Essays on John Donne*, edited by Arthur F. Marotti, 123–40. New York: G. K. Hall, 1994.

————. "Go Ask Alice: Daughter, Patron, and Poet in *A Mask Presented at Ludlow Castle*." In *Milton Studies*, vol. 44, edited by Albert C. Labriola, 111–128. Pittsburgh: University of Pittsburgh Press, 2005.

The Coverdale Bible 1535. Introduction by S. L. Greenslade. London: Dawson, 1975.

Cox, Catherine I. "The Garden Within: Milton's Ludlow Masque and the Tradition of Canticles." In *Milton Studies*, vol. 31, edited by Albert C. Labriola, 23–43. Pittsburgh: University of Pittsburgh Press, 1994.

Creaser, John. "'The present aid of this occasion': The Setting of Comus." In Lindley, *The Court Masque*, 111–34.

Cressy, David. *Birth, Marriage, and Death: Ritual, Religion, and the Life-Cycle in Tudor and Stuart England*. Oxford: Oxford University Press, 1997.

Cunnar, Eugene R., and Jeffrey Johnson, eds. *Discovering and (Re)covering the Seventeenth-Century Religious Lyric*. Pittsburgh: Duquesne University Press, 2001.

Daniel, Samuel. *The vision of the 12. goddesses*. London: T. C. for Simon Waterson, 1604.

Danielson, Dennis. "Through the Telescope of Typology: What Adam Should Have Done." *Milton Quarterly* 23, no. 3 (1989): 121–27.

Davies, Stevie. *The Feminine Reclaimed: The Idea of Woman in Spenser, Shakespeare, and Milton*. Lexington: University Press of Kentucky, 1986.

Davies, Stevie, and William B. Hunter. "Milton's Urania: 'The Meaning, Not the Name I Call.'" In William B. Hunter, *The Descent of Urania: Studies in Milton 1946–1988*, 31–45. Lewisburg, Pa.: Bucknell University Press, 1989.

Diekhoff, John S., ed. A Maske at Ludlow: *Essays on Milton's Comus*. Cleveland: The Press of Case Western Reserve University, 1968.

DiPasquale, Theresa. *Literature and Sacrament: The Sacred and the Secular in John Donne*. Pittsburgh: Duquesne University Press, 1999.

———. "Woman's Desire for Man in Lanyer's *Salve Deus Rex Judaeorum*." *Journal of English and Germanic Philology* 99, no. 3 (2000): 356–78.

———. "Donne's *Epigrams*: A Sequential Reading." *Modern Philology* 104.3 (February 2007): 329–78.

Docherty, Thomas. *John Donne, Undone*. London: Methuen, 1986.

Doerksen, Daniel. "Polemist or Pastor? Donne and Moderate Calvinist Conformity." In Papazian, *John Donne*, 12–34.

Doerksen, Daniel W., and Christopher Hodgkins, eds. *Centered on the Word: Literature, Scripture, and the Tudor-Stuart Middle Way*. Newark: University of Delaware Press, 2004.

Donne, John. *The Sermons of John Donne*. 10 vols. Edited by George R. Potter and Evelyn M. Simpson. Berkeley and Los Angeles: University of California Press, 1953–62.

———. *The Complete Poetry of John Donne*. Edited by John T. Shawcross. Garden City, N.Y.: Doubleday, 1967.

———. *Pseudo-Martyr: A Facsimile Reproduction.* 1610. Delmar, N.J.: Scholars' Facsimiles and Reprints, 1974.

———. *Letters to Several Persons of Honour.* London: J. Flesher for Richard Marriot, 1651. Introduction by M. Thomas Hester. Delmar, N.Y.: Scholars' Facsimiles and Reprints, 1977. Facsimile reprint.

———. *Devotions Upon Emergent Occasions Together with Death's Duel.* Ann Arbor: University of Michigan Press, 1978.

———. *The Anniversaries and the Epicedes and Obsequies.* Edited by Ted-Larry Pebworth et al. Vol. 6, *The Variorum Edition of the Poetry of John Donne.* Gen. ed. Gary A. Stringer. Bloomington: Indiana University Press, 1995.

———. *The Epigrams, Epithalamions, Epitaphs, Inscriptions, and Miscellaneous Poems.* Edited by Ted-Larry Pebworth et al. Vol. 8, *The Variorum Edition of the Poetry of John Donne,* gen. ed. Gary A. Stringer. Bloomington: Indiana University Press, 1995.

———. *The Elegies.* Edited by Ted-Larry Pebworth et al. Vol. 2, *The Variorum Edition of the Poetry of John Donne,* gen. ed. Gary A. Stringer. Bloomington: Indiana University Press, 2000.

———. *The Holy Sonnets.* Edited by Dennis Flynn et al. Vol. 7, part 1, *The Variorum Edition of the Poetry of John Donne,* gen. ed. Gary A. Stringer. Bloomington: Indiana University Press, 2005.

Dubrow, Heather. "The Masquing of Genre in *Comus.*" In *Milton Studies,* vol. 44, edited by Albert C. Labriola, 62–83. Pittsburgh: University of Pittsburgh Press, 2005.

Duerden, Richard. "Crossings: Class, Gender, Chiasmus, and the Cross in Aemilia Lanyer's *Salve Deus Rex Judaeorum.*" *Literature and Belief* 19 (1999): 131–52.

Eggert, Katherine. *Showing Like a Queen: Female Authority and Literary Experiment in Spenser, Shakespeare, and Milton.* Philadelphia: University of Pennsylvania Press, 2000.

Elyot, Thomas. *The Boke named the Gouernour.* 2 vols. Edited by H. H. S. Croft. London: K. Paul, Trench, 1880.

Empson, William. *English Pastoral Poetry.* New York: Norton, 1938.

Erne, Lukas. "Donne and Christ's Spouse." *Essays in Criticism* 51, no. 2 (2001): 208–29.

Faulkner, Eleanor and Edgar F. Daniels. "Donne's *Holy Sonnets* XVII (Since she whom I lovd), 1–2." *Explicator* 34 (1976): item 68.

Ferry, Anne D. *Milton's Epic Voice: The Narrator in* Paradise Lost. Cambridge, Mass.: Harvard University Press, 1963.

Fielding, Edwina. "John Donne and the New Christianity." *The Month* 42 (1969): 194–202.

Fish, Stanley. "Masculine Persuasive Force: Donne and Verbal Power." In *Soliciting Interpretation: Literary Theory and Seventeenth-Century English Poetry*, edited by Elizabeth D. Harvey and Katharine Eisaman Maus, 223–52. Chicago: University of Chicago Press, 1990.

———. "Why Milton Matters: Or, Against Historicism." In *Milton Studies*, vol. 44, edited by Albert C. Labriola, 1–12. Pittsburgh: University of Pittsburgh Press, 2005.

Fisken, Beth Wynne. "Mary Sidney's *Psalmes*: Education and Wisdom." In Hannay, *Silent But for the Word*, 166–83.

Flynn, Dennis. "Irony in Donne's *Biathanatos* and *Pseudo-Martyr*." *Recusant History* 12 (1973): 49–69.

———. "Donne's Catholicism: I." *Recusant History* 13 (1975): 1–17.

———. "Donne's Catholicism: II." *Recusant History* 13 (1975): 178–95.

———. "The 'Annales School' and the Catholicism of Donne's Family." *John Donne Journal* 2 (1983): 1–9.

———. "Donne the Survivor." In Summers and Pebworth, *The Eagle and the Dove*, 15–24.

———. "Donne's *Ignatius His Conclave* and Other Libels on Sir Robert Cecil." *John Donne Journal* 6 (1987): 163–83.

———. "'Awry and Squint': The Dating of Donne's Holy Sonnets." *John Donne Journal* 7 (1988): 35–46.

———. "A Biographical Prolusion to Study of Donne's Religious Imagination." In Frontain and Malpezzi, *John Donne's Religious Imagination*, 28–44.

———. "Donne, Henry Wotton, and the Earl of Essex." *John Donne Journal* 14 (1995): 185–218.

———. *John Donne and the Ancient Catholic Nobility*. Bloomington: Indiana University Press, 1995.

Fogle, French R. "'Such a Rural Queen': The Countess Dowager of Derby as Patron." In *Patronage in Late Renaissance England*, edited by French R. Fogle and Louis A. Knafla, 1–29. Los Angeles: William Andrews Clark Memorial Library, 1983.

Fowler, Alastair, ed. *Milton: Paradise Lost*. New York, London: Longman, 1971.

Frere, W. H. *The English Church in the Reigns of Elizabeth and James I*. New York: AMS, [1968].

Frontain, Raymond-Jean. "Donne's Imperfect Resurrection." *Papers on Language and Literature* 26 (1990): 539–45.

———. "Donne's Protestant *Paradiso*: The Johannine Vision of the *Second Anniversary*." In Papazian, *John Donne*, 113–42.

———. "Law, Song, and Memory: The Mosaic Voice of Donne's *First Anniversarie*." *Literature and Belief* 19 (1999): 154–74.

———. "'The Name of Shee': The Biblical Logocentrism of Donne's *Anniversaries*." *Publications of the Missouri Philological Association* 22 (1997): 28–39.

Frontain, Raymond-Jean, and Frances M. Malpezzi, eds. *John Donne's Religious Imagination: Essays in Honor of John T. Shawcross*. Conway, Ariz.: University of Central Arkansas Press, 1995.

Frost, Kate Gartner. "*Magnus Pan Mortuus Est*: A Subtextual and Contextual Reading of Donne's 'Resurrection, imperfect.'" In Frontain and Malpezzi, *John Donne's Religious Imagination*, 231–61.

Gardner, Helen, ed. *The Divine Poems of John Donne*. 2nd ed. Oxford: Clarendon, 1982.

The Geneva Bible: A facsimile of the 1560 edition. Madison: University of Wisconsin Press, 1969.

The Geneva Bible: A facsimile of the 1599 edition with undated Sternhold & Hopkins Psalms. Ozark, Mo.: L. L. Brown, 1995.

Goldberg, Jonathan. *James I and the Politics of Literature*. Baltimore: Johns Hopkins University Press, 1983.

———. *Desiring Women Writing: English Renaissance Examples*. Stanford, Calif.: Stanford University Press, 1998.

The Golden Legend; or, Lives of the Saints, as Englished by William Caxton. 7 vols. Edited by F. S. Ellis. London: J. M. Dent, 1900.

Good, Deirdre, ed. *Mariam, the Magdalen, and the Mother*. Bloomington: Indiana University Press, 2005.

Gosse, Edmund. *The Life and Letters of John Donne*. 2 vols. Gloucester, Mass.: Peter Smith, 1959.

Gosynhill, Edward. *The Prayse of all women called Mulieru[m] Pean*. London: W. Myddylton, [1542?].

Graef, Hilda. *Mary: A History of Doctrine and Devotion*. 2 vols. in 1. Westminster, Md.: Christian Classics, 1985.

The Great Bible: A Facsimile of the 1539 Edition. Introduction by Yoshio Teresawa. Tokyo: Elpis, 1991.

Grenander, M. E. "Holy Sonnets VIII and XVII: John Donne." *Boston University Studies in English* 4, no. 2 (1960): 95–105.

Grierson, Herbert J. C. *Criticism and Creation: Essays and Addresses*. London: Chatto and Windus, 1944.

Grierson, Herbert J. C., ed. *The Poems of John Donne*. 2 vols. Oxford: Clarendon, 1912.

Grossman, Marshall. "The Genders of God and the Redemption of the Flesh in *Paradise Lost*." In Martin, *Milton and Gender*, 95–114.

Grossman, Marshall, ed. *Aemilia Lanyer: Gender, Genre, and the Canon*. Lexington: University Press of Kentucky, 1998.

Guibbory, Achsah. "'Oh, Let Mee Not Serve So': The Politics of Love in Donne's Elegies." *ELH* 57 (1990): 811–33.

———. "Donne, Milton, and Holy Sex." In *Milton Studies*, vol. 32, edited by Albert C. Labriola, 3–21. Pittsburgh: University of Pittsburgh Press, 1996.

———. "Fear of 'loving more': Death and the Loss of Sacramental Love." In Hester, *John Donne's "desire,"* 204–27.

———. "The Gospel According to Aemilia: Women and the Sacred in Aemilia Lanyer's *Salve Deus Rex Judaeorum.*" In Grossman, *Aemilia Lanyer*, 191–211.

———. "'The Relique,' *The Song of Songs*, and Donne's *Songs and Sonets.*" *John Donne Journal* 15 (1996): 23–44.

Guibbory, Achsah, ed. *The Cambridge Companion to John Donne.* Cambridge: Cambridge University Press, 2006.

Hackett, Helen. *Virgin Mother, Maiden Queen: Elizabeth I and the Cult of the Virgin Mary.* New York: St. Martin's, 1995.

Hadfield, Andrew. "Literary Contexts: Predecessors and Contemporaries." In Guibbory, *Cambridge Companion to John Donne*, 49–64.

Haller, William. "'Hail Wedded Love.'" *ELH* 13, no. 2 (1946): 79–97.

Hanford, James Holly. "Haemony (*Comus* 616–648)." *Times Literary Supplement*, November 3, 1932, 815.

Hannay, Margaret P. "'House-Confinèd Maids': The Presentation of Woman's Role in the Psalmes of the Countess of Pembroke." *English Literary Renaissance* 24, no. 1 (1994): 44–71.

Hannay, Margaret P., ed. *Silent But for the Word: Tudor Women as Patrons, Translators, and Writers of Religious Works.* Kent, Ohio: Kent State University Press, 1985.

Hardison, O. B. *The Enduring Monument: A Study of the Idea of Praise in Renaissance Literary Theory and Practice.* Chapel Hill: University of North Carolina Press, 1962.

Harington, John. "Welcome to the King." In *The Progresses, Processions, and Magnificent Festivities, of King James the First, his Royal Consort, Family, and Court; Collected from Original Manuscripts*, vol. 1, edited by John Nichols, 49. New York: Burt Franklin, 1965.

Harvey, Elizabeth D. "Ventriloquizing Sappho: Or, the Lesbian Muse." In *Re-Reading Sappho: Reception and Transmission*, edited by Ellen Greene, 79–104. Berkeley and Los Angeles: University of California Press, 1996.

Haskin, Dayton. "Matthew, Mary, Luke, and John: The Mother of the Word in Milton's Poetry." *Proceedings of the PMR Conference* 10 (1985): 75–86.

———. "Milton's Portrait of Mary as Bearer of the Word." In *Milton and the Idea of Woman*, edited by Julia M. Walker, 169–84. Urbana: University of Illinois Press, 1988.

Haskins, Susan. *Mary Magdalen: Myth and Metaphor*. London: HarperCollins, 1993.

Heale, William. *An Apologie for Women*. Oxford: Joseph Barnes, 1609.

Healy, T. S., ed. *Ignatius His Conclave*, by John Donne. Oxford: Clarendon, 1969.

Herbert, George. *The Works of George Herbert*. Edited by F. E. Hutchinson. Oxford: Clarendon, 1941.

Herz, Judith Scherer. "Aemilia Lanyer and the Pathos of Literary History." In *Representing Women in Renaissance England*, edited by Claude J. Summers and Ted-Larry Pebworth, 121–35. Columbia: University of Missouri Press, 1997.

Hester, M. Thomas. *'Kinde Pitty and Brave Scorne': John Donne's 'Satyres.'* Durham, N.C.: Duke University Press, 1982.

———. "Donne's (Re)Annunciation of the Virgin(ia Colony) in Elegy XIX." *South Central Review* 4 (1987): 49–64.

———. "'This cannot be said': A Preface to the Reader of Donne's Lyrics." *Christianity and Literature* 39 (1990): 365–85.

———. "'Fæminæ lectissimæ': Reading Anne Donne." In Hester, *John Donne's "desire,"* 17–34.

———. "'Let me love': Reading the Sacred 'Currant' of Donne's Profane Lyrics." In Wilcox, Todd, and MacDonald, *Sacred and Profane*, 129–50.

Hester, M. Thomas, ed. *John Donne's "desire of more": The Subject of Anne More Donne in His Poetry*. Newark: University of Delaware Press, 1996.

Hill, Elizabeth. "The Parable of the Absent Lover: Joy and Anguish in Quarles' Emblemes." *Greyfriar: Siena Studies in Literature* 30 (1989–90): 13–34.

Hodgson, Elizabeth. *Gender and the Sacred Self in John Donne*. Newark: University of Delaware Press, 1999.

Holmes, Michael Morgan. "The Love of Other Women: Rich Chains and Sweet Kisses." In Grossman, *Aemilia Lanyer*, 167–90.

Holstun, James. "'Will you rent our ancient love asunder?' Lesbian Elegy in Donne, Marvell, and Milton." *ELH* 54, no. 4 (1987): 835–67.

The Holy Bible... Set Forth in 1611 and Commonly Known as the King James Version. New York: American Bible Society, n.d.

The Holy Bible, Translated from the Latin Vulgate... the Old Testament first published by the English college at Douay, A.D. 1609, and the New Testament first published by the English college at Rheims, A.D. 1582. Rockford, Ill.: Tan Books, 1971.

Honeygosky, Stephen R. *Milton's House of God: The Invisible and Visible Church*. Columbia: University of Missouri Press, 1993.

Hooker, Richard. *Of the Laws of Ecclesiastical Polity: And Other Works*. 3 vols. Edited by John Keble. Revised by R. W. Church and F. Paget. Ellicott City, Md.: Via Media, 1994.

Hughes, Merritt Y., ed. *Paradise Lost: A Poem in Twelve Books*, by John Milton. New York: Macmillan, 1962.

Hughes, Richard E. "The Woman in Donne's *Anniversaries*." *ELH* 34 (1967): 307–26.

Hunter, William B. "Prophetic Dreams and Visions in *Paradise Lost*." *Modern Language Quarterly* 9 (1948): 277–85.

Hutson, Lorna. "Why the Lady's Eyes Are Nothing Like the Sun." In *Women, Texts, and Histories 1575–1760*, edited by Clare Brant and Diane Purkiss, 13–38. London: Routledge, 1992.

I. G. *An Apologie For Womenkinde*. London: Ed. Allde for William Ferebrand, 1605.

Infante, Cecilia. "Donne's Incarnate Muse and His Claim to Poetic Control in 'Sapho to Philaenis.'" In *Representing Women in Renaissance England*, edited by Claude J. Summers and Ted-Larry Pebworth, 93–106. Columbia: University of Missouri Press, 1997.

Jackson, Robert S. *John Donne's Christian Vocation*. Evanston, Ill.: Northwestern University Press, 1970.

James I, King of England and Scotland. *Triplici nodo, triplex cuneus. Or an Apologie for the Oath of Allegiance*. London: Robert Barker, 1607. Facsimile reprint as *De Triplici Nodo: The Corrected Copy for the Second Edition*. Alburgh: Archival Facsimiles, 1987.

———. *Political Works of James I*. Edited by C. H. McIlwain. Cambridge, Mass.: Harvard University Press, 1918.

———. *Letters of King James VI & I*. Edited by G. P. V. Akrigg. Berkeley and Los Angeles: University of California Press, 1984.

———. *Political Writings*. Edited by Johann P. Sommerville. Cambridge: Cambridge University Press, 1994.

———. *Selected Writings*. Edited by Neil Rhodes, Jennifer Richards, and Joseph Marshall. Aldershot: Ashgate, 2003.

Jayne, Sears. "The Subject of Milton's Ludlow Masque." In Diekhoff, *Essays on Milton's Comus*, 165–87.

Johnson, Jeffrey. *The Theology of John Donne*. Woodbridge: D. S. Brewer, 1999.

Jonson, Ben. "Ben Jonson's Conversations with William Drummond of Hawthornden." 1619. In *Ben Jonson*, 11 vols., edited by C. H. Herford and Percy Simpson, 1:128–78. Oxford: Clarendon, 1925.

————. *The Complete Masques.* Edited by Stephen Orgel. New Haven: Yale University Press, 1969.

————. *The Complete Poems.* Edited by George Parfitt. New Haven: Yale University Press, 1982.

Jordan, Richard Douglas. *The Quiet Hero: Figures of Temperance in Spenser, Donne, Milton, and Joyce.* Washington, D.C.: Catholic University of America Press, 1989.

Keohane, Catherine. "'That blindest Weaknesse be not over-bold': Aemilia Lanyer's Radical Unfolding of the Passion." *ELH* 64, no. 2 (1997): 359–90.

Kermode, Frank, ed. *The Poems of John Donne.* New York: Heritage Press, 1970.

Kerrigan, William. *The Sacred Complex: On the Psychogenesis of Paradise Lost.* Cambridge, Mass.: Harvard University Press, 1983.

————. "The Politically Correct Comus: A Reply to John Leonard." *Milton Quarterly* 27, no. 4 (1993): 147–53.

Kerrigan, William W., and Gordon Braden. "Milton's Coy Eve: *Paradise Lost* and Renaissance Love Poetry." *ELH* 53 (1986): 27–51.

King, John. "Milton and the Bishops: Ecclesiastical Controversy and the Early Poems." In Doerksen and Hodgkins, *Centered on the Word,* 277–97.

Kirkpatrick, Hugh. "Donne's 'Upon the Annunciation and Passion Falling upon One Day. 1608.'" *Explicator* 30 (1972): item 39.

Klawitter, George. "John Donne's Attitude toward the Virgin Mary: The Public versus the Private Voice." In Frontain and Malpezzi, *John Donne's Religious Imagination,* 122–40.

Kremen, Kathryn R. *The Imagination of the Resurrection: The Poetic Continuity of a Religious Motif in Donne, Blake, and Yeats.* Lewisburg, Pa.: Bucknell University Press, 1972.

Krontiris, Tina. *Oppositional Voices: Women as Writers and Translators of Literature in the English Renaissance.* London: Routledge, 1992.

Labriola, Albert C. "Painting and Poetry of the Cult of Elizabeth I: The Ditchley Portrait and Donne's 'Elegie: Going to Bed.'" *Studies in Philology* 93, no. 1 (1996): 42–63.

Lamb, Mary Ellen. "Patronage and Class in Aemilia Lanyer's *Salve Deus Rex Judaeorum.*" In *Women, Writing, and the Reproduction of Culture in Tudor and Stuart Britain,* edited by Mary E. Burke, Jane Donawerth, Linda L. Dove, and Karen Nelson, 38–57. Syracuse, N.Y.: Syracuse University Press, 2000.

Lanyer, Aemilia. *The Poems of Aemilia Lanyer: Salve Deus Rex Judaeorum*. Edited by Susanne Woods. New York: Oxford University Press, 1993.

Lee, Maurice, Jr. *Great Britain's Solomon: James VI and I in His Three Kingdoms*. Urbana: University of Illinois Press, 1990.

Leonard, John. "'Good things': A Reply to William Kerrigan." *Milton Quarterly* 30, no. 3 (1996): 117–27.

———. *Naming in Paradise: Milton and the Language of Adam and Eve*. Oxford: Clarendon, 1990.

———. "Saying 'No' to Freud: Milton's *A Mask* and Sexual Assault." *Milton Quarterly* 25, no. 4 (1991): 29–40.

Levine, Amy-Jill, and Marianne Blickenstaff, eds. *A Feminist Companion to Paul*. Cleveland, Ohio: Pilgrim Press, 2004.

———. *A Feminist Companion to the Deutero-Pauline Epistles*. Cleveland, Ohio: Pilgrim Press, 2003.

Lewalski, Barbara K. *Milton's Brief Epic: The Genre, Meaning, and Art of* Paradise Regained. Providence, R.I.: Brown University Press, 1966.

———. *Donne's* Anniversaries *and the Poetry of Praise: The Creation of a Symbolic Mode*. Princeton, N.J.: Princeton University Press, 1973.

———. *Protestant Poetics and the Seventeenth-Century Religious Lyric*. Princeton, N.J.: Princeton University Press, 1979.

———. "Of God and Good Women: The Poems of Aemilia Lanyer." In Hannay, *Silent But for the Word*, 203–24.

———. Paradise Lost *and the Rhetoric of Literary Forms*. Princeton, N.J.: Princeton University Press, 1985.

———. "Re-Writing Patriarchy and Patronage: Margaret Clifford, Anne Clifford, and Aemilia Lanyer." *The Yearbook of English Studies* 21 (1991): 87–106.

———. *Writing Women in Jacobean England*. Cambridge, Mass.: Harvard University Press, 1993.

———. "Milton's *Comus* and the Politics of Masquing." In *The Politics of the Stuart Court Masque*, edited by David Bevington and Peter Holbrook. Cambridge: Cambridge University Press, 1998.

Lindley, David. *The Trials of Frances Howard: Fact and Fiction at the Court of King James*. London: Routledge, 1993.

Lindley, David, ed. *The Court Masque*. Manchester: Manchester University Press, 1984.

———. *Court Masques: Jacobean and Caroline Entertainments, 1605–1640*. New York: Oxford University Press, 1995.

Linsley, Joy L. "A Holy Puzzle: John Donne's 'Holy Sonnet XVII.'" In Frontain and Malpezzi, *John Donne's Religious Imagination*, 202–13.

Long, Mary Beth. "Contextualizing Eve's and Milton's Solitudes in Book 9 of *Paradise Lost.*" *Milton Quarterly* 37, no. 2 (2003): 100–115.

Loughlin, Marie H. "'Fast ti'd unto them in a golden Chaine': Typology, Apocalypse, and Woman's Genealogy in Aemilia Lanyer's *Salve Deus Rex Judaeorum.*" *Renaissance Quarterly* 53, no. 1 (2000): 133–79.

Love, Harold. "The Argument of Donne's *First Anniversary.*" In *Essential Articles for the Study of John Donne's Poetry*, edited by John R. Roberts, 355–62. Hamden, Conn.: Archon Books, 1975.

Lovelace, Richard. *The Poems of Richard Lovelace*, edited by C. H. Wilkinson. Oxford: Clarendon, 1953.

Low, Anthony. "Eve's Additions to the Command: Milton and Donne." *Milton Quarterly* 13 (1979): 20.

———. *The Reinvention of Love: Poetry, Politics, and Culture from Sidney to Milton.* Cambridge: Cambridge University Press, 1993.

MacLure, Millar. "Nature and Art in *The Faerie Queene.*" *ELH* 28, no. 1 (1961): 1–20.

Madsen, William G. *From Shadowy Types to Truth: Studies in Milton's Symbolism.* New Haven: Yale University Press, 1968.

Malpezzi, Frances. "Adam, Christ, and Mr. Tilman: God's Blest Hermaphrodites." *American Benedictine Review* 40 (1989): 250–60.

———. "Donne's Transcendent Imagination: The Divine Poems as Hierophantic Experience." In Frontain and Malpezzi, *John Donne's Religious Imagination*, 141–61.

———. "Love's Liquidity in 'Since she whome I lovd.'" In Hester, *John Donne's "desire,"* 196–203.

Manley, Frank, ed. *John Donne: The Anniversaries.* Baltimore: Johns Hopkins Press, 1963.

Mann, Lindsay A. "The Typology of Woman in Donne's *Anniversaries.*" *Renaissance and Reformation* 23 (1987): 337–50.

Manningham, John. *The Diary of John Manningham of the Middle Temple, 1602–1603: Newly Edited in Complete and Unexpurgated Form from the Original Manuscript in the British Museum.* Edited by Robert Parker Sorlien. Hanover, N.H.: University Press of New England, 1976.

Marcus, Leah. *The Politics of Mirth: Jonson, Herrick, Milton, Marvell, and Defense of Old Holiday Pastimes.* Chicago: University of Chicago Press, 1986.

Martin, Catherine Gimelli. "Demystifying Disguises: Adam, Eve, and the Subject of Desire." In *Renaissance Discourses of Desire*, edited by Claude J. Summers and Ted-Larry Pebworth, 237–258. Columbia: University of Missouri Press, 1993.

———. "The Non-Puritan Ethics, Metaphysics, and Aesthetics of Milton's Spensarian Masque." *Milton Quarterly* 37, no. 4 (2003): 215–44.

———. "Unmeete Contraryes: The Reformed Subject and the Triangulation of Religious Desire in Donne's *Anniversaries* and *Holy Sonnets*." In Papazian, *John Donne*, 193–220.

Martin, Catherine Gimelli, ed. *Milton and Gender*. Cambridge: Cambridge University Press, 2004.

Martz, Louis L. *The Poetry of Meditation: A Study in English Religious Literature of the Seventeenth Century*. New Haven: Yale University Press, 1954.

———. "The Action of the Self: Devotional Poetry in the Seventeenth Century." In *Metaphysical Poetry*, edited by Malcolm Bradbury and David Palmer, 101–21. Stratford-upon-Avon Studies 11. London: Edward Arnold, 1970.

Maurer, Margaret. "The Real Presence of Lucy Russell, Countess of Bedford, and the Terms of John Donne's 'Honour is so sublime perfection.'" *ELH* 47 (1980): 205–34.

McBride, Kari Boyd. "Remembering Orpheus in the Poems of Aemilia Lanyer." *SEL: Studies in English Literature, 1500–1900* 38, no. 1 (1998): 87–108.

———. "Sacred Celebration: The Patronage Poems." In Grossman, *Aemilia Lanyer*, 60–82.

———. *Country House Discourse in Early Modern England*. Aldershot: Ashgate, 2001.

———. "Gender and Judaism in Meditations on the Passion: Middleton, Southwell, Lanyer, and Fletcher." In Cunnar and Johnson, *Discovering and (Re)covering*, 17–40.

McBride, Kari Boyd, and John C. Ulreich. "'Eve's Apologie': Agrippa, Lanyer, and Milton." In *"All in All": Unity, Diversity, and the Miltonic Perspective*, edited by Charles W. Durham and Kristin A. Pruitt, 100–111. London: Associated University Presses, 1999.

———. "Answerable Styles: Biblical Poetics and Biblical Politics in the Poetry of Lanyer and Milton." *Journal of English and Germanic Philology* 100, no. 3 (2001): 333–54.

McColley, Diane Kelsey. *Milton's Eve*. Urbana: University of Illinois Press, 1983.

———. *A Gust For Paradise: Milton's Eden and the Visual Arts*. Urbana: University of Illinois Press, 1993.

———. "Milton and Ecology." In Corns, *A Companion to Milton*, 157–73.

McDuffie, Felicia Wright. *To Our Bodies Turn We Then: Body as Word and Sacrament in the Works of John Donne*. New York: Continuum, 2005.

McGrath, Lynnette. "Metaphoric Subversions: Feasts and Mirrors in Amelia Lanier's *Salve Deus Rex Judaeorum*." *LIT: Literature-Interpretation-Theory* 3 (1991): 101–13.

———. "'Let Us Have Our Libertie Againe': Aemilia Lanyer's Seventeenth-Century Feminist Voice." *Women's Studies* 20 (1992): 331–48.

———. *Subjectivity and Women's Poetry in Early Modern England*. Aldershot: Ashgate, 2002.

McGuire, Maryann Cale. *Milton's Puritan Masque*. Athens: University of Georgia Press, 1983.

McMichaels, John. "The Lady Rises: Stoicism and Spenser in Milton's *Comus*." *Renaissance Papers* (1998): 151–63.

Meakin, H. L. *John Donne's Articulations of the Feminine*. Oxford: Clarendon, 1998.

Milgate, Wesley, ed. *John Donne: The Epithalamions, Anniversaries, and Epicedes*. Oxford: Clarendon, 1978.

Miller, Naomi J. "(M)other Tongues: Maternity and Subjectivity." In Grossman, *Aemilia Lanyer*, 143–66.

Milton, John. *Complete Poems and Major Prose*. Edited by Merritt Y. Hughes. New York: Macmillan, 1957.

———. *Complete Prose Works of John Milton*. 8 vols. Edited by Don M. Wolfe et al. New Haven: Yale University Press, 1953–82.

Mollenkott, Virginia R. "The Pervasive Influence of the Apocrypha in Milton's Thought and Art." In *Milton and the Art of Sacred Song*, edited by J. Max Patrick and Roger H. Sundell, 23–43. Madison, Wis.: University of Wisconsin Press, 1979.

Moloney, Michael F. *John Donne: His Flight from Medievalism*. New York: Russell & Russell, 1965.

Morris, Harry. "John Donne's Terrifying Pun." *Papers on Language and Literature* 9, no. 2 (1973): 128–37.

Morris, June. "A Study of Humor in Donne's Anniversaries: 'How Witty's Ruin?'" *English Miscellany* 28 (1979): 157–70.

Mueller, Janel. "Lesbian Erotics: The Utopian Trope of Donne's 'Sapho to Philaenis.'" In *Homosexuality in Renaissance and Enlightenment England: Literary Representations in Historical Context*, edited by Claude J. Summers, 103–34. New York: Haworth Press, 1992.

———. "The Feminist Poetics of Aemilia Lanyer's 'Salve Deus Rex Judaeorum.'" In Grossman, *Aemilia Lanyer*, 99–127.

Neff, Amy. "The Pain of *Compassio:* Mary's Labor at the Foot of the Cross." *The Art Bulletin* 80, no. 2 (1998): 254–73.

Nelson, Holly Faith. "Gender and Politics in the Writings of Henry Vaughan." *Scintilla* 7 (2003): 99–115.

Newman, Barbara. *Sister of Wisdom: St. Hildegard's Theology of the Feminine.* Berkeley and Los Angeles: University of California Press, 1987.

——. *God and the Goddesses: Vision, Poetry, and Belief in the Middle Ages.* Philadelphia: University of Pennsylvania Press, 2003.

The New Oxford Annotated Bible with the Apocryphal / Deuterocanonical Books. Edited by Bruce M. Metzger and Roland E. Murphy. New York: Oxford University Press, 1994.

The New Testament, translated by W. Tyndale 1534. Edited by N. H. Wallis and I. Foot. Cambridge: Cambridge University Press, 1938.

Ng, Su Fang. "Aemilia Lanyer and the Politics of Praise." *ELH* 67 (2000): 433–51.

Nicolson, Marjorie. *The Breaking of the Circle: Studies in the Effect of the 'New Science' upon Seventeenth Century Poetry.* New York: Columbia University Press, 1960.

Norbrook, David. "The Reformation of the Masque." In Lindley, *The Court Masque,* 94–110.

——. *Poetry and Politics in the English Renaissance.* Rev. ed. Oxford, New York: Oxford University Press, 2002.

Novarr, David. *The Disinterred Muse: Donne's Texts and Contexts.* Ithaca, N.Y.: Cornell University Press, 1980.

Obertino, James. "Milton's Use of Aquinas in *Comus.*" In *Milton Studies,* vol. 22, edited by James D. Simmonds, 21–43. Pittsburgh: University of Pittsburgh Press, 1986.

Papazian, Mary Arshagouni, ed. *John Donne and the Protestant Reformation.* Detroit: Wayne State University Press, 2003.

Parrish, Paul. "'A Funerall Elegie': Donne's Achievement in Traditional Form." *Concerning Poetry* 19 (1986): 55–66.

——. "Poet, Audience, and the Word: An Approach to the *Anniversaries.*" In *New Essays on Donne,* edited by Gary A. Stringer, 110–39. Salzburg: Institut für Englische Sprache und Literatur, 1977.

Parrish, Paul, ed. Commentary on the *Anniversaries* in *The Variorum Edition of the Poetry of John Donne.* Gen. ed. Gary A. Stringer. Vol. 6, *The Anniversaries and the Epicedes and Obsequies,* 237–536. Bloomington: Indiana University Press, 1995.

Parry, Graham. *The Golden Age Restor'd: The Culture of the Stuart Court, 1603–42.* New York: St. Martin's, 1981.

Pearson, Jacqueline. "Women Writers and Women Readers: The Case of Aemilia Lanyer." In *Voicing Women: Gender and Sexuality in Early Modern Writing,* edited by Kate Chedgzoy, Melanie Hansen, and Suzanne Trill, 45–54. Pittsburgh: Duquesne University Press, 1997.

Pecheux, Mother Mary Christopher. "The Concept of the Second Eve in *Paradise Lost.*" *PMLA* 75 (1960): 359–66.

Pelikan, Jaroslav. *Eternal Feminines: Three Theological Allegories in Dante's Paradiso.* New Brunswick, N.J.: Rutgers University Press, 1990.

Petit, Herbert H. "The Second Eve in *Paradise Regained.*" *Papers of the Michigan Academy of Science, Arts, and Letters* 44 (1959): 365–69.

Philby, H. St. John. *The Queen of Sheba.* London: Quartet Books, 1981.

Phillippy, Patricia. "Sisters of Magdalen: Women's Mourning in Aemilia Lanyer's *Salve Deus Rex Judaeorum.*" *English Literary Renaissance* 31, no. 1 (2001): 78–106.

Polaski, Sandra Hack. *A Feminist Introduction to Paul.* St. Louis, Mo.: Chalice Press, 2005.

Pollock, Zailig. "'The Object, and the Wit': The Smell of Donne's *First Anniversary.*" *English Literary Renaissance* 13 (1983): 301–18.

Potter, George R. "Milton's Early Poems, The School of Donne, and the Elizabethan Sonneteers." *Philological Quarterly* 6 (1927): 396–400.

Powell, Brenda J. "'Witnesse thy wife (O *Pilate*) speakes for all': Aemilia Lanyer's Strategic Self-Positioning." *Christianity and Literature* 46, no. 1 (1996): 5–23.

Prescott, Anne Lake. "Male Lesbian Voices: Ronsard, Tyard and Donne Play Sappho." In *Reading the Renaissance: Ideas and Idioms from Shakespeare to Milton,* edited by Marc Berley, 109–29. Pittsburgh: Duquesne University Press, 2003.

———. "Refusing Translation: The Gregorian Calendar and Early Modern English Writers." *Yearbook of English Studies* 36, no. 1 (2006): 112–22.

Pritchard, James B., ed. *Solomon and Sheba.* London: Phaidon, 1974.

Questier, M. C. "Loyalty, Religion and State Power in Early Modern England: English Romanism and the Jacobean Oath of Allegiance." *The Historical Journal* 40, no. 2 (1997): 311–29.

Quilligan, Maureen. *The Language of Allegory: Defining the Genre.* Ithaca: Cornell University Press, 1979.

Quinn, Dennis. "Donne's *Anniversaries* as Celebration." In *Essential Articles for the Study of John Donne's Poetry*, edited by John R. Roberts, 368–73. Hamden, Conn.: Archon Books, 1975.

Quitslund, Jon A. "Spenser's Image of Sapience." *Studies in the Renaissance* 16 (1969): 181–213.

Raming, Ida. *The Exclusion of Women from the Priesthood: Divine Law or Sex Discrimination? A Historical Investigation of the Juridical and Doctrinal Foundations of the Code of Canon Law, Canon 968, §1.* Translated by Norman R. Adams. Metuchen, N.J.: Scarecrow Press, 1976.

Reichert, John. "'Against His Better Knowledge': A Case for Adam." *ELH* 48, no. 1 (1981): 83–109.

———. *Milton's Wisdom: Nature and Scripture in* Paradise Lost. Ann Arbor: University of Michigan Press, 1992.

Revard, Stella P. "The Sapphic Voice in Donne's 'Sapho to Philaenis.'" In *Renaissance Discourses of Desire*, edited by Claude J. Summers and Ted-Larry Pebworth, 63–76. Columbia: University of Missouri Press, 1993.

———. *Milton and the Tangles of Neaera's Hair: The Making of the 1645 Poems.* Columbia: University of Missouri Press, 1997.

Rice, Eugene F., Jr. *The Renaissance Idea of Wisdom.* Westport, Conn.: Greenwood Press, 1973.

Richey, Esther Gilman. "'To Undo the Booke': Cornelius Agrippa, Aemilia Lanyer, and the Subversion of Pauline Authority." *English Literary Renaissance* 27 (1997): 106–28.

———. *The Politics of Revelation in the English Renaissance.* Columbia: University of Missouri Press, 1998.

Ricks, Christopher. *Milton's Grand Style.* Oxford: Clarendon, 1963.

Rienstra, Debra. "Dreaming Authorship: Aemilia Lanyer and the Countess of Pembroke." In Cunnar and Johnson, *Discovering and (Re)covering*, 80–103.

Roberts, Gareth. *The Mirror of Alchemy: Alchemical Ideas and Images in Manuscripts and Books from Antiquity to the Seventeenth Century.* Toronto: University of Toronto Press, 1994.

Roberts, John R., ed. Commentary on *The Anniversaries* in *The Variorum Edition of the Poetry of John Donne.* Gen. ed. Gary A. Stringer. Vol. 6, *The Anniversaries and the Epicedes and Obsequies*, 237–536. Bloomington: Indiana University Press, 1995.

Roberts, Josephine A. "Diabolic Dreamscape in Lanyer and Milton." In *Teaching Tudor and Stuart Women Writers*, edited by

Susanne Woods and Margaret P. Hannay, 299–302. New York: Modern Language Association of America, 2000.

Rogers, John. "The Passion of a Female Literary Tradition: Aemilia Lanyer's *Salve Deus Rex Judaeorum.*" *Huntington Library Quarterly* 63, no. 4 (2000): 435–46.

———. "Transported Touch: The Fruit of Marriage in *Paradise Lost.*" In Martin, *Milton and Gender,* 115–32.

Rollin, Roger B. "'Fantastique Ague': The Holy Sonnets and Religious Melancholy." In Summers and Pebworth, *The Eagle and the Dove,* 131–46.

Roman Catholic Church. *The Primer, or Office of the Blessed Virgin Marie, in Latin and English.* Antwerp: Arnold Conings, 1599. Facsimile reprint, London: Scolar Press, 1975.

———. *The Canons and Decrees of the Council of Trent.* Translated by H. J. Schroeder. Rockford, Ill.: Tan Books, 1978.

———. Litany of Loreto. *Thesaurus Precum Latinarum; Treasury of Latin Prayers,* edited and translated by Michael W. Martin. Available at home.earthlink.net/~thesaurus/index.htm.

Rostenberg, Leona. *The Minority Press & the English Crown; A Study in Repression, 1558–1625.* Nieuwkoop, The Netherlands: B. De Graaf, 1971.

Rubin, Deborah. "The Mourner in the Flesh: George Herbert's Commemoration of Magdalen Herbert in *Memoriae Matris Sacrum.*" In *Men Writing the Feminine: Literature, Theory, and the Question of Genders,* edited by Thaïs E. Morgan, 13–28. Albany: State University of New York Press, 1994.

Rudnytsky, Peter L. "'The Sight of God': Donne's Poetics of Transcendence." *Texas Studies in Literature and Language* 24, no. 2 (1982): 185–207.

Ruether, Rosmary Radford. *Mary—The Feminine Face of the Church.* Philadelphia: Westminster Press, 1977.

Rumrich, John P. *Milton Unbound: Controversy and Reinterpretation.* Cambridge: Cambridge University Press, 1996.

———. "Radical Heterodoxy and Heresy." In Corns, *A Companion to Milton,* 141–56.

———. "Milton's *Theanthropos*: The Body of Christ in *Paradise Regained.*" In *Milton Studies,* vol. 42, *Paradise Regained in Context: Genre, Politics, Religion,* edited by Albert C. Labriola and David Loewenstein, 50–67. Pittsburgh: University of Pittsburgh Press, 2002.

Sabine, Maureen. *Feminine Engendered Faith: The Poetry of John Donne and Richard Crashaw.* Basingstoke: Macmillan, 1992.

———. "No Marriage in Heaven: John Donne, Anne Donne, and the Kingdom Come." In Hester, *John Donne's "desire,"* 228–55.

Sandys, George. *Ovid's Metamorphosis Englished, Mythologized, and Represented in Figures*. Edited by Karl K. Hulley and Stanley T. Vandersall. Lincoln: University of Nebraska Press, 1970.

Schnell, Lisa. "'So Great a Difference Is There in Degree': Aemilia Lanyer and the Aims of Feminist Criticism." *Modern Language Quarterly* 57, no. 1 (1996): 23–35.

————. "Breaking 'the rule of Cortezia': Aemilia Lanyer's Dedications to *Salve Deus Rex Judaeorum*." *Journal of Medieval and Early Modern Studies* 27, no. 1 (1997): 77–101.

Schoenfeldt, Michael C. *Prayer and Power: George Herbert and Renaissance Courtship*. Chicago: University of Chicago Press, 1991.

————. "The Gender of Religious Devotion: Aemilia Lanyer and John Donne." In *Religion and Culture in Renaissance England*, edited by Claire McEachern and Debora Shuger, 209–33. Cambridge: Cambridge University Press, 1997.

————. "Obedience and Autonomy in *Paradise Lost*." In Corns, *A Companion to Milton*, 363–79.

Schwartz, Regina M. "Redemption and *Paradise Regained*." In *Milton Studies*, vol. 42, *Paradise Regained in Context: Genre, Politics, Religion*, edited by Albert C. Labriola and David Loewenstein, 26–49. Pittsburgh: University of Pittsburgh Press, 2002.

Scoufos, Alice-Lyle. "The Mysteries in Milton's Masque." In *Milton Studies*, vol. 6, edited by James D. Simmonds, 113–42. Pittsburgh: University of Pittsburgh Press, 1974.

Seelig, Sharon Cadman. "'To all vertuous Ladies in generall': Aemilia Lanyer's Community of Strong Women." In *Literary Circles and Cultural Communities in Renaissance England*, edited by Claude J. Summers and Ted-Larry Pebworth, 44–58. Columbia: University of Missouri Press, 2000.

Shakespeare, William. *The Riverside Shakespeare*. 2nd ed. Edited by G. Blakemore Evans and J. J. M. Tobin. Boston: Houghton Mifflin, 1997.

Shawcross, John T. Paradise Regain'd: *Worthy T'have Not Remain'd So Long Unsung*. Pittsburgh: Duquesne University Press, 1988.

————. "Allegory, Typology, and Didacticism: *Paradise Lost* in the Eighteenth Century." In *Enlightening Allegory: Theory, Practice, and Contexts of Allegory in the Late Seventeenth and Eighteenth Centuries*, edited by Kevin L. Cope, 41–74. New York: AMS Press, 1993.

Shell, Alison, and Arnold Hunt. "Donne's Religious World." In Guibbory, *Cambridge Companion to John Donne*, 65–82.

Shuger, Deborah K. "'Gums of Glutinous Heat' and the Stream of Consciousness: The Theology of Milton's Maske." *Representations* 60 (1997): 1–21.

Shullenberger, William. "Girl, Interrupted: Spenserian Bondage and Release in Milton's Ludlow *Mask*." *Milton Quarterly* 37, no. 4 (2003): 184–204.

———. "The Profession of Virginity in *A Maske Presented at Ludlow Castle*." In Martin, *Milton and Gender*, 77–94.

Sidney, Sir Philip. *Sir Philip Sidney: A Critical Edition of the Major Works*. Edited by Katherine Duncan-Jones. Oxford: Oxford University Press, 1989.

Simpson, Evelyn. *A Study of the Prose Works of John Donne*. Oxford: Clarendon, 1948.

Simpson, Ken. "Lingering Voices, Telling Silences: Silence and the Word in *Paradise Regained*." In *Milton Studies*, vol. 35, edited by Albert C. Labriola, 179–95. Pittsburgh: University of Pittsburgh Press, 1997.

Sims, James H. *The Bible in Milton's Epics*. Gainesville: University of Florida Press, 1962.

Smith, A. J. "Two Notes on Donne." *Modern Language Review* 51 (1956): 405–07.

———. *John Donne: The Complete English Poems*. London: Penguin, 1986.

Smith, A. J., ed. *John Donne: Essays in Celebration*. London: Methuen, 1972.

Smith, Carolyn. "The Virgin Mary in *Paradise Regain'd*." *South Atlantic Quarterly* 71 (1972): 557–64.

Spenser, Edmund. *Works. A Variorum Edition*. 9 vols. in 10. Edited by Edwin Greenlaw, Charles Grosvenor Osgood, and Frederick Morgan Padelford. Baltimore: The Johns Hopkins University Press, 1932–49.

———. *The Poetical Works of Edmund Spenser*. Edited by J. C. Smith and E. DeSelincourt. London: Oxford University Press, 1952.

———. *The Faerie Queene*. Edited by A. C. Hamilton. London: Longman, 1977.

Stachniewski, John. "The Despair of the Holy Sonnets." *ELH* 48 (1981): 677–705.

Stanwood, Paul. "'Essential Joye' in Donne's *Anniversaries*." In *Essential Articles for the Study of John Donne's Poetry*, edited by John R. Roberts, 387–96. Hamden, Conn.: Archon Books, 1975.

———. "Donne's Reinvention of the Fathers: Sacred Truths Suitably Expressed." In Wilcox, Todd, and Macdonald, *Sacred and Profane*, 195–201.

Startzman, L. Eugene. "Wisdom and Beauty: Two Principles in *Paradise Lost.*" *Christianity and Literature* 36, no. 3 (1987): 26–39.

Steadman, John M. "Milton's Haemony: Etymology and Allegory." *PMLA* 77, no. 3 (1962): 200–207.

———. *Milton's Biblical and Classical Imagery.* Pittsburgh: Duquesne University Press, 1984.

Steinberg, Leo. *The Sexuality of Christ in Renaissance Art and in Modern Oblivion.* New York: Pantheon, 1983.

Stewart, Alan. *The Cradle King: The Life of James VI & I, the First Monarch of a United Great Britain.* New York: St. Martin's, 2003.

Stewart, Stanley. *The Enclosed Garden: The Tradition and the Image in Seventeenth-Century Poetry.* Madison: University of Wisconsin Press, 1966.

———. *"Renaissance" Talk: Ordinary Language and the Mystique of Critical Problems.* Pittsburgh: Duquesne University Press, 1997.

Strong, Roy C. *The Cult of Elizabeth: Elizabethan Portraiture and Pageantry.* London: Thames and Hudson, 1977.

Stull, William L. "'Why are not *Sonnets* Made of Thee?' A New Context for the 'Holy Sonnets' of Donne, Herbert, and Milton." *Modern Philology* 80 (1982): 129–35.

———. "Sonnets Courtly and Christian." *University of Hartford Studies in Literature* 15–16 (1983–84): 1–15.

Summers, Claude J. "The Bride of the Apocalypse and the Quest for True Religion: Donne, Herbert, and Spenser." In *"Bright Shootes of Everlastingnesse": The Seventeenth-Century Religious Lyric,* edited by Claude J. Summers and Ted-Larry Pebworth, 72–95. Columbia: University of Missouri Press, 1987.

Summers, Claude J., and Ted-Larry Pebworth, eds. *The Eagle and the Dove: Reassessing John Donne.* Columbia: University of Missouri Press, 1986.

Summers, Joseph H. *The Muse's Method: An Introduction to Paradise Lost.* Cambridge, Mass.: Harvard University Press, 1962.

Swancutt, Diana M. "Sexy Stoics and the Rereading of Romans 1.18–2.16." In Levine and Blickenstaff, *A Feminist Companion to Paul,* 42–73.

Tayler, Edward W. *Donne's Idea of a Woman: Structure and Meaning in* The Anniversaries. New York: Columbia University Press, 1991.

Thérel, Marie-Louise. *Les Symboles de l'Ecclesia dans la création iconographique de l'art Chrétien du IIIe au VIe siècle.* Rome: Edizioni di storia e letteratura, 1973.

Tillyard, E. M. W. "The Action of *Comus.*" In Diekhoff, *A Maske at Ludlow*, 17–57.

———. *The Metaphysicals and Milton*. London: Chatto & Windus, 1956.

Turner, James Grantham. *One Flesh: Paradisal Marriage and Sexual Relations in the Age of Milton*. Oxford: Clarendon Press, 1987.

von Raumer, Frederick. *History of the Sixteenth and Seventeenth Centuries, Illustrated by Original Sources*. Translated by H. E. Lloyd. London, 1835.

Walker, Julia M. *Medusa's Mirrors: Spenser, Shakespeare, Milton, and the Metamorphosis of the Female Self*. Newark: University of Delaware Press, 1998.

Walker, Julia M., ed. *Dissing Elizabeth: Negative Representations of Gloriana*. Durham, N.C.: Duke University Press, 1998.

———. *Milton and the Idea of Woman*. Urbana: University of Illinois Press, 1988.

Wall, Wendy. *The Imprint of Gender: Authorship and Publication in the English Renaissance*. Ithaca, N.Y.: Cornell University Press, 1993.

Wallace, John M. "Milton's *Arcades.*" In *Milton: Modern Essays in Criticism*, edited by Arthur E. Barker, 77–87. New York: Oxford University Press, 1965.

Waller, Gary F. "The Countess of Pembroke and Gendered Reading." In *The Renaissance Englishwoman in Print: Counterbalancing the Canon*, edited by Anne M. Haselkorn and Betty S. Travitsky, 327–45. Amherst: University of Massachusetts Press, 1990.

Warner, Marina. *Alone of All Her Sex: The Myth and Cult of the Virgin Mary*. New York: Knopf, 1976.

Watson, Paul F. "The Queen of Sheba in Christian Tradition." In *Solomon and Sheba*, edited by James B. Pritchard, 115–45. London: Phaidon, 1974.

Whalen, Robert. *The Poetry of Immanence: Sacrament in Donne and Herbert*. Toronto: University of Toronto Press, 2002.

White, Micheline. "A Woman with Saint Peter's Keys? Aemilia Lanyer's *Salve Deus Rex Judaeorum* (1611) and the Priestly Gifts of Women." *Criticism: A Quarterly for Literature and the Arts* 45, no. 3 (2003): 323–41.

Wiggins, Elizabeth L. "Logic in the Poetry of John Donne." *Studies in Philology* 42 (1945): 41–60.

Wilcox, Helen. "Exploring the Language of Devotion in the English Revolution." In *Literature and the English Civil War*, edited by Thomas Healy and Jonathan Sawday, 75–88. Cambridge: Cambridge University Press, 1990.

Wilcox, Helen, Richard Todd, and Alasdair MacDonald, eds. *Sacred and Profane: Secular and Devotional Interplay in Early Modern British Literature*. Amsterdam: Vrije Universiteit Press, 1996.

Wittreich, Joseph. *Feminist Milton*. Ithaca, N.Y.: Cornell University Press, 1987.

Woodhouse, A. S. P. "The Argument of Milton's *Comus*." In Diekhoff, *Essays on Milton's Comus*, 17–42.

———. "*Comus* Once More." *University of Toronto Quarterly* 19 (1950): 218–23.

Woods, Susanne, ed. *The Poems of Aemilia Lanyer: Salve Deus Rex Judaeorum*. New York: Oxford University Press, 1993.

———. "Aemilia Lanyer and Ben Jonson: Patronage, Authority, and Gender." *The Ben Jonson Journal* 1 (1994): 15–30.

———. "Vocation and Authority: Born to Write." *Aemilia Lanyer: Gender, Genre, and the Canon*. Grossman, *Aemilia Lanyer*, 83–98.

———. *Lanyer: A Renaissance Woman Poet*. New York: Oxford University Press, 1999.

———. "Lanyer and Southwell: A Protestant Woman's Re-Vision of St. Peter." In Doerksen and Hodgkins, *Centered on the Word*, 73–86.

Yates, Frances. *Astraea: The Imperial Theme in the Sixteenth Century*. London: Routledge & Keegan Paul, 1975.

Young, Michael B. *King James and the History of Homosexuality*. New York: New York University Press, 2000.

Young, R. V. "'O My America, My New-Found-Land': Pornography and Imperial Politics in Donne's Elegies." *South Central Review* 4, no. 2 (1987): 35–48.

———. *Doctrine and Devotion in Seventeenth-Century Poetry: Studies in Donne, Herbert, Crashaw, and Vaughan*. Cambridge: D. S. Brewer, 2000.

Zwicky, Laurie B. "Kairos in *Paradise Regained*: The Divine Plan." *ELH* 38 (1964): 271–77.

Index

Adam, 82, 142, 162–63, 257–84, 286–87, 302
Agrippa, Cornelius, 105
Ambrose, Saint, 65
Anabaptism, 60
Andrew (apostle), 160
Anglican Church. *See* Church of England
Anne of Denmark, Queen of England, 45–46, 50, 70, 109, 111, 114–18, 121, 193, 198–99, 221, 331n7
Anniversaries (Donne), 8
Annunciation, 132–33, 174–77, 298
Apocrypha, 343n4
Apollo, 224–25
apostolic succession, 138, 149–62
Aquinas, Thomas, 65, 67, 96, 98, 102, 237, 342n3
Arianism, 4, 292
Arminianism, 4, 233, 292, 305
art, and nature, 128–29, 203–05
atonement, 141
Augustine, Saint: on chastity, 238; on church unity, 59–62; *Confessions*, 56; Donne and, 8, 56, 65; *Expositions of the Psalms*, 56; on love, 46; on resurrection, 96, 98–99; on sacraments, 68, 77; and sexuality, 57–58, 99, 249; and Trinity, 24, 30; and wisdom, 56–59, 232, 284–85, 342n3; and women, 99

Bale, John, 90
baptism, 43, 75
Barker, Arthur E., 4
Barlow, William, 109, 123
beauty, 166–69
Bedford, Countess of. *See* Russell, Lucy Harrington, Countess of Bedford
Bellarmine, Robert, 22
Bernard of Clairvaux, 174
Bertie, Susan, Countess Dowager of Kent, 164, 194–95
Bewley, Marius, 71–72
Bishop's Bible, 133
Blackwell, George, 22
Boccaccio, Giovanni, 189
body: Christ's, 130–31, 138, 144, 171–72; Lanyer and, 166; resurrection and, 99; of woman, 130–31, 166. *See also* flesh
Book of Common Prayer, The, 121, 141, 158
Boss, Sarah Jane, 134, 333n26
Boyle, Marjorie O'Rourke, 300, 302
Bradburie, Thomas, 19
Braden, Gordon, 264
bride of Christ. *See* Jesus Christ: spouse of
Brooks, Cleanth, 252
Brown, Cedric, 218–19, 227, 247, 251
Brucioli, Antonio, 235
Byng, Thomas, 19

383

Calvin, John: and Cana wedding feast, 301–02; Donne and, 65; on Jesus' intellectual development, 292–93; and Mary, 133, 295–97, 301–02; on Real Presence, 93; on sacraments, 77; on transubstantiation, 91
Calvinism, 2, 4, 68, 127
Cana wedding feast, 301–02
Carew, Thomas, "A Rapture," 276
Carey, John, 230, 244, 285
Catholicism. *See* Roman Catholicism
celibacy, 171, 184. *See also* chastity
Charles I, King of England, 217, 227–28, 254
Charles II, King of England, 11
chastity, 178, 190, 232–33, 237–38, 243–51. *See also* celibacy
Chaucer, Geoffrey, 165, 272
childbirth, 38, 79, 183
Christian humanism, 217
Christian IV, King of Denmark, 193
Christina, Queen of Sweden, 191
Christology, 285
church. *See* Ecclesia
Church Militant, 231, 232, 234–35, 237, 241, 246
Church of England (Anglican Church), 52, 72
Cleopatra, 168–69
Clifford, Anne, Countess of Dorset, 111, 147, 150–51, 178, 205, 208–11
Clifford, George, 183
Clifford, Margaret, Countess Dowager of Cumberland, 10, 70, 111–13, 115–16, 125, 129–30, 141–43, 146–48, 150, 155, 158–59, 161–62, 171–72, 178, 183–85, 188, 194–97, 207–08, 210–12, 217, 251, 253
Coiro, Anne Baynes, 212
Conti, Natale, 244–46
Cook, Patrick, 213

Corinthians, Letters to, 139
Corthell, Ronald, 83, 249
Cox, Catherine I., 233, 235–36
Creaser, John, 228
Cumberland, Countess of. *See* Clifford, Margaret, Countess Dowager of Cumberland
Curle, Edward, 17, 20
Cybele, 224–25

Daniel, Samuel, *The Vision of the Twelve Goddesses,* 114
Daniels, Edgar F., 38
Danielson, Dennis, 280, 282
death, 30–31
De Critz, John, 166
Derby, Dowager Countess of. *See* Egerton, Alice Spencer Stanley, Dowager Countess of Derby
desire: Christ as object of, 164, 171–72; female, 164, 174, 182–85, 189, 194; human nature and, 184; Lanyer's, 197–200; Mary and, 172–74; Queen of Sheba and, 184–85, 188–90. *See also* eros; sexuality
Dobranski, Stephen B., 4
Donatism, 59–60
Donne, John: on Adam, 82; and alchemy, 84–86; *An Anatomie of the World,* 83, 90; *Anniversaries,* 8, 64–78, 312–13 (see also *The First Anniversarie; The Second Anniversarie*); "The Annunciation and Passion," 7, 20–35, 65, 312; and baptism, 43; "Batter my hart," 164; *Biathanatos,* 23, 313; "The Broken Heart," 62; "The Canonization," 86, 304; and Catholicism, 3, 53–54, 56, 71–72, 84, 101; and Christ, 25–26; Christ and Elizabeth Drury compared by, 76–77, 83–84, 88, 91–93; and Christian divisions, 59–60, 62–63, 75; and Christ's spouse, 51–53,

89–90, 92–93, 132; Lanyer and,
118–20, 123–24, 126–37, 154,
196, 207–08, 313–14; Milton
and, 315; as sacrament, 65–66,
79, 94; Spenser and, 221
Potter, George R., 45
priesthood: apostolic succession
and, 149–62; Catholicism
and, 139–40; Donne and,
3, 13, 32, 48–49, 55, 63, 68;
Lanyer and, 126–28, 132, 138;
Protestantism and, 140;
women and, 3, 5, 9–10, 106,
120, 138–62, 311, 334n31
Protestantism: and Apocrypha,
343n4; Donne and, 54–56,
95–96, 101, 318n7; and
Eucharist, 68, 91, 326n58;
and priesthood of all believers,
140
Proverbs, book of, 1, 6, 17, 46, 50,
57, 186, 256–57, 262–63, 268,
342n3, 349n48
Psalms, book of, 32
Puritanism, 292

Quarles, Francis, 2, 235
Queen of Sheba, 145–47, 184–85,
188–94, 201, 223, 224
Questier, M. C., 22

Ralegh, Walter, 16
Raming, Ida, 139–40, 149
Real Presence, 93–94, 101
recusants, 3, 13, 21–23, 60
Reformed theology, 2
Reichert, John, 260–61
religion: Donne and, 2–3; Lanyer
and, 2–4; Milton and, 2–4
resurrection: Augustine on, 96,
99; Donne and, 40, 47, 91–92,
206
Revelation, book of, 1, 44, 232,
234
Rienstra, Debra, 126
Roman Catholicism: anti-
Catholic sentiment, 53; Donne
and, 3, 53–54, 56, 71–72,
84, 101; and Eucharist, 91;
Henrietta Maria and, 218; and
heresies, 4; James I and, 21–22;

and Mary, 133; and priesthood,
139–40; and purgatory, 77; and
sacraments, 68
Romans, Letter to, 42–43,
194–95, 202, 206
Ruether, Rosemary Radford, 2
Rumrich, John P., 4, 215, 240,
305
Russell, Lucy Harrington,
Countess of Bedford, 107, 111,
165–66, 171–72, 200, 328n68

Sabine, Maureen, 95, 97
sacraments: Donne and, 36–37,
39–40, 65, 76–78, 91, 127, 311;
form and matter of, 66–68;
nature of, 77, 100; poems
as, 65–66, 79, 94; Roman
Catholicism and, 68; women
as, 36–37, 39–40, 72–75, 77–79,
100–101, 311
sacred feminine: central figures
of, 1; Donne and, 1–2, 5, 8,
14–15, 23, 311–12; Lanyer
and, 1–2, 5, 9–10, 311–12;
Milton and, 1–2, 5, 10–12,
216–17, 311–12; poets and, 1–2;
tradition of, 1
Sandys, George, 224–25
Sapientia: Augustine and,
57–58; created versus
uncreated, 342n3; historical
interpretations of, 6; Milton
and, 11, 218–19, 290;
Neoplatonic, 263; as sacred
feminine, 1. *See also* Wisdom
Satan: and Eve, 260, 262, 281,
289; and Jesus, 285–92
Schoenfeldt, Michael, 4, 164, 190
Schwartz, Regina, 306–07
Scotus, John Duns, 65, 237,
333n26
Scoufos, Alice-Lyle, 233, 234
Sebastian, Saint, 172, 200
sexuality: Augustine and, 57–58,
99, 249; Christianity and, 163;
Donne and, 6–8, 38–39, 52, 58,
62–63, 99, 202–03; after Fall,
276–77, 283; homoeroticism,
196–213; Jesus and, 171–72,
200; Lanyer and, 10, 162–81,